Legal Duties of Fiduciaries

Definitions, Duties and Remedies

Legal Duties of Fiduciaries

Definitions, Duties and Remedies

Tamar Frankel
Professor of Law
Boston University School of Law

Fathom Publishing Company
Anchorage, Alaska

ISBN 978-1-888215-20-5

Fathom Publishing Company
P.O. Box 200448
Anchorage, Alaska 99520-0448
Telephone 907-272-3305
Fax 907-272-3305

www.teachfiduciarylaw.com

Printed in the United States of America
2012

Dedication

In memory of my parents, Judith and Lothar Hofmann.
They taught me how to learn.

And to Ray and my children, Anat and Michael,
with much love.

Tamar Frankel

Acknowledgments

This teaching book is the product of many years of learning from others. My article "Fiduciary Law" in 1983 benefited from the thoughtful comments of Professor Robert Clark. The Regulation of Money Managers, a treatise published in the late 1970s, gained greatly from the guidance of Dean Robert Mundheim.

Thanks to Dean Maureen O'Rourke for her support; and to my colleagues, Professor Ward Farnsworth and Professor William Ryckman, Jr., for their invaluable critical comments.

I am deeply grateful to Ann Taylor Schwing who has taken the time to read the manuscript and enrich it with her incisive comments. William Hecker, Esq., was, as usual, tremendously helpful. So was Margaret Ashbury (2L). Debra Daugherty's editing and suggestions contributed much. I cannot thank all three enough.

Thanks to my students in the Spring seminar 2007 LAW JD860A1, named here. Their papers and comments are embodied in this book: Abdulmalik Majed Almarshad, Christopher D. Carlson, Joselyn Chico, Tzung-Wei Chou, Ian D. Engstrand, Hang Yeun Leung, Yao Liu, Erin C. Loomis, Stefanie Marazzi, Yoshihisa Masaki, Paul G. Nikhinson, Ryuichi Nozaki, Timothy M. Riffin, Judah S. Skoff, Adrian Kit ChunWong, and Qing Ye.

Heartfelt thanks to two ultimate fiduciaries: Dr. Marshall Wolf and Dr. Ralph Morton Bolman III of the Brigham and Women's Hospital. They are master physicians, committed to their calling. Without them, this book might not have been completed.

Tamar Frankel

Publication Notes

This teaching book (originally published in 2007) was designed for teaching the law of fiduciaries.

I wrote another book under the name Fiduciary Law by Oxford University Press (2010) which is a general theoretical, explanatory discussion of fiduciary law. It is aimed at the general public.

Table of Contents

Introduction

The purpose of this book is to study fiduciary law by uncovering its underlying structure, principles, themes and objectives. Fiduciaries appear everywhere in the law. They emerge in contract, in tort, in corporate law, agency law, partnership law, criminal law, environmental law, employment law, and constitutional law, in property law, in procedure, and in other areas. But rarely are the policies of the fiduciary law examined as such, in its own context. This book examines fiduciary law's reach and its limits separately from the other categories.

Fiduciaries are not unfamiliar to law students. Under the same name, the student meets many kinds of fiduciaries. Like members of a family, they are similar yet far from identical. Here are the bailees, such as parking lot attendants, the agents, such as brokers, the partners and co-venturers, the professionals, such as lawyers and physicians, the directors and officers of corporations, the trustees and money managers, and of late—the clergymen who abused trust.[1] But rarely are fiduciaries viewed together in a systematic manner. The purpose of this book is to study them together.

Why change our focus? Why not continue to view fiduciaries as we now do, that is, in each specific context?

There are good reasons to study the disparate members of the fiduciary family and the different rules that govern them and to view them as belonging to one category.

First, even though fiduciary relationships are embedded in many legal categories, somehow they do not find a comfortable home in any category. Fiduciary relationships *look* like contracts among the parties. After all, most of these relationships are based on the parties' consent. But, as we will see, fiduciary relationships lack many of the features of contract, raise different expectations, and are subject to different community values.

Violations of fiduciary duties are *similar* to torts (civil wrongs) as well. Abuse of trust carries the stigma of a wrongful act. Therefore, a breach of fiduciary duties can be punished like torts, not only by damages but also by punitive damages. But a breach of fiduciary duties differs from many torts because the breach is committed within a

---

1.   *E.g.,* Martinelli v. Bridgeport Roman Catholic Diocesan Corp., 10 F. Supp. 2d 138 (D. Conn. 1998).

1

consensual arrangement, unlike most torts that are not based on consent. Some violations of fiduciary duties reach the level of crimes, such as embezzlement and species of frauds. But not all violations are crimes. Thus, these relationships and the duties they carry do not fit any legal branch even as they reside in most legal branches. This book helps find out why this is so and what we can learn when we put all fiduciaries in one category.

Second, as diverse as fiduciary law is in terms of the contexts in which it arises, it is quite cohesive in terms of the problems it addresses, the principles it presents, and the solutions it mandates. For example, a single person might occupy different roles. Both roles would make the person a fiduciary. But each would involve different powers and obligations.

Thus, both trustees and corporate directors manage other people's money. Both are fiduciaries. Trustees receive the money or assets from trustors with directions to manage and distribute the assets in particular ways and usually over time. A trustee could be required to distribute the income from trust assets to specific beneficiaries (e.g., the wife of the trustor) and hand over the rest of the property to others, after the income beneficiary dies.

Directors are elected by the shareholders of a corporation to supervise the management of the enterprises of the corporation. The directors hire the corporation's officers that operate the day-to-day operations of the corporation's business. Shareholders have no power to interfere in the day-to-day corporate operations, but they can vote for, or deny their vote for, the directors, and have a number of other specific powers that do not relate to the everyday management of the corporation. Shareholders receive payments ("dividends") on their shares, generally representing the profits of the corporation.

Thus, both trustees and directors distribute income from entrusted assets; the trustee—to income beneficiaries; the directors—to the shareholders. But the power of these two fiduciaries to determine if, when, and how much money to distribute is different. In most cases, trust documents direct the trustees with respect to the distribution of income from entrusted assets. In contrast, directors have, and should have, far greater discretion to decide if and when to distribute the corporation's profits. After all, they are running a business. Directors may decide not to distribute the profits but to reinvest the profits and expand the business. The trustees typically have no such discretion. The different businesses entrusted to these fiduciaries dictate the extent of the discretion that they should exercise in performing their services. When we study the two together, we can better understand the rules that apply to each of them.

Third, the seemingly disparate rules, which apply to the different types of fiduciaries, are in fact consistent with one another. They reflect the costs of verifying the fiduciaries' statements and monitoring the fiduciaries' actions. The higher the costs, the stricter the rules are likely to be. Complicating the calculation is an additional factor: the cost of legal restrictions to the fiduciaries. Viewing all fiduciaries' types together makes it easier to rationally design different rules that apply to each. If we deal with each situation separately, in different legal categories, the meaning of, and need for, fiduciary law, its underlying principle and the arguments about them, are hard to grasp and harder to remember. If we look at all fiduciaries together, then fiduciary rules make far more sense and are easier to understand, to evaluate and criticize.

Fourth, in a changing environment, a view of the foundations of fiduciary law helps apply and shape fiduciary rules to new situations or to relieve existing situations from the burden of legal restrictions. A study of fiduciary law assists the lawyer to predict who the new members in the fiduciary family are likely to be, and which of the existing ones will die out.

Therefore, this book is not about bailment, or corporate governance, or agency, or partnership, or presidential powers (Yes. Presidents are fiduciaries!). This book is about the conceptual basis on which all these situations and relationships are intertwined and regulated in a similar way. If we understand the bases and the arguments that surround fiduciary law, we can understand each type of fiduciaries and the detailed rules that apply to each type.

The style of this book is a bit different from the usual law school casebooks and a bit closer to books used in practice. Practice starts with the client's story. It requires an analysis of the story, and research tools such as treatises, relevant cases, and secondary sources. The book adopts some of the style used in treatises. It has more than the usual number of footnotes. Students who wish to pursue a certain point can be helped by these footnotes.

This book is organized as follows. Chapter One highlights the roots of fiduciary law and the impact of culture, psychology, religion, and commerce on the changes that the law has undergone. Against the background of over 3,000 years, the colors of the present law emerge sharper and more vividly.

Chapter Two defines fiduciary relationships by outlining the elements that compose these relationships. Each element is examined by cases, discussion topics, often by problems, and exposure of gray areas in which fiduciary relationships might arise. The dark side of fiduciary relationships and their potential abuse is exposed as well.

Chapter Three deals with fiduciary law duties and the rationales of the different degree of such duties in different situations.

Chapter Four covers the way in which fiduciary duties can be relaxed and changed by the consent of the parties to the fiduciaries (the entrustors). It shows that many fiduciary duties are default rules that can be waived by the entrustors, provided the entrustors are independent and received full disclosure of all relevant facts necessary to determine whether to waive their rights.

In Chapter Five, we review fiduciaries as arbitrators. Fiduciaries can be obligated to many parties. For example, corporate directors can be fiduciaries to hundreds or thousands of shareholders and to various classes of shareholders. These shareholders may have different and perhaps conflicting interests. Although sometimes fiduciaries are unable to serve the conflicting interests, in many situations they can, depending on the circumstances and guidelines.

Chapter Six focuses on the question: why fiduciary law should be recognized as a category. Besides, what is so important about categories? It turns out that the issue is not merely theoretical but also very practical. The previous Chapters demonstrate the unique nature of fiduciary law as a hybrid: it is part property and part contract; it rubs shoulders with tort and with criminal law. This body of law intersects with many other categories of law. The question is whether it should remain unique. There are loud voices that seek to place fiduciary law as a subcategory of contract law. This Chapter raises the issue, the arguments, and the implications of categorizing fiduciary law as contract.

Chapter Seven proceeds to discuss the courts' discretion in fashioning fiduciary rules, the courts' self-imposed limitation in exercising their discretion, and the remedies that can be meted out on breach of fiduciary duties.

In Chapter Eight, we travel abroad and peek at fiduciary law outside the United States. We compare United States laws with the laws of a select group of countries: Japan, China, Taiwan, the United Kingdom, and the European Union. The main purpose of the comparison is not to learn the rules in each of these systems but rather to recognize differences that must be explored by lawyers who deal with businesses and lawyers in other systems. The Chapter notes issues to which lawyers should be sensitive. These include not merely the legal rules but also the social, cultural, and economic pressures that may render law less prominent or necessary. These pressures can provide the substitutes for the law because they aim and achieve at the same purposes that fiduciary law aims to achieve in the United States.

Chapter Nine deals with the idea and practice of trust. Even though most human relationships are based on some degree of trust, fiduciary law aims at situations that require a high degree of trust. The Chapter explores the nature and reasons for the law's interference in support of trusting relationships among the parties.

We close our study with an Epilogue: maintaining and restoring trust. This subject is not necessarily part of the specific rules that govern fiduciaries. However, lawyers serve clients (whether fiduciaries or not) who have lost the trust of their investors, or employees, or customers. These clients attempt to restore that trust or they might go out of business. In such cases, lawyers can no longer merely recount legal rules to their clients. Besides, many lawyers advise clients in far more than mere legal rules. The contexts, whether business context or personal or others, must be taken into consideration.

Further, increasingly, laws and regulations offer more standards to the clients who are fiduciaries and require the clients to implement the standards in light of the clients' environment, nature of the business, competition, and personnel. Corporate governance is no longer merely a list of rules to follow. Partnerships are no longer moral dictates. Moreover, the lawyer might be the one who sets the rules for the parties in the contracts and other documents that the lawyer prepares. These documents affect the trustworthiness of the client and should focus on that aspect of the relationship.

Therefore, the issue of maintaining and restoring trust is linked to the nature of trust as well as to the standards that the Congress, the courts, the regulators, and the markets are fashioning. Like any other branch of the law, fiduciary law is affected by social, economic, mores, and psychological standards, which this Epilogue highlights. Fiduciary law is based on the need to create and maintain trust among actors in our society's systems. Examining trust and its implications helps review the present law and predict its possible developments in the future.

Chapter One
Where Does Fiduciary Law Come From?

The heritage of fiduciaries and the rules that govern them is ancient. The following materials present a very short and far from complete survey of a number of recognized fiduciary relationships and rules that have existed for over 3,000 years. The purpose of this survey is to highlight the problems that brought about the need for fiduciary duties, and the rules that addressed these problems. Our search is for the social and economic origins of fiduciary law.

A. The Laws of Hammurabi

In Ancient Mesopotamia (currently Iraq), laws of agency developed with commerce. These laws were unique to Hammurabi's laws and reflected the environment in which they developed. The laws discuss primarily situations in which a *tamkarum*, or principal/merchant, gives a *samallum*, or agent, either money to use for travel and for investments or purchases, or goods for trading or selling. Under the laws, an agent is generally required to keep a written receipt of transactions he performs for the principal and tabulate the loans that are due to present at the return of an expedition. An agent also has a duty to account to the principal for interest on the entrusted money over the period of the agency.[1]

Hammurabi's laws required an agent to generate a profit for the principal. An agent who failed to do so had to pay the principal double the amount originally entrusted to him. Another rule stated that an agent who incurred a loss had to return the amount of the capital sum entrusted but not more. In Hammurabi's times, travel and trade could be very dangerous. Therefore, the laws excused agents who had to abandon their goods when attacked by enemies. Basically, an agent would be excused from performing when failure to perform or the losses were not the agent's fault.[2]

Examples of laws from Hammurabi's Code include the following:

If a man fills a boat with goods, such as clothes and corn, and hires a sailor to bring the boat to a certain destination, and the sailor negligently causes the boat and the goods to be damaged, the sailor must compensate the man for the entire damage.

---

1.   Russ VerSteeg, *Early Mesopotamian Commercial Law*, 30 U. Tol. L. Rev. 183, 202 (1999).
2.   *Id.*

This is a rule of negligence that applies in American law today, except that the remedy might differ.

Another rule in Hammurabi's laws is that if a herdsman hired to take care of cattle or sheep falsely accounts for the natural growth of the herd or fraudulently sells the newborn cattle or sheep, the herdsman must pay the owner ten times the owner's loss. This is a rule concerning an entrustor's fraudulent misappropriation, which applies today, except that the remedy might differ.

Another rule holds that a landowner who has abandoned his land because of a misfortune, such as being captured in battle, may reclaim the land when he returns to it. The rule of abandoned property today might be somewhat different and might not belong to the category of fiduciary duties but both rules share the flavor of justice that disallows a person who did not pay for the land to benefit from the owner's misfortune.[3]

Hammurabi's laws deal with bailment contracts. A bailment usually takes place "when an owner of personal property (the bailor) temporarily transfers the property to another person (bailee)."[4] Hammurabi's laws state that in order for a bailment contract to be valid, the transfer of possession must be in writing and public: "the agreement had to be in writing, and the [property being bailed] had to be shown to witnesses."[5] Thus, if a person claimed to own property in the possession of another, the burden of proof was on the claimant. Liability of the bailee under Hammurabi's laws attaches to fault and negligence.[6] A bailee who negligently, or by physical abuse, caused the death of a rented animal was legally bound to replace the animal.[7] If a rented ox were killed by a lion, for example, or by some other "act of god" event, the bailee was not liable.[8] A renter of an ox must pay if the rented ox is injured. The amount of compensation varies depending on the seriousness of the injury.[9]

The trustee's duty of loyalty is an ancient concept. The Babylonian Code of Hammurabi held that a man's hand will be cut if the man was hired to manage another person's farm and stole seed grain or the fodder. However, the stolen good must be found in the man's hands.[10]

Andrew Simmonds describes the Laws of Eshnunna, predating "both the laws of Hammurabi and Moses. . . . Eshnunna was an independent city-state," "near modern Baghdad." It lost its independence to Hammurabi. Its Laws concerning the goring ox rule[11]

---

3. The quoted materials are translations, derived from a text on Google, summarized and edited. THE CODE OF HAMMURABI (L.W. King trans., Richard Hooker ed., 1996), *available at* http://www.wsu.edu/~dee/MESO/CODE.HTM (last visited Aug. 26, 2007).
4. Russ VerSteeg, *Early Mesopotamian Commercial Law*, 30 U. TOL. L. REV. 183, 196 (1999).
5. *Id.*
6. *Id.* at 197.
7. *Id.*
8. *Id.*
9. *Id.* at 196-97.
10. Daniel Jack Chasan, *A Trust for All the People: Rethinking the Management of Washington's State Forests*, 24 SEATTLE UNIV. L. REV. 1, 33 (2000) (citing H.L. MENCKEN, A NEW DICTIONARY OF QUOTATIONS 1220 (1960)).

"offer[] the closest parallel between Biblical law and another ancient Near Eastern code."[12] Under the Laws of Eshnunna, a bailee was liable for goods that were stored in a house if he was unable to prove that the house had been broken into and the goods stolen.[13] If, however, the bailee could prove the theft and show that some of the bailee's own property was stolen as well, the bailee would not be liable to the bailor. This rule was changed by Hammurabi's Laws, which made a bailee of grain strictly liable to his bailor.[14] Another rule applied to a careless resident of a house. He was required to restore lost property that was given to him for safe keeping.[15] Another interesting parallel to current laws is that Hammurabi's code included punitive damages [16]

The concept of restitution was also known in ancient times. "Restitution is an 'act of restoring; restoration of anything to its rightful owner; the act of making good or giving equivalent for any loss, damage or injury; and indemnification.'"[17] "Payment for wrongs committed in the form of restitution to victims has a long history. It has always been closely intertwined with conceptions of punishment and justice. The law of Moses required fourfold restitution for stolen sheep and fivefold for the more useful ox; the Middle Eastern law Code of Hammurabi (c. 1700 B.C.), which focused on implementing deterrent measures through severe and cruel punishments and imposition of restitution for property offenses, could demand up to thirty times the value of damage caused."[18]

Some rules that seem very cruel may have been prompted by the desire for fairness. For example, it seems that "[T]he 'eye for an eye and tooth for a tooth' formulation in the Hammurabi Code" was a benign punishment. It was "intended to restrict revenge by requiring a

---

11. Under the rule, found in Exodus, "if an ox (not known to be a habitual gorer . . .) [i.e., a "tame" ox] gores and kills another ox, the live ox is sold and the proceeds of the sale together with the meat of the dead ox are divided equally between the two owners." "[I]n the case of a [tame ox] one pays [one-] half damages from the body of [the animal], whereas in the case of a [habitual gorer] one pays full damages from the . . . [choicest of the owner of the [gorer's] properties]." "[T]he case of the [tame] ox that gores another ox. . . is the famous rule of one-half damages." A literal interpretation of the rule could lead to anomalies, as if the gorer killed an ox worth more than twice its value, "the owner of the gorer would make a profit," and if the gorer killed a much less valuable ox, "the owner of the inexpensive dead ox might make a profit." Consequently, in the Talmud version of the rule, "damages were half the value of the victim, rather than half the value of the gorer." "The Talmudic modification was sensible in that damages should be viewed from the perspective of the injury done to the victim." Andrew R. Simmonds, *Indirect Causation: A Reminder from the Biblical Goring Ox Rule for Fraud on the Market Securities Litigation,* 88 KY. L.J. 641, 644-46 (2000).
12. Andrew R. Simmonds, *Indirect Causation: A Reminder from the Biblical Goring Ox Rule for Fraud on the Market Securities Litigation,* 88 KY. L.J. 641, 646-47 (2000).
13. Russ VerSteeg, *Early Mesopotamian Commercial Law,* 30 U. TOL. L. REV. 183, 198 (1999).
14. *Id.*
15. *Id.* (quoting Laws of Hammurabi, ¶ 125, at 105, *in* Martha T. Roth, Law Collections from Mesopotamia and Asia Minor (1995)).
16. David G. Owen, *Problems in Assessing Punitive Damages Against Manufacturers of Defective Products,* 49 U. CHI. L. REV. 1, 9-10 (1982).
17. United States v. Ferranti, 928 F. Supp. 206, 220 (E.D.N.Y. 1996) (citing BLACK'S LAW DICTIONARY 1477 (4th ed. 1968)).

measured, proportional response."[19] The laws of Hammurabi regulated the charging of interest rates. In 1750 B.C., the rules limited annual interest rates "to about 20% . . . for loans on silver and 33% on loans of grain."[20] The rules limited, rather than prohibited, the charging of interest, as the Moslem and Catholic Middle Ages rules did.

Similarly, Hammurabi's laws prohibited bribery.[21] After all, he was a successful ruler who seemed to fight against the corruption of his officers and managers. Further, Mesopotamian merchants were aware of ethical principles. A Mesopotamian letter, discovered in Ur, was written by a merchant that reminded another merchant "of the obligation of being a *mar awelim*[,] i.e. to adhere to certain ethical and social standards in business transactions."[22] "Very similar phrases can be found in the correspondence of the Old-Assyrian merchants . . . , such as . . . 'act as gentleman!', . . . [and] 'act according to your status as gentleman!'"[23]

Nelson P. Miller discusses the moral and religious influence on Hammurabi's laws. Hammurabi's Code is not a code like modern codes but a series of statements, based on circumstances and not necessarily principles. The Code's introduction or preamble has references to the gods in the Babylonian pantheon and recognizes the notions of good and evil and right and wrong. Scholars note his desire to protect the weak and the oppressed, and his mission "to further the welfare of the people."[24] The themes of fairness, prohibition of corruption, ethical

---

18.   928 F. Supp. at 219-20 (citing Charles F. Abel & Frank H. Marsh, *Punishment and Restitution, A Restitutionary Approach to Crime and the Criminal,* 25-30 (1984); Tamar Frankel, *Lessons from The Past: Revenge Yesterday and Today,* 76 B.U. L. REV. 157, 158 (1996); STEPHEN SCHAFER, COMPENSATION AND RESTITUTION TO VICTIMS OF CRIME 4 (1970); Daniel W. Van Ness, *Restorative Justice,* in CRIMINAL JUSTICE, RESTITUTION, AND RECONCILIATION 7-14 (Burt Galaway & Joe Hudson eds., (1990)). *See also id.* at 221 ("The Roman Law of the Twelve Tables (449 B.C.) required thieves to make restitution payments to their victims starting at double the value of the stolen goods. The value of the payment due would increase depending on the circumstance in which such stolen goods were found or confiscated. In England, prior to the Middle Ages, elaborate and detailed systems of victim compensation were developed by the Anglo-Saxons, placing the victim's right to compensation at the forefront of punishment considerations.") (citations omitted) (citing Van Ness, *supra,* at 7).
19.   Robert E. Scott & Paul B. Stephan, *Self-Enforcing International Agreements and the Limits of Coercion,* 2004 WIS. L. REV. 551, 569 n.48 (2004) (citing THE HAMMURABI CODE AND THE SINAITIC LEGISLATION 61-62 (Chilperic Edwards trans., Kennikat Press ed. 1971) (1904)).
20.   Christopher L. Peterson, *Truth, Understanding, and High-Cost Consumer Credit: The Historical Context of the Truth in Lending Act,* 55 FLA. L. REV. 807, 815-32 (2003).
21.   Philip M. Nichols, *The Fit Between Changes to the International Corruption Regime and Indigenous Perceptions of Corruption in Kazakhstan,* 22 U. PA. J. INT'L. ECON. L. 863, 876 n.38 (2001) (proscription of public bribery existed in "the most ancient laws" such as the Code of Hammurabi and the Edict of Harmab) (citing THE CODE OF HAMMURABI 4 (Robert F. Harper trans., 1904); JAMES HENRY BREASTED, A HISTORY OF EGYPT: FROM THE EARLIEST TIMES TO THE PERSIAN CONQUEST 405-06 (2nd ed. 1919)).
22.   A.L. Oppenheim, *The Seafaring Merchants of Ur,* 74 J. AM. ORIENTAL SOC. 6, 12 (1954).
23.   *Id.* at 12-13.
24.   Nelson P. Miller, *The Nobility of the American Lawyer: The Ennobling History, Philosophy, and Morality of a Maligned Profession,* 22 T.M. COOLEY L. REV. 209, 275-77 (2005).

behavior and consideration of the common good reverberate in fiduciary law throughout the ages to form a common thread.

B. Fiduciary Duties in the New Testament

The New Testament contains the values underlying fiduciary law today. In this case the principle is the duty to take care of the person who entrusted the fiduciary and exclude the fiduciary's interests from consideration. In an article about the fiduciary principle, Austin W. Scott discussed a story found in the New Testament:[25]

> There was a certain rich man, which had a steward; and the same was accused unto him that he had wasted his goods. And he called him, and said unto him, How is it that I hear this of thee? [G]ive an account of thy stewardship; for thou mayest be no longer steward. Then the steward said within himself, What shall I do? [F]or my lord taketh away from me the stewardship: I cannot dig; to beg I am ashamed. I am resolved what to do, that, when I am put out of the stewardship, they may receive me into their houses. So he called every one of his lord's debtors unto him, and said unto the first, How much owest thou unto my lord? And he said, An hundred measure of oil. And he said unto him, Take thy bill, and sit down quickly, and write fifty. Then said he to another, And how much owest thou? And he said, An hundred measures of wheat. And he said unto him, Take thy bill, and write fourscore. And the lord commended the unjust steward, because he had done wisely: for the children of this world are in their generation wiser than the children of light.[26]

In discussing the story, Scott wrote that the steward was a fiduciary. "He was entrusted with the management of his master's property" and had a "duty dealing with his master's affairs to act solely in the interest of his master." However, he relieved the master's debtors of some of their debts. If the debtors were unable to repay the full debts, and by settling with them the steward could at least collect something, the steward did not act improperly. However, it seems more likely that he was trying to obtain the favor of the debtors for when he left the stewardship. If so, he violated his fiduciary duty, and if he were a trustee, he would have violated his duty under the *Restatement of Trusts* "to administer the trust solely in the interest of the beneficiary."[27]

C. Fiduciaries Under Sharia Islamic Law[28]

Islamic law (Sharia) recognizes and regulates fiduciaries. For example, under the law, a fiduciary is someone who is deposited (entrusted) with property. That person might include non-fiduciaries as well. A "depositor" is entrusted with the owner's property and not presumed to have taken the property of the true owner against the

---

25. Austin W. Scott, *The Fiduciary Principle*, 37 CAL. L. REV. 539, 539-40 (1949), *quoted in* DEBORAH DEMOTT, FIDUCIARY OBLIGATION, AGENCY AND PARTNERSHIP: DUTIES IN ONGOING BUSINESS RELATIONSHIPS 3 (1991).

26. *Luke* 16:1-8.

27. Austin W. Scott, *The Fiduciary Principle*, 37 CAL. L. REV. 539, 539-40 (1949) (citing RESTATEMENT OF TRUSTS § 170 (1935)), *quoted in* DEBORAH DEMOTT, FIDUCIARY OBLIGATION, AGENCY AND PARTNERSHIP: DUTIES IN ONGOING BUSINESS RELATIONSHIPS 3 (1991)).

28. This material is drawn, with consent, from a paper by Majed Al-Marshad, in satisfaction of a seminar requirements on fiduciary law at Boston University Law School, Spring 2007. The paper is edited and abridged, and some of the footnotes were omitted.

owner's wishes. He is not liable for the property, as a thief is. A depositor is an "agent, private employee, guardian, curator of an orphan and the supervisor of an endowment or a financial institution." The depositor doesn't intend to have it for himself. ("Hand"). He holds it in the interest of the owner. Or "he may be a tenant, borrower, mortgager and the potential buyer who tries the item before buying it or to show it to another. A depositor may also hold an item with others for their mutual interest, such as the "speculator, partner, farmer and irrigator."[29]

A depositor is not responsible for damage to the entrusted property unless he commits "trespass or negligence."[30] In the case of trespass or negligence, the deposit turns into a "guarantee," that is, into "responsibility." Therefore, the responsibility of the depositor for the property will arise only if the depositor has been negligent or has trespassed—dealt with the property for his own benefit.[31]

The parties' freedom to design their relationships as they wish is recognized in the Sharia. Their freedom, however, is limited by the rules of the Koran; for example, the agreement may not involve a prohibited payment of interest on a loan. The prohibitions of these rules may not be waived.[32]

Even though the Sharia is subject to different interpretations, the differences relate to particulars that are all anchored in similar principles of fiduciary relationships. It seems that Sharia law deals with entrustment (deposit); the depositors are not liable for damage to entrusted property unless they are negligent or breach their duty of loyalty (trespass), which involves misappropriation of the entrusted property. Finally, a relationship whose terms provide for violation of the positive law (the Koran) is not enforceable. This rule is similar to a rule that agreements in violation of the law are not enforceable.

The trust (waqf) is an important institution in Islamic law and serves as an alternative to the institution of corporations. Timur Kuran noted[33] that the need for a long-term corporate-type legal structure to house the mosques and schools, among others, existed in the Islamic world. While Europe adopted the corporation, the Islam adopted the waqf. The choice was successful in some respect but did not easily suit commercial and business activities.

There was a "dazzling variety of waqfs," dedicated to a variety of uses.[34] The waqf was based on the concept of a trust in Roman law.

---

29.   Majed Al-Marshad paper, citing PHD.Ahmed Nazeh, *AlShart fe Alfeghh Al-Islame*, at 14. A person may hold other person's property without a contract or intention as when the wind blows something into a neighbor's house. When this happens, it is not a deposit, but just a matter of honesty "trust."
30.   PHD.Ahmed Nazeh, *AlShart fe Alfeghh Al-Islame*, at 15.
31.   Al-Marshad paper.
32,   Al-Marshad paper.
33.   Timur Kuran, *The Absence of the Corporation in Islamic Law: Origins and Persistence,* 53 AM. J. COMP. L. 785 (2005).
34.   *Id.* at 799-802.

Muslims may have selected it over the corporation perhaps because "the waqf accords with Islam's communal vision," and indication of "generosity and prestige," as well as self-interest in providing money for the "founder and his family." By appointing the founder as the "mutawalli (manager-trustee)," collecting salary for himself and his relatives, and appointing his successors, the waqf allowed "bypassing Islam's inheritance regulations" and protected the assets from expropriation.[35]

The waqf was subject to the principles that it purported to be. "[W]aqfs were designed as inflexible in order to mitigate the agency problem inherent in delegating implementation of the founder's instructions to successive individuals liable to divert assets to their own uses. . . . The 'static perpetuity' principle of the waqf emerged, then, as part of an implicit social bargain between rulers and the owners of private property." [36] The result of the waqf, however, was to limit its use for commerce and trade in its assets, and thus was an inefficient mechanism for trade.

"The early universities of Europe, such as Paris (1180) and Oxford (1249), were founded as trusts resembling the waqf. But they quickly became self-governing and self-renewing organizations through incorporation."[37] For our purpose, it is important to note the ancient origin of the institution of trust, its positive commitment to God and community, and its flip side, of enabling the trustees to benefit at the expense of the beneficiaries, with the support of the rulers.

D. Jewish Law of Agency

Like the Sharia, Jewish law makes little distinction between secular and religious law.[38] Law and religion end up together, as the law derives from the Bible or from tradition based on the Bible.[39] Thus, the Talmud is not a legal code written by a legislative body, but is more an interpretation of Scripture. In addition to law, it covers many other subjects.[40] The Bible actually contains few rules of civil law. As commerce developed and spread, a system of civil laws had to be constructed.[41] It is possible as well that old Jewish civil law was influenced by Babylonia, a far more commercial nation.[42]

A few examples of Jewish law relating to fiduciaries are available. In the Jewish law of agency, the person who is serving another as an agent is known as *Shaliah*, or "one who is sent," and the person who is sending the *Shaliah* is known as the *Sholeah*, or "one who sends."[43]

35.　*Id.* at 799-802.
36.　*Id.* at 799-802.
37.　*Id.* at 799-802.
38.　Israel Herbert Levinthal, *The Jewish Law of Agency*, 13 JEWISH Q. REV. (n.s.) 117, 119 (1922).
39.　*Id.* at 120.
40.　*Id.* at 123.
41.　*Id.* at 121.
42.　*Id.* at 121-22.
43.　*Id.* at 125.

The agency relationship is known as *Shelihut* which can mean agency.[44] The Jewish law of agency provides that an agent in a for-profit corporation must maximize the principal's profits.[45] An agent may deviate from profit maximization only if the principal clearly directs the agent to do so.[46] Therefore, generally an agent may not act to promote a socially desirable outcome, unless it also maximizes the principal's profits.[47] Further, Jewish law of agency is founded upon the principle that "a man's agent is like himself," and that a man can generally do through a representative anything that he could do in person.[48] These rules are quite similar to the current American rules of agency and rules governing the behavior of corporate directors.

Most Jewish law authorities "characterize a corporation . . . as a type of partnership." "One view considers all shareholders to be partners." Another "treats only the owners of voting shares as partners." And a third view holds that partners are "only those possessing enough shares to have meaningful input into corporate decision-making."[49] Actors for the corporation serve as agents for the partners. Agents "must act in the manner desired by" the partners, or principals.[50] These rules, too, are similar to the current rules in the United States.

A major issue in Jewish law is whether actions are moral.[51] Jewish law forbids a person from harming another, either directly or indirectly. In addition, a person must take steps to make sure that no injury is caused.[52] People are forbidden from aiding others or allowing others to violate Jewish law. People must take affirmative actions to prevent others from violating the law.[53] These rules apply to professionals who, under secular law, are judged by a different set of morals.[54] Lawyers, for example, may not assist their clients to commit a wrong. Lawyers may have to reveal clients' confidences, because the lawyers' responsibilities to their clients do not trump their pre-existing duties under Jewish law to protect prospective victims.[55] Arguably, Jewish law forbids a corporation from doing business with a corrupt government, because by doing that the corporation would be aiding or allowing corruption.[56] Agents do not escape these rules. Agents may

---

44.   *Id.*
45.   Steven H. Resnicoff, *Jewish Law and Socially Responsible Corporate Conduct*, 11 FORDHAM J. CORP. & FIN. L. 681, 691-92 (2006).
46.   *Id.*
47.   *Id.*
48.   Israel Herbert Levinthal, *The Jewish Law of Agency*, 13 JEWISH Q. REV. (n.s.) 117, 133 (1922).
49.   Steven H. Resnicoff, *Jewish Law and Socially Responsible Corporate Conduct*, 11 FORDHAM J. CORP. & FIN. L. 681, 691 (2006).
50.   *Id.* at 691-92.
51.   *Id.* at 683-84.
52.   *Id.* at 685.
53.   *Id.* at 686.
54.   *Id.*
55.   *See id.* at 686-87.
56.   *Id.* at 686.

not justify a violation of Jewish law by claiming that they were acting as agents for others.[57]

Thus, Hammurabi's rules, Moslem law and Jewish law, deal with people who control other people's assets or money in order to provide services. Interestingly, these legal systems introduce themes of ethics, reliability and trust and barriers to negligence and dishonesty.

— — — — — — — — — — -

Discussion Topics

a. How do the agent and principal divide between them the benefits and losses from the relationships in the ancient systems described above?

b. How similar and different are the Hammurabi rules as compared to the rules in Moslem and Jewish laws? If there are differences, what do you think affected the differences?

— — — — — — — — — — -

E. Roman Law

Roman fiduciary law may have begun with property and inheritance law.[58] "Roman law developed the *fideicommissum* [and] *fiducia* [that] allowed fiduciaries to hold property [for others]." The *fideicommissio,* or trust, permitted Roman testators to leave property to a beneficiary who could not inherit the property, such as a criminal or a foreigner. The testator would leave a legacy to a legally qualified beneficiary. His obligation to obey the request was moral.[59] Similarly, the creditor received a collateral from the debtor, which had to be returned upon payment. Therefore, the creditor was prohibited from selling the property.[60] Roman law then recognized situations in which ownership is held in "suspended animation." It is ownership in the hands of persons who seem to be the owner, and may even act as owners, but are not the true owners. Like agents, described below, these persons could deal with specific property but had to act in accordance with the requirements of the previous true owners. Their rights and duties are similar to those of modern trustees.

Agency in Roman Law.[61] Roman slavery law posed a problem for slave owners who wished to take advantage of their slaves' abilities to shop and bargain well. Slaves could not enter into binding contracts because they were considered property rather than persons. Thus, the issue was how to allow the slaves to bargain for their masters. This problem was resolved by amending the law. A slave was allowed to bind the master to legal obligation, even though the slave himself was incapable of entering into a binding contract.

---

57. *Id.* at 688.
58. Mary Szto, *Limited Liability Company Morality: Fiduciary Duties in Historical Context,* 23 QUINNIPIAC L. REV. 61, 89 (2004).
59. *Id.*
60. *Id.*
61. *See generally* DAVID JOHNSTON, THE ROMAN LAW OF TRUSTS (1988).

Modern agency law has retained an aspect of Roman law. Today, agency is defined as: "the fiduciary relation which results from the joint manifestation of consent by one person that another shall act on his behalf and subject to his control, and of consent by that other so to act."[62] The agent has the power to bind another person to legal obligations without binding himself.[63] Like in Roman law, an agent will be "transparent." Liability for the obligations which he undertook for the master will be imposed on the agent only in special circumstances. He binds to a legal obligation the party with whom he negotiated and the master for whom he negotiated while he himself is not liable for these obligations (with some exceptions).

In an article on the history of firms, Henry Hansmann, Reinier Kraakman, and Richard Squire discuss the commercial firms that developed in Rome. One form was the *societas* ("partnership"), an agreement to share profits and losses. However, unlike in the modern partnership, partners were not agents of each other and were not jointly and severally liable for all the partnership debts, but only liable on a pro rata basis. In addition, the *societas'* assets were not distinguished from the assets of its members.

Another organizational structure was the *familia* ("family")—an entity composed of "the oldest living male in the male line of descent" (*pater familias*), his children and slaves, and his adult male descendants and members of their households. The *pater familias* formally owned entity property, but members were liable for debts incurred on behalf of the entity.

Another form of organization was the *peculium* which consisted of assets provided by a master to a slave for business use. The master was the formal owner of the asset, and was liable as owner for the *peculium* debts but only up to the *peculium* value and any distributions received. However, it is believed that the *peculium* assets were not protected from the master's creditors.

The last form of organization was the *societas publicanorum* ("tradable limited partnership"): an entity that invested in public contracts. The lead investor pledged personal assets as security. General partners had control but were personally liable for entity debts; limited partners had no control but had limited liability. It is believed that limited partners in large *societates publicanorum* were trading their interests, and that the entity's assets were protected from the limited partners' creditors.[64]

---

62.   Nelson v. Serwold, 687 F.2d 278, 282 (9th Cir. 1982) (citing Grace Line, Inc. v. Todd Shipyards Corp., 500 F.2d 361 (9th Cir. 1974); RESTATEMENT (SECOND) OF AGENCY § 1(1) (1958)); *see also* RESTATEMENT (THIRD) OF AGENCY § 1.01 (2006). "The agent acts for or on behalf of the principal . . . ." 687 F.2d at 282 (citing NLRB v. United Brotherhood of Carpenters, 531 F.2d 424 (9th Cir. 1976)); *see also* RESTATEMENT (THIRD) OF AGENCY § 1.01 (2006).

63.   *See, e.g.,* Griffin v. United States, 588 F.2d 521, 528 (5th Cir. 1979) (stating that "an essential characteristic of an agency is the power of the agent to commit his principal to business relationships with third parties").

_ _ _ _ _ _ _ _ _ _ -

Discussion Topics

a. What was the problem that Roman agency law was designed to solve? How different is the problem from the issues that the current agency law addresses?

b. What was the situation of agents in Rome if they did not perform to their master's satisfaction? What is the situation of such agents of today?

c. Has the value of a "transparent" owner or agent diminished in modern times? Has it increased? What are the incentives to create this transparency? How does it affect existing rules?

_ _ _ _ _ _ _ _ _ _ -

F. Ancient and Middle Ages Partnership Law

Early partnership law. During the High Middle Ages, Europe "emerged from manorial society and developed commercial trading markets and organizations to respond to the pressures of rapid urbanization and a world that now stretched beyond the local village."[65] The villages brought with them their customary law.[66]

Throughout the Middle Ages, the Catholic Church had enormous influence and served as the creator of the social and legal norms.[67] "Canon law provided the normative framework for canonists and theologians, and together with the comprehensive Roman law formed the foundation" of the new, separate discipline of law.[68] Also, the jurisdiction claimed by ecclesiastical courts was "virtually limitless,"[69] and hence the ecclesiastical courts became the courts for the merchants.[70]

Medieval Europe partnership law was based on Roman law.[71] Traders need to cooperate brought about partnership law in Medieval Europe. The Church had difficulty in accepting this partnership[72] (*"societas"*) because it served to circumvent the

---

64.   Henry Hansmann, Reinier Kraakman, & Richard Squire, *Law and the Rise of the Firm,* 119 HARV. L. REV. 1333, 1356-61 (2006) (summarized).
65.   Dennis J. Callahan, *Medieval Church Norms and Fiduciary Duties in Partnership,* 26 CARDOZO L. REV. 215, 229 (2004) (citing 1 SCOTT ROWLEY, THE MODERN LAW OF PARTNERSHIP 1-6 (1916)).
66.   *Id.* at 220-21.
67.   David J. Gerber, *Prometheus Born: The High Middle Ages and the Relationship Between Law and Economic Conduct,* 38 ST. LOUIS L.J. 673, 683-84 (1994).
68.   *Id.* (footnote omitted).
69.   *Id.* at 222 (citing THEODORE F. T. PLUCKNETT, A CONCISE HISTORY OF THE COMMON LAW 271 (2d ed. 1936)).
70.   *Id.* at 223.
71.   JOHN T. NOONAN, JR., THE SCHOLASTIC ANALYSIS OF USURY 133 (1957), *cited in* Dennis J. Callahan, *Medieval Church Norms and Fiduciary Duties in Partnership,* 26 CARDOZO L. REV. 215, 230 (2004).
72.   David J. Gerber, *Prometheus Born: The High Middle Ages and the Relationship Between Law and Economic Conduct,* 38 ST. LOUIS L.J. 673, 703 (1994) (The prohibition on usury was not, in the opinion of the writer, the main reason for the rise of partnership, even though that prohibition was considered "the single most important economic conduct norm during this period and for centuries afterward.").

prohibition on usury, by introducing investing partners that contributed only capital but no labor. They are "money partners," like lenders.[73]

In Roman law, a *societas* "created a certain right of fraternity." *Societas* could not exist unless all partners were exposed to equal burdens and risks of losses.[74] Partners had to bear equal risks and burdens.[75] *Societas* was a fraternity and that determined the partners' fiduciary duties.[76] Partners (1) had to "share[] loss and gain in proportion to their contributions";[77] (2) "were liable in common for harm done in the conduct of partnership business";[78] (3) "owed each other a duty of forthcomingness": "If a partner keeps back part of the partnership's profit and uses it for his own benefit before restoring it to the common fund, he is held to pay his partner for the damages caused by this delay."[79] (4) While Roman law "limited [partners'] money liability to [their] capital investment, "the . . . partnership form of the canonists allowed partners to bind each other to contracts (a fiduciary model)."[80]

The Church imposed its long-held communal values on the new economic and market organizations."[81] For example, pursuant to the prohibition of Church law on charging interest the Church prohibited the breach of duties to business partners,[82] imposed communal values of justice and fairness on the international trading community,[83] prohibited "disproportionate allocations of risk or profit," and limited "a partner's liability at the expense of other partners, self-dealing in the distribution of partnership profits, and binding partners to contracts outside the scope of the partnership."[84] All these are in fact prevalent in fiduciary law today.

The reliable person relationship [The Salic law]. Although our previous examples examined agency and partnership, other forms of fiduciary relationships developed early to forge other useful rules.

---

73.   JOHN T. NOONAN, JR., THE SCHOLASTIC ANALYSIS OF USURY 134, 134 (1957), *cited in* Dennis J. Callahan, *Medieval Church Norms and Fiduciary Duties in Partnership*, 26 CARDOZO L. REV. 215, 229-30 (2004) [Callahan, *supra* note 517, at 229-30].

74.   Dennis J. Callahan, Medieval Church Norms and Fiduciary Duties in Partnership, 26 CARDOZO L. REV. 215, 23 at 231 (quoting JOHN T. NOONAN, JR., THE SCHOLASTIC ANALYSIS OF USURY 141 (1957)) (citing R. H. Tawney, *Introduction* to THOMAS WILSON, A DISCOURSE UPON USURY 128 (2d ed. 1963 (1925)).

75.   *Id.* (citing R. H. Tawney, *Introduction* to THOMAS WILSON, A DISCOURSE UPON USURY 128 (2d ed. 1963 (1925)).

76.   *Id.* at 232.

77.   JOHN T. NOONAN, JR., THE SCHOLASTIC ANALYSIS OF USURY 147 (1957), *quoted in* Dennis J. Callahan, *Medieval Church Norms and Fiduciary Duties in Partnership*, 26 CARDOZO L. REV. 215, 232 (2004).

78.   Dennis J. Callahan, *Medieval Church Norms and Fiduciary Duties in Partnership*, 26 CARDOZO L. REV. 215, 232 (2004).

79.   *Id.* [Callahan, *supra* note 517, at 232] (quoting JOHN T. NOONAN, JR., THE SCHOLASTIC ANALYSIS OF USURY 106 (1957).

80.   *Id.*

81.   *Id.* at 233.

82.   *Id.*

83.   *Id.*

84.   *Id.*

"Salic law influenced development of the use." Under 6th century Salic law, a trusted person (Salman or Treuhand) could become a trustee by receiving "property from a grantor on behalf of beneficiaries. Usually grantors held on to their property until death and the Salman transferred the grantor's property after the grantor's death," although he might not have been legally required to do so.[85]

The "use" and "Trust" in medieval England. The "use" dates from about the 9th century and was influenced by the doctrine of utilitas ecclesiae. The term "ad opus" in 9th century England "referred to a fiduciary relationship in favor of a beneficiary with no legal enforcement." The term "use" was drawn from Gallic 'al os' and 'ues' in the Laws of William the Conqueror and the Domesday Book and became 'use.'" In addition, the French term "cestui a qui oes le feffement fut fait" became "cestui que use," a term for a beneficiary. Thus, the use was drawn from secular sources (Roman and Salic law) and religious sources (including the Franciscans, who popularized it).[86]

The "use" and fiduciary rules developed in England during the Middle Ages to address specific problems. For example, vows of poverty prohibited Franciscan Friars from owning land. Therefore, charitable persons transferred houses to trusted persons for the use of the Friars. The trusted persons were bound by good conscience to treat the houses they legally owned for the exclusive use of the beneficiaries. The duties constituted a social practice, which the courts enforced on the ground of trust and confidence related to good conscience.[87] The Middle Ages Church doctrine of utilitas ecclesiae allowed clerics to have stewardship or beneficial ownership of Church property for personal maintenance, and prevented the property from passing to clerics' relatives after death.[88]

Before the Statute of Uses was passed in 1535, England recognized special (or "active") trusts and general (or "passive" or "simple") trusts. The special trust was for a "temporary purpose, such as for the care or management of the property." "The more common general trust, otherwise known as the *use*, entailed the transfer of legal title (*enfeoffment*) to a person who was to hold the property (the *feoffee to uses*) for the benefit of another (the *cestui que use*)."

The English common law imposed burdens on the holders of legal title to land. It limited the property transfers during the owner's life and did not allow property transfers after the death of the owner. The use allowed people to circumvent legal burdens on the holders of legal title, under the feudal system. For example, by transferring the legal

---

85. Mary Szto, *Limited Liability Company Morality: Fiduciary Duties in Historical Context*, 23 QUINNIPIAC L. REV. 61, 93-94 (2004) (footnote omitted).

86. *Id.* at 93 (footnotes omitted).

87. J.H. BAKER, AN INTRODUCTION TO ENGLISH LEGAL HISTORY 284 (3d ed. 1990); *see* MICHAEL WALZER, SPHERES OF JUSTICE: A DEFENSE OF PLURALISM AND EQUALITY (1983) 9 (footnotes omitted).

88. Mary Szto, *Limited Liability Company Morality: Fiduciary Duties in Historical Context*, 23 QUINNIPIAC L. REV. 61, 92 (2004) (footnotes omitted).

title to their property they could avoid paying the dues to the "lord." Similarly, if the holders committed certain offenses they might try to avoid the forfeiture of their property by transferring title to third parties. Debtors could do the same to avoid repayment while they continued to use the property. In addition, one could transfer a "use" without publicity, as required by transfer of legal title.

The "use" was adopted when the Crusaders left for the Holy Land and transferred the ownership of their lands to trusted persons temporarily on the understanding that the ownership of the trustees would expire when the real owners returned. Similarly, the "use" was designed to overcome the prohibition of transferring land by will. Land was transferred to a trusted person for the donor's benefit and by the trustee—to the donor's heirs. A daughter was disqualified from holding land. The "use" enabled her father to give her the beneficial ownership through a trust person who vowed to use the property for her benefit. The "use" was also useful as a means of tax evasion.[89] Thus, one could view the "use" as a means of evading the law.

Under common law "uses" were not enforceable. If the trusted person refused to return the land or reaped the land's profits the true owners had recourse. But in early fifteenth century, such unfaithful trustees could be sued in the Court of Chancery and forced to abide by their promises.[90]

The use came to an end in 1535 under the Statute of Uses. The preamble [to the Statute of Uses (1535)] lists "the evil effects of the system and legal writers of a later day have regarded the words of this preamble as though they stated a generally admitted evil. As a matter of historical fact this is not true. The Statute of Uses was forced upon an extremely unwilling parliament by an extremely strong-willed king. It was very unpopular and was one of the excuses, if not one of the causes, of the great Catholic Rebellion. . . . It was at once seen that it would deprive men of that testamentary power, that power of purchasing the repose of their souls, which they had long enjoyed. The kind was the one person who had all to gain and nothing to lose by the abolition of uses. . . . The statute abolished the power of devising a use which men had heretofore enjoyed."[91] The result of the Statute of Uses was to convert uses into legal estates, which forced the "use" into the old order and its limitations on making wills, for example, just as an "estate" was limited. The Statute legitimized illegal "uses" by recognizing the transfers as binding transfers. The trustee because the true recipient of the property. The true owners could no longer be hidden.

---

89.   *See also* GEORGE T. BOGERT, TRUSTS § 2, at 6, 7-8 (6th ed. 1987).
90.   Avisheh Avini, *The Origins of the Modern English Trust Revisited*, 70 TUL. L. REV. 1139, 1143-1145 (1996) (summarized) (footnote omitted). *See also* J.H. BAKER, AN INTRODUCTION TO ENGLISH LEGAL HISTORY 283-87 (3d ed. 1990) (discussing origins of the use); *id.* at 288-89 (the use provided "an escape" from feudal law and allowed flexibility).
91.   F.W. MAITLAND, EQUITY: A COURSE OF LECTURES 34 (1936).

Our judgment of the "uses" depends on whether we believe that "uses" were employed for good causes or were employed to circumvent the law (no matter whether the law was good or bad). Most importantly, uses demonstrated the way in which law can be avoided by interpositioning other persons between the true actors and the outside world. This is a feature of many fiduciary relationships today as well. One could use a trust or agency to avoid paying taxes, or hide the identity of the voters who control a corporation (whether upright citizens or members of the Mafia). We will revisit this issue and the solutions under modern fiduciary law in the next Chapter.

— — — — — — — — — — -

Discussion Topics

a. Is anything wrong with the "use" arrangement?

b. If that is not an acceptable state of affairs, how would you correct it? Would you follow the Statute of Uses and declare the voting trustee to be the true owner? Or would you find another solution?

c. Is there a difference between a permanent and a temporary "use"? If a difference exists, which kind would be more suspect as a method of circumventing the law?

— — — — — — — — — — -

G. Recent U.S. History

Lawrence M. Friedman discussed the history of fiduciary duties in corporate law.[92]

As private corporations became more dominant in the economy by the late 19th century, corporate law generally developed to allow corporations and their management more freedom to act. Because some states prohibited state investments in private corporations, these corporations sought private capital. The market for private capital, however, was largely unregulated, and corporate promoters cheated investors. Shareholder lawsuits brought about new doctrines. Corporate case law borrowed from trust law, analogizing officers and directors to trustees and adopted the duty to avoid self-dealing and the duty to account for profits from self-dealing transactions.

Case law had previously adopted a "trust fund" doctrine, awarding creditors of a corporation priority over the stockholders. The doctrine was expanded in the late 19th century. For example, in a 1875 Supreme Court case, a defendant had subscribed to stock in a corporation that had gone bankrupt and paid 20% of the face value. He claimed not to be liable for the remainder, arguing that the company agent said that he would be liable for only the 20%.

Justice Hunt wrote:

[The capital stock] is a trust fund, of which the directors are the trustees. It is a trust to be managed for the benefit of its shareholders during its life, and for the benefit of its creditors in the event of its dissolution. This duty is a sacred one, and cannot be

---

92. LAWRENCE M. FRIEDMAN, A HISTORY OF AMERICAN LAW 446-52 (1973) (summarized).

disregarded. Its violation will not be undertaken by any just-minded man, and will not be permitted by the courts. The idea that the capital of a corporation is a foot-ball to be thrown into the market for the purposes of speculation, that its value may be elevated or depressed to advance the interests of its managers, is a modern and wicked invention. Equally unsound is the opinion, that the obligation of a subscriber to pay his subscription may be released or surrendered to him by the trustees of the company. This has been often attempted, but never successfully. The capital paid in, and promised to be paid in, is a fund which the trustees cannot squander or give away.[93]

States have usually provided that "until *all* of the capital (as measured by par value)[94] was paid in, stockholders were doubly liable on their stock." In addition, states often provided that "stockholders were liable for debts due from the corporation to its employees." However, some states later diluted the provisions to attract corporations to their jurisdiction.

In an 1891 case, directors and officers purchased stock at par value knowing that the stock was worth much more. The Kansas Supreme Court, upholding an injunction for equitable relief, said, "The officers and directors of a corporation are trustees of the shareholders, and in securing to themselves an advantage not common to all the stockholders, they commit a plain breach of duty."[95] And in an 1889 case, the officers and directors of a bank neglected to supervise the bank's affairs while the bank lost money through fraud and improvident loans. In holding the defendants personally liable for the losses, the Virginia Supreme Court said, "The high degree of confidence and responsibility resting upon directors of corporations has often led the courts to regard them as trustees, and to declare the relationship existing between them and the stockholders to be that of trustees and *cestuis que trust*, respectively."[96]

Arguably, the adoption of fiduciary duties in corporate law was not sufficient to prevent abuses, as lawsuits were expensive and often the corporation or the director or officer had no assets.[97]

In *The Law of Fiduciary Duty in New York, 1920-1980,* William E. Nelson concluded that fiduciary law of the 1980s did not differ much from that of the 1920s although the context of the law has broadened to include public policy considerations.[98] The author notes that "[n]o

---

93. Upton v. Tribilcock, 91 U.S. 45, 47-48 (1875).
94. Par value was the price that the promoters decided to require for the corporation's shares. During the 1800, the par value signified the value of the corporation as compared, for example, to "penny stock." It later became clear that the par value, which may have represented the value of the corporation accurately at one point, did not continue to be accurate. The value of the shares could be higher or lower. Today, par value is a cent or less, and stock prices are determined by the market price or a valuation of the corporate business at any particular time. Hence, the aggregate par value of corporate shares no longer supports the creditors' claims as a "trust fund."
95. Ark. Valley Agric. Soc'y v. Eichholtz, 25 P. 613, 613 (Kan. 1891).
96. Marshall v. Farmers' & Mechs.' Sav. Bank, 8 S.E. 586, 589 (Va. 1889).
97. LAWRENCE M. FRIEDMAN, A HISTORY OF AMERICAN LAW 446-52 (1973) (summarized).
98. William E. Nelson, *The Law of Fiduciary Duty in New York, 1920-1980,* 53 SMU L. REV. 285 (2000), LEXIS, Lawrev Library, Smulr File (LEXIS summary).

explicit changes in doctrine occurred over the course of the century in the black-letter law of fiduciary duty."

Another interesting observation relates to the movement of fiduciary law from the courts to regulation and legislation and the continuing influence and citation of Justice Cardozo's statement in *Meinhard v. Salmon*.[99] In discussing fiduciary duties, Robert W. Hillman[100] noted that the lofty ethical level established by Justice Cardozo in 1928 has been cited continuously to this very day, even though the attitude and decisions of the courts have become far more conservative. It seems that the underlying ethical standard that Justice Cardozo has proposed is influential even in the changing jurisprudence, and even though legislation is playing an increasing role in fiduciary law regulation of business associations and the markets.

H. Chapter Review

How similar and different was fiduciary law in ancient Rome and Middle Ages societies? What drove fiduciary law in each era? Were fiduciary rules beneficial to society? If so, in what way? Does the history of fiduciary help understand fiduciary rules in our 21st century?

---

99.   Meinhard v. Salmon, 164 N.E. 545, 546 (N.Y. 1928) ("Joint adventurers, like copartners, owe to one another . . . the duty of the finest loyalty. Many forms of conduct permissible in a workaday world for those acting at arm's length, are forbidden to those bound by fiduciary ties. A trustee is held to something stricter than the morals of the market place. Not honesty alone, but the punctilio of an honor the most sensitive, is then the standard of behavior. As to this there has developed a tradition that is unbending and inveterate. Uncompromising rigidity has been the attitude of courts of equity when petitioned to undermine the rule of undivided loyalty by the "disintegrating erosion" of particular exceptions. Only thus has the level of conduct for fiduciaries been kept at a level higher than that trodden by the crowd. It will not consciously be lowered by any judgment of this court." (citation omitted)).
100.   Robert W. Hillman, *Closely-Held Firms and the Common Law of Fiduciary Duty: What Explains the Enduring Qualities of a Punctilio?*, 41 TULSA L. REV. 441 (2006).

Chapter Two
The Nature of Fiduciary Relationships

Nearly all men can stand adversity, but if you want to test a man's character, give him power
— Abraham Lincoln.[1]

Power does not corrupt men; fools, however, if they get into a position of power, corrupt power.
— George Bernard Shaw.[2]

Introduction. A study of fiduciary law poses the problem of a chicken and an egg. What should come first, fiduciaries or their duties? Defining fiduciaries first leaves us with the questions: So what? What are the consequences of these definitions, and what are the duties of such a fiduciary? Starting with fiduciary duties first leaves us with the questions: Who are we talking about? Who are the fiduciaries that bear these duties? And why are their duties similar in principle but different in details? Selecting each type of fiduciary and attaching the duties to that fiduciary leaves out the most important questions with which we are dealing, that is: How do we recognize fiduciaries? How are they different? And should these differences bring about different rules to govern them? Are these rules justified?

There is no fully satisfactory answer to this dilemma. Therefore, this Chapter starts with looking at specific fiduciaries and examining the features that are common to all, yet distinct for each of them. We then outline the features that all fiduciaries share and examine each feature by examples. Later, having established these similar and different features, we can determine how the differences are reflected in the rules that govern the particular fiduciaries. When we read the various definitions of different fiduciaries, let us think about the problems that they raise and imagine how the law would address and resolve them. The next Chapters will focus on those solutions.

In the study of fiduciary law, an issue of naming arises. Agents, advisers, money managers, lawyers, physicians, have a general name in common. They are called fiduciaries. However, principals (who engage agents), investors (who engage advisers and money managers), clients (who engage lawyers), and patients (who engage physicians) do not have one name in common. They have only a specific one related to

---

1.   QUOTEDB, http://www.quotedb.com/quotes/1654 (last visited Sept. 7, 2006).
2.   *George Bernard Shaw,* http://www.whale.to/v/shaw1.html (last visited Aug. 7, 2007).

their relationship to a particular fiduciary. The absence of the general name is a question to ponder. In this book, we call the parties to whom fiduciaries owe fiduciary duties: *Entrustors*. This name is derived from the word "entrustment" which all parties to relationships with fiduciaries do. The word is also a derivative of the word "trust" on which all fiduciary relationships must be based.

A. Definitions of Fiduciary Relationships

We start with the definitions of particular fiduciaries and then move to generalize what these definitions teach us. Court decisions and legislation rarely provide a general definition of fiduciary relationships. Definitions of particular fiduciaries are more available in cases, statutes,[3] the Restatements of the Law (ALI),[4] in treatises,[5] and in Uniform Codes and Statutes, such as the Uniform Trust Code.[6]

At the end of the next three chapters, we may paint the following picture, for example. The parking garage attendant where I park my car is my bailee. He may not use my car for any purpose except perhaps moving it to a safer place. The money manager who manages my life savings has control and possession of my money. She is my fiduciary as well. She may not use any of the money I entrusted to her for any purpose except for the purpose that was specified in the entrustment, and she may deal with my money only for my benefit or the benefit of those whom I specified.

If the garage attendant violates his duty and drives my car, he might cause me damage: the cost of the gas that he used, or the cost of the overuse of the car, or the value of the car that he may have smashed in an accident while driving. I am unlikely to be responsible for any harm he has done with my car to anyone else. But that is another risk for me, even if he drives my car without my permission. In any event, the chances are that he is covered by insurance of the parking lot

---

3.   *See, e.g.,* Investment Company Act of 1940, 15 U.S.C. § 80a-2(a)(3) (2000) (definition of "affiliated person"); *id.* 15 U.S.C. § 80a-2(a)(9) (2000) (definition of "control"); *id.* 15 U.S.C. § 80a-35(b) (2000) (investment adviser of registered investment company has fiduciary duty with respect to compensation or payments by investment company to adviser or affiliate); Employee Retirement Income Security Act of 1974, 29 U.S.C. § 1002(21) (2000) (definition of "fiduciary" with respect to pension plan); DEL. CODE ANN. tit. 12, § 3301(b) (2001) (definition of "fiduciary" for fiduciary relations law); MD. CODE ANN., EST. & TRUSTS § 15-114(a)(2) (West 2001) (definition of "fiduciary" for guidelines and standards for investment of assets).

4.   *See* RESTATEMENT (SECOND) OF AGENCY (1958); RESTATEMENT (THIRD) OF TRUSTS (2003); AMERICAN LAW INSTITUTE, PRINCIPLES OF CORPORATE GOVERNANCE: ANALYSIS AND RECOMMENDATIONS (1994).

5.   See, e.g., WILLIAM A. GREGORY, THE LAW OF AGENCY AND PARTNERSHIP (3d ed. 2001); AUSTIN WAKEMAN SCOTT, WILLIAM FRANKLIN FRATCHER, & MARK L. ASCHER, SCOTT AND ASCHER ON TRUSTS (5th ed. 2006); FRANKLIN A. GEVURTZ, CORPORATION LAW (2000).

6.   UNIFORM TRUST CODE § 103(20) defines a "trustee" to include "an original, additional, and successor trustee, and a cotrustee." Note: The duties/powers of a trustee are outlined in sections 801-817. Specifically the duties are at sections 801-814 and the powers at 815-817. UNIFORM TRUST CODE (2005), http://www.law.upenn.edu/bll/archives/ulc/uta/2005final.txt (last visited Aug. 13, 2007). States that have enacted the Prudent Investor Act are encouraged to reenact that Act as Section 9 of the Code, less certain duplicative provisions. The Uniform Trusts Act (1937) is incorporated into/superseded by the Uniform Trust Code.

against any harm he might cause me if he violates his duty, or that the garage owner will be responsible for the damage and could pay for it. Moreover, my own insurance may protect me.

If my money manager makes use of my money or gambles with it against the directives I gave her, my losses can be substantial and affect my life and when I can retire. The money manager may be covered by insurance against embezzlement, but she is unlikely to get insurance against losses from gambling with my money against my specific or implied directions.

If the incidence of parking attendants taking parked cars for joy riding happens in one parking lot, the word is likely to spread around and the parking lot owner is either going to control the attendants or buy insurance against damages to the parked cars or go out of business. The market will take care of this situation. If joy riding by attendants becomes an epidemic in the city and causes serious jams in traffic, the law might respond by imposing on managers of parking lots a requirement to have insurance coverage for possible damage to the cars that are deposited there. But that is less likely.

The law is far more invasive in the case of my money manager. She may be required to buy insurance against embezzlement of my savings. But that may not be enough, especially if I have saved a significant amount and that presents a far greater temptation to misappropriate or "borrow." In her case, there are many rules to prevent the abuse of my entrustment, including specific prohibitions on specific activities and even criminal prohibitions.

You will find that, while the definitions of fiduciaries reproduced below are not identical, they share the same flavor. All definitions point to the need of an entrustor to trust the fiduciary, a need that is inherent in the relationship. Most definitions relate to property and financial relationships. But in addition to these two features, can a more detailed and precise general definition emerge? How do the elements of the definitions below differ from each other? How do they differ from the elements that were established in the cases above? In search for the elements that all fiduciaries and their relationships have in common, as well as the differences between them, examine the following definitions:

1. Definition of agency

"Agency is the fiduciary relation which results from the joint manifestation of consent by one person that another shall act on his behalf and subject to his control, and of consent by that other so to act."[7]

"The agent acts for or on behalf of the principal . . . ."[8]

---

7.   Nelson v. Serwold, 687 F.2d 278, 282 (9th Cir. 1982) (citing Grace Line, Inc. v. Todd Shipyards Corp., 500 F.2d 361 (9th Cir. 1974); RESTATEMENT (SECOND) OF AGENCY § 1(1) (1958)); *see also* RESTATEMENT (THIRD) OF AGENCY § 1.01 (2006).
8.   687 F.2d at 282 (citing NLRB v. United Brotherhood of Carpenters, 531 F.2d 424 (9th Cir. 1976)); *see also* RESTATEMENT (THIRD) OF AGENCY § 1.01 (2006).

2. Definition of trust

"A trust is created when a settlor conveys property to a trustee with a manifest intent to impose a fiduciary duty on that person requiring that the property be used for a specific benefit of others."[9]

3. DEL. CODE ANN. tit. 12, § 3301 (2001 & Supp. 2004):[10] Application of chapter; definitions

(a) This chapter shall govern fiduciaries, as well as agents in certain instances, now or hereafter acting under governing instruments.

(b) The term "fiduciary" shall mean trustees, personal representatives, guardians and custodians under the Uniform Gifts to Minors Act (Chapter 45 of this title) and other fiduciaries.

(c) The term "agents" shall mean custodians (other than those acting under the Uniform Gifts to Minors Act, Chapter 45 of this title), escrow agents, managing agents and other persons holding, other than in the capacity of a fiduciary as above defined, property belonging to another person whether that other person is a fiduciary or a nonfiduciary.

(d) The term "governing instrument" shall mean a will, agreement, court order or other instrument creating or defining the duties and powers of a fiduciary or agent.

(e) The terms "legal investment" or "authorized investment" or words of similar import, as used in any governing instrument, shall mean any investment which is permitted by the terms of § 3302 of this title . . . .

– – – – – – – – – – –

Discussion Topics

a. What are the services performed by each of the fiduciaries described in these definitions? What is similar and different in these services and in these definitions?

b. What question would you ask a client to determine whether the client is a fiduciary and what kind of fiduciary the client is? What tests do the definitions apply in terms of the fiduciary's functions, entrustment, and level of the entrustors' trust?

c. Are legislative definitions of fiduciaries helpful in determining whether (and what) fiduciary duties arise in different circumstances?

– – – – – – – – – – –

B. Suggested General Definition of Fiduciaries

As noted and as the legislative definitions of fiduciary show, situations that give rise to fiduciary duties vary. Nonetheless, these situations share a "family resemblance." The following list suggests the factors that give rise to fiduciary relationships and attendant duties. Not everyone agrees with this list of factors or even with the existence of fiduciary law as a separate category. We will deal with these arguments later in our inquiry. Now we follow the suggested "family resemblance." These are the features that all fiduciaries seem to have in common.

---

9. Branson Sch. Dist. RE-82 v. Romer, 161 F.3d 619, 633 (10th Cir. 1998) (citing RESTATEMENT (SECOND) OF TRUSTS §§ 2, 17, 23, 23 cmt. a (1959)), *cert. denied,* 526 U.S. 1068 (1999); *see also* RESTATEMENT (THIRD) OF TRUSTS § 2 (2003).
10. DEL. CODE ANN. tit. 12, § 3301 (2001 & Supp. 2004).

First, the services that fiduciaries offer are usually socially desirable and often involve expertise, such as healing, or legal services, or business partnering, or teaching. Of a later vintage are asset management, corporate management, and religious services.

Second, in order to perform these services effectively, fiduciaries must be entrusted with property or power. One commentator suggested substituting property or power by "critical resource." We will use the terms "property" and "power" and attempt to define them in the context of the relationship.[11]

Third, entrustment poses risks to entrustors. First, for various reasons, the services that fiduciaries offer are hard to evaluate at the time of the bargain. That difficulty is what distinguishes the services from the sale of items. To be sure, some items are also hard to evaluate without expertise. But at least the items can be evaluated before the bargain is closed. Fiduciaries' services, in contrast, are different. Entrustment is a condition precedent to the performance of fiduciaries' services. The services cannot be performed unless the property or power is entrusted *first*. The services can be evaluated only afterwards. In addition, the services involve various degrees of discretion that must be vested in fiduciaries. The fiduciaries must have the ability to act without resorting to the prior approval of the entrustor. Fiduciaries cannot be fully directed or controlled in the use of entrusted property or power or in the performance of their services. Depending on the nature of the services, greater specifications, constraints or control over the fiduciaries' performance would undermine the very utility of the relationship.

Fourth, monitoring fiduciaries in the performance of their services is costly to entrustors. Absent intervention, the costs are presumably higher than the benefits from the relationship. Establishing trustworthiness is presumably more costly to fiduciaries than the rewards from the relationship. And the markets fail to protect entrustors from the risks posed by a fiduciary relationship. In that situation, it is likely that the parties will not interact. As a result, it is likely that the law will interfere to support the interaction by reducing the costs to the parties.

Let us discuss each of these features in more detail.

1. The services that fiduciaries offer are usually socially desirable and often involve expertise.

Our society, like any society with a developed economy, is based in large part on specialization. Each of us specializes in an activity. Others rely on us to perform our services for them, and we rely on others' activities to meet our other needs. Fiduciary services usually involve expertise, such as medicine, law, investment management and teaching. These service givers have greater knowledge than the service

---

11.   D. Gordon Smith, *The Critical Resource Theory of Fiduciary Duty,* 55 VAND. L. REV. 1399, 1404 (2002) (noting that "property" is a difficult concept to define).

receivers. These services are also valuable, and others are encouraged to rely on them, for example, medical service. However, the very expertise of the service givers renders the receivers of the services more vulnerable to abuse of trust and to lack of care.

Nonetheless, the expert services are doubly socially desirable. Not only because the services are useful to the public but also because duplication of the expertise is more costly to society. It takes many years to study medicine and law. It takes years of experience to be an effective manager of a large enterprise. Therefore it is important that people will resort to experts to avoid wasteful duplication. We have expert organizations as well. Banks, insurance companies, and the financial system as a whole took years to develop. They form the channels for our everyday interaction and exchange. A threat to public trust in these institutions and systems poses a treat to our way of life and standard of living. In sum, expertise, the value of certain services, and society's drive to specialization mean also vesting decision power—discretion—in experts.

Fiduciaries have discretion in different degrees, but some degree of discretion is necessary for the performance of any fiduciary service. Little discretion is required of a parking lot attendant, and far more is required of the investment specialist. The parking lot attendant should be able to drive a car so as to place cars in convenient places or move them. But the money manager must have far more knowledge of the markets and investments.

Even if an entrustor could perform the services of a fiduciary, the entrustor might have to be engaged in doing something else. Then the person who performs the services for the entrustor becomes a fiduciary. Thus, it does not necessarily matter that the entrustor himself could perform the services, for example, that he is an expert money manager. He may decide to entrust his money to another manager while he goes on vacation. The entrusted manager will then have to perform the service both honestly and well, as any fiduciary must.

– – – – – – – – – – – – –

Discussion Topics

a. Whose services do you consider more important to society? The services of a electrician, plumber, lawyer, partner, or the president of the United States? Which of these services raises greater danger to the entrustor? Should any or all of these services be supported by greater judicial supervision?

b. Should we distinguish between (a) an adviser that controls and manages clients' assets; (b) an adviser who gives clients advice on how to manage their own investments, if they control the investments; (c) a software designer who designs the software for the adviser by automatically suggesting the trend of the markets to guide investments in stock; (d) a reporter on financial news, and (e) a publisher of the *Wall*

Street Journal that contains evaluations of corporations and money managers? Which of these actors should be deemed a fiduciary?

— — — — — — — — — — -

2. In order to perform these services effectively, fiduciaries must be entrusted with property or power

Assume that the definition of fiduciaries is "people who are entrusted with property or power for the purpose of performing services to others." Let us view an example from everyday life. Jane gives her friend John $100 to buy groceries for her. John is an astute businessman. He goes to the market on Saturday before closing, and buys all the groceries for $75. Jane is very pleased with the groceries but is angered when she finds out that John pocketed the $25, that is, the difference between the amount she gave him and the amount he spent on the groceries. She demanded the $25. John denies that he owes her the money. He claims it to be his.

Who is entitled to the $25? How would you define the legal relationship between Jane and John? Is there more than one possible legal definition? What additional facts would you seek to elicit in order to determine the ownership of the $25?

What if John was robbed on the train while traveling to the market and lost the money through no fault of his? Who should bear the loss? Would the legal relationships determine this result as well? Does it make a difference that the two (former) friends did not mention any remuneration for John's services and that he offered the service free of charge?

Who owned the $100 when Jane gave the money to John? Consider the summaries of the following three cases that highlight the issue of entrustment. What is the difference between entrustment and full transfer of property? When is the transfer of property entrustment, and when is it a full transfer of the property?

a. What is entrustment?

The following case deals with entrustments that will be recognized by the court to constitute a fiduciary relationship called a trust. In this case the question is: to what extent did the trustor or settlor—the person who handed over the asset to the trustee in order to create the trust—really hand over the asset? Did the trustor or settlor in fact hand over the control of the asset in one hand, and take back the control in the other hand?

In *Denver National Bank v. Von Brecht,* the plaintiffs sought to set aside and avoid a trust agreement executed by plaintiff's settlor—the person who entrusted the property—the entrustor to—the trustee—the fiduciary.[12] One of the issues in this case was whether the "trust agreement" was a trust in the first place. If it was not (because the settlor retained too much power over the entrusted property), then the

---

12. Denver Nat'l Bank v. Von Brecht, 322 P.2d 667 (Colo. 1958).

agreement constituted a will that required the bank to act in a certain way only after the settlor's death. After all, there are wills that establish trusts. But if the instrument was a will and not a trust established during the life of the trustor, then the instrument was invalid because it did not comply with the necessary form of a will (e.g., witnesses). Note how the court describes entrustment.

[By the trust agreement] the settlor transferred to the Bank as Trustee two thousand seven hundred ninety-two and two-thirds shares of the capital stock of Don-Vir Investment Company, and by the terms thereof it was the duty of the Bank to pay the settlor the net income from the trust estate in monthly or quarterly installments, "as convenient to the Trustee"; and "From time to time, upon the written request of the Settlor, to pay over to him any part or all of the corpus of the trust estate." Provision was made for disbursement of funds from the trust for the care and medical attention of the Settlor in the event of his illness. After the death of the Settlor all of the trust estate not required to meet debts incident to his last illness "shall be distributed . . . to such of Settlor's brother and sister . . . and their lawful lineal descendents as are living at the time of each respective distribution, but if none of such persons is living, then to Ida Vet Funk."

The Trustee was authorized to "transfer all or any part of the trust estate into its name or its nominee with the right to exercise full powers or ownership thereof, including the right to execute proxies, whether discretionary or otherwise, with respect to any stocks constituting a part thereof," and "To retain the property received from the Settlor to invest and reinvest the money and property at any time comprising the trust estate in such securities and other property, real or personal, as the Trustee may select, whether or not legal investments for trustees under any statute or rule of law, and . . . from time to time to change such investments in such manner as the Trustee shall deem best; provided, however, that the Trustee shall not sell or otherwise dispose of any of the trust properties in value in excess of One Thousand Dollars (\$ 1,000.00), or invest trust funds in an amount in excess of One Thousand Dollars (\$ 1,000.00), unless it shall first have notified the Settlor in writing, delivered to him or mailed to his address last on file with the Trustee, and shall have requested his approval of the action proposed by the Trustee. If the Settlor shall file with the Trustee his written disapproval the Trustee shall not take such action. If the Trustee shall not receive such written disapproval within five (5) days after such delivery or mailing, the Trustee shall be free to act regarding the proposed matter in such manner as it shall deem advisable." The Settlor reserved the right to designate some other person than himself to receive such notice from the Trustee, such person to have the same right to disapprove any such proposed action of the Trustee.

The Trustee was empowered "To sell, assign, transfer, collect, alter and change, and to compromise and adjust any part or all of the trust estate, and to execute, acknowledge and deliver all proper assignments, bills of sale, receipts, transfers, deeds, conveyances and other instruments in its judgment needful or desirable . . . [and] to add to the trust by depositing additional property with the Trustee "to be held and administered thereafter as part of the trust estate."

[Among other powers,] [t]he settlor reserved the "right to revoke, modify or amend the Trust agreement." . . .

[The court held that these reserved powers were] not inconsistent with the creation of the trust, and withdrawals made in exercise of that reserved power will be treated as [partial] revocation. . . . [Did sufficient interests pass to the trustee to constitute a trust during the lifetime of the settlor?]

... "In this case, ... the interest of all beneficiaries vested at the creation of the trust, [not at the time of the trustor's death] subject to being divested by the exercise of the reserved power to amend or revoke the indenture of trust. ..." ...

... *"A reservation by a settlor of the power to control investments does not impair the validity of the trust.'*

Where, as here, the property involved in a trust is assigned, transferred and set over to the trustee and remains in the name of the trustee, the interest of the settlor therein passes to the trustee in presenti and while the settlor remains alive the transfer is inter vivos [during his life time] and not testamentary. ...

... The settlor specifically reserved to himself three matters, viz. (1) The income from the trust estate; (2) the right to change or entirely revoke the trust, and (3) the right to disapprove investments of more than $ 1,000 suggested by the trustee. It is agreed by counsel on both sides that a settlor may reserve a life income for himself, together with the right to revoke the trust, and he may reserve additional powers if he does not go too far. We are satisfied that settlor did not go too far in reserving the so-called 'veto' power concerning investments proposed by the trustee. ... "The intended trust is not testamentary merely because the Settlor reserves power to direct the trustee as to making of investments or the exercise of other particular powers, or power to appoint a substitute trustee." ...

The trust involved is not invalidated by the reservations made therein by the settlor, nor is it invalid as a testamentary document in violation of the statute relating to the execution of wills.

[The court held that sufficient property passed to the trustee during the lifetime of the trustor. Hence, the trust was not testamentary. The trust would have been invalid for lack of formalities, had it been testamentary. For our purposes, the case demonstrates the extent of entrustment that is sufficient to create fiduciary relationships—the trust.]

_ _ _ _ _ _ _ _ _ _ _

Discussion Topics

a. What difference did it make if the arrangement was a trust or was not a trust? Who cared? Who do you think brought the case? What was the argument in this case?

b. Assume that the trustor had been alive. Would the bank be a fiduciary of the trustor?

c. Recall the definitions of "agency" and "trust." How would you describe the fiduciary relationship in *Denver National Bank v. Von Brecht*?

_ _ _ _ _ _ _ _ _ _ _

b. What property or power is entrusted?

Let us start by exploring entrusted property. Is public office a form of entrusted property for our purposes? What property can be entrusted? When you studied property law you may have concluded that property would be anything on which the courts assign certain rights to the "owners" in relationship to others. Courts can "propertize" many things. For example, information can become property in law by judicial caveat. This book is property but is the information imported in this book property, if covered by copyright? The concept of power is not clearer or more specific. Let us derive the meaning of "property" and "power" from the cases described below.

In *John D. Hoke v. Henderson,* the Supreme Court of North Carolina discussed the nature of public office as property.[13] In that case, a clerk was appointed under an act of the legislature in 1806. In 1832, another legislative enactment in effect fired this clerk and assigned the clerkship to another person. The clerk who was removed sued to be reinstated. The analysis of the court focused on the authority of the legislature to remove the clerk. That authority depended on whether the clerk had an estate or property right in the office. If he did, he could not be removed by the legislature. Under the constitution, the legislature is authorized to pass general laws, such as establishing the criteria for removal or qualifications of the clerk. It is the judiciary that is authorized to apply these criteria to a specific individual clerk, such as determining the removal of the clerk. If the legislature removed the clerk as a judicial action, the removal would be unconstitutional and void.[14] In addition, the legislature may not deprive the citizens of property. Therefore, the question of whether the public office of a clerk was property was essential to the court's decision, especially after the court determined that the removal of the clerk in this case is a judicial action.

The court wrote:

The sole inquiry that remains is, whether the office of which the act deprives Mr. *Henderson,* is property.... For what is *property;* that is, what do we understand by the term? It means, in reference to the thing, whatever a person can possess and enjoy by right; and in reference to the person, he who has that right to the exclusion of others, is said to have the property. That an office is the subject of property thus explained, is well understood by every one, as well as distinctly stated in the law books from the earliest times. An office ... is defined to be the right to exercise a public or private employment, and to take the fees and emoluments thereunto belonging. A public office has been well described to be this: when one man is specially set by law, and is compellable to do another's business against his will and without his leave, and can demand therefor such compensation, by way of salary or fees, as by law is assigned; to the doing of which business no other person but the officer, or one deputed by him, is legally competent. That the purpose of creating public offices is the common good is not doubted. Hence, most of the rules regulating them have a reference

---

13. Hoke v. Henderson, 15 N.C. (4 Dev.) 1 (1833) (affirming the judgment of the lower court that maintained the right of the defendant to an estate in is office).

14. *Id.* ("The office of clerk is recognized in the constitution; but the tenure is not prescribed in any part of that instrument, and is doubtless, within the discretion of the Legislature. Very soon after the adoption of the Constitution the Act of 1777, . . . for the establishment of Courts of law passed and provided, that the Courts should appoint clerks of skill and probity, who should execute official bonds and take certain oaths of office; and enacts in the fourth section, *that the clerks so appointed shall hold their offices during their good behavior therein.* In 1806 a new law passed which established a Superior Court of Law and a Court of Equity in each county, and provided that the Judges should appoint clerks . . . . Under this law the defendant was in April, 1807 appointed. The legal tenure of his office is therefore that created by the act of 1777, during his good behavior therein, and, as additionally qualified by the act of 1806, during his residence in the County of Lincoln. He has not been found guilty of any misdemeanor in office . . . . The act of 1832 removes him from office and confers it on the applicant").

to the discharge of the duties, and the promotion of the public convenience; they are *pro commodo populi*. Hence they are not the subjects of property in the sense of that full and absolute dominion which is recognized in many other things. They are only the subjects of property, as far as they can be so in safety to the general interest, involved in the discharge of their duties. This principal (sic) demands that different rights of property should be recognized in different offices. It is one of the ordinary rights of property to alien and dispose of it at pleasure; but that is inadmissible in public offices, because the public require a responsible person to answer for defaults. Besides, the power of alienation is not the test of property; for doubtless, it is within the scope of legislative authority to restrict it or to deny it, as in the laws which prescribe the ceremonies necessary to the validity of wills, or conveyances of infants and married women, and which deny altogether the power of conveying, and which interdict all conveyances made in *mortman* (sic). It is another ordinary right of property to have the power of substituting another person to manage it, or to let it lie idle and unmanaged. But the former is not allowable in some offices and the latter in none. The chief executive office and judicial offices cannot be delegated, while subordinate ministerial ones may; for there would be no security that, in the former cases the delegate would be competent, and no responsibility of the superior would be adequate to answer the consequences: though in the latter it is otherwise. But non user is punishable in all public officers and, at the election of the public, is a forfeiture. So a misdemeanor or corruption in office may be punished by judicial sentence in any manner prescribed by law, including a motion as for a forfeiture. These are all restrictions and penalties to secure the public service, which is the object in creating the office. But with these limitations and the like, a public office is the subject of property, as every other thing corporeal or incorporeal, from which men can earn a livelihood and make gain. The office is created for public purposes; but it is conferred on a particular man and accepted by him as a source of individual emolument. To the extent of that emolument it is private property, as much as the land which he tills, or the horse he rides or the debt which is owing to him. Between him and another man, none will deny the right of property. For if one usurp an office which belongs to another, the owner may have an action for damages for the expulsion, for the fees of office received, and a remedy by *quo warranto* to enquire into the right of the usurper, and by *mandamus* to be himself restored. When we find these remedies established to enforce the right of admission into office, to secure the possession of it and its emoluments, we can no longer doubt that in law, an office is deemed the subject of property and valuable property to the officer, as well as an institution for the convenience of the people. If it be so, it falls within those provisions of the Constitution which secure private interests; and cannot be divested without some default of the officer, or the cesser of the office itself.

These are the general principles that lead the Court to the conclusion that the act of Assembly is invalid.

In opposition to them, several arguments have been urged, which the Court has anxiously considered; but without a change of opinion.

It was principally urged, that, whatever may be the rule of the common law, yet in this country and under our Republican institutions, public offices cannot be admitted to be private property; but the offices must be regarded as created solely for the public use, and therefore as subject to abolition when required by the general interest, of which the Legislature is exclusively to judge. [Otherwise] a system requiring officers for its execution, once fixed, would be unchangeably permanent . . . .

. . . Undoubtedly, the creation of an office is a question of political expediency; so is the qualification of the officer; and so are his duties, perquisites, punishment, and the tenure by which he holds his office . . . subjects of legislative regulation . . . [as is] the continuance of the office . . . . If the Legislature increase his duties and responsibilities, or diminish his emoluments, he must submit . . . . It is competent therefore to call for large official bonds and to increase or diminish the fees; *for all that concerns the interest of the community at large.* . . . [F]or the like reasons, . . . the office itself, when it ceases to be required for the benefit of the people, may be abolished. . . . [A person] takes the office with the tacit understanding, that the existence of the office depends on the public necessity for it; and that the Legislature is [the] judge of that.

But while these postulates are conceded, the conclusions drawn from them, cannot be admitted. They are, that there cannot be private property in public offices . . . . The sole concern of the community is that they should be performed, and well performed, by somebody. . . . It is true that a clerk, like all other officers, is a public servant; but he has also a private interest. He is not merely a public servant and political agent. If he were, and had no interest of his own, he might be discharged at pleasure. The distinction in principle, between agencies of the two kinds is obvious. The one is for the public use exclusively, and is often neither lucrative nor honorary, but is onerous. To be deprived of such an office is often a relief, and never can be an injury. The other is for the public service conjointly with a benefit to the officer. To be deprived in this last case is a loss to the officer. . . . [See, for example] the difference between the public agency exercised in appointing a clerk, and that exercised in discharging the duties of a clerk. . . . That power is an *office* in the extended sense of that word, which originally signifies *duty,* generally; but it is not a lucrative or a valuable office. It was a duty to be performed exclusively for the public convenience, and with reference to it alone, without any benefit, immediate or remote, to the Judges and Justices as individuals; who were required, by oath, not to make any private advantage from it, but to give their voice for the appointment of only such persons as appeared to them to be sufficiently qualified, and to do that without reward or hope of it, or any private motive whatsoever. . . .

. . . It has been said, that the obligation to continue in office ought to be mutual, to be complete, and that such is not the case, because the officer may at his pleasure resign. . . . [Yet an] officer may certainly resign; but without acceptance, his resignation is nothing and he remains in office. It is not true, that an office is held at the will of either party. It is held at the will of both. . . . The obligation is therefore strictly mutual. . . .

It is lastly said, that it can be no injury to remove an officer: because the salary is taken to be but a just compensation for his time and labor . . . . It is true that to the officer is left the command of his own time, and the application of his own labor and the fruits of it. But it is not true that he does not suffer by being deprived. . . . [He is deprived of] an employment— the immediate source of livelihood . . . . True, he is free to work at other employments; but he is fit for none . . . . *Per Curiam.* Judgment affirmed.[15]

Compare this case with *State ex Rel. Bonner, Governor v. District Court,* in which the court stated:

Who, *under the law,* is entitled to hold and exercise the office?

At common law, an officer could only be removed for cause and after a hearing. This was because at common law in England, a public office was considered as an incorporeal hereditament grantable by the Crown in which the holder acquired and had an estate.

That conception of a public office does not obtain in this country. Here a public office is considered a public trust. "With us, a public office has never been regarded as an incorporeal hereditament, or as having the character or qualities of a grant. That a public office is the property of him to whom the execution of its duties is intrusted (sic) is

---

15.   *Id.* (citations omitted).

repugnant to the institutions of our country, and at issue with that universal understanding of the community which is the result of those institutions. With us, public offices are public agencies or trusts, and the nature of the relation of a public officer to the public is inconsistent with either a property or a contract right. Every public office is created in the interest and for the benefit of the people, and belongs to them. The right, it has been said, is not the right of the incumbent to the place, but of the people to the officer. . . . The incumbent has no vested right in the office which he holds." "Public officers, in other words, are but the servants of the people, and not their rulers."[16]

– – – – – – – – – – -

Discussion Topics

a. Why is a public officer a fiduciary? What was entrusted to the officer? To whom is the officer a fiduciary? With which of the two decisions would you agree? Why?

b. What precisely is entrusted to directors, officers or employees of a corporation? Do they have property rights in their job? Do they have property rights in anything else related to their jobs?

c. Clearly, the public clerks in both cases were entitled to payment for their service. So is a lawyer, a physician or a trustee, who has contracted to perform services. What, then, belongs to them, and what does not? If a money manager is entrusted with another people's life savings, and agrees to manage the savings for a fee, is his "position" his property? Is any part of the arrangement his property? How would you distinguish what is and what is not his property?

– – – – – – – – – – -

c. Is information "property" that could be entrusted?

[Frank Snepp was a CIA agent.[17] After he left the agency, Snepp published a book about CIA activities in South Vietnam. The manuscript was not submitted to the CIA for review, as required by Snepp's agreement with the agency in 1968. That agreement prohibited him from publishing "any information or material relating to the Agency, its activities or intelligence activities generally, either during or after the term of [his] employment . . . without specific prior approval by the Agency."] The promise was an integral part of Snepp's concurrent undertaking "not to disclose any classified information relating to the Agency without proper authorization." Thus, Snepp had pledged not to divulge *classified* information and not to publish any information without prepublication clearance.[18] [The Government sued Snepp seeking a] declaration that Snepp had breached the contract, and an injunction requiring Snepp to submit future writings for prepublication review. The government also sought an order imposing a constructive trust for the Government's benefit on all profits that Snepp might earn from publishing the book in violation of his fiduciary obligations to the Agency.[19]

---

16.   Bonner v. District Court, 206 P.2d 166, 169 (Sup. Ct. Mont. 1949) (citations omitted).

17.   Snepp v. United States, 444 U.S. 507 (1980) (some footnotes omitted) (citations omitted).

18.   Upon the eve of his departure from the Agency in 1976, Snepp also executed a "termination secrecy agreement." That document reaffirmed his obligation "never" to reveal "any classified information, or any information concerning intelligence or CIA that has not been made public by CIA . . . without the express written consent of the Director of Central Intelligence or his representative."

19.   At the time of suit, Snepp already had received about $ 60,000 in advance payments. His contract with his publisher provides for royalties and other potential profits.

[The District Court found that Snepp had] "willfully, deliberately and surreptitiously breached his position of trust with the CIA and the [1968] secrecy agreement" by publishing his book without submitting it for prepublication review. The court also found that Snepp deliberately misled CIA officials into believing that he would submit the book for prepublication clearance. Finally, the court determined as a fact that publication of the book had "caused the United States irreparable harm and loss." The District Court therefore enjoined future breaches of Snepp's agreement and imposed a constructive trust on Snepp's profits." [Thus, Snepp's profits from the book had to be paid over to the government.]

The Court of Appeals accepted the findings of the District Court and agreed that Snepp had breached a valid contract.[20] It specifically affirmed the finding that Snepp's failure to submit his manuscript for prepublication review had inflicted "irreparable harm" on intelligence activities vital to our national security. Thus, the court upheld the injunction against future violations of Snepp's prepublication obligation. The court, however, concluded that the record did not support imposition of a constructive trust. The conclusion rested on the court's perception that Snepp had a First Amendment right to publish unclassified information and the Government's concession -- for the purposes of this litigation -- that Snepp's book divulged no classified intelligence. In other words, the court thought that Snepp's fiduciary obligation extended only to preserving the confidentiality of classified material. It therefore limited recovery to nominal damages and to the possibility of punitive damages if the Government -- in a jury trial -- could prove tortious conduct.

Judge Hoffman, sitting by designation, dissented from the refusal to find a constructive trust. The 1968 agreement, he wrote, "was no ordinary contract; it gave life to a fiduciary relationship and invested in Snepp the trust of the CIA." Prepublication clearance was part of Snepp's undertaking to protect confidences associated with his trust. Punitive damages, Judge Hoffman argued, were both a speculative and inappropriate remedy for Snepp's breach. We agree with Judge Hoffman that Snepp breached a fiduciary obligation and that the proceeds of his breach are impressed with a constructive trust.

Snepp's employment with the CIA involved an extremely high degree of trust. In the opening sentence of the agreement that he signed, Snepp explicitly recognized that he was entering a trust relationship.[21] The trust agreement specifically imposed the obligation not to publish any information relating to the Agency without submitting the information for clearance. Snepp stipulated at trial that—after undertaking this obligation—he had been "assigned to various positions of trust" and that he had been granted "frequent access to classified information, including information regarding intelligence sources and methods." Snepp published his book about CIA activities on the basis of this background and exposure. He deliberately and surreptitiously violated his obligation to submit all material

---

20.   [The court noted that Snepp signed the contract freely, and the] agreement is an entirely appropriate exercise of the CIA Director's statutory mandate to "[protect] intelligence sources and methods from unauthorized disclosure" . . . . [E]ven in the absence of an express agreement—the CIA could have acted to protect substantial government interests by imposing reasonable restrictions on employee activities that in other contexts might be protected by the First Amendment. The Government has a compelling interest in protecting both the secrecy of information important to our national security and the appearance of confidentiality so essential to the effective operation of our foreign intelligence service. The agreement that Snepp signed is a reasonable means for protecting this vital interest.

21.   The first sentence of the 1968 agreement read: "I, Frank W. Snepp, III, understand that upon entering duty with the Central Intelligence Agency I am undertaking a position of trust in that Agency of the Government . . . ."

for prepublication review. Thus, he exposed the classified information with which he had been entrusted to the risk of disclosure.

Whether Snepp violated his trust does not depend upon whether his book actually contained classified information. The Government does not deny -- as a general principle -- Snepp's right to publish unclassified information. Nor does it contend -- at this stage of the litigation -- that Snepp's book contains classified material. The Government simply claims that, in light of the special trust reposed in him and the agreement that he signed, Snepp should have given the CIA an opportunity to determine whether the material he proposed to publish would compromise classified information or sources. Neither of the Government's concessions undercuts its claim that Snepp's failure to submit to prepublication review was a breach of his trust.

Both the District Court and the Court of Appeals found that a former intelligence agent's publication of unreviewed material relating to intelligence activities can be detrimental to vital national interests even if the published information is unclassified. When a former agent relies on his own judgment about what information is detrimental, he may reveal information that the CIA--with its broader understanding of what may expose classified information and confidential sources--could have identified as harmful. In addition to receiving intelligence from domestically based or controlled sources, the CIA obtains information from the intelligence services of friendly nations[22]and from agents operating in foreign countries. The continued availability of these foreign sources depends upon the CIA's ability to guarantee the security of information that might compromise them and even endanger the personal safety of foreign agents. . . .

[But what should be the appropriate remedy? The Court ruled:]

The decision of the Court of Appeals denies the Government the most appropriate remedy for Snepp's acknowledged wrong. Indeed, as a practical matter, the decision may well leave the Government with no reliable deterrent against similar breaches of security. No one disputes that the actual damages attributable to a publication such as Snepp's generally are unquantifiable. Nominal damages are a hollow alternative, certain to deter no one. The punitive damages recoverable after a jury trial are speculative and unusual. Even if recovered, they may bear no relation to either the Government's irreparable loss or Snepp's unjust gain.

The Government could not pursue the only remedy that the Court of Appeals left it without losing the benefit of the bargain it seeks to enforce. Proof of the tortious conduct necessary to sustain an award of punitive damages might force the Government to disclose some of the very confidences that Snepp promised to protect. The trial of such a suit, before a jury if the defendant so elects, would subject the CIA and its officials to probing discovery into the Agency's highly confidential affairs. Rarely would the Government run this risk. In a letter introduced at Snepp's trial, former CIA Director Colby noted the analogous problem in criminal cases. Existing law, he stated, "requires the revelation in open court of confirming or additional information of such a nature that the potential damage to the national security precludes prosecution." When the Government cannot secure its remedy without unacceptable risks, it has no remedy at all.

A constructive trust, on the other hand, protects both the Government and the former agent from unwarranted risks. This remedy is the natural and customary consequence of a

---

22.   Every major nation in the world has an intelligence service. Whatever fairly may be said about some of its past activities, the CIA (or its predecessor the Office of Strategic Services) is an agency thought by every President since Franklin D. Roosevelt to be essential to the security of the United States and—in a sense—the free world. It is impossible for a government wisely to make critical decisions about foreign policy and national defense without the benefit of dependable foreign intelligence.

breach of trust. It deals fairly with both parties by conforming relief to the dimensions of the wrong. If the agent secures prepublication clearance, he can publish with no fear of liability. If the agent publishes unreviewed material in violation of his fiduciary and contractual obligation, the trust remedy simply requires him to disgorge the benefits of his faithlessness. Since the remedy is swift and sure, it is tailored to deter those who would place sensitive information at risk. And since the remedy reaches only funds attributable to the breach, it cannot saddle the former agent with exemplary damages out of all proportion to his gain. . . . We therefore reverse the judgment of the Court of Appeals insofar as it refused to impose a constructive trust on Snepp's profits, and we remand the cases to the Court of Appeals for reinstatement of the full judgment of the District Court. *So ordered.*[23]

d. Can "virtual" property, created in a game on the Internet, be entrusted property?[24]

With the development of the Internet, new forms of possible property and property rights have emerged. A most interesting issue arose with respect to stealing "virtual property." A virtual world produced by game developers houses numerous participants from the real world who interact inside it. It creates a parallel, second life. It is the new genre of games referred to as "Massively Multiplayer Online Role Playing Game."[25] As the name itself suggests, participants in the game play their roles via their "avatar," their online identity. These players interact, "fight" together to win their "rewards," in the form of "virtual property" in game "currencies" and "items." The players then "trade" with each other and put their "items" in game "auction houses." Some games involve "virtual real property" that the players can "acquire," and on which they can build and develop.

The games seem a child's fantasyland. Yet this fantasy had real impact in the real world not merely by providing revenues to entertainment companies that offer these game services. The players themselves are selling and trading virtual items in the real world, for real world U.S. currency. The average participants are adults,[26] and have attached real world money value to their items. The players take their "virtual property" seriously.

MMORPG is a game through the Internet, which involves a rare virtual weapon. In March 2005, one player acquired the weapon and that started a quarrel with another player. The other player borrowed and promised to return the weapon. Instead he sold it for the equivalent of more than $1000. The weapon "owner" reported the theft,

---

23. Snepp v. United States, 444 U.S. 507 (1980).
24. This material is drawn, with consent, from a paper by Adrian Wong Chun Kit in satisfaction of a seminar requirements on fiduciary law at Boston University Law School, Spring 2007. The paper is edited and abridged, and some of the footnotes were omitted.
25. Popular games of this genre includes games like *"World of Warcraft," "Everquest II."*
26. Theodore J. Westbrook, Comment, *Owned: Finding a Place for Virtual World Property Rights*, 2006 MICH. ST. L. REV. 779, 785 (2006) ("The average age of users and the amount of time spent by these users in virtual worlds are also indicative of the social and economic impact of MMGs. It may be surprising to some that most users of popular MMGs are adults. For example, the average age of an Everquest user is 25.7 years. While women make up a small percentage of Everquest users, their average age is 29, somewhat higher than the overall average") (footnotes omitted).

but the authorities did not take it seriously. They doubted whether it was a theft. After all, the item was a virtual weapon. The owner then met with the "thief" and stabbed him "repeatedly in the left chest and killed him."[27]

While this might be a unique bizarre incident, it is not difficult to imagine similar disputes and lawsuits in the foreseeable future. Questions arise (1) whether it would be easier for the developers to solve the disputes; for example, in the above situation, by restoring the item; (2) whether the developers have a duty to protect the virtual property; and particularly (3) whether virtual property should be considered property under the law.

The following is reportedly an actual online conversation between two players ("Q" and "A"), held to ascertain the views of a layperson player ("A").[28]

Q: Have you read the entire agreement before setting up the game account and playing the game?

A: Not really, I just assumed its reasonable . . . have you?

Q: For the purpose of writing my essay [this essay] Ya, but frankly not really when I was starting the account. Do you know that under the contract/ terms of use Blizzard [the game developer] stipulates that we [the players] have no property right whatsoever over any data, items or character [otherwise known as the "avatar"] that we used; that our rights on this contract are limited to the license to use and enjoy the game; and that they have no liability over any loss or damage to these data, and they reserve the right to full control and destroy of these data?

A: Well there is no way to prove that you have what you have, so they have no way to compensate unless you keep a printout of your status [the attributes of the "avatar"] and stuff [the virtual items].

A: And if another player steal my stuff . . . its not like they can regulate all the players day by day?

Q: So with that distrust why are you still playing the game?

A: Addiction lol [i.e. laugh out loud] aren't you also playing? . . . well I guess it's a gamble that this doesn't happen.

Q: So you are taking the risk despite knowing the risk, and knowing that you might have no way of verifying/ increasing the trust you have on blizzard?

A: If their stuff messes up a lot they will lose clients so I guess they will do their best to accommodate [the clients]. The trust works both ways, our trust on their ability and intention to keep customers.

---

27. This material is drawn, with consent, from a paper by Adrian Wong Chun Kit, in satisfaction of a seminar requirement on fiduciary law at Boston University Law School, Spring 2007 entitled *Fiduciary Duty in the Virtual Property?: Looking into the New Challenges the Virtual Internet World Poses into the Relationship Between Internet Service Providers and Users.* The paper is summarized. For a more detailed report of the incident, *see* Amalie Finlayson & Reuters, *Online Gamer Killed for Selling Virtual Weapon,* SYDNEY MORNING HERALD, Mar. 30, 2005, http://www.smh.com.au/news/World/Online-gamer-killed-for-selling-virtual-weapon/2005/03/30/1111862440188.html.
28. Conversation conducted on April 17, 2007 in the "guild chat channel" of the game "World of Warcraft." Some of the language has been altered to avoid using less than pleasant language or otherwise to accommodate better understanding due to short forms that players commonly use. The other player is actually (he purports) a 42-year old father of 3, and all but one of the family actually regularly play the game, which also shows how wide the MMORPG market actually is today, and how it is changing from a teenager-only activity into almost a family activity.

Q: What about remedies? Don't you want to be compensated?

A: I think they did give this one guy his stuff back but I am not sure. I mean if you sell bbq ribs and customers sue you will lose out, but if they are good you will win?

Q: Problem is here you might not have any claim because its not a property per se.

A: I think we should be entitled to what we lost, but ya I guess its hard for the moment . . . . "

This conversation sheds some light on the current trend in Internet use. Misinformation and lack of knowledge as to the mechanism and legal implications of online actions seems to be what, ironically, prevents the users from recognizing the risks that lie in Internet use. Other than the property rights issues, there are also many hidden traps, for example, by service providers use of personal information.[29]

Is the current law adequate to address the issue of the virtual property?[30] Young users seem to consider it to be; at least there are no court decisions on the issue.[31] Yet, after all, we speak of "identity theft" and "privacy invasion" on the Internet.

The virtual world provider earns subscription revenue from users, who in turn "earn" money and "items" in the game, and by fighting monsters. Within the world the users have the right to use and transfer the items and money. According to John Locke, "Whatsoever then he removes out of the State that Nature hath provided, and left it in, he hath mixed his Labour with it, and joyned to it something that is his own, and thereby makes it his Property."[32] From the users' viewpoint, they should have rights in the property, and the fact that the property is intangible should not prevent recognition of these rights, as the law recognizes intangible property in other contexts.[33] However, to avoid liability, and to avoid third party intrusion into the game or service, service providers restrict the rights of the users through contract terms that restrict the rights in/to the underlying data.[34]

---

29. As laid down by the Electronic Privacy Information Center in the article *Privacy Self Regulation: A Decade of Disappointment*: "Today, there are many more methods through which users can be tracked, profiled and monitored in the online world. . . . Entirely new technologies have emerged as well, some of which are all but unknown to consumers. Few of these methods are regulated, either internally by industry or externally by government. . . ." Chris Jay Hoofnagle, *Privacy Self Regulation: A Decade of Disappointment*, EPIC (2005) (further explaining technologies such as cookies, virus, google email content extraction that allow the service providers or third parties to acquire information and data that are not voluntary provided by the users).

30.   Adrian Wong Chun Kit, *Fiduciary Duty in the Virtual Property?: Looking into the New Challenges the Virtual Internet World Poses into the Relationship Between Internet Service Providers and Users* (2007) (student paper, Boston University School of Law), *citing* Corey A. Ciocchetti, *E-Commerce and Information Privacy: Privacy Policies as Personal Information Protectors*, 44 AM. BUS. L.J. 55 (2007).

31.   *Id.* (a more detailed account of the virtual world phenomenon can be seen in Greg Lastowka, *Decoding Cyberproperty*, 40 IND. L. REV. 23 (2007); and Theodore J. Westbrook, Comment, *Owned: Finding a Place for Virtual World Property Rights*, 2006 MICH. ST. L. REV. 779 (2006)).

32.   JOHN LOCKE, TWO TREATISES OF GOVERNMENT 306 (Cambridge Univ. Press 2d ed. 1967) (1690).

33.   Adrian Wong Chun Kit, *Fiduciary Duty in the Virtual Property?: Looking into the New Challenges the Virtual Internet World Poses into the Relationship Between Internet Service Providers and Users* (2007) (student paper, Boston University School of Law).

Arguably, the service providers need not restrict the users' rights in the virtual property. They could retain rights to the data and intellectual property rights related to the items and the game, while allowing property rights in the items, at least the right to use or transfer the items in the game context. According to Judge Mosk in his dissent in *Moore v. Regents of University of California,*[35] "the concept of property is often said to refer to a 'bundle of rights'"[36] and "'[s]ince property or title is a complex bundle of rights, duties, powers and immunities, the pruning away of some or a great many of these elements does not entirely destroy the title.'"[37]

As more people participate in such games, the value of virtual property is increasing, along with the potential for abuse due to the lack of recognition of virtual property rights. Arguably, with no recognition of such rights, users have little or no remedy for abuse and service providers have no incentive to prevent it.[38]

Viktor Mayer-Schonberger and John Crowley examined "the phenomenon of virtual worlds like Lineage, EverQuest and Second Life": In their article the authors describe and analyze virtual worlds governance and law through the lenses of law and economics. They note the fact that virtual worlds must compete with the real world in terms of governance, law, and markets. The authors examine various possibilities by which real world lawmakers should reach to regulate the virtual world. Rather than compete or impose their rule on the virtual world the authors recommend "the creation of robust self-governance within virtual worlds."

... [The authors offer] options for real-world lawmakers. They speculate that "as economic pressures make it difficult for virtual world providers to resist granting IP rights to users, virtual world providers may find themselves in competition with each other, based not in small part on the regulatory framework they can offer their users. [The authors] predicted that these cross-jurisdictional dynamics among virtual worlds could restrict the ability of real-world lawmakers to exert control over virtual worlds."[39]

---

34.   *Id.* (under the standard end-user license agreement, the provider retains all ownership and intellectual property rights in/to the data related to the world. This implies that, since the "items" in the games are comprised of this data, the users have no right to the items and no remedy if the items are taken by the provider or lost if the game is invaded by a third party).

35.   Moore v. Regents of University of California, 793 P.2d 479 (Cal. 1990) (Mosk, J., dissenting), *cert. denied,* 499 U.S. 936 (1991).

36.   Moore v. Regents of University of California, 793 P.2d 479, 509 (Cal. 1990) (Mosk, J., dissenting), *cert. denied,* 499 U.S. 936 (1991).

37.   *Id.* at 510 (Mosk, J., dissenting) (quoting People v. Walker, 90 P.2d 854, 855 (Cal. Ct. App. 1939)).

38.   Adrian Wong Chun Kit, *Fiduciary Duty in the Virtual Property?: Looking into the New Challenges the Virtual Internet World Poses into the Relationship Between Internet Service Providers and Users* (2007).

39.   Viktor Mayer-Schonberger & John Crowley, *Napster's Second Life?: The Regulatory Changes of Virtual Worlds,* 100 Nw. U.L. Rev. 1775, 1779-80, 1826 (2006) (footnotes omitted).

- - - - - - - - - - -

Discussion Topics

a. Should courts worldwide recognize property rights to virtual property and personal data? If so, would courts recognize fiduciary relationships between service providers and subscribers, and the attendant duties of the service providers, for example, to refrain from misusing subscribers' data for their own gain, and ensuring reasonable protection against third parties from doing the same?

b. Comment on this sentence: "By a general fiduciary duty, a wider and expandable variety of cases can then be under control, granting the users remedies and offering incentive to providers to be trustworthy in its service in the future."

c. What would be the role of service providers in the governance and legal regime of the virtual world?

- - - - - - - - - - -

e. Can power be entrusted?

The following case, *Moore v. Regents of University of California,*[40] discusses the question of the physician's power over the patient. We may describe the issues in this case differently than the description of the court. For our purposes two issues are raised. One is whether the physician has the power to do what this physician did, and the second is whether the patient entrusted the physician with that power.

I. Introduction

Plaintiff alleges that his physician failed to disclose preexisting research and economic interests in [his body] cells before obtaining consent to the medical procedures by which they were extracted. The superior court sustained all defendants' demurrers to the third amended complaint, and the Court of Appeal reversed. We hold that the complaint states a cause of action for breach of the physician's disclosure obligations, but not for conversion.

II. Facts ...

The plaintiff is John Moore (Moore), who underwent treatment for hairy-cell leukemia at the Medical Center of the University of California at Los Angeles (UCLA Medical Center). The five defendants are: (1) Dr. David W. Golde (Golde), a physician who attended Moore at UCLA Medical Center; (2) the Regents of the University of California (Regents), who own and operate the university; (3) Shirley G. Quan, a researcher employed by the Regents; (4) Genetics Institute, Inc. (Genetics Institute); and (5) Sandoz Pharmaceuticals Corporation and related entities (collectively Sandoz).

Moore first visited UCLA Medical Center on October 5, 1976, shortly after he learned that he had hairy-cell leukemia. After hospitalizing Moore and "withdr[awing] extensive amounts of blood, bone marrow aspirate, and other bodily substances," Golde confirmed that diagnosis. At this time all defendants, including Golde, were aware that "certain blood products and blood components were of great value in a number of commercial and scientific efforts" and that access to a patient whose blood contained these substances would provide "competitive, commercial, and scientific advantages."

---

40.   Moore v. Regents of University of California, 793 P.2d 479 (Cal. 1990) (footnotes omitted) (some citations omitted), *cert. denied,* 499 U.S. 936 (1991).

On October 8, 1976, Golde recommended that Moore's spleen be removed. Golde informed Moore "that he had reason to fear for his life, and that the proposed splenectomy operation . . . was necessary to slow down the progress of his disease." Based upon Golde's representations, Moore signed a written consent form authorizing the splenectomy.

Before the operation, Golde and Quan "formed the intent and made arrangements to obtain portions of [Moore's] spleen following its removal" and to take them to a separate research unit. Golde gave written instructions to this effect on October 18 and 19, 1976. These research activities "were not intended to have . . . any relation to [Moore's] medical . . . care." However, neither Golde nor Quan informed Moore of their plans to conduct this research or requested his permission. Surgeons at UCLA Medical Center, whom the complaint does not name as defendants, removed Moore's spleen on October 20, 1976.

Moore returned to the UCLA Medical Center several times between November 1976 and September 1983. He did so at Golde's direction and based upon representations "that such visits were necessary and required for his health and well-being, and based upon the trust inherent in and by virtue of the physician-patient relationship . . . ." On each of these visits Golde withdrew additional samples of "blood, blood serum, skin, bone marrow aspirate, and sperm." On each occasion Moore travelled to the UCLA Medical Center from his home in Seattle because he had been told that the procedures were to be performed only there and only under Golde's direction.

[While Moore was treated by Golde, Golde and other defendants were doing research on Moore's cells from which they planned to benefit financially without disclosing these facts to Moore.]

Sometime before August 1979, Golde established a cell line from Moore's T-lymphocytes. On January 30, 1981, the Regents applied for a patent on the cell line, listing Golde and Quan as inventors. "[B]y virtue of an established policy . . . , [the] Regents, Golde, and Quan would share in any royalties or profits . . . arising out of [the] patent." The patent issued on March 20, 1984, naming Golde and Quan as the inventors of the cell line and the Regents as the assignee of the patent. (U.S. Patent No. 4,438,032 (Mar. 20, 1984).]

The Regent's patent also covers various methods for using the cell line to produce lymphokines. . . .

With the Regents' assistance, Golde negotiated agreements for commercial development of the cell line and products to be derived from it. Under an agreement with Genetics Institute, Golde "became a paid consultant" and "acquired the rights to 75,000 shares of common stock." Genetics Institute also agreed to pay Golde and the Regents "at least $ 330,000 over three years, including a pro-rata share of [Golde's] salary and fringe benefits, in exchange for . . . exclusive access to the materials and research performed" on the cell line and products derived from it. On June 4, 1982, Sandoz "was added to the agreement," and compensation payable to Golde and the Regents was increased by $ 110,000. "[T]hroughout this period, . . . Quan spent as much as 70 [percent] of her time working for [the] Regents on research" related to the cell line.

Based upon these allegations, Moore attempted to state 13 causes of action [one of which was conversion of the cells, which the superior court considered and rejected. Having rejected this claim the judge rejected all the rest of the claims as well].

With one justice dissenting, the Court of Appeal reversed, holding that the complaint did state a cause of action for conversion. The Court of Appeal agreed with the superior court that the allegations against Genetics Institute and Sandoz were insufficient, but directed the superior court to give Moore leave to amend. The Court of Appeal also directed the superior court to decide "the remaining causes of action, which [had] never been expressly ruled upon."

III. Discussion

A. *Breach of Fiduciary Duty and Lack of Informed Consent*

Moore repeatedly alleges that Golde failed to disclose the extent of his research and economic interests in Moore's cells before obtaining consent to the medical procedures by which the cells were extracted. These allegations, in our view, state a cause of action against Golde for invading a legally protected interest of his patient. This cause of action can properly be characterized either as the breach of a fiduciary duty to disclose facts material to the patient's consent or, alternatively, as the performance of medical procedures without first having obtained the patient's informed consent.

Our analysis begins with three well-established principles. First, "a person of adult years and in sound mind has the right, in the exercise of control over his own body, to determine whether or not to submit to lawful medical treatment." Second, "the patient's consent to treatment, to be effective, must be an informed consent." Third, in soliciting the patient's consent, a physician has a fiduciary duty to disclose all information material to the patient's decision.

These principles lead to the following conclusions: (1) a physician must disclose personal interests unrelated to the patient's health, whether research or economic, that may affect the physician's professional judgment; and (2) a physician's failure to disclose such interests may give rise to a cause of action for performing medical procedures without informed consent or breach of fiduciary duty.[41]

The majority of the court rejected the claim that Moore's cells were property and hence rejected his claim to benefit from the patent that Golde and his collaborators established based on the cells which they developed from Moore's cells.

– – – – – – – – – – – –

Discussion Topics

a. Are all physicians fiduciaries of their patients? Suppose a physician treats a patient for a broken bone, is the physician a fiduciary of the patient for the patient's asthma or tendency to hysteria?

b. Are teachers fiduciaries? If they are, what makes them fiduciaries? What is the power with which they are entrusted?

c. Professionals have had a special place in the crowd of fiduciaries. They are distinguished from tradespersons. But there are doubts. Here are two views:

In the opinion of David Schmidt, some managers are more professional than the usual professionals, such as doctors. He distinguishes between professionals and "careerists," who are "self-centered" pursuing their interests excluding the public's interests. This difference reflects the difference between market exchange and professional exchange.

"The market exchange is 'merely *transactional* . . . , in the sense that it serves only to meet the self-perceived, stated wants of the customer. The professional exchange is *transformational* in the sense that it serves the 'deeper needs' of the client." [42]

---

41.   *Id.* This decision is discussed in Chapter Three, dealing with fiduciary duties, and in Chapter Six, dealing with classification of fiduciary law compared, among others, to tort, as well as in Chapter Seven, discussing remedies on breach of fiduciary duties.

Here is a view expressed through my e-mail correspondence with a brain surgeon who will remain nameless. I asked:

Tamar: Question: Are surgeons professionals or trades-persons?

Anonymous: Professionals, it's surely fair to say, but it really has that trade feel as time goes on. In practice, perhaps the only thing really separating a blue-collar worker from a brain surgeon is the CE requirements

Tamar: Just FYI-nothing separates me from a blue-collar person except the ingrained drive to meet public need and not only for $$$. The surgeon wants to heal the patient -- not only for the money. I do not sell my services to anyone who pays more. The shoe merchant does. That is the difference, as it should be. There are privileges that professionals receive for the commitment they should make. Sorry for the long answer to a short message.

Anonymous: I'm not sure why you consider it a professional distinction/privilege to serve others above and beyond $$$. To be sure, notoriously lawyers (and increasingly doctors on account of the evolution of insurance) go to the highest bidder. Most surgeons choose that specialty because it is the highest paying in medicine. And, I've known many craftsmen who were in their trade to serve as much as to survive (shoe merchant is probably not the best example), greatly motivated by the legacy and enhanced customer of quality life their work leaves. An outstanding example would be the superb young stone mason who just did my soapstone counters and then mentored me through my slate terrace. I've done tree work very part-time for many years (still climbing high at 50) and have experienced the same circumstance with a fellow who has been specializing in ornamentals after 25 years doing traditional tree work. The ornamentals lent too much more intimate contact with the customer and shared gratification with the process. Hmmmm. Do you have many "blue collar" friends? :-).

What is your position in this debate? Is it possible for a fiduciary to manage a business? Can law firms be viewed as businesses? Are there any differences between law businesses and shoe factories?

d. A difficult question regarding fiduciary relationships is raised in the case of organ harvesting. Consider this issue reported on by Cindy Chan.

In July 2006, David Matas, an international human rights lawyer, and David Kilgour, the former Canadian Secretary of State for Asia-Pacific, reported continuous "large-scale organ seizures from unwilling [persons]." [43]

While the possible harm to the patient in the *Moore* case was minimal, in this case, the persons whose organs are being harvested are likely to die. Is there a relationship between the physicians, who receive organs and perform the transplants, and the unknown persons whose organs are being removed?

Do those who take out the organs without authority owe a fiduciary duty to the persons whose organs they are harvesting? Should physicians who use harvested organs but do not know their origins, ask where the organs come from and whether they were removed from

---

42. David P. Schmidt, *Quilting Professional Identities in Business, in* RELIGION, MORALITY AND THE PROFESSIONS IN AMERICA 27, 27, 36-37 (1998), http://poynter. indiana.edu/publications/m-rmpa.pdf (endnotes omitted).
43. Cindy Chan, *Revised Report into Allegations of Organ Harvesting:* EPOCH TIMES, Feb. 1, 2007, http://en.epochtimes.com/news/7-2-1/51181.html (last visited Aug. 7, 2007).

consenting donors? What is the relationship of the physicians to people who donate their organs to other family members?

e. Are physicians fiduciaries of people that the physicians did not accept as patients? Read this excerpt from Robin Cook's *Godplayer*:

Many terminally ill patients at Boston Memorial Hospital are dying. This is not notable. However, what is notable is the fact they are dying before they were expected to die.

> Is Thomas Kingsley, a top cardiac surgeon, killing terminal patients? Does he kill patients if he does not treat them? Some may feel that it is a waste of time to help them when they are doomed to die soon, whether he treats them or not. By killing them, he has more time to devote to patients with a better prognosis (those who "deserve to live"). Resources are limited in the hospital where he works. He feels it is in the best interests of everyone involved if he can simply focus on those who have a better prognosis to live.[44]

Arguably, a doctor's duty is to treat all patients equally. Doctors should not pick or choose which patients to care for or care for better than others. Is this baseline of treatment obvious? Should certain patients be treated better than others (or mistreated, as one could interpret the situation)? Is giving better care to one patient over another a breach of the doctor's duty? Could it be a crime as well (and a breach of the Hippocratic Oath)? How should a surgeon choose patients? Kingsley was a leader in his field. Therefore other physicians are likely to follow his example. How should certain patients be selected for his services over others? Should the ones with the best chance of survival be chosen for his services? Should the ones who pose the biggest risks be selected as Kingsley is the surgeon most likely to provide a successful surgery? The old v. the young? The terminally ill v. those who have the chance to live? Patients with interesting unusual diseases?

Could rejected patients sue Kingsley? On what grounds? Is refusing to accept a patient permissible? Under all circumstances? What should the law be?

— — — — — — — — — — -

f. Should marriage be recognized as a fiduciary relationship?[45]

A good marriage is at least 80 percent good luck in finding the right person at the right time. The rest is trust.
—Nanette Newman[46]

---

44.   ROBIN COOK, GODPLAYER (1983) (summarized).
45.   The material in this section represents with the permission of the author a modified, edited and abridged paper of Paul Nikhinson written in satisfaction of the requirements of a seminar on Fiduciary Law, 2007, Boston University School of Law. Some footnotes omitted.
46.   QUOTATIONSBOOK, http://www.quotationsbook.com/quote/25487/ (last visited Oct. 17, 2007).

> *Take special care that thou never trust any friend or servant with any matter that may endanger thine estate; for so shalt thou make thyself a bond-slave to him that thou trustest, and leave thyself always to his mercy.*
> —**Sir Walter Raleigh**[47]

Most if not every relationship requires some measure of trust. The type of trust operating in "affect-based" relationships (i.e. husband-wife, parent-child) differs from that in "cognitive-based" relationships (i.e. entrustor-trustee, investor-money manager). Irrespective of form, however, a common characteristic in these cases is the presence of disproportionate levels of information, resource, knowledge or capacity among the parties. Such asymmetries can discourage or destroy proper functions. Consequently, trust in the conduct of others, and in the system's integrity, provides valuable social capital.

Cognitive-based relationships—the product of logic and experience—are more frequent in economic/market transactions. Trust in these relationships is often based on performance criteria. But it is undermined by costly and difficult monitoring and controls. "[F]iduciary law presupposes that trustees feel morally obligated to serve in the best interests of beneficiaries, and partners conduct themselves with 'a punctilio of honor,'[48] yet if (or when) those moral duties fail, default legal norms must protect the aggrieved and serve as the baseline mechanism of enforcement."

Affective relationships are rarely imposed with fiduciary duties under U.S. law. It may well be that the law views such duties as "superfluous to, or inconsistent with, the normative moral obligations of the institution." Marriage relationships are status-based rather than consent-based. And "focusing so greatly on status, the common law disregards marriage's progression towards a more contractual structure. Maine's perceptive examination of the move from status to contract[49] and the treatises of numerous respected commentators evidence the direction and scope of this development. While marriage once existed as a true constant in the social order, current statistics indicate otherwise. Societal confidence in marriage is low, breach of trust between parties commonplace, and the financial consequences quite grim."

In today's world divorces are increasing and so are the legal issues concerning finances in marriages. Perhaps the legal classification of marriage or at least some aspects of the marriage relationship should be deemed fiduciary. A background summary of the common law's treatment of marriage, divorce, and spousal duties in the past may be helpful for the future.

---

47.   GIGA QUOTES, http://www.giga-usa.com/quotes/topics/trust_t003.htm (last visited Oct. 17, 2007).
48.   Meinhard v. Salmon, 164 N.E. 545, 546 (N.Y. 1928).
49.   HENRY JAMES SUMNER MAINE, ANCIENT LAW (C. K. Allen ed. 1931) (1861).

Early ideas of marriage viewed the husband and wife as one person under the law, and that one person was the husband. The woman's personal property at the commencement of the marriage and thereafter during the marriage vested absolutely in the husband. The common law also barred married women from making contracts and undertaking independent investments of personal and real property. In the middle and late nineteenth century, however, most states passed laws to change the common law disabilities of married and divorced women, and balance the spouses' rights. Under these statutes married women had the rights to independently transact in property, to make a will, to sue and be sued individually, and to contract and keep their earnings separately.

In some states another system developed based on continental civil law principles, developing spousal fiduciary duties. "California's system is one of the oldest and most developed examples. It recognizes that spouses on the brink of divorce may engage in reckless behavior and unfair dealings. Over forty years ago, in *Vai v. Bank of America*,[50] California established spousal fiduciary duties. The *Vai* standard, however, imposed a rather high trustee-like fiduciary duty and presented the potential for many baseless claims brought out of mere spite. Consequently, the California Court of Appeal modified the duty, limiting it primarily to property settlements.[51] The legislature further narrowed the duty with the enactment of former Civil Code § 5125, providing for a spousal duty no more stringent than a 'good faith' standard. The California Supreme Court further limited spousal duty to the period prior to filing a petition for divorce."[52]

In 1991 the California legislature broadened the standard, in reaction to judicial ambiguity and the massive influx of divorce litigation. The legislature explicitly amended the pertinent statutes to replace the good faith standard with more concrete rules governing fiduciary relationships.[53] The courts are still struggling to fit a proper standard; one which would fall below *Vai's* trustee-like duties, and above good faith. The results conditioned the scale of duty upon level of spousal control.[54]

The legislature once again saw judicial development as somewhat ambiguous and reacted by amending California Family Code § 721 to set forth the relevant standard. The statute presumptively maintained

---

50. Vai v. Bank of America National Trust & Savings Ass'n 56 Cal.2d 329, 15 Cal. Rptr. 71, 364 P.2d 247 (1961) ("because of his management and control over the community property, the husband occupies the position of trustee for his wife in respect to her one-half interest in the community assets.").

51. Bank of Calif. v. Connolly, 111 Cal. Rptr. 468 (Ct. App. 1973).

52. *In re* Marriage of Connolly, 591 P.2d 911 (Cal. 1979) ("From the time that wife filed her petition seeking dissolution of the marriage . . . her relationship with her husband was an adversary one. Any obligation of trust between them [is] terminated").

53. CAL. CIV. CODE §§ 5103, 5125, 5125.1 (West 1991) (repealed 1994) (current versions at CAL. FAM. CODE §§ 721, 1100, 1101 (West 2004)).

54. *In re* Marriage of Brewer & Federici, 93 Cal. App. 4th 1334 (2001) (shifting evidentiary and proof burdens onto the spouse with control in the transaction and superior position to obtain records or financial information).

the scale of duty to scope of control idea. However, it specifically excluded California Probate Code § 16040. This section is synonymous with the "prudent investor rule."[55] The section was excluded from the definition of spousal fiduciary duties. Moreover, Section 721 cross-referenced California Corporations Code § 16404; requiring business partners to refrain from "engaging in grossly negligent or reckless conduct, intentional misconduct, or a knowing violation of the law."[56] This action constituted a limitation of the spousal fiduciary duty of care, excluding mere negligence from conduct necessary to hold spouses accountable.

Thus, California's spousal fiduciary duties are laced with business law analysis.

Many common law states accept the [marriage-business] analogy. These states have co-opted the language of model statutes such as the Uniform Marital Property Act,[57] to recognize fiduciary duties during divorce proceedings. This limited application of fiduciary duties solely to divorce created two different systems of obligations, one during the marriage, and one outside the marriage. This dichotomy offers temptations to commit financial wrongs before the divorce. For example, a spouse holding title to property obtained during the marriage is free to deal with it throughout the period leading to divorce. Yet courts found ways to read spousal fiduciary duties into the marriage period as well. In *Dunkin v. Dunkin,* the court imposed fiduciary duties on spouses and held that the husband's deceitful and reckless mismanagement of the parties' assets constituted a breach of his fiduciary duty.[58] And in *Despain v. Despain,* the court recognized the wife's proposed second amended complaint, validating specific allegations of breach of the husband's fiduciary duty during the marriage.[59]

These are the exceptions to the common law norm. Courts and legislatures continue to recognize the intimate bond among spouses and avoid disrupting the necessary high level of mutual trust on which a good marriage is grounded. Hence, for example, Federal Rule of Evidence Rule 501 "continues to recognize a marital communications privilege as effective by common law."[60] And "[m]ost jurisdictions now provide that both spouses hold the privilege."[61]

---

55.   CAL. PROB. CODE § 16040 (West 1991 & Supp. 2007) (requiring a trustee to administer a trust with "reasonable care, skill, and caution under the circumstances then prevailing that a prudent person acting in a like capacity would use").
56.   CAL. CORP. CODE § 16404 (West 2006).
57.   UNIF.MARITAL PROPERTY ACT § 2(a), 9A Part I U.L.A. 114 (1998) ("Each spouse shall act in good faith with respect to the other spouse in matters involving marital property or other property of the other spouse.").
58.   Dunkin v. Dunkin, 986 P.2d 706 (Or. App. 1999).
59.   Despain v. Despain, 682 P.2d 849 (Utah 1984).
60.   MCCORMICK ON EVIDENCE § 78, at 143 (Kenneth S. Brown et al. eds., 6th ed. 2006) (citing FED. R. EVID. 501).
61.   *Id.* § 83, at 146.

Thus, there is a tension between the common law rules that exclude judicial interference in marital affairs during the marriage, even in the case of disastrous financial consequences to one of the spouses, and the view of marriage parties as partners subject to fiduciary duties.

– – – – – – – – – – – –

Discussion Topics

a. Should marriage be viewed as a fiduciary relationship? Who entrusts what to whom? Are all power relationships in marriage similar? How helpful is the analogy of the relationship to other forms of fiduciaries, such as partners? How helpful is the list of features of fiduciaries listed in this Chapter?

b. Need all aspects of marriage be subject to fiduciary relationships?

c. Under what conditions should friendships be classified as fiduciary relationships?

Suppose a long-term friend confides in the other about an idea that he had developed for a number of years. The friend listens carefully and then sells the idea to a wealthy woman whom he has known. Could this selling friend be sued as a fiduciary, who violated a fiduciary duty?

Compare this story with the following: Abe and Bob are two shareholders in a corporation that operates a Small Business (SB). They have been working together for over 15 years. Abe is approached by a large corporation that is planning to build an office building and needs the land on which SB is located. The large corporation offers a $1 million for the land. Able offers to buy Bob's shares in the corporation for $500,000. Abe does not tell Bob about the large corporation's offer. Bob agrees to sell his shares to Abe for $500,000. After the sale, Abe sells the land to the large corporation and gains $500,000. Does Bob have a claim against Bob? Assume that Abe did not ask Bob whether there are offers on SB's land.

Now assume that Abe and Bob were good friends for many years. Each holds shares in a publicly held large corporation (LC). Abe learns from a reliable source and his own research that the shares of LC are going to fall and sells the shares without telling Bob. Is Abe a fiduciary of Bob's in this case? Does Bob have a claim against Abe for failing to disclose the information?

Problem

Many stories in good novels offer interesting legal issues concerning fiduciary relationships. Here is one such story derived from John Grisham: *The Broker*:[62]

Joel Backman was a Washington power broker who had been sent to a federal prison for various illegal activities (treason being the most notable). Backman was known as "the broker" due to the fact that he was a high-powered, highly paid attorney who had access at the highest

---

62.   JOHN GRISHAM, THE BROKER (2006).

levels. During his time as a Washingtonian power broker, Backman obtained secrets that compromised America's satellite surveillance system. These secrets were obtained when Backman attempted to broker a deal to sell the world's most powerful satellite surveillance system to another country. Anyone (or any country) who obtained this satellite surveillance system would be omnipotent and would know so much that all other countries would be brought to their collective knees.

Many of the key players involved in the creation and sale of the system were killed. Backman accepted the prison sentence, knowing he would be safest in a high-security detention system. This way those interested in obtaining this secret system (such as the Chinese, the Israelis, the Russians and the Saudis) would not be able to find him and torture him to obtain the secrets.

In a turn of events, the U.S. decides Backman would be useful to this country, as well. The Director of the CIA convinces the President to pardon Backman, relocate him to Italy and then leak his whereabouts to the U.S.' enemies. The reasoning is twofold: 1. The CIA will be able to monitor which group (or country) is most eager to kill Backman (and thus, which country was attempting to buy the sophisticated system), and 2. Backman won't ever be able to leak the secrets once he is killed. The CIA, and the United States, will profit by obtaining this knowledge along with keeping Backman silent.

Is the President a fiduciary of Backman—an American citizen?

Is the CIA a fiduciary of Backman? Think back to the organ-donating example, above. Compare the fiduciary duties you felt should be accorded prisoners to the duties that should be accorded to Backman. Do the following additional facts change your mind?

What if Backman were told about the CIA's reasoning? What if he consented to this reasoning? What if he didn't consent to this reasoning? After all, prosecutors reach settlement deals with the accused all the time. If Backman had consented, would this arrangement be permissible? Usually, when accused individuals reach a deal, they are not put in harm's way. Here, Backman would possibly be killed and, at the very least, would be put in an extremely dire situation. If Backman views this as a better alternative than being jailed, perhaps no duty is being breached since Backman is consenting? Is consent the main issue when it comes to this type of entrustment?

Consider the purpose and directive of the CIA. Take into account that the CIA's purpose is to protect the U.S. and its citizens. Does this mean that each citizen should be protected or should the greater good be protected? A prosecutor has a very different purpose and directive than the CIA does. So perhaps the entrustment issue is different for each. Perhaps the bottom line result of keeping the country safe is more important than the possible death of one prisoner. If the CIA's main entrusted power is to keep the country safe, is Backman's lack of consent still viewed as a breach of the CIA's duty, or is the CIA just carrying out the duty it owes to the U.S.?

Does the CIA's duty conflict with the entrusted power of the President of the United States? Are the two duties the same or are they different? Is it the President's duty to ensure the safety of individuals or the country as a whole? Does it matter that Backman was under the control of the federal system (as he was in a federal penitentiary), and thus under the indirect control of the President? Is the question similar to the United States' Japanese internment camps?

Problem

On May 4, 2007, the *Wall Street Journal* article entitled "Student Loan Probe Widens to Alumni Groups" reported about investigations of alumni groups:

A company in Nebraska had "affinity agreements" and license arrangements with 120 alumni associations. For a fee, the associations offered the company the contact information of their members as well as the associations' logos. The company used the information in its market efforts.[63]

What is the nature of the relationship between the alumni associations and the alumni? Even if their relationship is fiduciary, is there anything wrong with these arrangements?

g. When does influence become entrusted power?

[In *Lash v. Cheshire County Savings Bank, Inc.*, the plaintiffs operated a small business and became obligated to the defendant bank as well as to another person, Pappas.[64] Pappas was indebted to the bank as well. He helped the plaintiffs receive a $35,000 loan from the bank, secured by trucks and a second mortgage on their home.]

At the closing, the bank disbursed $5,622.94, and the plaintiffs later ratified additional disbursements of $5,086.38. The remaining $24,290.68 was never received by the plaintiffs, but was unilaterally credited by the bank to Mr. Pappas' account to reduce his debt. [The amount that the plaintiffs owed Pappas was lower and they never authorized the bank to reduce the loan to Pappas by that amount. The plaintiffs sued the bank for breach of contract as well as a breach of fiduciary duty.]

[The court held:] A fiduciary relationship has been defined as "a comprehensive [term] and exists wherever influence has been acquired and abused or confidence has been reposed and betrayed." In doubtful cases, whether the conduct of two parties was such that a fiduciary relationship existed between them is a question of fact for the trier of fact, and we will not set aside such a jury's determination unless it is not sustainable on the evidence.

The reason so many banks use names like "Trust," "Security," or "Guarantee" is that they hold themselves out as a safe and responsible place to entrust funds. The legislature has provided for detailed and extensive regulation of savings banks since 1895. The officers of a savings bank take an oath "to the faithful discharge of their duties," and are governed by [the rule requiring them to invest the money prudently]. The hundreds of pages of statutes and regulations affecting such banks clearly place them in a different category from all of the other corporations in this State who are not held to the high level of conduct we expect of a bank.

The Uniform Commercial Code sections of Article 4 devoted to bank deposits and collections even go so far as to make illegal any attempt by a bank to enter into an

---

63.   Suzanne Sataline, *Student Loan Probe Widens to Alumni Groups,* WALL ST. J., May 4, 2004, at B1, LEXIS, News Library, Wsj File.
64.   Lash v. Cheshire County Sav. Bank, Inc., 474 A.2d 980 (N.H. 1984) (citing Tamar Frankel, *Fiduciary Law,* 71 CAL. L. REV. 795 (1983)) (other citations omitted).

agreement to 'disclaim a bank's responsibility for its own lack of good faith or failure to exercise ordinary care' or to 'limit the measure of damages for such lack or failure.' Where a bank exercises "bad faith" in handling an item, consequential damages are awarded. While these sections of the law do not explicitly govern the instant facts, they are indicative that the laws of the market place do not set a high enough standard for the financial institutions to which we entrust our financial security.

Other courts, when faced with the varieties of relationships between a bank and a customer, have found that certain fact patterns were legally sufficient to constitute a fiduciary relationship. This is not to say that either a confidential relationship or the normal trustee beneficiary status is imposed upon banks in their dealings when the law does not specifically otherwise so provide. A fiduciary relation does not depend upon some technical relation created by, or defined in, law. It may exist under a variety of circumstances, and does exist in cases where there has been a special confidence reposed in one who, in equity and good conscience, is bound to act in good faith and with due regard to the interests of the one reposing the confidence. In this case, the bank retained the plaintiffs' funds, disbursed them without authorization, and now demands that the plaintiffs repay the loan. We conclude that a jury reasonably could have found this action to be a breach of a fiduciary duty. The jury was instructed that if it found that the Lashes failed to prove a breach of the contract but instead prevailed on the fiduciary duty count it could award damages for that count alone. The jury was instructed to measure damages the same way under either the contract or fiduciary duty count. Because no double damages were awarded, there being a defendant's verdict on the contract count, we find no inconsistency in those two verdicts.[65]

- - - - - - - - - - -

Discussion Topic

What facts induced the court to impose on this bank a fiduciary relationship towards the plaintiffs? Does every borrower's trust in a bank create a fiduciary relationship?

- - - - - - - - - - -

h. Insider trading. Who is the entrustor? The corporation or its shareholders?

Goodwin v. Agassiz is a 1933 case that did not lose its punch.[66] It raises the question of who is the entrustor of information—to whom do directors of a corporation owe a fiduciary duty? To the corporation or to the shareholders personally?

The defendant Agassiz was president of Cliff Mining Company. MacNaughton was a director and general manager. Both owned stock in the company. In May 1926, they bought additional stock, which was owned by the plaintiff. They did not buy the stock directly, however, but through brokers on the Boston stock exchange. The defendants decided to buy the stock on the basis of the information that in theory there might be copper deposits in the company's region. The plaintiff argued that the defendants owed him a duty, which they breached, to disclose the information under all circumstances.

---

65. *Id.*
66. Goodwin v. Agassiz, 186 N.E. 659 (Mass. 1933) (abridged and some citations omitted).

While the exploration for copper has been unsuccessful, and that fact was publicized (although not by the defendants), the theory, as speculative as it was held some hope and the defendants decided to test it under strict secrecy. They caused another company that they controlled to buy opinions on land adjacent to the "copper belt."

The defendants speculated that the price of Cliff Mining Company's stock might rise if copper were found. When the plaintiff heard of the unsuccessful exploration, which was publicized, he sold his shares of stock through brokers. Neither party knew of the activities of the other. The court found that the defendants were not guilty of fraud, nor breached their duty to Cliff Mining Company. The company was not harmed by any of their actions.

The court wrote:

The question presented is whether the decree dismissing the bill rightly was entered on the facts found.

The directors of a commercial corporation stand in a relation of trust to the corporation and are bound to exercise the strictest good faith in respect to its property and business. The contention that directors also occupy the position of trustee toward individual stockholders in the corporation is plainly contrary to repeated decisions of this court and cannot be supported. . . . [I]t was said by Chief Justice Shaw: "There is no legal privity, relation, or immediate connexion, between the holders of shares in a bank, in their individual capacity, on the one side, and the directors of the bank on the other. The directors are not the bailees, the factors, agents or trustees of such individual stockholders.". . . "The fact that the defendants were directors created no fiduciary relation between them and the plaintiff in the matter of the sale of his stock."

The principle thus established is supported by an imposing weight of authority in other jurisdictions. A rule holding that directors are trustees for individual stockholders with respect to their stock prevails in comparatively few States; but in view of our own adjudications it is not necessary to review decisions to that effect.

While the general principle is as stated, circumstances may exist requiring that transactions between a director and a stockholder as to stock in the corporation be set aside. The knowledge naturally in the possession of a director as to the condition of a corporation places upon him a peculiar obligation to observe every requirement of fair dealing when directly buying or selling its stock. Mere silence does not usually amount to a breach of duty, but parties may stand in such relation to each other that an equitable responsibility arises to communicate facts. Purchases and sales of stock dealt in on the stock exchange are commonly impersonal affairs. An honest director would be in a difficult situation if he could neither buy nor sell on the stock exchange shares of stock in his corporation without first seeking out the other actual ultimate party to the transaction and disclosing to him everything which a court or jury might later find that he then knew affecting the real or speculative value of such shares. Business of that nature is a matter to be governed by practical rules. Fiduciary obligations of directors ought not to be made so onerous that men of experience and ability will be deterred from accepting such office. Law in its sanctions is not coextensive with morality. It cannot undertake to put all parties to every contract on an equality as to knowledge, experience, skill and shrewdness. It cannot undertake to relieve against hard bargains made between competent parties without fraud. On the other hand, directors cannot rightly be allowed to indulge with impunity in practices which do violence to prevailing standards of upright business men. Therefore, where a director personally seeks a stockholder for the purpose of buying his shares without making disclosure of material facts within his peculiar knowledge and not within reach of the stockholder, the transaction will be closely scrutinized and relief may be granted in appropriate instances. The applicable legal principles "have almost always been the fundamental ethical rules of right and wrong."

... The Cliff Mining Company was not harmed by the nondisclosure. There would have been no advantage to it, so far as appears, from a disclosure. The disclosure would have been detrimental to the interests of another mining corporation in which the defendants were directors. In the circumstances there was no duty on the part of the defendants to set forth to the stockholders at the annual meeting their faith, aspirations and plans for the future. Events as they developed might render advisable radical changes in such views.

Disclosure of the theory, if it ultimately was proved to be erroneous or without foundation in fact, might involve the defendants in litigation with those who might act on the hypothesis that it was correct. The stock of the Cliff Mining Company was bought and sold on the stock exchange. The identity of buyers and seller of the stock in question in fact was not known to the parties and perhaps could not readily have been ascertained. The defendants caused the shares to be bought through brokers on the stock exchange. They said nothing to anybody as to the reasons actuating them. The plaintiff was no novice. He was a member of the Boston stock exchange and had kept a record of sales of Cliff Mining Company stock. He acted upon his own judgment in selling his stock. He made no inquiries of the defendants or of other officers of the company. The result is that the plaintiff cannot prevail. *Decree dismissing bill affirmed with costs.*[67]

- - - - - - - - - - - -

Discussion Topics

a. What facts were the most important in the court's consideration? How did the court categorize the relationship of the directors who controlled the corporation and its shareholders?

b. Do you agree with the decision? How would you rationalize the duties of the directors by making them fiduciaries of the shareholders and yet enable the directors to trade in the corporation's stock?

c. To what extent do the cases and definitions above validate the list of factors that might describe the existence of fiduciary relationships and to what extent do these cases negate the existence of these factors?

- - - - - - - - - - - -

i. Can an army uniform (or the authority it represents) be entrusted?

Reading v. Attorney-General is an old English case that teaches us both about entrustment and about remedies for violations of fiduciary duties.[68] We will deal with this case again in Chapter Seven, when we study remedies for breach of fiduciary duties. Here we examine the decision of the court to impose a fiduciary duty on an army sergeant and the rationale for doing so.

The court wrote:

---

67. *Id.*
68. Reading v. Attorney-General, 1 All E.R. 617 (House of Lords Mar. 1, 1951) (citations omitted).

My Lords, this is an appeal from an order of the Court of Appeal dated May 19, 1949, affirming the judgment of Denning J., and ordering that the appellant's appeal from the said judgment be dismissed with costs . . . .

. . . (A) In 1943 and 1944 the appellant was a sergeant in the Royal Army Medical Corps and receiving pay at the rate appropriate to his rank. He was employed as a sergeant in charge of medical stores at No. 63 General Hospital, Cairo. (B) On [Mar. 14, 1944], he dictated and signed a statement to Lieutenant Brooks of the Special Investigation Branch, Middle East, that he had received in all some £ 20,000 from a man named Manole in the following circumstances. Some time about the beginning of 1943, when having coffee at Alexandria while on leave, he was asked by a man, who, apparently, knew him, but whom he did not know, whether he would assist by selling cases of whisky and brandy to agents in Cairo for which he would get a few pounds. The appellant expressed his willingness and was told that someone would get into contact with him outside the hospital gates at Helmeih and tell him what he had to do. About a month later Manole met him there and told him a lorry was coming at a specified time to a place which was pointed out to him. When it arrived he was to board it and take it to another spot which again he was shown. At the specified time and place a lorry duly arrived, the appellant then boarded it and conducted it through Cairo to the appointed spot, where the contents were transferred to another lorry, but he was unable to see of what they consisted. He then went home, but by arrangement met Manole later on the same day at a restaurant in Cairo and received from him an envelope which on examination was found to contain £ 2,000. This process was repeated on a number of occasions on which, as in the first, a lorry arrived with cases the contents of which were undisclosed, and after each journey the appellant was given sums varying from £ 1,000 to £ 4,000. [And on Mar. 20, 1944], his statement was shown to the appellant by Sergeant-Major Jones of the Special Investigation Branch, and the appellant acknowledged that it was his statement and that it was true. He also told Sergeant-Major Jones that he had been dressed on each occasion in uniform, and on a later occasion he showed Corporal Read of the Special Investigation Branch a number of different places in Cairo as points at which he had met or left the lorries which he had accompanied from time to time. The appellant's case also alleges that at all material times it was obligatory for all service personnel in Cairo to wear uniform, except when engaged in sport or other specially excepted activity. I can find no evidence to this effect, but regard the allegation as immaterial to the decision which your Lordships are asked to reach.

In these circumstances Denning J, held that the Crown was entitled to the money in question. It was, in his view, immaterial to consider whether the method of seizure was justified or not. Even if it was not, the Crown had a valid counterclaim, and, avoiding a circuity of action, could thus defeat the appellant's claim.... His reasoning is to be found in the passage which succeeds that quoted. He says: . . .

"In my judgment, it is a principle of law that, if a servant takes advantage of his service and violates his duty of honesty and good faith to make a profit for himself, in the sense that the assets of which he has control, the facilities which he enjoys, or the position which he occupies, are the real cause of his obtaining the money as distinct from merely affording the opportunity for getting it, that is to say, if they play the predominant part in his obtaining the money, then he is accountable for it to the master. It matters not that the master has not lost any profit nor suffered any damage, nor does it matter that the master could not have done the act himself. If the servant has unjustly enriched himself by virtue of his service without his master's sanction, the law says that he ought not to be allowed to keep the money, but it shall be taken from him and given to his master, because he got it solely by reason of the position which he occupied as a servant of his master." . . .

"The uniform of the Crown and the position of the suppliant as a servant of the Crown were the only reasons why he was able to get this money, and that is sufficient to make him liable to hand it over to the Crown."

The learned judge, however, also writes: "There was not, in this case, a fiduciary relationship. The suppliant was not acting in the course of his employment."

If this means, as I think it does, that the appellant was neither a trustee nor in possession for some profit-earning chattel and that it was contrary to his duty to escort unwarranted traffic or, possibly, any traffic through the streets of Cairo, it is true, but, in my view, irrelevant. He, nevertheless, was using his position as a sergeant in His Majesty's army, and the uniform to which his rank entitled him, to obtain the money which he received. In my opinion, any official position, whether marked by a uniform or not, which enables the holder to earn money by its use gives his master a right to receive the money so earned even though it was earned by a criminal act. "You have earned," the master can say, "money by the use of your position as by servant. It is not for you, who have gained this advantage, to set up your own wrong as a defence to my claim."[69]

— — — — — — — — — — -

Discussion Topics

a. What were the underlying reasons for entitling the crown to the money that the army man earned?

b. Reread the *Snepp* decision. Is there a common theme to both cases?

— — — — — — — — — — -

j. The duality of entrustment: fiduciary law as duties *in personam* and *in rem*

Joshua Getzler wrote:[70]

It could be claimed that fiduciary obligations and trusts share a common origin in English Chancery jurisdiction, as *in personam* duties of conscience. The classical notion that 'equity acts *in personam*' meant that Chancery ordered the person affected by conscience to desist from claiming the full extent of his or her legal rights, or else be subjected to a contempt order binding the person, that is the body. [T]he institution of the trust can be modelled as a multiplication of fiduciary duties. . . . The trust title is constructed of a series of binding personal, good faith claims against nearly all takers of trusts assets. . .

An example of Professor Getzler's statement is the *Goodwin v. Agassiz* case we just studied. To whom do directors have a fiduciary relationship, and what is the nature of the relationship?

The relationship with the shareholders, under certain circumstances, and with the corporation generally, would be personal (*in personam*), and give rise to fiduciary duties. What about the directors' relationship with public investors? The *Goodwin* court, following the common law, did not recognize a relationship. There was no duty *in rem* to the whole world to deal fairly with investors in the impersonal market. However, Congress and the Securities and Exchange Commission did recognize a partial relationship on the ground that the information the directors use is not theirs but belongs

---

69. *Id.*
70. Joshua Getzler, *Rumford Market & the Genesis of Fiduciary Obligations in* MAPPING THE LAW: ESSAYS IN HONOUR OF PETER BIRKS 577-98 (A. Burrows & A. Rodger eds., 2006) (footnotes omitted).

to the source of the information, and more importantly, that the use of inside information may undermine investors' trust in the securities markets. To that extent the regulators recognized a fiduciary relationship between directors and the source of the inside information. When the directors and executives of Enron Corporation sold their shares, knowing that the corporation was in financial trouble, but declared that the corporation was in good shape, they misappropriated information given to them in trust and had a relationship with the corporation and the shareholders which required them to avoid misrepresentation and trading. That duty then extended to all traders under Section 10b-5 of the Securities Exchange Act of 1934 and Rule 10b-5, enacted under the section.[71]

3. Entrustment poses risks to entrustors

Fiduciary relationships pose risks for entrustors. However, the level of these risks varies, depending on the type of services that the fiduciaries offer and the value of the property and strength of the power with which they are entrusted as well as the ability and efficiency of control over the fiduciaries' performance. We start with listing the source of the risks that entrustors bear from fiduciary relationships.

a. Entrustment is a condition to the performance of fiduciaries' services

The weakness of the entrustor is inherent in the relationship. Compare the negotiation between an entrustor and a fiduciary before and after the deal is struck. The entrustor may have the money and ability to choose any available fiduciary, while the fiduciary may be desperately seeking clients in competition with other fiduciaries.

However, once the deal is struck, the entrustor must entrust property or power to the fiduciary. Otherwise, the fiduciary cannot perform the intended services. Therefore, entrustment must occur *before* the fiduciary performs his part of the bargain. To be sure, there are long-term contractual relationships that require entrustment to one party before the entrusting party can receive its part of the bargain. But in the case of fiduciary relationship, there is usually a greater risk of misappropriation by the fiduciary, as well as the vague specifications of the fiduciary's performance, if the fiduciary is allowed to perform well.

Compare a fiduciary relationship to a construction contract. The construction contract contains copious specifications. Usually, before any part of the building is covered, preventing examination of whether the specifications were met, a qualified architect or engineer inspects that part to make sure that the specifications were met. For example, the expert verifies that the amount of cement poured into the foundations was satisfactory before the foundation is covered.

---

71. Securities Exchange Act of 1934, 15 U.S.C. § 78j(b) (2000); 17 C.F.R. § 240.10b-5 (2007).

A similar specification cannot bind a lawyer in court presentation or a surgeon in the operating room. The decision in these cases must be left to the professionals, and sometimes must be determined on the spot. These individuals must possess the power to make the decision in advance and exercise it whenever it is required.

─ ─ ─ ─ ─ ─ ─ ─ ─ ─

Discussion Topic

A lawyer must have the power to conduct the case in litigation. Does this power include the power to settle the case? If not, why not?

─ ─ ─ ─ ─ ─ ─ ─ ─ ─

b. Fiduciaries' services involve various degrees of discretion. Fiduciaries cannot be fully controlled in the performance of their services

It is not possible to prescribe for fiduciaries the precise way in which they are to perform their services. The directives to fiduciaries must be general, and the precise ways in which they are to perform their services must be left to them, both because they are the experts, such as physicians, and because their performance is usually subject to a changing or unknown environment, such as investment management or the development of a potentially earthshaking patent. Any itemized controlling directives to fiduciaries are likely to undermine the utility of the services. This does not mean that some fiduciaries cannot be subject to more specific directives than others. It depends on their services.

In fact, as we shall see, the definition of various fiduciaries depends in part on the specificity of the directives that can be given to them without eliminating the utility of their services. The more specific the directives are, the less discretion they will have, and the lower their duties become. Low discretion presumes less entrustment and lower costs for the entrustors in supervising the fiduciaries. Thus, there comes a point where the persons who provide the services are not fiduciaries at all. Thus, as a general rule, a "servant" is generally not a fiduciary. Principals or employers can and should then protect themselves from the servant's abuse of trust and can do so without undermining the benefits from the servant's services.

Consider the following case of *Brophy v. Cities Serv. Co.*:

Kennedy . . . was employed in an "executive capacity" and as "confidential secretary" to the defendant, W. Alton Jones, a director and officer of Cities Service Company; [and] in those capacities "he had access to confidential information concerning Cities Service Company" and its operations and the operations of its subsidiaries. The acts of Kennedy labelled fraudulent are briefly, that by reason of his employment he knew in advance from 1932 to the date of filing the amended complaint when Cities Service Company, or its controlled subsidiaries, intended to purchase shares of Cities Service Company's stock on the open market in quantities sufficient to cause a rise in its market price; that knowing in advance when such purchases were to be made Kennedy acquired for his personal account, or for the account of his nominees, Cities Service Company's shares prior to the purchase by the company, and thereafter sold them at a profit resulting from the rise in the market price incident to the purchase by Cities Service Company; that by reason of Kennedy's employment as an executive and as the confidential secretary to an officer and director of Cities Service Company he occupied a position of trust and confidence toward the corporation, with respect to the information so acquired, and the purchase of its stock for his own account was a breach of the duty he owed to Cities Service Company.[72]

4. Law interferes to support fiduciary relationships

Law interferes to support fiduciary relationships when 1. Monitoring the fiduciaries in the performance of their services is more costly to the entrustors than their benefits from the relationships; and 2. Establishing trustworthiness is more costly to the fiduciaries than the rewards from the relationships; and 3. The markets or other private sector parties fail to protect entrustors from the risks posed by fiduciary relationships.

a. The cost of monitoring

Joshua Getzler wrote: "The policy [underlying fiduciary law] can also be put in evidential terms . . . fiduciary law erects its prophylactic rules and prohibits profit-taking precisely because the stronger party to a fiduciary relationship controls all evidence of the relationship and can easily conceal wrongdoing from the vulnerable party or the court."[73] In fact, the author noted, fiduciaries control all the evidence and sometimes create the evidence as part of their services.

When examining fiduciary law, one is likely to find a relationship between the strictness of the rules and the balance between the risks for entrustors in engaging in fiduciary relationship and the cost which the rules impose on the fiduciaries. The arguments about regulating fiduciaries are usually centered around one or more of these items. The analysis of the types of fiduciaries is closely related to these items as well. That is why fiduciaries resemble members of a family, and that is why they differ from each other. Learning about their similarities and differences enhances our ability to evaluate the risks they pose, the necessary level of self-protection against those risks, and the rules that help these protections on the one hand and our ability to enhance the trustworthiness of fiduciaries on the other hand.

"In different language we can say that the costs of monitoring a fiduciary are high, since the fiduciary has extensive powers and discretionary control over the running of the relationship, including extensive powers to deal with the beneficial assets."[74]

In the case of fiduciaries, market monitoring and evaluation of their performance are often ineffective. For example, corporate executives' compensation has been criticized and publicized for quite some time. However, executives are powerful, and investors value market performance of the stock more than they criticize high compensation. If performance is poor, investors would rather "exit"—

---

72.   Brophy v. Cities Serv. Co, 70 A.2d 5, 7 (Del. Ch. 1949) (footnote omitted).
73.   Joshua Getzler, *Rumford Market and the Genesis of Fiduciary Obligations in* MAPPING THE LAW: ESSAYS IN HONOUR OF PETER BIRKS 577-598 (A. Burrows & A. Rodger eds., 2006) (footnote omitted).
74.   *Id.*

sell their stock, than "voice"—fight the executives about executive compensation. The market for executives (not entrustors-investors) is fairly small. For many other reasons too long and complicated to list here, it took years for some directors and executives to heed the pressures. It took a long time for the Securities and Exchange Commission to respond with a requirement for a more itemized disclosure.[75]

Further, the use of the fiduciaries' service involves various kinds and degrees of risks for entrustors, relating to the fiduciaries' poor performance and dishonest behavior. The rules that govern fiduciaries are usually linked to the risks of the entrustors as well as to the benefits for the fiduciaries. Therefore, when you "meet a fiduciary," examine the difference between the new one and some you know and ask the questions that might distinguish the new one in terms of the risk you may be willing to take in trusting this type of fiduciary.

– — — — — — — — — — – -

Discussion Topic

a. Saul Levmore listed among the market monitors of trustworthiness: secured and unsecured creditors, and corporate outside directors, capital markets, shareholders suits, and corporate financial structure.[76] How do these parties help monitor trustworthiness? What determines their effectiveness? Do we need so many monitors? If they do their job, should fiduciary duties be reduced, or the very fiduciary relationship be eliminated? Why is the law necessary in this area?

– — — — — — — — — — – -

b. Establishing trustworthiness is more costly to the fiduciaries than the rewards from the relationships

Consider the following summary from Donald Langevoort's article *Selling Hope, Selling Risk: Some Lessons for Law from Behavioral Economics About Stockbrokers and Sophisticated Customers:*[77]

When investors lose money they might sue their brokers, blaming them for the losses. The issue would be whether the investors knew the risks, were sophisticated to understand it, "and simply made . . . bad decision[s]" or whether the brokers gave their trusting clients bad advice for gain. Professor Langevoort suggests that the reason for brokers' lack of disclosure and the investors' bad investment decisions is trust, from which both parties can benefit, and which both parties can "exploit." The difficult question is not related to unsophisticated

---

75. Executive Compensation and Related Person Disclosure, Securities Act Release No. 8732A (Aug. 29, 2006), 71 Fed. Reg. 53,158 (Sept. 8, 2006) (codified as amended in scattered sections of 17 C.F.R.).

76. Saul Levmore, *Monitors and Freeriders in Commercial and Corporate Settings,* 92 YALE L.J. 49 (1982).

77. Donald C. Langevoort, *Selling Hope, Selling Risk: Some Lessons for Law from Behavioral Economics About Stockbrokers and Sophisticated Customers,* 84 CAL. L. REV. 627, 627-31 (1996) (footnotes omitted).

clients. They are protected by law. But what about wealthy and experienced investors who seem naïve and fall for risky investments?

Courts are likely to resolve the conflict by resorting to "some rough heuristics to decide the merits of each case. They will invoke social constructs drawn from their own experience and imagination about the ways in which brokers normally deal with their customers, and how customers normally choose investments."

Professor Langevoort offers "a more nuanced view" to "generate better strategies for regulating the brokerage industry ex ante. . . . [T]he issue of trust emerges as the pivotal consideration." If a broker gained the clients' trust, writes Professor Langevoort, the broker may not be shielded by the client's sophistication. The "broad-based trust" does not apply only to the unsophisticated investor. The sophisticated investors may need to rely on the broker as well.[78] Thus, the test of the broker's liability is the depth of the trust relationship with the client and not the client's sophistication. However, the client's trust must be reasonable. A gullible client that unreasonably trusts the broker ought not to be protected. The law is designed to balance trust with self-protection and responsibility for oneself. Otherwise, society will breed persons who do not take care of themselves and fully rely on others.

– – – – – – – – – – – –

Discussion Topics

a. Should the law protect people who can protect themselves? If not, why should sophisticated persons who make bad investment choices be protected by the law? Or are they protected because they trusted the brokers? Is there a social objective to render people trusting of the brokers? Is there a business reason for the brokers to be trusted? If so, what induces broker to offer trusting clients speculative, risky investments?

b. In evaluating the risk to entrustors from the fiduciaries, does it matter if the relationship is between the fiduciary and one entrustor, as compared to the fiduciary and many entrustors? Or between entrustors and one fiduciary as compared to entrustors and many fiduciaries? How would you measure the risks to entrustors from the relationship? How does the number of entrustors and fiduciaries shape the power relationship of the parties?

c. When will organizations such as corporations, business trusts, partnerships and medical institutions be deemed fiduciaries? Are the people who work at these entities entrusted with power? Are the organizations entrusted with power? What then would distinguish them? Is their culture relevant to the discussion here?

d. How different is the fiduciary status of corporate management from that of corporate employees? After all, management has an employment contract with the corporation. Why do employees

---

78. *Id.*

(especially those who have no contract with the corporation and can be fired with little notice) organize in unions? Why is management not organized in a union?

e. Who should be compensated more: Those managers that are entrepreneurs and promoters that create an enterprise and make it grow, or the management of mammoth corporations that grow by acquiring these enterprises? Which of these types of managers is subject to greater supervision? Who is better paid? Why?

f. Do you agree with Evan J. Criddle, who wrote:

> [T]he fiduciary model of entrustment, residual control, and fiduciary duty offers a lucid lens for examining the role of [administrative] agency discretion in contemporary administrative law because it deftly interweaves the law's disparate thematic strands - delegation, discretion, fidelity, rationality, impartiality, and accountability - into a coherent and intelligible whole. . . . Where a fiduciary relation involves multiple beneficiaries, the duty of loyalty takes on an antidiscrimination aspect. . . . The terms of an administrative agency's enabling statute reflect the type and degree of trust that the people, through their elected representatives, have chosen to repose in the agency. . . .[79]

g. Are the police fiduciaries? What is entrusted to them and by whom? To what extent should the law interfere to protect entrustors from the police?

— — — — — — — — — — -

Problem

John and Linda (Authors) wrote a book and signed a contract with Publisher to deliver the book within a certain time frame. The contract provided that (1) Publisher will hold the copyright to the book; (2) Authors will receive 10% of the proceeds of the sales of the book; (3) Publisher will provide authors with an account every three months and pay the royalties within 30 days of the date of the report. Authors received a report which showed a very small number of books sold, and they suspect that Publisher does not provide a truthful report nor pay them the royalties due. Is Publisher a fiduciary to Authors?

c. The markets or other private sector parties fail to protect entrustors from the risks posed by fiduciary relationships

Regulation of the securities markets is based on the policy that all traders should have access to material information with respect to the traded securities. Some traders may do better research than others or have better expertise than others. But all can resort to the same material information. That is why those who have "insider information" that is not available to the public are not permitted to trade on the basis of such information. If they do, other traders in the market can sue. Also the source of the information can sue, if the "insider trader" was a fiduciary of the source of the information (or in

---

79. Evan J. Criddle, *Fiduciary Foundations of Administrative Law*, 54 U.C.L.A. L. Rev. 117 (2006) (LEXIS summary), LEXIS, Lawrev Library, Uclalr File.

some cases the received a tip from the source of the information) and traded without permission.[80]

The following case raises an interesting issue in this area. It involves Ginnie Mae, a government corporation that pools mortgage loans, converts them into tradable securities that are bought by investors, and creates a market in these loans. Thus, Ginnie Mae enables middle income and low income persons to buy and own their homes by making affordable mortgage loans for them. Because Ginnie Mae guarantees the payments on the loans regardless of the creditworthiness of the borrowers, these loans carry a far lower interest. In *United States v. York,*[81] the government sued York for violations of its fiduciary duties to Ginnie Mae.

York acted as a buyer of the securities that Ginnie Mae created and also serviced these loans, by collecting the borrowers' payments and distributing the payments to the investors. Information on whether a borrower is likely to default on the loan is valuable to investors because Ginnie Mae will pay the entire amount of the loan upon default pursuant to its guarantee rather than the periodic payments that investors would normally receive.

York engaged in purchasing securities from private investors upon information that it gained by virtue of its position as a servicer. York bought the securities after finding out, as a servicer, that the mortgagor defaulted and the Ginnie Mae guarantee was going to kick in. This information was not known to the public. Therefore, the price of the securities would be lower than after the information that the loan would be paid in full became known to investors. York often offered select investors this information, so that they would benefit from buying the securities at a lower price and converting their full face amount from Ginnie Mae.

Upon discovering of the practice, Ginnie Mae sued York. Ginnie Mae argued that York violated its fiduciary duty to Ginnie Mae by misappropriating the information that it was supposed to hold in trust and creating conflicting interests for itself. The court of appeals held that there was no legal basis for holding York to be a fiduciary of Ginnie Mae. Therefore, York did not misappropriate the information it received as a servicer and as a buyer of the mortgages.

- - - - - - - - - - -

Discussion Topics

a. Upon this defeat, how could Ginnie Mae prevent York or other servicers from using the information that it received as servicers to trade on the information or sell it to others?

---

80.   *See* United States v. O'Hagan, 521 U.S. 642 (1997); Dirks v. SEC, 463 U.S. 646 (1983); SEC v. Hirshberg, Nos. 97-6171, 97-6259, 1999 U.S. App. LEXIS 4764 (2d Cir. Mar. 18, 1999). As an unpublished opinion filed before January 1, 2007, *Hirshberg* may not be cited except in certain limited circumstances. 2d CIR. LOCAL R. 32.1(c)(2).
81.   United States v. York, 112 F.3d 1218 (D.D.C. 1997).

b. Does this solution explain why York need not be a fiduciary of Ginnie Mae?

- - - - - - - - - - - -

C. How Do Courts Recognize Fiduciary Relationships?

1. General

Courts rarely provide specific definitions of fiduciaries or fiduciary relationships.[82] Rather they view the relationships as the parties have designed them and then, when appropriate, classify the relationships as fiduciary. In contrast, legislatures define fiduciary relationships and fiduciary duties more specifically. In such cases, the courts follow the legislatures' intent.

Let us track the courts' journey to discover where the courts find the guiding principles to determine whether the parties' relationship was fiduciary. And where do they find the guiding principles for distinguishing between different types of fiduciaries, such as partners, agents or trustees? In determining the legal nature of the relationship, to what extent do the courts consider or follow the parties' own classification of fiduciary relationship?

Consider the following excerpts of the following three cases: *Wolf v. Superior Court of Los Angeles County,*[83] *Roberts v. Sears, Roebuck & Co.,*[84] and *Martinelli v. Bridgeport Roman Catholic Diocesan Corp.*[85] In each of these three cases cited below, what approach did the courts take to determine that the parties' relationship was fiduciary? Why are some courts more reluctant than others to define fiduciary relationships or find new fiduciary relationships? Which one is a better approach, in your opinion? What philosophy drove the courts to view the issues differently? As a lawyer for the parties in each of the cases, how would you act to avoid the conflicts and the need to resort to the courts?

We start with *Wolf v. Superior Court of Los Angeles County.*[86] The court wrote:

Gary Wolf is the author of the novel entitled Who Censored Roger Rabbit? (1981). In or about August 1983, Wolf entered into a written agreement with Disney (the 1983 Agreement) in which Wolf assigned to Disney the rights to the novel and the Roger Rabbit characters. In exchange for acquiring the rights, Disney agreed to pay Wolf a stated, fixed compensation upon execution of the agreement; a percentage of the "net profits," as defined by the parties, from a motion picture based on the novel; and additional,

---

82. SEC v. Chenery Corp., 318 U.S. 80, 85-86 (1942) ("But to say that a man is a fiduciary only begins analysis; it gives direction to further inquiry. To whom is he a fiduciary? What obligations does he owe as a fiduciary? In what respect has he failed to discharge these obligations? And what are the consequences of his deviation from duty?").
83. Wolf v. Superior Court, 107 Cal. App. 4th 25 (Ct. App. 2003), *remanded,* 114 Cal. App. 4th 1343 (Ct. App. 2004).
84. Roberts v. Sears, Roebuck & Co., 573 F.2d 976 (7th Cir. 1978).
85. Martinelli v. Bridgeport Roman Catholic Diocesan Corp., 10 F. Supp. 2d 138 (D. Conn. 1998).
86. Wolf v. Superior Court, 107 Cal. App. 4th 25 (Ct. App. 2003), *remanded,* 114 Cal. App. 4th 1343 (Ct. App. 2004) (some citations omitted).

contingent compensation in the amount of 5 percent of any future gross receipts Disney earned from merchandising or other exploitation of the Roger Rabbit characters. The 1983 Agreement provided that Disney was not "under any obligation to exercise any of the rights" granted to it and could assign or license any and all rights granted under the 1983 Agreement as Disney "s[aw] fit."

Disney then developed and coproduced, along with Steven Spielberg's Amblin Entertainment, a motion picture entitled Who Framed Roger Rabbit (1988) based upon Wolf's novel and its characters. After a dispute arose between Wolf and Disney regarding certain terms contained in the 1983 Agreement, the parties entered into a 1989 agreement that confirmed Wolf's entitlement to the contingent compensation set forth in the 1983 Agreement. In addition, the 1989 agreement granted Wolf certain audit rights.

According to the complaint, each time Wolf attempted to exercise its audit rights, Disney failed to provide access to pertinent records. In addition, Disney allegedly underreported revenues it received in connection with the Roger Rabbit characters and failed to disclose the nature of its third party agreements concerning the characters and the compensation received. Wolf alleges such conduct not only constitutes a breach of contract but also amounts to a breach of fiduciary duty. Wolf claims that Disney is a fiduciary because Disney enjoyed "exclusive control over the books, records and information concerning the exploitation [of the Roger Rabbit characters] and the revenue and Gross Receipts Royalties derived therefrom."

[The trial court held "that the contract between [Wolf] and [Disney] d[id] not create a fiduciary relationship" as a matter of law, and the issue was now before the court of appeal.]

2. *The Trial Court Did Not Err in Sustaining Without Leave to Amend the Demurrer to the Breach of Fiduciary Duty Cause of Action*

A fiduciary relationship is "'any relation existing between parties to a transaction wherein one of the parties is in duty bound to act with the utmost good faith for the benefit of the other party. Such a relation ordinarily arises where a confidence is reposed by one person in the integrity of another, and in such a relation the party in whom the confidence is reposed, if he voluntarily accepts or assumes to accept the confidence, can take no advantage from his acts relating to the interest of the other party without the latter's knowledge or consent. . . .'"

Traditional examples of fiduciary relationships in the commercial context include trustee/beneficiary, directors and majority shareholders of a corporation, business partners, joint adventurers, and agent/principal.

Inherent in each of these relationships is the duty of undivided loyalty the fiduciary owes to its beneficiary, imposing on the fiduciary obligations far more stringent than those required of ordinary contractors. As Justice Cardozo observed, "Many forms of conduct permissible in a workaday world for those acting at arm's length, are forbidden to those bound by fiduciary ties. A trustee is held to something stricter than the morals of the market place. Not honesty alone, but the punctilio of an honor the most sensitive is then the standard of behavior."

Wolf concedes that the complaint is devoid of allegations showing an agency, trust, joint venture, partnership or other 'traditionally recognized' fiduciary relationship and further admits that the complaint cannot be amended to state facts alleging such a relationship. Nonetheless, he argues that the absence of a 'traditionally recognized' fiduciary relationship is not dispositive on the question whether a fiduciary duty exists. Because Wolf's contractual right to contingent compensation necessarily required Wolf to repose 'trust and confidence' in Disney to account for the revenues received, and because such revenues and their sources are in the exclusive knowledge and control of Disney, Wolf claims the relationship is "confidential" in nature and necessarily imposes a fiduciary duty upon Disney, at least with respect to accounting to Wolf for the gross revenues received.

   a. *A Contingent Entitlement to Future Compensation Does Not, Alone, Give Rise to a Fiduciary Relationship.*

   Contrary to Wolf's contention, the contractual right to contingent compensation in the control of another has never, by itself, been sufficient to create a fiduciary relationship where one would not otherwise exist.

   Equally without merit is Wolf's contention that a fiduciary relationship exists because he necessarily reposed "trust and confidence" in Disney to perform its contractual obligation--that is, to account for and pay Wolf the contingent compensation agreed upon in the contract. Every contract requires one party to repose an element of trust and confidence in the other to perform. For this reason, every contract contains an implied covenant of good faith and fair dealing, obligating the contracting parties to refrain from "'doing anything which will have the effect of destroying or injuring the right of the other party to receive the fruits of the contract . . . .'"

   b. *The Profit-sharing Aspect of an Agreement Alone Does Not Give Rise to a Fiduciary Relationship. . . .*

   c. *Wolf's Contractual Right to an Accounting Does Not Create a Fiduciary Relationship.*

   Relying on *Waverly*, Wolf alternatively argues that fiduciary duties exist with respect to Disney's obligation to provide an accounting even though the relationship itself is not otherwise fiduciary in character. In *Waverly*, a distribution company (RKO) entered into an agreement with a producer to distribute two of the producer's motion pictures. The distributor then entered into sublicensing agreements with foreign distributors. The producer sued RKO, claiming RKO breached its fiduciary duty by subcontracting the distribution duties to foreign distributors who made little or no effort to distribute the films. Rejecting the producer's claim that the distributor was a fiduciary, the court held, "The [distribution] contract is an elaborate one which undertakes to define the respective rights and duties of the parties . . . . A mere contract or a debt does not constitute a trust or create a fiduciary relationship." Noting that the trial court had correctly held that although not a fiduciary, RKO did have an obligation to account to the producer for rentals received from its sublicensees, the court also stated its holding in the following language: "We think it clear that RKO was not a fiduciary with respect to the performance of the terms of this contract (except as to accounting for rentals received) and that arguments predicated on the assumption that it was are directed to a false issue." . . .

   The duty to provide an accounting of profits under the profit-sharing agreement in Waverly is appropriately premised on the principle, also expressed in Nelson, that a party to a profit-sharing agreement may have a right to an accounting, even absent a fiduciary relationship, when such a right is inherent in the nature of the contract itself. . . .

   d. *The Need to Shift the Burden of Proof in Profit-sharing Cases Does Not Create a Fiduciary Relationship. . . .*

   . . . We agree with Wolf that, in contingent compensation and other profit-sharing cases where essential financial records are in the exclusive control of the defendant who would benefit from any incompleteness, public policy is best served by shifting the burden of proof to the defendant, thereby imposing the risk of any incompleteness in the records on the party obligated to maintain them. . .

Johnson, J., Concurring and Dissenting.

   I agree with . . . the majority opinion suggesting the burden of proof will shift to Disney with respect to whether it accurately reported and paid Wolf the full royalties owed for its exploitation of Wolf's characters. . . .

I write separately, however, to register my disagreement with the majority opinion affirming the trial court's order . . . . This ruling is based on a finding Disney owed no fiduciary duty, *as a matter of law,* to accurately and honestly account to Wolf for his 5 percent share of the gross receipts attributable to the company's exploitation of Wolf's intellectual product. . . .

But in any event, there remains the question whether there *is or should be* such a fiduciary duty, and under what circumstances, when two parties enter into a profit-sharing relationship but one of those parties retains full control over the books. This issue, in turn, depends on whether the other party's right to audit the books provides a strong enough incentive to ensure an honest report of those receipts and profits. Or does it require imposition of a fiduciary duty and the threat of the attendant remedies to encourage a proper performance of this critical responsibility?

The majority opinion implies there can be no fiduciary duty to keep honest and accurate books--and none of the traditional remedies enforcing such a duty--unless the relationship between the two parties is a fiduciary relationship for all purposes. The majority argues the relationship defined in this contract falls short of being a joint venture, largely because Disney lacks a contractual duty to exploit any of Wolf's figures or other intellectual property, and thus does not qualify as a fiduciary relationship. Consequently, according to the majority rationale, Disney owes no fiduciary duty to maintain honest accounts even as to the exploitations of Wolf's intellectual property it does choose to undertake.

I differ with the majority opinion on both counts.

First, in my view, evidence may develop establishing Disney and Wolf were involved in a joint venture . . . . Intellectual property is not the same as "widgets" and cannot be treated as such. Whether a joint venture exists is to be determined from the statements and conduct of the parties, not just the written contract they may have executed as part of the venture . . . .

Furthermore, no amount of contractual disclaimers avowing this was a debtor-creditor relationship instead of a joint venture can turn it into something it was not. As this court held 20 years ago, "[T]he conduct of the parties may create a joint venture despite an express declaration to the contrary." So if it hops like a rabbit and has big floppy ears like a rabbit and eats carrots like a rabbit, Roger is a rabbit--even if the contract says he is a duck (or a mouse). . . .

Second, even if the arrangement ultimately fails to qualify as a true joint venture that does not end the matter. Disney does not necessarily escape a fiduciary duty to honestly and accurately account to the author of the intellectual property for the receipts earned from the intellectual property on which that author's compensation is based. Under the terms of this contract, Disney undertook the accounting responsibility for the author as well as itself--a responsibility arguably carrying with it a fiduciary duty to accurately and honestly report the true receipts and profits. Accountants, like lawyers, owe a fiduciary duty to their clients. Accountants also owe a duty not to supply negligently or intentionally false information to nonclients who the accountant knows with substantial certainty will rely on that information in their dealings with the client.

Disney may not be an accounting firm, but it employs the accountants and bookkeepers who perform the accounting function Disney contracted to carry out. In a very real sense, Disney is Wolf's accountant with respect to the complete and accurate and honest maintenance of the books as to any transactions involving exploitation of Wolf's characters. . . .

In either event, contrary to a bank-depositor relationship or many other relationships where one business entity maintains records for another, in this instance Wolf necessarily depended entirely on Disney's accounting department and the other Disney employees providing raw information to that department. He was not able to "reconcile" his checkbook based on his own records, or the equivalent. Nor was Wolf in a position to verify the accuracy and completeness of the raw data--the true gross receipts from exploitation of his characters--purportedly recorded in the reports he received. . . .

As one leading commentator wrote in describing what justifies the imposition of fiduciary duties: "Because fiduciaries manage or have some control over very substantial property interests of others, they have the potential to inflict great losses on those property owners. [The] economic interests of fiduciaries are frequently substantially affected by the discretionary decisions they make on behalf of others. . . As a result . . . *fiduciaries have unusually great opportunities to cheat without detection and they have unusually great incentives to do so.* Moreover, the relative costs which their cheating may impose on those whose property they manage are frequently much greater than the relative costs that can be imposed without detection or remedy in simpler contractual exchanges."

"Fiduciary duties and conflict of interest regulation both provide standardized terms to minimize transaction costs and impose unwaivable quality requirements which *prevent fiduciaries from taking unfair advantage of the superior bargaining power* resulting from their specialized information and skills."

The opportunity and temptation to cheat are present in the relationship here just as much as in the trustee-beneficiary, partnership, or other traditional fiduciary relationships. Wolf must depend entirely on the honesty and accuracy of Disney in the performance of the accounting function Disney is carrying out for both of them. Every sale of a toy "Roger Rabbit" that Disney fails to include in its report of receipts from exploitation of Wolf's characters means less money for Wolf and more profit for Disney. The conflict of interest inherent in this relationship, therefore, is more than apparent. So there appears to be just as great a need to impose a fiduciary duty on the performance of that accounting responsibility in order to discourage Disney "from taking unfair advantage of" its special position as there is for partners who manage a partnership business or for trustees who keep the books for a beneficiary's property interests. . . ."[87]

*   *   *

Now read the case of *Roberts v. Sears, Roebuck & Co.*[88]

This case involves the efforts of one of this nation's largest retail companies, Sears, Roebuck & Co. (Sears), to acquire through deceit the monetary benefits of an invention of a new type of socket wrench created by one of its sales clerks during his off-duty hours. That sales clerk, Peter M. Roberts (Plaintiff), initiated the unfortunate events that led to this appeal in 1963, when at the age of 18 he began work on a ratchet or socket wrench that would permit the easy removal of the sockets from the wrench. He, in fact, designed and constructed a prototype tool with a quick-release feature in it that succeeded in permitting its user to change sockets with one hand. Based on that prototype, plaintiff filed an application for a United States patent. In addition, since he was in the employ of Sears, a company that sold over a million wrenches per year, and since he had only a high school education and no business experience, he decided to show his invention to the manager of the Sears store in Gardner, Massachusetts where he worked. Plaintiff was persuaded to submit formally his invention as a suggestion to Sears. In May 1964, the prototype, along with a completed suggestion form, was sent to Sears' main office in Chicago, Illinois. Plaintiff, thereafter, left Sears' employ when his parents moved to Tennessee.

---

87. Wolf, 107 Cal. App. 4th 25.
88. Roberts v. Sears, Roebuck & Co., 573 F.2d 976 (7th Cir. 1978).

It was from this point on that Sears' conduct became the basis for the jury's determination that Sears appropriated the value of the plaintiff's invention by fraudulent means. Plaintiff's evidence proved that Sears took steps to ascertain the utility of the invention and that based on the information it acquired, Sears became convinced that the invention was in fact valuable. . . .

. . . Thus, by early 1965, it was clear to Sears that this invention was very useful and probably would be quite profitable.

Sears also took pains to ascertain the patentability of the quick-release feature. . . .

[Then it negotiated with the plaintiff to buy the invention, while] Sears' lawyer told the plaintiff that the invention was not new and that the claims in any patent that would be permitted would be "quite limited." [and] that the cost of the quick-release feature would be 40-50 cents [and not 20 cents as Sears knew]. Third, he told plaintiff the feature would sell only to the extent it would be promoted and thus $10,000 was all that the feature was worth. Finally, and perhaps most ironically, Schram wrote to plaintiff that "once we have paid off the royalty expense, then we would probably take the amount previously allocated to said expense and use it for promotional expenses *if we desire to maintain sales on the item.*" (Emphasis added).

Based on this letter, plaintiff entered into the agreement on July 29, 1965, which provided for a two cent royalty per unit up to a maximum of $10,000 to be paid in return for a complete *assignment* of all of plaintiff's rights. In fact, for no extra charge, plaintiff's [own] attorney gave Sears all of plaintiff's foreign patent rights. A provision was included in the contract regarding what would happen if Sears failed to sell 50,000 wrenches in a given year, thus reinforcing the impression that the wrenches might not sell very well. Also, a provision was inserted dealing with the contingency that a patent might not be issued, notwithstanding that Sears already knew, and plaintiff did not, that the patent had been granted.

By July, Sears knew that it planned to sell several hundred thousand wrenches with a cost per item increase of only 20 cents, that a patent had issued and that this product in all likelihood would have tremendous appeal with mechanics. Nonetheless, it entered into this agreement both having failed to disclose vital information about the product's appeal and structural utility and having made representations to plaintiff that were either false at the time they were made or became false without disclosure prior to the time of the signing of the contract.

Within days after the signing of the contract, Sears was manufacturing 44,000 of plaintiff's wrenches per week - all with plaintiff's patent number prominently stamped on them - and within three months, Sears was marketing them as a tremendous breakthrough. Within *nine months,* Sears had sold over 500,000 wrenches and paid plaintiff his maximum royalty thereby acquiring all of plaintiff's rights. Between 1965 and 1975, Sears sold in excess of 19 million wrenches, many at a premium of one to two dollars profit because no competition was able to market a comparable product for several years. To say the least, plaintiff's invention has been a commercial success.

Plaintiff, a Tennessee resident, filed suit against Sears, an Illinois Corporation, in federal district court in December 1969, based on diversity jurisdiction, seeking alternatively return of the patent and restitution or damages for fraud, breach of a confidential relationship and negligent misrepresentation. A jury trial was held from December 20, 1976, until January 18, 1977. During the trial plaintiff basically proved the facts as presented above. Sears argued that it did not misrepresent any facts to plaintiff, that he had a lawyer and thus there was no confidential relationship and that the success of the wrenches was a function of advertising and the unforeseeable boom in do-it-yourself repairs, and thus Sears did not misrepresent the salability of plaintiff's wrenches. . . . The jury apparently believed the plaintiff's evidence because it found Sears guilty on all three counts and entered judgment for one million dollars on each count, but the award was not cumulative.

Both parties filed post-trial motions. Sears filed for judgment NOV and plaintiff sought rescission of the contract and restitution. The district court denied both motions holding as to Sears' motion that the jury verdict was in accordance with the evidence and that the damages award was reasonable and holding as to plaintiff's motion that when he permitted the case to go to the jury he had elected his legal remedy and could not later also seek his equitable relief. Plaintiff appealed seeking equitable relief and Sears cross-appealed the one million dollar judgment against it. . . .

Sears' final argument in its cross-appeal is that plaintiff failed to prove the existence of a confidential relationship between himself and Sears. In assessing that argument, we recognize at the outset that there are no hard and fast rules for determining whether a confidential relationship exists. The trier of fact must examine all of the circumstances surrounding the relationship between the parties and determine whether "one person reposes trust and confidence in another who thereby gains a resulting influence and superiority over the first."

Various factors have been recognized judicially as being of particular relevance to that inquiry. Among them are disparity of age, education and business experience between the parties. Additional factors are the existence of an employment relationship and the exchange of confidential information from one party to the other. All five of those factors are present in this case. In addition, one of Sears' witnesses admitted that the company expected plaintiff to "believe" and to "rely" on various representations that Sears made to him. Obviously, this question is best left to the trier of fact, and this court under any circumstances would hesitate to disturb the jury's findings. That hesitation is especially strong here where so many factors suggest that a confidential relationship in fact existed.

Sears argues, however, that there are two factors involved here that eliminate any possible confidential relationship. They are that plaintiff never proved that Sears had knowledge of the confidential relationship upon which plaintiff was relying and that plaintiff retained counsel to guide him, and therefore, did not rely on Sears. We find neither factor sufficient to justify overturning the jury's verdict on this issue.

[Although] a confidential relationship cannot be thrust upon an unknowing party [it does not mean] that a plaintiff must demonstrate by direct evidence that the defendant actually was aware of the confidential relationship. All that must be proved is that the parties engaged in activities under circumstances that created a confidential relationship and that defendant breached that relationship.

In the cases cited by Sears, all of the circumstances surrounding the transactions that were being attacked suggested an arms-length arrangement, and thus the plaintiffs in those cases attempted to thrust a confidential relationship on the unknowing defendants after the fact. Here, Sears' knowledge is circumstantially proved by all of the facts surrounding its dealings with plaintiff. In addition, as suggested above, there was direct testimony to the effect that Sears expected plaintiff to rely on its representations.

With regard to the existence of counsel representing plaintiff, we conclude that that is merely one factor to be considered along with all of the others. In fact, once plaintiff established the existence of a confidential relationship through proof of the five factors previously discussed, the burden was on Sears to prove that plaintiff had competent and independent advice. The judge instructed the jury on this issue and it obviously rejected Sears' argument. There is no basis for this court to disturb that determination. Thus, we conclude that a jury could reasonably find that a confidential relationship existed between the parties and that Sears breached its duties created by that relationship.

For all of the above-stated reasons, we find no merit to any of the issues raised in Sears' cross-appeal. We, therefore, affirm the district court's judgment of liability against Sears on all three counts of plaintiff's complaint....

[Judgment against Sears was affirmed on all three counts in plaintiff's complaint.][89]

*   *   *

Finally, examine the case of *Martinelli v. Bridgeport Roman Catholic Diocesan Corp.*[90]

The parishioner suffered sexual abuse as a minor by a church priest. Almost 25 years after reaching the age of majority, the parishioner filed an action against the church for the church's failure to investigate, warn, and take remedial action following its knowledge of the sexual misconduct. A jury awarded damages to the parishioner after finding that a fiduciary relationship existed between the church and parishioner and that the fiduciary duty was breached. The jury also found that there was fraudulent concealment by the church by its deceptive response to the parishioner's allegation, and therefore, the statute of limitations did not bar the action. The church filed a motion for judgment as a matter of law, which the court denied. The court held that there was no violation of the First Amendment because neither the court nor the jury had to evaluate or weigh ecclesiastical standards or church doctrine. Instead, the court held that neutral principles could be applied to evaluate the church's conduct and response to the minors in its care. The court held that the jury's determination regarding the church's duty, breach, proximate cause, and resulting damages were reasonable.... [91]

... [O]ne commentator has urged courts to resist the urge to develop fiduciary law through analogy to the prototypical fiduciary relations, and instead follow an approach in which it is the power relationship and its potential for abuse that is examined. Guided by this model as well, it is apparent that a party who has critical information available to it by virtue of its position, and yet unavailable to anyone, ... has tremendous opportunity to abuse the power relationships here, by dissembling and nondisclosure.[92]

– – – – – – – – – – –

Discussion Topics

a. In *Wolf*, the court noted a distinction between debt and fiduciary relationships. How would you distinguish these relationships? Note the following definition of debt:

The basic idea of "debt", as a legal term, is that an obligation has arisen out of contract, express or implied, which entitles the creditor unconditionally to receive from the debtor a sum of money which the debtor is under legal, equitable, or moral obligation to pay without regard to any future contingency.[93]

Note that "[a] sum of money which is payable is a debt, 'without regard to whether it be payable now or at a future time.'"[94] How does the dissent in *Wolf* differ from the majority's opinion with respect to the

89.   Roberts v. Sears, Roebuck & Co., 573 F.2d 976 (7th Cir. 1978).
90.   Martinelli v. Bridgeport Roman Catholic Diocesan Corp., 10 F. Supp. 2d 138 (D. Conn. 1998).
91.   *Id.,* LEXIS, Genfed Library, Dist File (LEXIS summary).
92.   *Id.* at 156 (citing Tamar Frankel, *Fiduciary Law,* 71 CAL. L. REV. 795, 836 (1983)).
93.   Evans v. Kroh, 284 S.W.2d 329, 330-31 (Ky. 1955).
94.   Nelson v. Wilson, 264 P. 679, 683 (Mont. 1928) (quoting People v. Arguello. 37 Cal. 524, 525 (1969)).

method of recognizing fiduciaries and their duties? What role does the burden of proof play in the majority's opinion and in the opinion of the dissent?

c. What is a confidential relationship? What factors suggest that it existed and between whom exactly does it exist? Which of Sears' actions constituted violations of confidentiality? Was it the lawyer that breached confidentiality? Did Sears' capacity as a provider of legal advice make the relationship confidential?

d. How can a transaction be structured in a way that would protect the contract party from violations by the other party? Assume that a bank lent a sum of money to a corporation according to the bank's loan forms. Thereafter, the directors of the corporation found a way to reduce the corporation's assets and thereby (indirectly) the bank's collateral. The terms of the loan did not address such a situation. Can the bank argue that the directors owed the bank a fiduciary duty and seek an injunction against the behavior that is harmful to the bank, even if the contract did not prohibit it?

e. There are cases of temporary fiduciary relationships. For example, consider how most people structure the sale of a house. The transaction undergoes a number of stages. Usually, after the parties agree on price and date of possession, the buyer pays the seller a small amount for an informal contract. A few days later they sign a formal contract. At this point, the seller wants the buyer to pay a significant amount of money because the seller is going to take the building off the market. The buyer, however, is not ready to hand over a significant amount of money in exchange of a more detailed contract. After all, the buyer will cease to look for another house. If the seller decides to sell the house to someone else (for a higher price) or demands a higher price from the buyer, the buyer would have to sue for the return of the money and will lose time in finding another home.

How do the parties solve this problem? They appoint the broker as the escrow agent of the buyer's payment. What is the function and legal position of the broker with respect to the deposited money? Can the broker be the agent of both parties? At what point and with respect to what part of the transaction does a broker represent both parties?

- - - - - - - - - - - - - -

2. Is it fair to extend the definition of fiduciary relationships and attendant duties to new situations?

The expansion of fiduciary duties to new situations raises a fundamental issue of fairness to the fiduciaries. *Martinelli v. Bridgeport Roman Catholic Diocesan Corp.*[95] presented a new factual situation. In the United States, fiduciary law did not apply to priests until this case arose. Neither was a claim such as this brought before (although it was raised in Canada).

---

95. Martinelli v. Bridgeport Roman Catholic Diocesan Corp., 10 F. Supp. 2d 138 (D. Conn. 1998).

The issue of expanding the law to new situations is not limited to fiduciary law. In our country, the rule of law applies. People ought to know whether they are subject to prohibitions and be free to act outside the legal prohibitions. Liability should not be imposed without prior notice. Therefore, one could argue that people ought to know whether or not they are fiduciaries and consequently what prohibitions apply to them. They should be free to engage in non-prohibited activities.[96] Even though we deal with the definition of who is a fiduciary in this section, the same problem exists when the courts include in the category of wrongful acts those acts that were not specifically declared wrongful before.

Samuel Buell has dealt with a similar problem although more serious, concerning the definition of fraud in criminal law. There are an increasing number of new general anti-fraud provisions in criminal statutes. He noted that markets tend to innovate and law tends to provide general prohibitions, such as the prohibition on fraud. Yet criminal law requires specificity and prohibits retroactive punishable prohibitions. He wrote that in criminal law this tension was reduced by weighing the "actor's observable awareness of the wrongfulness of her actions. This mechanism is a coping device, not a means of settling the unending contest over novel fraud. Novelty never ceases; neither will doubt about criminality."[97]

– – – – – – – – – – –

Discussion Topics

a. Can you justify the extension of fiduciary duties to new situations without notifying the would-be fiduciaries that they will be subject to increasing limitations and duties?

b. Assuming that expansion to new situations is desirable, how would you mitigate the unfairness to the fiduciaries in such cases?

– – – – – – – – – – –

3. In determining the nature of the relationships, to what extent do the courts defer to the parties?

In *Martin v. Peyton,* the issue was whether an arrangement, which was framed as a loan, was in fact a partnership.[98] The result of the classification was not to impose fiduciary duties on the "lenders" but to make them responsible for the partnership debts. However, the court

---

96.   The issue is similar to the constitutional the principle against retroactive laws. 16B AM. JUR. 2D *Constitutional Law* § 696 (2007) ("A constitutional provision prohibiting retrospective laws covers laws which create a right where none before existed and which relate back so as to confer on a party the benefit of such right, and also all such laws as take away or impair any vested right acquired under existing laws, create a new obligation, impose a new duty, or attach a new disability in respect of transactions or considerations already past. The purpose of the constitutional prohibition against retroactive laws is to safeguard rights not guaranteed by other constitutional provisions such as the impairment of the obligation of contracts."); Jan G. Laitos, *Natural Resources Interests and Retroactive Laws*, 32 ROCKY MTN. MIN. L. INST. 3 (1992).
97.   Samuel W. Buell, *Novel Criminal Fraud*, 81 N.Y.U.L. REV. 1971 (2006).
98.   Martin v. Peyton, 158 N.E. 77 (N.Y. 1927) (citations omitted).

discusses the extent to which it would consider the parties' classification of their relationship, and that part is of interest to us here.

The court wrote:

Assuming some written contract between the parties the question may arise whether it creates a partnership. If it be complete; if it expresses in good faith the full understanding and obligation of the parties, then it is for the court to say whether a partnership exists. It may, however, be a mere sham intended to hide the real relationship. Then other results follow. In passing upon it effect is to be given to each provision. Mere words will not blind us to realities. Statements that no partnership is intended are not conclusive. If as a whole a contract contemplates an association of two or more persons to carry on as co-owners a business for profit a partnership there is. On the other hand, if it be less than this no partnership exists. Passing on the contract as a whole, an arrangement for sharing profits is to be considered. It is to be given its due weight. But it is to be weighed in connection with all the rest. It is not decisive. It may be merely the method adopted to pay a debt or wages, as interest on a loan or for other reasons.

An existing contract may be modified later by subsequent agreement, oral or written. A partnership may be so created where there was none before. And again, that the original agreement has been so modified may be proved by circumstantial evidence -- by showing the conduct of the parties.

In the case before us the claim that the defendants became partners in the firm of Knauth, Nachod & Kuhne, doing business as bankers and brokers, depends upon the interpretation of certain instruments. There is nothing in their subsequent acts determinative of or indeed material upon this question. And we are relieved of questions that sometimes arise. "The plaintiff's position is not," we are told, "that the agreements of June 4, 1921, were a false expression or incomplete expression of the intention of the parties. We say that they express defendants' intention and that that intention was to create a relationship which as a matter of law constitutes a partnership." Nor may the claim of the plaintiff be rested on any question of estoppel. "The plaintiff's claim," he stipulates, 'is a claim of actual partnership . . . , and liability is not sought to be predicated upon article 27 of the New York Partnership Law.

Remitted then, as we are, to the documents themselves, we refer to circumstances surrounding their execution only so far as is necessary to make them intelligible. And we are to remember that although the intention of the parties to avoid liability as partners is clear, although in language precise and definite they deny any design to then join the firm of K. N. & K.; although they say their interests in profits should be construed merely as a measure of compensation for loans, not an interest in profits as such; although they provide that they shall not be liable for any losses or treated as partners, the question still remains whether in fact they agree to so associate themselves with the firm as to "carry on as co-owners a business for profit."

- - - - - - - - - - - - -

Discussion Topics

a. Did the court defer to the parties' desires to classify their relationship as a loan?

b. Where did the court draw the line between a loan (not a fiduciary relationship) and a partnership (a fiduciary relationship)?

c. How would a court determine whether the terms of a relationship were a "sham"?

— — — — — — — — — — — -

The approach of the Federal Court of Australia was different from the U.S. court approach.[99] The Federal Court of Australia gave the parties far more power to determine the legal effect of their relationships. Here is the summary of the case and a detailed statement by the court concerning this issue. Because the Court has an interesting approach to the entrustors' consents, we will return to this case in the Chapter dealing with that topic. A summary of the Court's decision follows.

1. In accordance with the practice of the Federal Court in some cases of public interest, the following summary has been prepared to accompany the reasons for judgment delivered today. The summary is intended to assist understanding of the decision of the Court. It is not a complete statement of the conclusions reached by the Court or the reasons for those conclusions. The only authoritative statement of the Court's reasons is that contained in the published reasons for judgment. The published reasons for judgment and this summary will be available on the Internet at www.fedcourt.gov.au.

2. Citigroup Global Markets Australia Pty Ltd ('Citigroup') is the Australian arm of Citigroup Inc, a global financial services company. Citigroup's business in Australia is conducted through various divisions and business segments. They include investment banking and equities trading.

3. Citigroup has established 'Chinese walls' to restrict the flow of information between different departments. Employees who work in areas such as the Investment Banking Division and who are exposed to confidential, market sensitive information, are known as private side employees. Those who work in areas such as Equities and who are not so exposed, are known as public side employees.

4. These proceedings arise out of the purchase by a public side employee of Citigroup of over 1 million shares in Patrick Corporation Limited ('Patrick') at a time when private side employees working in the Investment Banking Division were acting for Citigroup's client, Toll Holdings Ltd ('Toll') on a proposed takeover bid for Patrick. The shares were purchased by the proprietary trader for Citigroup's own account on the last trading day before Toll announced its bid for Patrick.

5. The Australian Securities and Investments Commission ('ASIC') does not allege that the proprietary trader was in possession of inside information when he purchased the shares. However, when private side employees became aware of the proprietary trader's purchase of the shares, steps were taken from within the private side that resulted in an instruction to the trader to stop buying any more shares in Patrick. The trader did not buy more shares but in the half hour before the close of trading, he sold nearly 200,000 of the parcel of Patrick shares that he had purchased earlier that day.

6. ASIC contends that Citigroup, as an adviser to Toll, occupied a relationship that was in critical respects, fiduciary. ASIC also contends that in purchasing the shares in Patrick, Citigroup placed itself in a position where its duty of loyalty to Toll conflicted with its interests arising from the purchase of the shares in Patrick. The gravamen of the claim is that Citigroup contravened its obligations under s 912A(1)(aa) of the *Corporations Act* to have in place adequate arrangements for the management of conflicts of interest.

---

99. Australian Sec. & Inv. Comm'n v. Citigroup Global Markets Australia Pty. Ltd., [2007] FCA 963 (June 28, 2007).

7. All of the claims of conflict of interest and duty and breach of s 912A(1)(aa) depended upon the existence of a fiduciary relationship between Citigroup and Toll. However, the claims failed at the outset because the letter of engagement under which Toll retained Citigroup as its adviser specifically excluded the existence of such a relationship. The Court held that the law does not prevent an investment bank from contracting out of a fiduciary capacity; whether it should be able to do so is a matter for the legislature, not the courts.

8. ASIC relied on a number of propositions of law to overcome the effect of the engagement letter and sought to impose on Citigroup a duty to obtain Toll's express consent to proprietary trading in Patrick shares. The Court held that the propositions relied on by ASIC had no application in the present case. . . . [100]

The Court wrote: [101]

. . . [T]he term "investment bank" is not capable of precise definition but the influence and importance of investment banks in the financial system is vast; they are integral to the efficient operation of the system.

Major investment banks are listed public companies which operate internationally. They describe themselves, and are referred to, as global financial services firms and financial services conglomerates. They provide a diverse range of services including financial advisory services to corporations on mergers and acquisitions, issuing, buying and selling securities, investment research and transaction financing. This is not an exhaustive list.

. . . [T]he UK Law Commission [pointed out] that the organisational structure of the modern financial conglomerate has enhanced the possibility that the providers of these services will be exposed to potential conflicts of interest or duty with or to their clients.

The UK Law Commission observed . . . that conflicts of interest and of duty and interest that arise from the organisational structure of financial conglomerates are primarily due to three factors. These are first, the range of products and services provided by the firms, second, the breadth of their customer bases and, third, the different capacities in which they conduct their businesses. . . .

[A cited paper] goes so far as to observe that these factors have the result that conflicts are regarded as an inescapable feature of the business of investment banking.

[Another paper] gives examples of conflicts which may occur in takeovers. One such example is where the investment bank's corporate advisory department is advising a corporation which is making a hostile share swap bid for another company but another department of the bank, such as the department managing discretionary share trading accounts, is selling shares in the bidder. This could have the effect of depressing the bidder's share price contrary to its interests.

---

100. Alternatively, ASIC claimed that Citigroup breached the prohibitions in the *Corporations Act* and the *ASIC Act* on misleading and deceptive conduct and unconscionable conduct. Yet, these claims depended on Citigroup and Toll fiduciary relationships. Since there were none—the claims failed. ASIC also argued a violation of the insider trading in the *Corporations Act*. Patrick sold the shares in late afternoon, after receiving instructions not to buy the shares. He could have assumed that Citigroup was acting for Toll in the proposed takeover. This claim failed because the trader was not Citicorp's "officer." His knowledge was not attributable to Citigroup. Besides, he did not make the alleged supposition. Another insider trading claim failed because when Citigroup traded in the shares, it had arrangements (Chinese walls) that could reasonably be expected precent information from reaching the trader. However, while the defence in s 1043F of the *Corporations Act* was upheld, the Court endorsed warnings given in an earlier authority about the risk of leakage of information through Chinese walls.
101. Australian Sec. & Inv. Comm'n v. Citigroup Global Markets Australia Pty. Ltd., [2007] FCA 963 (June 28, 2007) (page numbers and citations omitted).

This example is indistinguishable from the events which occurred in the present case. Purchase by another department of the bank of shares in the target company may well be contrary to the bidder's interests.

[C]lients who are involved in, or considering undertaking, transactions such as mergers and acquisitions, will ordinarily engage an investment bank to provide financial advisory services for the transaction. . . . [F]or large transactions it is usual to engage several investment banks. . . . [T]ypically, the parties will enter into an engagement letter which details the terms of the contract between the parties.

The financial advisory services supplied by an investment bank in a takeover involve decisions that go to the very core of the transaction. They include advising on the merits of entering into the transaction, valuation analyses, recommendations on strategy, advising as to timing, structure, and pricing of the transaction, advising on finance, and assisting in implementation of the takeover.

Investment banks, together with the law firm(s) engaged by the client, work together as a team; they are integrated into the client's working group for the acquisition. They are involved in almost every aspect of it. A relationship of trust and confidence is implicit in the investment banks' role. It is not unusual for fees of tens of millions of dollars to be earned.

The thesis put forward . . . is that the relationship between the client and the investment bank engaged to advise on a takeover is fiduciary in character. . . .

However, . . . the question of whether a fiduciary relationship exists, and the scope of any duty, will depend upon the factual circumstances and an examination of the contractual terms between the parties.

No doubt, for this reason, investment banks have developed contractual techniques to modify or displace fiduciary obligations. The question of whether the mandate letter between Toll and Citigroup is effective to exclude a fiduciary relationship between the parties is at the heart of the present case.

The other techniques developed by investment banks to deal with potential conflicts of interest are structural techniques under which the bank is organised in a way which effectively manages conflicts, or perhaps eliminates them. A favoured technique for dealing with conflicts that arise from carrying on a financial services business in a conglomerate is the use of Chinese walls.

An issue which arises in the proceedings is whether Citigroup's Chinese walls were sufficient to eliminate or adequately manage conflicts of interest.

The Identification of a Fiduciary Relationship

As Gaudron and McHugh JJ observed, . . . "Australian courts have consciously refrained from attempting to provide a general test for determining when persons [. . .] stand in a fiduciary relationship". It may be, as their Honours said, that the term "fiduciary relationship" defies definition. This is because of the difficulty of stating a comprehensive principle suitable for application to different types of relationships that carry different obligations.

The courts have recognised certain classes of persons as falling within established categories of fiduciary relationships. Examples of these include trustee and beneficiary, agent and principal, solicitor and client, director and company, employee and employer, and partners.

Apart from the established categories, perhaps the most than can be said is that a fiduciary relationship exists where a person has undertaken to act in the interests of another and not in his or her own interests but all of the facts and circumstances must be carefully examined to see whether the relationship is, in substance, fiduciary.

Other factors that have been referred to in the authorities as pointing to the existence of a fiduciary relationship will also be important. But they will be so only to the extent that they disclose an expectation in one party that the other will act in his or her interests.

This is encapsulated in the following remarks of Professor Finn (as his Honour then was) in "The Fiduciary Principle":

"What must be shown, in the writer's view, is that the actual circumstances of a relationship are such that one party is entitled to expect that the other will act in his interests in and for the purposes of the relationship. Ascendancy, influence, vulnerability, trust, confidence or dependence doubtless will be of importance in making this out, but they will be important only to the extent that they evidence a relationship suggesting that entitlement. The critical matter in the end is the role that the alleged fiduciary has, or should be taken to have, in the relationship. It must so implicate that party in the other's affairs or so align him with the protection or advancement of that other's interests that foundation exists for the 'fiduciary expectation."

... La Forest J [Supreme Court of Canada] also agreed with Professor Finn's remarks....

The Co-existence of Contractual and Fiduciary Relationships and the Effect of Exclusion Clauses

... Mason J observed that "contractual and fiduciary relationships may co-exist". His Honour said that if a fiduciary relationship is to exist between parties to a contract, the fiduciary relationship must conform to the terms of the contract. He went on to say that:

"The fiduciary relationship cannot be superimposed upon the contract in such a way as to alter the operation which the contract was intended to have according to its true construction."

The observations of Gummow J ... are to the same effect. But his Honour also pointed out that a contractual term may be so precise in its regulation of what a party may do that there is no scope for the creation of a fiduciary duty.

It follows from these statements of principle that it is open to the parties to a contract to exclude or modify the operation of fiduciary duties....

It may well be that a fiduciary cannot exclude liability for fraud or deliberate dereliction of duty but beyond that there appears to be no restriction in the law to prevent a fiduciary from contracting out of, or modifying, his or her fiduciary duties, particularly where no prior fiduciary relationship existed and the contract defines the rights and duties of the parties.

The effect of the Australian and English authorities referred to above is that where a fiduciary relationship is said to be founded upon a contract, the ordinary rules of construction of contracts apply. Thus, whether a party is subject to fiduciary obligations, and the scope of any fiduciary duties, is to be determined by construing the contract as a whole in the light of the surrounding circumstances known to the parties and the purpose and object of the transaction ....

PART V: THE CONFLICTS CLAIMS – DETERMINATION OF ISSUES

Issue 1 – Fiduciary Relationship, Construction of the Mandate Letter

The authorities to which I have referred above ... make it clear that the question of whether any fiduciary relationship existed between Citigroup and Toll is to be determined by the proper construction of the mandate letter.

... Deane J said in plain terms that the parties to a partnership agreement could provide "that any fiduciary relationship between the partners was excluded." The observations of Mahoney JA ... were to the same effect. His Honour said that fiduciary duties could be "varied or released" by contract. Also, in *News Limited,* a Full Court of this

Court . . . said that whether there are any fiduciary obligations at all may depend on the terms of the contract.

It is difficult to see that the words of the mandate letter have anything other than their plain meaning. Citigroup was retained solely as an adviser to Toll, as an independent contractor and not as a fiduciary. The engagement of Citigroup as an 'independent contractor and not in any other capacity' suggested that the parties had in mind the distinction between independent contractors and employees or agents . . . . Thus, these words also point against the assumption of any fiduciary capacity.

It is true . . . that an adviser may have fiduciary obligations to the client. But for the express terms of the mandate letter, the pre-contract dealings between Citigroup and Toll would have pointed strongly toward the existence of a fiduciary relationship in Citigroup's role as an adviser.

I have set out the pre-contract dealings in some detail because they were referred to by Mr Walker and they contain all of the indicia of a fiduciary relationship of adviser and client.

In summary, Citigroup gave Toll advice as to the wisdom and merits of making a bid for Patrick. Citigroup gave strategic advice which involved the use of its financial acumen, judgment and expertise to further Toll's interests. Citigroup worked closely with Toll as is evidenced by the presentations made before the execution of the mandate, as well as the large number of communications between them, both oral and by email.

Moreover, Citigroup actively "pitched" to obtain the mandate and it sought a primary role, comparing itself favourably with Carnegie Wylie from an advisory perspective. It emphasised its "access to global players" and its abilities, not just as a funder but also as an adviser. It promised to back the transaction "to the hilt even if it gets a little hairy".

In addition, Citigroup gave advice to Toll about many aspects of the transaction, including, in particular, extensive advice, prior to the execution of the mandate letter, as to the pricing of the offer and the calculation of the premium. Citigroup's advice was that the premium should be calculated so as "to convey the most optically appealing bid".

There were substantial negotiations as to the fees payable to Citigroup, and Citigroup ultimately secured success fees in the range of AUD$10 million to AUD$18 million. Fees of that order are testimony in themselves to a finding that Citigroup held itself out as an expert adviser on mergers and acquisitions, which points to the existence of a fiduciary relationship.

The mandate letter does not spell out the advisory services to be supplied by Citigroup, other than to describe them as financial advisory and investment banking services in connection with the proposed transaction as are customary and appropriate.

Customary financial advisory services would include those described [above], such as advising on the merits of entering into the transaction, strategic advice and advising on timing, structure and pricing. The services which would be considered to be appropriate would also be determined by reference to those supplied by Citigroup before the execution of the mandate letter, as part of the relevant factual matrix.

However, ASIC did not suggest that the factual matrix, or the object or purpose of the mandate letter, could bear upon the proper construction of the acknowledgment that the relationship between the parties was not fiduciary.

Nor did ASIC argue that the words "including as a fiduciary" should be limited or read down by anything else in the terms of the lengthy acknowledgment.

It is true, as Frankfurter J said in *Securities and Exchange Commission v Chenery Corporation,* that "to say a man is a fiduciary only begins the analysis." But it is otherwise where the parties acknowledge that they are not in a fiduciary relationship. In my view, those words mean what they say and should be enforced accordingly, unless the mandate letter was vitiated as a matter of law.

ASIC did not contend that the mandate letter was unenforceable in accordance with its terms. There was of course no allegation of mistake or misrepresentation. Nor did ASIC argue that the exclusion of a fiduciary relationship was contrary to the regulatory obligations imposed on Citigroup by s. 912A(1)(aa) of the Corporations Act to have in place adequate arrangements for the management of conflicts of interest.

It seems to me to follow that the exclusion of the fiduciary relationship was effective, notwithstanding the fact that Citigroup undertook to provide financial advisory services to Toll and that both parties' interests were "well aligned" in the fee structure set out in the mandate letter.

The exclusion of the fiduciary relationship in the mandate letter is to be contrasted with the more extensive acknowledgments contained in the Custodian & Nominee Appointment. There, the form of appointment authorised Citigroup to have a variety of specified conflicts and to carry on business through the operation of Chinese walls.

However, those documents cannot bear upon the proper construction of the mandate letter itself. At most, they may point to Toll's informed consent to proprietary trading by Citigroup.

Issue 2 – Whether Informed Consent was Required

ASIC submitted that the acknowledgment in the mandate letter that Citigroup was neither an agent nor a fiduciary raises the question of the ability of a person who would otherwise be a fiduciary to include in the retainer letter a provision limiting or excluding that role.

ASIC advanced eleven propositions in support of its contentions that the acknowledgment in the mandate letter was ineffective without Toll's informed consent.

I do not propose to set out each of the propositions. The first was that a fiduciary relationship, if it is to exist, must accommodate itself to the terms of the contract. For reasons given above, the proposition is plainly correct but it does not provide an answer favourable to ASIC upon the terms of the mandate letter.

The remaining propositions have at their core the submission that where the inclusion of a particular term in "a putative *fiduciary's* retainer agreement" would create an actual or potential conflict between the interests of the fiduciary and those of the client, then the "would be fiduciary" must obtain the informed consent of the client to the inclusion of that term.

This submission is said to be based upon the principles stated in the authorities dealing with time charging by solicitors. ASIC submitted that the principle is not limited to solicitors and applies generally to all fiduciaries.

However, for reasons given above, I do not consider that this principle applies in the present case. In particular, even if the principle stated by Mahoney JA in **Foreman** is of general application to fiduciaries, it cannot apply unless the fiduciary is within an established category or is subject to fiduciary obligations before entering into the contract.

To hold otherwise would be to say that a person who is not a fiduciary may nevertheless owe an obligation which flows from a fiduciary relationship. That could hardly be correct. [102]

---

102. *Id.* (page numbers and citations omitted).

Discussion Topics

a. What is the difference between the attitude of the American court and Australian courts' views? Do these views depend on the different culture in the two countries, or their different economic and financial contexts? Are the public policy objectives in the two countries different? Or is there greater need for judicial intervention in the United States than in Australia to achieve the same objectives? Which of these views do you favor? What principles would you suggest to guide Citicorp in the future?

b. As noted, an agent is a fiduciary while generally a servant is not. Can you explain the reasons for the difference? What are the risks posed by servants who clean the home while the owner is present as compared with servants that clean the home when the owner is absent? What kinds of risks do servants pose? How can the homeowners protect themselves from these risks? How can the cleaning service offer trustworthy services and reduce the risks? Would the same analysis apply to the *Brophy* case?

c. A bailee is someone who obtains possession of another person's property for safekeeping, or in connection with service, such as a garage attendant, a car mechanic or a tailor entrusted with clothes for mending. The bailee's fiduciary duties are very limited in contrast to the other types of fiduciaries. Why is that so? What are the risks that bailees pose for entrustors? For example, the garage attendant may use your car to sit and listen to music on your radio. He may use your car for a joy ride. Or he may use your car to bring a client who has had a heart attack to the hospital. A car mechanic may do the same. Do both pose the same risks or are the risks different, and if so, which one of these bailees is riskier to the entrustor?

d. Who poses greater risks to shareholders-entrustors? Corporate directors (who are elected by the shareholders to supervise the affairs of the corporation), or top management (that is appointed by the board to operate the corporation full time)? How do both compare with investment advisers to individuals v. investment advisers to mutual funds that are pools of individuals' money managed together?

e. What about brokers and dealers? Do they owe any fiduciary duty to all or some customers? Note that brokers execute transactions for customers, for example, selling and buying stocks for customers or bringing buyers and sellers of real estate to transact. Dealers sell stock to customers or buy stock from customers at the dealers' own account. Usually when brokers cannot find buyers (or sellers) for customers in the markets, the brokers offer their customers to buy (or sell) their stock as dealers.

4. The fiduciary business

We have reviewed fiduciaries in personal relationships with entrustors and those in relationship with many entrustors, as well as fiduciaries of an entity that contains the assets of many entrustors. An additional situation is people or entities that are in the business of offering fiduciary services. Large law firms and accounting firms are of this sort. These entities may face an issue of whether they act as fiduciaries or as businesses.

For example, mutual funds are entities that hold investors' money. Advisers are organizations that manage the investors' money held in the mutual funds.[103] Advisers invest and own the infrastructure necessary to manage large amounts of financial assets. These include portfolio managers and analysts, legal and accounting staff, stock transfer agents, brokers and trading desks and the investor contact personnel. The advisers invest their own money in these services and receive from the mutual funds payment for some of their expenses as well as fees for their services. Advisers in this case are similar to a law firm that serves many clients and employs the staff to manage complex litigation and transactions. These independent advisers to mutual funds service millions of investors.

Now suppose that an adviser use its financial clout and manages to negotiate a 30% reduction in the cost of services to the funds, such as calculations and statistical services. Who should benefit from this deduction? Should the adviser pocket this deduction and charge the "client" funds the market price of the services? Or should the advisers charge the funds the deducted fees that it negotiated? What should determine the question? What are the adviser's duties in this case?

D. The Dark Side of Fiduciary Relationships

Our judgment of the historical "uses" of the past and fiduciary relationships of the present and the future depends on whether we view the relationships as employed for good causes or whether they are employed to circumvent the law (whether the circumvented law is good or bad). The "uses" and "trusts" in the past, and fiduciary relationships in the present, offer a method to avoid the law by interpositioning other persons between what are the true actors and what seem to be the true actors. While the Statute of Uses attempted to erase uses and trusts in one broad sweep, the legislators and the courts in later centuries judged these relationships on a one-to-one basis, and distinguished between their desirable and undesirable results.

For example, one could use agency to hide the identity of the true owner.[104] One could interpose between the wealthy owner and the world a less wealthy "owner." A 1892 case demonstrates such a use of a fiduciary relationship. In *Watteau v. Fenwick*[105] a hotel manager

---

103. Rashid Bahar & Luc Thévenoz, *Conflicts of Interest: Disclosure, Incentives, and the Market, in* CONFLICTS OF INTEREST: CORPORATE GOVERNANCE & FINANCIAL MARKETS 1, 3-4 (Luc Thévenoz & Rashid Bahar eds., 2007); *accord,* 2 TAMAR FRANKEL & ANN TAYLOR SCHWING, THE REGULATION OF MONEY MANAGERS: MUTUAL FUNDS AND ADVISERS § 12.01, at 12-5 (2d ed. 2001) ("[A]dvisers for investment companies occupy a special position, in that they substitute for managing directors and paid officers of the investment company.").
104. Watteau v. Fenwick, 1 Q.B. 346, (1893) LEXIS, Uk Library, Iclr File.
105. *Id.*

seemed to be the hotel owner; for example, his name was posted on the hotel's entrance door. In fact, he was an agent of the owners. These owners authorized the manager to buy only certain kinds of drinks. He violated their directive and bought other goods as well. These unauthorized goods remained unpaid. The supplier sued the hotel manager-agent for the price, and when he discovered the true owners, the supplier sued the true owners as well. The court held that the owners-principals were liable for the price of the unauthorized goods.

The court analogized the liability of undisclosed principals for the acts of their agents to the liabilities of dormant (undisclosed) partners for their partnership's debts. Partners are liable for these debts regardless of whether the creditors know of the partners' existence. A similar rule should apply to the principals in the *Watteau* case. They should be liable for their agent's obligations, regardless of whether the creditor knew of the principal's existence. To be sure, the supplier-creditor received an additional (and better) debtor from whom to collect the debt. After all he gave credit to the agent only. But the principals should pay the debt because they enabled their agent to masquerade as owner.

The court wrote:

Here the defendants have so conducted themselves as to enable their agent to hold himself out to the world as the proprietor of their business, and they are clearly undisclosed principals .... All that the plaintiff has to do, therefore, in order to charge the principals, is to shew that the goods supplied were such as were ordinarily used in the business—that is to say, that they were within the reasonable scope of the agent's authority.[106]

A voting trust is another example of using fiduciary relationships to hide the true actors. Assume that a few shareholders decide to unite and vote together on particular issues or the choice of directors. Assume, however, that the shareholders are not sure about the reliability of each other's promise to vote according to certain guidelines. Or perhaps they want to hide their identity for good or bad reasons. So they create a "voting trust." They transfer their shares to a trusted person to be their trustee, and direct him on how to vote the shares. The trustee must transfer to the shareholders all benefits from the shareholdings, such as dividends; all benefits except the power to vote. No one need know who the real owners are. The courts and the legislatures looked on voting trusts with disfavor, but did not ban them altogether.[107] Rather they were regulated. Thus, in *Smith v. Biggs Boiler Works Co.* the court wrote:

No voting trust may now be created in this state unless it complies with that statute. When the Legislature passed the statute setting up the terms and conditions under which a voting trust would be valid, it occupied the whole field. Sec. 18 provides: (1) that the stock must be deposited with the voting trustee or trustees; (2) that the trustee or trustees may vote said stock for a period not exceeding ten years; (3) that a copy of the agreement shall

---

106. *Id.*
107. *See, e.g.,* Watts v. Des Moines Registrar & Tribune, 525 F. Supp. 1311 (S.D. Iowa 1981).

be filed in the principal office of the corporation in the State of Delaware; (4) that certificates of stock shall be issued to the voting trustees to represent any stock so deposited with them; (5) that in the certificates so issued it shall appear that they are issued pursuant to the voting trust agreement; and, (6) that in the entry of such voting trustees as owners of such stock in the proper books of the issuing corporation that fact shall be noted.[108]

Last but not least is the use of trusts for tax avoidance. In *United States v. Scherping*[109] the government sought to foreclose on property that the taxpayers transferred to two business trusts. The government argued that the trusts were the taxpayers' alter egos and the transfers were fraudulent. The court affirmed a district court decision in favor of the government. The court upheld the district court's use of the "reverse piercing" doctrine to hold a trust liable for individual liabilities, finding the trusts "alter egos" of the taxpayers and not separate persons, and called them "sham entities." The court noted policy reasons for the reverse piercing, i.e., "avoiding fraud and collecting delinquent federal taxes." Finally the court held the transfers to be fraudulent conveyances under state law.[110]

Similarly, trusts were used to establish monopolies that led to the prohibition of antitrust laws in the United States. Yet, trusts were not prohibited altogether. In each case, the use and abuse of trust was noted, and attempts were made to avoid the abuses while keeping the beneficial uses available.

- - - - - - - - - - -

Discussion Topic

a. Is there anything wrong with voting trusts? What precisely did the legislatures regulate with respect to voting trusts? Please articulate the problems that the legislatures attempted to address.

- - - - - - - - - - -

E. Chapter Review

The discussion and materials in this Chapter can be confusing. There are so many actors and situations. So please re-focus and review the outline in the introduction to this Chapter. What are the features that all fiduciaries have in common and what are the differences among them? The features are (1) Services; (2) Entrustment of property and power; (3) Inability of the entrustor to specify the power of the fiduciaries without undermining the utility of the relationship; (4) Inability of the entrustor to monitor the fiduciaries closely and make sure that the fiduciary complies with the terms of the entrustment.

---

108. Smith v. Biggs Boiler Works Co., 91 A.2d 193, 197 (Del. Ch. 1952) (citations omitted) (citing DEL. CODE ANN. tit. 8, § 218) (the agreement was held invalid and the trustee of the agreement was ordered removed. The supplemental agreement, which was conditioned on a refunding agreement and an option to purchase, failed to comply with § 18 of the General Corporation Law. The bitter relationship between plaintiff and defendant trustees prevented them from managing the corporation properly).
109. United States v. Scherping, 187 F.3d 796 (8th Cir. 1999).
110. *Id.*

Then we question the value of fiduciary relationships to society and show their more seamy side. In the next Chapter, we discuss fiduciary duties and link the duties to the features we listed and discussed in this Chapter. We also focus some of our discussion on the limitations on the use of fiduciary relationships by entrustors.

We review this Chapter by problems. Clients differ and so do the following stories. Please read them and determine the legal relationships among the parties.

Problem

The bank and borrower. In *Brooks v. Valley National Bank,* the bank made a loan to Brooks, secured by a mortgage. Under the terms of the loan, Brooks made monthly payments to the bank to cover his insurance and taxes on the mortgaged home (before these amounts were due). The bank invested these payments and received income from the investments until it made the annual payments on the insurance and property tax. Brooks sued the bank, demanding the income from these invested payments. The mortgage terms did not state whether the bank may invest the payments or who had the right to the income from such investments. Was the bank a fiduciary with respect to these payments? How should the court decide the issue?[111]

Problem

The mortgage brokers. Mortgage brokers connect lenders with borrowers who offer a security of their home as collateral (mortgages). Some brokers work for particular lenders and some for many. Some wait for the borrowers to approach them and some search for borrowers. The brokers' compensations differ as well. Some receive a salary and some work on commissions and some receive both salaries and commissions. Mortgage brokers perform a useful function of reducing the cost for both borrowers and lenders in connecting with each other. However, the mortgage brokers' function and ways of bringing borrowers to the lenders have raised questions. The 2005-06 rise in real estate values and the low interest rates enabled high-risk borrowers to acquire homes which they could not afford. They also hoped that the price of the homes will continue to rise and they could sell the homes at a profit. When interest rates rose, and home prices fell, many high-risk borrowers defaulted.

In most cases, mortgage loans did not stay with the original lenders. Rather they were pooled and transferred into an entity that offered investors securities (a pro rata share of the cash flow). Thus, the lenders could get these risky loans off their books. The brokers collected their fees (which at times were very high) and disappeared from the scene. The borrowers, who did not evaluate their risk of losing their homes, and the investors, who did not evaluate correctly the price they paid for the investments in these mortgages, remained "holding the

111. *See* Brooks v. Valley Nat'l Bank, 539 P.2d 958 (Ct. App. Ariz. 1975), *aff'd,* 548 P.2d 1166 (Ariz. 1976).

bag." Not surprisingly, they complained, and some sued the brokers. The main complaints were based on misrepresentation or lack of full information. The latter requires that the brokers be fiduciaries. If their relationships to the lenders or the borrowers are that of contract-service givers, then they have no duty to inform the other parties, unless they are asked.

Mortgage brokers argued that they were fiduciaries neither to the lenders nor to the borrowers. "They are fighting efforts by federal and state politicians to impose a fiduciary duty on them to put their customers' interests first, as lawyers, real-estate agents and financial planners generally are required to do with their clients."[112]

Are mortgage brokers fiduciaries of the lenders, the borrowers, or neither? How would you decide?

Problem

The story of a writer's legacy. What are the kinds of legal relationships that this story uncovers? Are any of these relationships fiduciary relationships?

Youngblood Hawke by Herman Wouk is a novel that describes the successes, tribulations, and, ultimately, the death of a young novelist in New York in the late 1940s and early 50s.[113] The following summary from the book deals with events following the death of the novelist, Arthur Youngblood Hawke. The key characters in the passages are Jeanne Green, who was Hawke's editor and fiancee and who married much later after his death; Ferdie Lax, Hawke's literary agent, who is apparently still managing Hawke's copyrights for his legatees; and Sara Hawke, the author's mother. The properties Sara received under her son's will included the copyright to the novel *Evelyn Biggers,* a critical and popular failure when it was first published, but which lately was enjoying a "late blooming vogue." Lax saw new ways to exploit Hawke's copyright in Television, for example. Another book *The Lady From Letchworth* was shown on TV and won a prize. So Lax looked through the author's other works in order to sell to TV. The view of the author's work began to change and the books had new and larger followings among the critics as well. Some of the author's writings even became required readings in high schools and colleges. This acclaim focuses on the novel *Evelyn Biggers.*

Lax met with Jeanne and told her of a famous film star who was interested in playing the lead part in *Evelyn Biggers.* He tried unsuccessfully to persuade Sarah Hauk to consent the film. She refused, reminding him of the film of another of her son's book that failed miserably because of faulty production. Yet, Lax persisted. If the film were made with this famous actress, Lax's career would flourish; the film would bring millions! Therefore, Lax pressed Jeanne to

---

112. James R. Hagerty, *Mortgage Brokers: Friends or Foes?*, WALL ST. J., May 24, 2007, at D1, LEXIS, News Library, Wsj File.
113. HERMAN WOUK, YOUNGBLOOD HAWKE, Epilogue. Selected passages from pages 771-783 (1962).

persuade Sarah to consent to the deal on *Evelyn Biggers* and offered her half of his commission.[114]

Lax invited the screen writer and director to meet with Ms. Hawke and asked Jeanne and her husband to join the group. Jeanne subsequently met with Lax and the director, Fred Mannes, at dinner and like him. He read all of the author's books and promised a good picture. Thus, Jeanne, her husband Gus, Lax, and Roberto Luzzatto, a producer, subsequently flew down to Hovey, Kentucky, where Mrs. Hawke lived, to persuade her to allow a movie to be made of *Evelyn Biggers*.

"Mrs. Hawke was a little slower, a little grayer, a little heavier in her movements, but otherwise unchanged, and she apparently was making a career of keeping the old house on High Street, where she still lived, unchanged." Jeanne who has not been in the house since the author's death noted no change, except that the house was turned into a museum commemorating the author. His mother offered tours of the house not only to her guests but also to tourists. They visited the place he was born, the kitchen where he ate, his bedroom, and where he worked. Ms. Hawke was furious at the town's mayor who refused to spend over $30,000 for a museum dedicated to her son, after all the tourists that his name and fame attracted to the town.

After the meal the visitors described to Ms. Hawke the film they were contemplating and Jeanne and her husband did their share in persuading the mother to agree to make a film based on the book. Then, Jeanne's voice cut sharply into the jubilation and the congratulations. And she said, addressing Ms. Hawke: "I have some good news for you. Mr. Lax has already told me that, if this deal works out, he'll give half his commission to the town of Hovey." And Lax, nonplused, lowered his eyes and said that this was the least he could do.

— — — — — — — — — — — —

Discussion Topics

a. Review the materials in this Chapter and apply them to the actors in this story. Analyze the relationship among the various actors. Which relationship was a fiduciary relationship and what kind of obligations did or should the fiduciary have followed? For example, did Jean violate any legal duties to Mrs. Hawke? Had she shared the commissions with Lax, would she be legally liable to Mrs. Hawke?

b. What did Mother really want? Money or sentiment? Can you distinguish between them? Is the question relevant? What model would you apply? The market model, the family/social model, quantifiable legal rule?

---

114. *Id.* at 773.

c. What if Jean was merely a friend of Mother? Is that relevant to whether the law should interfere in the relationship?

— — — — — — — — — — -

Problem

How Steve Jobs Played Hardball in iPhone Birth.[115] The iPhone was developed by Apple Computers and Cingular—a cell company. The phone has a touch-screen, allowing users to "view contacts, dial numbers and flip through photos with the swipe of a finger."

While developing iPhone, Apple avoided the rules of the cellphone industry that usually controls the development and details of phones. Although Cingular, Job's partner in developing the iPhone, is a cellphone company, Cingular agreed to remove its brand from the phone's body, and did not insist (as most phone makers do) on "carrying its software for Web surfing, ringtones and other services." In fact, Cingular had little information about the development of iPhone. In addition, Cingular agreed that iPhone will be distributed solely through Cingular and Apple retail systems. Other wireless providers refuse to leave their retail partners. Thus, Cingular gave up control in developing iPhone for "the privilege of being the exclusive U.S. provider of one of the most highly anticipated consumer electronics devices in years—and to deny rivals a chance to do the same . . . ."[116]

— — — — — — — — — — -

Discussion Topics

a. What is the nature of the relationship between Jobs and Cingular? Apart from contract relationship, Jobs had more freedom to operate and Cingular had very little say in Jobs' creation of the iPhone. It is very unusual for a wireless carrier to cede this type of control. Does Jobs' discretion trigger a fiduciary relationship?

b. What if Jobs sold his idea to another wireless company?

c. What if Cingular, after Jobs created the iPhone, allowed others, such as Circuit City, to sell the phone?

d. What if Jobs failed to create an iPhone?

— — — — — — — — — — -

Problem

Check Cashing Institutions and H & R Block.[117] Check-cashing outlets charge for cashing mostly government or paychecks, although in some states they might cash personal checks, as loans for future paychecks. These may be viewed as short-term loans or check cashing (which are not subject to statutes limiting charges on consumer loans). The charges cover the costs of check cashing business and profits.[118]

---

115. Amot Sharma et al., *Apple Coup: How Steve Jobs Played Hardball in iPhone Birth — In Deal With Cingular He Called the Shots; Flirting With Verizon*, WALL ST. J., Feb. 17, 2007, at A1, LEXIS, News Library, Wsj File (abridged and summarized; footnotes omitted).
116. *Id.*
117. JOHN P. CASKEY, FRINGE BANKING: CHECK-CASHING OUTLETS, PAWNSHOPS, AND THE POOR 30, 55, 57-59, 61 (1994) (footnote omitted).

A survey of the Consumer Federation of America in 1989 covering 60 check-cashing outlets in 20 major cities across the United States found that charges for cashing local payroll checks were 0.9% of the check amounts to 3%. The average rate was 1.74%. Charges for cashing government assistance checks were 0.9% to 3.25% (average: 1.73%) and personal check cashing: 1.66% to 20% of the checks' amounts (average: 7.7%).

Consumers paid for convenience of business hours and locations, as well as the willingness of the check cashing business to take a risk which the banks are less willing to take, that the checks will bounce.

H & R Block's tax preparation is similar to the check cashing services. Clients pay at least $20 for electronic filing of their returns and another $30 for an anticipated refund loan. "[T]he average refund was $916 for the 1990 year. Therefore, the typical H & R Block customer who [used the service] pa[id] an annual interest rate of [85%] on the loan."[119]

- - - - - - - - - - - -

Discussion Topics

a. Is there a distinction between CCOs and H & R Block's tax preparation?

b. Is there a fiduciary duty in some cases regarding CCOs and not others? When you go to a store to buy a good (food, clothing, etc.), that good may cost more than if you had bought it at another store. There is no fiduciary duty on the part of the employees of the store to tell the consumer that the good can be bought more cheaply elsewhere. Is this a good analogy to CCO consumers, or are there other factors at play?

c. What is H & R Block's relationship with its customers? With respect to what activity? Would you agree to represent a suit against H & R Block as a class action? What would you claim?

d. There are consumer protection statutes that prohibit charging consumers excessive service fees, and require relevant disclosure to consumers. For example, a car dealership that sells cars by installment payments must disclose the APR in bold print. Should these laws extend from the purchasing of a vehicle to other areas, such as this H & R Block example or CCOs?

e. Consider *Carazo v. Lopez*.[120] In that case, the sellers of real estate brought a successful action against their real estate agent for breach of fiduciary duty in the sale of the sellers' real estate. The real estate agent had concealed from the sellers, who could not read or write English, the true compensation she received from the sale. The court held that the real estate agent violated her fiduciary duty to sellers by

---

118. *Id.*

119. *Id.* at 80-81 (citation omitted) (citing Scott R. Schmedel, *A Special Summary and Forecast of Federal and State Tax Developments*, WALL ST. J., Mar. 20, 1991, at A1, LEXIS, News Library, Wsj File).

120. Carazo v. Lopez, 169 Cal. Rptr. 182 (Ct. App. 1980).

taking advantage of their inability to speak English. As a result, the sellers had to hire counsel and wait over four years before receiving a judgment for the amount of damages that they had sustained. The real estate agent subsequently filed a frivolous appeal and forced sellers to incur further attorney's fees and court costs. The court awarded the sellers additional damages of $1,000 as costs on appeal. How different is this case from the case of a CCO?

Problem

Jack and the Beanstalk.[121]

There was a poor widow, her son, Jack, and a cow, Milky-white. The cow gave milk which Jack and his mother sold in the market. One day the cow gave no milk, so Jack's mother told him to sell to cow. He agreed.

On his way to the market, Jack met a man who offered to buy the cow for five beans that would "grow right to the sky." Jack accepted. When Jack returned with the beans, his mother threw the beans out. The next day Jack saw a giant beanstalk leading to the sky. He climbed the beanstalk and reached a giant house and saw a giant woman. The woman told Jack to leave because her husband is an ogre who eats boys. Jack begged for food and she offered him some. When Jack finished eating, the ogre had arrived. Jack did not have time to escape and the ogre's wife hid Jack in the oven." The ogre noted the smell. He growled: "Alive or dead, I want the Englishman's bones."

The ogre's wife answered that he was imagining, no Englishman was around. Then the ogre took bags of gold to count, but fell asleep. Jack crept out of the oven, stole a bag of gold, and slid down the beanstalk to his home.

After Jack and his mother used all the gold, Jack climbed up the beanstalk again. The ogre's wife told him to leave, noting that the ogre's gold has been stolen, but as they heard the ogre coming, she hid Jack in the oven again and after the ogre completed his breakfast, he asked for his hen that lays golden eggs. The ogre commanded the hen to lay a golden egg, and the hen complied. As the ogre fell asleep, Jack took the hen and slid down the beanstalk. Jack's third visit to the ogre enabled him to grab the ogre's golden harp. But this time the harp cried to the ogre, who woke and chased after Jack. Jack managed to reach down, and chopped the beanstalk. The ogre and the beanstalk fell down and did not rise again. Jack and his mother became wealthy, he married a great princess, and they lived happily ever after.[122]

— — — — — — — — — — -

Discussion Topics

a. What fiduciary relationships arise in this story?

---

121. *The Annotated Jack and the Beanstalk,* http://www.surlalunefairytales.com/jackbeanstalk/index.html (last visited Aug. 8, 2007) (summarized and edited).
122. *Id.*

b. Does Jack have any fiduciary relationship with the ogre? Since the planting of the beans occurred as a result of Jack's trade, the beans sprouted and led to the ogre. Does this create a relationship?

c. What was the relationship between Jack and his mother when she sent him to the market to sell Milky-white? She did not, however, specify that he should collect money for the cow. Jack exchanged the cow for seemingly worthless beans. Was this a breach of duty? Once the beans produced gold, to whom did the gold belong?

d. What was the relationship between the ogre's wife and Jack? She did invite him into her house to eat. She knew of hidden dangers (i.e., the ogre eats little boys) when inviting Jack into her home.

e. As a wife, what were her relationships to the ogre? Did she breach a duty by allowing Jack in the first time? Or did she breach a duty the second time she let Jack in when the danger that they would be robbed was more foreseeable?

— — — — — — — — — — —

Chapter Three
The Duties of Fiduciaries

A. Introduction. The Fundamentals

1. Much is about human nature

Like many legal rules, fiduciary duties are based on assumptions about human nature. The following story is instructive: One evening an old man said to his grandson: "My son, the battle is between two 'wolves' inside us all. . . . One is Evil. It is anger, envy, jealousy, sorrow, regret, greed, arrogance, self-pity, guilt, resentment, inferiority, lies, false pride, superiority, and ego. The other wolf is Good. It is joy, peace, love, hope, serenity, humility, kindness, benevolence, empathy, generosity, truth, compassion and faith." The grandson thought about it for a minute and then asked his grandfather: "Which wolf wins?" The old Cherokee replied simply, "The one you feed."

Thus, it is assumed that some persons who are entrusted with property or power for the purpose of benefiting others might be tempted to benefit themselves as well, especially when there are no police around. Further, they may fail to follow the instructions that they receive with respect to the use of the entrusted property or power. Or they may fail to perform in a reasonably expected way the services they promised to perform.

Would it not be simple to require these persons to commit to satisfy other persons' interests or always to follow the given directives and always to perform skillfully and well? It would be simple but too much to ask of humans. Besides, it may not be healthy for society to require all people always to tend to the needs and desires of others and never to their own needs and desires. Therefore, the duties that bind fiduciaries must be weighed and balanced. In addition, the extent and severity of fiduciary duties depend on non-legal controls and social monitoring of fiduciaries. The intervention of the law reflects the extent to which these controls and monitoring are effective.

In addition, fiduciary duties reflect the culture of society and its needs. If society enforces the desirable behavior, the law may be dormant. If it fails to enforce—the laws will be more useful. The rules will change with the changing mores of society.

2. What do fiduciary duties aim at?
a. What do fiduciary duties regulate?

The fiduciaries' temptations relate to *entrusted property or power* and not to other parts of the relationship that may involve *exchanged property or power*. Therefore, the focus of fiduciary law is on entrustment. For example, suppose John entrusts $10,000 to Jane, his stockbroker, to buy and trade in securities and promises to pay her a commission of 1% of the traded assets. If Jane then deducts from John's account 1%, this deduction is permitted, and she can do with the money whatever she wishes. But if she takes more than the percentage due to her, or fails to perform the services as expected or does not trade in a reasonably efficient way, she breaches her fiduciary duties to John.

Like any other law, fiduciary duties can be designed and expressed by standards and principles, or by specific rules. However, even when the duties are specified, they are usually established against the background of standards and principles. Duncan Kennedy distinguishes between altruistic and individualistic (self-interested) views of private law. He suggested that the "altruist views on substantive private law issues lead to willingness to resort to standards in administration, while individualism seems to harmonize with an insistence on rigid rules rigidly applied."[1] Although his observation was made in the context of contract law, perhaps it could apply with even greater strength in the context of fiduciary law. As you go through the materials in this Chapter, consider whether this observation is correct, and whether there is a connection between the standards—orientation, altruism, and fiduciary law on the one hand, and specific rule orientation, individualism, and contract law on the other hand.

How do fiduciary duties arise? According to one commentator:[2]

Fiduciary law creates causes of action for entrustors against their fiduciaries, even if the parties did not contract. A trustee has obligations towards beneficiaries of a trust absent any agreement between them. The courts provide protection to entrustors by imposing on fiduciaries restrictive obligations. Arguably, the parties would have agreed on these obligations if the need for giving the fiduciaries broad discretion, which could not be specified in advance had not precluded them from doing so by contract. Others suggest that fiduciary rules reflect not only the parties' presumed agreements but policy considerations as well.

The extent of a fiduciary duty varies with the degree of potential abuse of power stemming from the relationship. The standards are stricter for trustees than for corporate directors because the beneficiary does not control the trustee and is locked into the relationship, whereas shareholders can terminate the directors or sell their shares if they are dissatisfied with the directors' performance. In either case, however, even though the fiduciary's promise to act for a particular purpose does not create a contractual obligation, fiduciary laws fills the void by imposing a legal duty on him to act for that purpose once he chooses to enter into the relationship. . . .

---

1.   Duncan Kennedy, *Form and Substance in Private Law Adjudication,* 89 HARV. L. REV. 1685, 1685, 1713-22, 1731-33 (1976).
2.   Tamar Frankel, *Fiduciary Law,* 71 CAL. L. REV. 795, 825-27 (1983) (summarized and edited).

Control over fiduciaries, whether directly or by rules, creates a tension. On the one hand, fiduciaries must be free to use their expertise and respond to future unanticipated event. Otherwise they will not maximize their benefit to the entrustors benefit of entrustors. On the other hand, it is necessary to restrict them their freedom and prevent possible abuse of their power. Consequently, the courts defer to fiduciaries in some areas, so long as there is no showing of conflicts of interest and other possible abuses of trust. In the corporate area the courts' deference is called "the business judgment rule."[3]

[We noted in Chapter Two that entrustors are vulnerable because they are not able to control their fiduciaries strictly.] Fiduciary law strengthens the entrustor's ability to monitor the fiduciary. Substantive rules may be motivated by hidden concerns regarding accountability and monitoring. For example, in *Dodge v. Ford Motor Co.*, the defendant Henry Ford had declared his intention to reduce the future price of Ford cars for the benefit of society.[4] The minority shareholders, the Dodge brothers, objected. The court held that a corporation is not a charitable institution. It is organized to make profits for its shareholders. The price reduction was an inappropriate corporate act. Yet in *A.P. Smith Mfg. Co. v. Barlow*,[5] when a minority shareholder objected to a $1,500 corporate donation to Princeton University, the court held that the gift was valid and attempted to redefine the corporation's role in society as the contributor to the pool of talent and knowledge.

The cases offer conflicting principles on the role of a corporation in society. And yet, both *Ford* and *Smith* are good law. The "donation" in Ford was flawed because it was of an indeterminate amount to an unspecified number of unknown recipients. If Ford had been allowed to reduce the price of the cars as a gift to society, the courts and the minority shareholders would have lost the ability to control the amount of the donation and its purpose.[6] In contrast, the donation in *Smith* was for a specific amount to a known recipient. The minority shareholders, and eventually the courts, could therefore pass judgment on whether the donation was appropriate.[7]

The courts may also strengthen the monitoring process of fiduciaries by acting in a role akin to that of a middleman, thus encouraging the markets for fiduciary services. For example, recent Supreme Court decisions have stricken down restrictions on advertising of lawyers' fiduciary services and have imposed strict antitrust rules regarding fee-fixing. The Supreme Court was clearly dissatisfied with the self-regulation of lawyers and physicians, and responded by strengthening the markets for their services and the protections given to entrustors.[8]

b. When do fiduciary duties arise?

The commonsense answer to the question of when fiduciary duties arise could be: "When the parties agreed to enter the relationship." They could do so by writing, or verbally or by action.

---

3.   Duncan Kennedy, *Form and Substance in Private Law Adjudication*, 89 HARV. L. REV. 1685, 1713-22, 1731-33 (1976).
4.   Dodge v. Ford Motor Co., 170 N.W. 668 (Mich. 1919).
5.   A.P. Smith Mfg. Co. v. Barlow, 98 A.2d 581 (N.J. 1953).
6.   Dodge v. Ford Motor Co., 170 N.W. 668 (Mich. 1919) (Ford could have based the price reduction on business grounds of increasing the number of sales, although in the case of his company there were long-term orders).
7.   A.P. Smith Mfg. Co. v. Barlow, 98 A.2d 581 (N.J. 1953).
8.   *E.g.*, Bates v. State Bar of Arizona, 433 U.S. 350 (1977).

Or perhaps the birth of the relationship occurs when the entrustor entrusted the property or power to the fiduciary. After all, before that moment, there are no reasons to protect the entrustor more than any other contract party.

But if fiduciary duties do not arise before the parties have closed the bargain and established the relationship, why do lawyers owe fiduciary duties to potential clients under the common law as well as under the rules of professional conduct? Similarly, why do investment advisers owe fiduciary duties to potential clients under the common law as well as the Investment Advisers Act of 1940? Besides, if the common law were sufficient, why were these duties established by statute or rules? What are the reasons for imposing any duties of disclosure or confidentiality on these fiduciaries even before they close the deal with the entrustors?

The answer seems to be that in order to enter the relationship, some of the conditions for the establishment of fiduciary relationships have already occurred. Therefore, the fiduciary duties or pre-fiduciary relationships arise. Therefore, not all, but some, pre-fiduciary relationships involve fiduciary duties.

— — — — — — — — — — -

Discussion Topics

a. List the possible components of fiduciary relationships that arise when a potential client meets with a lawyer, or a physician.

b. In light of these components, what is the justification of requiring advisers in the securities area to offer potential clients brochures (prescribed by law)? The brochures contain information about the advisers, their education, their fees and sometimes even the fact that their fees exceed the level of fees usual in the market.

— — — — — — — — — — -

3. What are the main fiduciary duties?

Fiduciary duties relate to entrusted property or power. They do not apply to other parts of the relationships, for example, the relationships that involve exchange. We already noted the promise of the entrustor to pay the fiduciary fees constitutes an exchange. The fiduciaries may then use the fees they earned as they wish. A gray area applies to agreements regarding the fees after the fiduciary relationships have been established. The fees are not entrusted, but the level of the fees may be subject to limitations under fiduciary law. Once the relationship has commenced, the beneficiary is entitled to trust the fiduciary, and the relation is no longer arms' length.

As to entrustment, two fundamental fiduciary duties cover all species of fiduciaries. The first duty is the duty of loyalty, focusing on the use of entrusted property or power for the benefit of the entrustor or its designees. The second duty is the duty of care, which focuses on the quality of the service that the fiduciary undertook to perform, and the level of care attached to the performance. For example, when John entrusts Jane with $1 million to buy a house for him, and, looking for his house, Jane finds a suitable one, that she buys for herself, Jane may have violated her duty of loyalty to John, even if she used her own money to buy the house. She was supposed to use the time she spent in searching and apply her skills to serve his interests. If Jane used the entrusted money to buy a house as an agent for John—the principal—but failed to inquire whether there are termites in the basement or failed to ensure that the house is properly registered in John's name, Jane has breached her duty of care to John. She did not use her skill reasonably to protect John's interests.

In addition, there are a number of related duties. One duty, derived from the duty of loyalty, is the fiduciary's duty to follow the directives of entrustment with respect to the entrusted power or property. A second duty that derives from the notion of entrustment is the duty to account, and a close relative of such duty is the duty to disclose. Accounting relates to assets. Disclosure relates to activities. A third duty requires a fiduciary to treat entrustors fairly, and a fourth is a duty to act in good faith in performing fiduciary services. Finally, the fifth duty is a prohibition on delegating the fiduciary services. Because fiduciary relationships are personal, the rule limits the extent to which fiduciaries may delegate their services to others.

Thus, in our example, if Jane signed a purchase contract on a house on John's behalf to pay $1.2 million, Jane breached a related duty to comply with John's directives. That is, even if Jane (or anyone else except the seller) did not benefit from the violation. If Jane did not give John an account of what was done with the money he entrusted to her, she has breached the duty to account, even if John did not ask her for an account. He would not be bound by the account—which she had, but did not give to him. If Jane did not give John information pertinent to the house and the process of the purchase, she has breached the duty to disclose, again, regardless of whether he asked her to tell him the facts. If there were faults in the home or unusual legal limitations on building connected with the house, Jane might be liable for the lower value of the house. And finally, she may not send someone else to negotiate and to close the deal. If she did, she would be responsible for any misdeeds that her delegate has committed. We expound on these duties later.

B. The Duty of Loyalty

What does the duty of loyalty mean? What does it mean to be loyal? It could mean following the directives of someone to whom one is loyal. But that is not necessarily loyalty. It may be obedience. Obedience can be the outward sign of loyalty. In fact, loyalty may require disobedience in order to protect the person to whom one is loyal.

Among the synonyms of the word "loyalty" are the words "trustworthiness" and "faithfulness." Thus, loyalty is a state of mind and a manner of behavior. It means identifying with the other persons' interests. Loyalty is not required in business relationships. None of the contract parties is obligated to be loyal to the interests of the other. A faithful servant who works under a contract can be cast out at the end of the contract term when his usefulness has been exploited and a better servant or a cheaper one is available. Yet many people do not behave this way. They reward loyalty with loyalty. The faithful servant may be relegated to a lower position or be paid sufficiently to retire.

In arms' length transactions, the law does not require loyalty or reward it. But there is an exception to this legal "hands-off" attitude with respect to the fiduciaries' loyalty to entrustors, applicable, however, only to entrusted property or power.

The legal duty of loyalty takes two forms. One form is a requirement that fiduciaries act for the sole benefit of the entrustors. The other form is a prohibition on fiduciaries from acting in conflict of interests with the interests of the entrustors (always in relationship to the entrustor property or power). In certain cases, the prohibition extends to the fiduciaries who put themselves in conflict of interest situations where none existed before, such as lawyers who take new clients whose interests conflict with those of existing clients.

The duty of loyalty supports the main purpose of fiduciary law: to prohibit the fiduciary from misappropriating or misusing entrusted property or power. Property, however, is a vague term as is demonstrated in the cases discussed in Chapter Two. Property includes information but does not, at least in California, include human body cells. The rules that govern the duty of loyalty consist of prohibited actions that damage or could damage the entrustors' interests in relation to the entrusted property or power. Among these rules, there are important preventive rules. In and by themselves the prohibited actions in these preventive rules might not injure the entrustors. Yet, the rules prohibit the actions in order to dampen the fiduciaries' temptation to do such injury.

For example, fiduciaries are prohibited from buying entrusted property for their own account even at market price or even at a price higher than the market price and even if the purchase saves the entrustor a broker's commission. That is, unless the entrustor or some other authorized person or regulators consent to the transaction after receiving full information from the fiduciary.

Many debates concerning preventive rules in fiduciary law focus on the degree to which the rules should prohibit non-harmful actions by fiduciaries. How costly are the rules for fiduciaries? Why should fiduciaries be prohibited from profiting if the entrustors are not harmed? The counter calculation of cost is sometimes forgotten. The question then is how costly is it to monitor and control the fiduciaries and what are the probabilities that sooner or later the entrustors would be harmed unless the fiduciaries are conditioned to avoid first step actions that lead to temptation?

A second debate regarding fiduciary duties is based on the extent to which the entrustors can protect themselves against abuse of trust without the protection of the law. How costly would self-protection be for entrustors, compared to the costs of the fiduciaries in complying with the rules and perhaps the costs of government in enforcing the rules?

A third debate regarding fiduciary duties involves the evaluation of market effectiveness as enforcer of fiduciaries' honesty. After all, restrictive fiduciary rules should not apply if the markets are likely to provide protection to the entrustors against abuse of trust. In such a case, the question is whether law should step back and let the markets take its place.

1. Curbing temptation by prohibiting conflicts of interest

A major rule, which is designed to prevent violation of fiduciary duties, is the rule prohibiting the fiduciaries from acting in conflicts of interest. Joshua Getzler discussed the origins of the rule against conflicts of interest.[9] One example of the prohibition on conflicts of interest is a rule, established in England in the 1700s, that prohibits trustees from acquiring trust property for themselves, even if they paid the market price for the property. The rule was established as a preventive measure.[10] In part the policy underlying the rule is based on the idea of inequality. The cost of monitoring the fiduciary also may have played a role in establishing the rule against conflicts of interest.[11] The rule is not popular with some modern commentators. They argue that the automatic

"finding of impropriety should be replaced by a rebuttable presumption, partly because modern law and accounting is more apt to deal with fiduciary power; partly out of unease at the penal or deterrent application of private law remedies to pursue public policy goals. But equity has maintained the rule, allowing only informed consent to suspend its operation."[12]

Fiduciaries are prohibited from acting on behalf of their entrustors when the fiduciaries' interests conflict with those of the entrustors. The prohibition applies regardless of the fairness of the terms of the deals. The following case demonstrates the rule.[13]

Singer was an employee in charge of soliciting buyers for certain widgets, which the employer—Automotive—produced. Singer was approached by potential clients for widgets that his employer did not and could not currently produce. Singer did not merely send the potential buyers away. He established a brokerage business and directed potential buyers for products, which Automotive could not produce, to other producers. Those other producers paid him a commission for the reference. When Automotive discovered the arrangement, and recognized that Singer gained over $60,000 from the side business, Automotive sued for the amount and interest.

---

9.   Joshua Getzler, The Road to Rumford Market: History and Classification of Fiduciary Obligations (footnotes omitted) (on file with author).
10.   *Id.*
11.   *Id.*
12.   *Id.*
13.   *Id.*

The court held that Singer must account to Automotive for all his profits from this side business. The reason is that Singer had a conflict of interest. He was the one to determine whether Automotive could not produce the desired products. It matters not that his judgment was correct. He benefited from his decision to divert the buyers elsewhere and receive commissions. He did not disclose this side dealing to his employer. Had he done so, Automotive could have either increased its personnel to meet the demand for the products or would have engaged in the brokerage business itself for its own benefit. So long as the buyers came to the employer, Automotive, the information about them and their needs belonged to the employer. Even if the buyers came to Singer, it is unclear to what extent he could start the side dealing without disclosing his conflict to his employer.[14]

a. Brokers

Brokers include stockbrokers and real estate brokers, among others. Brokers are agents, who undertake to act for others. Therefore, they are fiduciaries with respect to the execution of the transaction on behalf of their clients. Brokers may become fiduciaries as advisers, depending on the circumstances. Sometimes they hold their clients' money and assets as escrow agents or in order to be able to buy or sell for clients.

What about mortgage brokers, that is, people who connect prospective home buyers, who need financing, with lenders? David Unseth wrote that "[s]ome courts hold that mortgage brokers do not owe their borrowers a general fiduciary duty, reasoning that the loan transaction is conducted at arm's length," similar to the relationship between the borrower and the lender. [15] "Where courts have imposed this general fiduciary duty, mortgage brokers have typically breached this duty to their borrower in one of three scenarios: failure to disclose loan terms; failure to disclose loan fees; and failure to provide the most favorable loan terms or lowest loan fees." Unseth notes that the California Supreme Court held a mortgage broker to be a fiduciary because the broker is customarily serving "as the borrower's agent in negotiating an acceptable loan."[16] One can see the important implications from this holding, if the broker does not inform and explain to the borrower the implications of all the terms of the mortgage loan (including the small print).

Stockbrokers play multiple roles, especially in the financial area. For example, brokers are usually also dealers and sometimes advisers and financial planners as well. These multiple roles of the actors, especially in the financial area, make economic sense, but can raise difficult legal issues when the actors' relationships with others combine contractual and fiduciary relationships and present conflicts of

---

14. *Id; see* Gen. Auto. Mfg. Co. v. Singer, 120 N.W.2d 659 (Wis. 1963).
15. David Unseth, Note, *What Level of Fiduciary Duty Should Mortgage Brokers Owe Their Borrowers?*, 75 WASH. U. L.Q. 1737, 1741 (1997).
16. *Id.* at 1742 (citing Wyatt v. Union Mortg. Co.,598 P.2d 45, 50 (Cal. 1979) (en banc)).

interest. Broker-dealers offer a telling example. Brokers are agents and therefore fiduciaries. They represent and find, for client buyers or sellers, their counter-parties. In the securities markets brokers execute the transactions among these parties. Brokers are entrusted with the buyers' or sellers' assets or cash and are fiduciaries with respect to these entrusted assets and cash.

In fact, brokers perform a very useful role in preventing either transacting party from reneging on the deals. In the securities markets, the transactions are not executed immediately upon the clients' orders. In these markets volatility is the name of the game. Therefore, when prices move up or down either sellers or buyers are likely to regret their decision. Brokers, however, would regret transactions only if they did not occur; because execution of the transactions is a condition for the brokers' payment. Therefore, brokers have an incentive to execute the transactions; the more the merrier. Hence brokers are willing to comply with the rules that require them to prevent the parties from reneging. Brokers must control the clients' cash or securities and prevent clients from changing their minds. This is one reason why notwithstanding securities markets' volatility there are very few court cases on breach of agreements and these occur usually when the parties negotiate directly and not through a broker.[17]

When brokers cannot find a counterparty for their clients, the brokers are likely to become dealers. That is, they provide clients with liquidity by offering to buy the clients' securities or sell the clients the securities the clients wish to buy. In this posture the brokers are no longer agents or fiduciaries. The transactions with the clients are sales or purchases. The securities and cash that the dealers receive are not entrusted to them but given to them in an exchange.

Broker-dealers live off transactions. Therefore, they seek to advertise their wares—the securities, and their promised profits. In the securities markets the clients not only buy the products, but also sell them. The more the clients trade, the more broker-dealers earn. Therefore, volatility is the desirable state of affairs for broker-dealers. Volatility, however, must move forward. If clients continuously lose on their investments, they might cease trading. Therefore, broker-dealers advertise their services and emphasize that trading is likely to increase their clients' wealth.

The status of broker-dealers as advertisers increases their ambiguous posture. Advertising renders them advisers as well as salespersons. Clients who do not know much about the securities markets seek the broker-dealers' advice. Some clients are entirely dependent on the advice. In fact, clients might entrust their assets to the broker-dealers for management, at the broker-dealers' discretion. Yet in this posture the broker-dealers are also salespersons, tending to their own affairs and well being.

---

17. *See, e.g.,* Essex Universal Corp. v. Yates, 305 F.2d 572 (2d Cir. 1962).

Thus, broker-dealers' position is ambiguous on both grounds. They act as fiduciary-agents as well as buyers and sellers under contracts. They act as fiduciary advisers and money managers as well as salespersons. The rules that apply to broker-dealers demonstrate their ambiguous status. For example, the Securities and Exchange Commission imposed duties on broker-dealers not on the ground that they are fiduciaries but rather on the basis of the "shingle theory." The Commission stated that when broker-dealers hang out their shingles and offer services to the public, they are presumed to promise the public a fair treatment.[18] Thus, many duties have been imposed on broker-dealers not on fiduciary law grounds but on misrepresentation grounds. Even so, there are cases in which brokers' duties are not waivable and disclosure is not helpful. For example, when clients obviously act as uncontrolled gamblers, and require brokers to execute transactions that are obviously "suicidal," brokers must at some point stop complying and cease trading on the clients' behalf. In that respect the brokers are similar to the bartenders who must stop serving drunken customers prepared to drive.

Broker-dealers who hold the clients' assets and cash are not required to segregate them as trustees would. However, brokers are required to be financially sound[19] and to carry compulsory insurance.[20] Unless clients ask broker-dealers to execute specified transactions for them, broker-dealers are subject to a "suitability rule."[21] They must advise clients to acquire investments that are suitable for the clients, under the clients' circumstances.

If broker-dealers advise clients without charging them a special fee they are excluded from the definition of adviser under the Advisers Act of 1940.[22] But when brokers offer free "financial planning" but not free brokerage services to implement the planning, their status is more complicated. Thus, broker-dealers' relationships with clients present a mixture of contract and fiduciary law subject to regulation.

Why should we bother about these classifications? The answer is that many regulations are implicitly based on these classifications. Consider the example of advisers to hedge funds. The hedge funds are not regulated under the Investment Company Act of 1940.[23] The advisers need not register with the Securities and Exchange Commission so long as they have fewer than 15 clients.[24] But these unregistered advisers are subject to the antifraud provision of section 206 of the Investment Advisers Act of 1940.[25] That section authorizes the Securities and Exchange Commission to promulgate rules under

---

18.   8 Louis Loss & Joel Seligman, Securities Regulation 3814 (3d ed. rev. 2004) (quoting Charles Hughes & Co., Inc., v. SEC, 139 F.2d 434 (2d Cir. 1943), *cert. denied,* 321 U.S. 786 (1944)).
19.   17 C.F.R. § 240.15c3-1 (2007) (net capital rule).
20.   15 U.S.C. § 78ccc(a)(2)(A) (2000) (members of Securities Investor protection Corporation (SIPC) generally include all registered brokers and dealers).
21.   NASD Manual (CCH) Rule 2310(a) (Mar. 2007).
22.   *See* 15 U.S.C. § 80b-2(a)(11) (2000) (definition of "investment adviser" requires that person advises "for compensation").

various conditions. The Commission adopted a Rule that prohibits such advisers from defrauding investors.[26]

It is important to notice that the Commission stated that the Rule does not classify these advisers as fiduciaries.[27] Nonetheless, the Rule authorizes the Commission to prosecute advisers who have violated their fiduciary duties under state laws.[28] For example, if the adviser to a hedge fund violated his fiduciary duties as the general partner in a limited partnership, federal law would authorize the Commission to sue the adviser pursuant to the Rule.

Federal law in this case did not absorb the common law but it provided federal enforcement of fiduciary duties under common law when the violators are advisers as defined by the federal law. Hence, the classification of fiduciaries can help guide the lawyer in identifying fiduciary principles even in this case.

The following cases demonstrate the complexities of the rule against conflicts of interest.

b. Physicians

We visited *Moore v. Regents of University of California*[29] when we dealt with entrustment of power. Please read pages 39-40. Here we revisit the case in connection with the physician's conflicts of interest. When a conflict exists, the physician and every fiduciary under such circumstances must disclose the conflict to the entrustor and obtain his consent. Otherwise, the physician may not continue to entertain the conflicting interest and serve the patient at the same time. The court wrote:

Plaintiff alleges that his physician failed to disclose preexisting research and economic interests in [his body] cells before obtaining consent to the medical procedures by which they were extracted.... We hold that the complaint states a cause of action for breach of the physician's disclosure obligations....

" ... [T]hroughout the period of time that [Moore] was under [Golde's] care and treatment, ... the defendants were actively involved in a number of activities which they concealed from [Moore] ...." Specifically, defendants were conducting research on Moore's cells and planned to "benefit financially and competitively ... [by exploiting the cells] and

---

23.   15 U.S.C. § 80a-3(c)(1) (2000) (excluding from definition of "investment company" "[a]ny issuer whose outstanding securities (other than short-term paper) are beneficially owned by not more than one hundred persons and which is not making and does not presently propose to make a public offering of its securities"); 15 U.S.C. § 80a-3(c)(7)(A) (2000) (excluding from definition of "investment company" "[a]ny issuer, the outstanding securities of which are owned exclusively by persons who, at the time of acquisition of such securities, are qualified purchasers, and which is not making and does not at that time propose to make a public offering of such securities").

24.   15 U.S.C. § 80b-3(b)(3) (2000).

25.   15 U.S.C. § 80b-6(4) (2000).

26.   Prohibition of Fraud by Advisers to Certain Pooled Investment Vehicles, Advisers Act Release No. 2628 (Aug. 3, 2007), 72 Fed. Reg. 44,756 (Aug. 9, 2007) (to be codified at 17 C.F.R. § 275.206(4)-8).

27.   *Id.* at 44,760.

28.   *Id.*

29.   Moore v. Regents of University of California, 793 P.2d 479 (Cal. 1990) (Mosk, J., dissenting), *cert. denied,* 499 U.S. 936 (1991) (some citations omitted).

[their] exclusive access to [the cells] by virtue of [Golde's] ongoing physician-patient relationship . . . ."

[Golde developed the cells for commercial use without disclosing the fact to Moore.] . . . .

A. *Breach of Fiduciary Duty and Lack of Informed Consent*

Moore repeatedly alleges that Golde failed to disclose the extent of his research and economic interests in Moore's cells before obtaining consent to the medical procedures by which the cells were extracted. These allegations, in our view, state a cause of action against Golde for invading a legally protected interest of his patient. This cause of action can properly be characterized either as the breach of a fiduciary duty to disclose facts material to the patient's consent or, alternatively, as the performance of medical procedures without first having obtained the patient's informed consent.

Our analysis begins with three well-established principles. First, "a person of adult years and in sound mind has the right, in the exercise of control over his own body, to determine whether or not to submit to lawful medical treatment." Second, "the patient's consent to treatment, to be effective, must be an informed consent." Third, in soliciting the patient's consent, a physician has a fiduciary duty to disclose all information material to the patient's decision.

These principles lead to the following conclusions: (1) a physician must disclose personal interests unrelated to the patient's health, whether research or economic, that may affect the physician's professional judgment; and (2) a physician's failure to disclose such interests may give rise to a cause of action for performing medical procedures without informed consent or breach of fiduciary duty.

To be sure, questions about the validity of a patient's consent to a procedure typically arise when the patient alleges that the physician failed to disclose medical risks, as in malpractice cases, and not when the patient alleges that the physician had a personal interest, as in this case. The concept of informed consent, however, is broad enough to encompass the latter. "The scope of the physician's communication to the patient . . . must be measured by the patient's need, and that need is whatever information is material to the decision."

Indeed, the law already recognizes that a reasonable patient would want to know whether a physician has an economic interest that might affect the physician's professional judgment. As the Court of Appeal has said, "[c]ertainly a sick patient deserves to be free of any reasonable suspicion that his doctor's judgment is influenced by a profit motive." The desire to protect patients from possible conflicts of interest has also motivated legislative enactments. Among these is Business and Professions Code section 654.2. Under that section, a physician may not charge a patient on behalf of, or refer a patient to, any organization in which the physician has a "significant beneficial interest, unless [the physician] first discloses in writing to the patient, that there is such an interest and advises the patient that the patient may choose any organization for the purposes of obtaining the services ordered or requested by [the physician]." Similarly, under Health and Safety Code section 24173, a physician who plans to conduct a medical experiment on a patient must, among other things, inform the patient of "[t]he name of the sponsor or funding source, if any, . . . and the organization, if any, under whose general aegis the experiment is being conducted."

It is important to note that no law prohibits a physician from conducting research in the same area in which he practices. Progress in medicine often depends upon physicians, such as those practicing at the university hospital where Moore received treatment, who conduct research while caring for their patients.

Yet a physician who treats a patient in whom he also has a research interest has potentially conflicting loyalties. This is because medical treatment decisions are made on the basis of proportionality -- weighing the benefits to the patient against the risks to the patient. As another court has said, "the determination as to whether the burdens of treatment are worth enduring for any individual patient depends upon the facts unique in each case," and "the patient's interests and desires are the key ingredients of the decision-making process." A physician who adds his own research interests to this balance may be tempted to order a scientifically useful procedure or test that offers marginal, or no, benefits to the patient. The possibility that an interest extraneous to the patient's health has affected the physician's judgment is something that a reasonable patient would want to know in deciding whether to consent to a proposed course of treatment. It is material to the patient's decision and, thus, a prerequisite to informed consent.

Golde argues that the scientific use of cells that have already been removed cannot possibly affect the patient's medical interests. The argument is correct in one instance but not in another. If a physician has no plans to conduct research on a patient's cells at the time he recommends the medical procedure by which they are taken, then the patient's medical interests have not been impaired. In that instance the argument is correct. On the other hand, a physician who does have a preexisting research interest might, consciously or unconsciously, take that into consideration in recommending the procedure. In that instance the argument is incorrect: the physician's extraneous motivation may affect his judgment and is, thus, material to the patient's consent.

We acknowledge that there is a competing consideration. To require disclosure of research and economic interests may corrupt the patient's own judgment by distracting him from the requirements of his health. But California law does not grant physicians unlimited discretion to decide what to disclose. Instead, "it is the prerogative of the patient, not the physician, to determine for himself the direction in which he believes his interests lie." 'Unlimited discretion in the physician is irreconcilable with the basic right of the patient to make the ultimate informed decision . . . .'

Accordingly, we hold that a physician who is seeking a patient's consent for a medical procedure must, in order to satisfy his fiduciary duty and to obtain the patient's informed consent, disclose personal interests unrelated to the patient's health, whether research or economic, that may affect his medical judgment. . . .

. . . Moore was never informed prior to the splenectomy of Golde's "prior formed intent" to obtain a portion of his spleen. In our view, these allegations adequately show that Golde had an undisclosed research interest in Moore's cells at the time he sought Moore's consent to the splenectomy. Accordingly, Moore has stated a cause of action for breach of fiduciary duty, or lack of informed consent, based upon the disclosures accompanying that medical procedure.

We next discuss the adequacy of Golde's alleged disclosures regarding the postoperative takings of blood and other samples. In this context, Moore alleges that Golde "expressly, affirmatively and impliedly represented . . . that these withdrawals of his Blood and Bodily Substances were necessary and required for his health and well-being." However, Moore also alleges that Golde actively concealed his economic interest in Moore's cells during this time period. "[D]uring each of these visits . . ., and even when [Moore] inquired as to whether there was any possible or potential commercial or financial value or significance of his Blood and Bodily Substances, or whether the defendants had discovered anything . . . which was or might be . . . related to any scientific activity resulting in commercial or financial benefits . . . , the defendants repeatedly and affirmatively represented to [Moore] that there was no commercial or financial value to his Blood and Bodily Substances . . . and in fact actively discouraged such inquiries."

Moore admits in his complaint that defendants disclosed they "were engaged in strictly academic and purely scientific medical research . . . ." However, Golde's representation that he had no financial interest in this research became false, based upon the allegations, at least by May 1979, when he "began to investigate and initiate the procedures . . . for [obtaining] a patent" on the cell line developed from Moore's cells.

In these allegations, Moore plainly asserts that Golde concealed an economic interest in the postoperative procedures. Therefore, applying the principles already discussed, the allegations state a cause of action for breach of fiduciary duty or lack of informed consent. . . .

Thus, Moore can state a cause of action based upon Golde's alleged failure to disclose that interest before the splenectomy.

The superior court also held that the lack of essential allegations prevented Moore from stating a cause of action based on the splenectomy. According to the superior court, Moore failed to allege that the operation lacked a therapeutic purpose or that the procedure was totally unrelated to therapeutic purposes. In our view, however, neither allegation is essential. Even if the splenectomy had a therapeutic purpose, it does not follow that Golde had no duty to disclose his additional research and economic interests. As we have already discussed, the existence of a motivation for a medical procedure unrelated to the patient's health is a potential conflict of interest and a fact material to the patient's decision.[30]

— — — — — — — — — — -

Discussion Topics

a. What are the ways in which the court defined the duties of the physician to his patient? List the reasons why Dr. Golde committed wrongs in treating Mr. Moore.

b. Should Dr. Golde have refused to treat Mr. Moore, or could he treat him under certain conditions?

c. Was Dr. Golde justified in requiring Mr. Moore to continue coming in for tests?

d. Did the court reject the possibility that courts would create fiduciary duties when none existed before? If such a possibility is not ruled out, what self-guidelines does the court adopt?

e. If a physician receives substantial research grants or contracts from a large pharmaceutical company and recommends to patients the use of drugs or other products of that company, does the physician have a duty to disclose his interest to the patient? Assume that the drugs are the best for the patient, what relevance does such disclosure have?

— — — — — — — — — — -

Another issue which arises in the medical area concerns physicians that engage in sexual relationships with clients or with the spouses of clients.[31] In such cases the physician's duties indirectly relate to their entrusted power.

---

30.   *Id.* at 480-86.
31.   Linda J. Demaine, *"Playing Doctor" with the Patient's Spouse: Alternative Conceptions of Health Professional Liability,* 14 VA. J. SOC. POL'Y & L. 308 (2007).

In *Long v. Ostroff,* an appeals court found that a physician has no duty to refrain from sexual activity with the patient's spouse:

In this appeal, we are asked to consider whether Pennsylvania recognizes a claim for professional negligence where a doctor has a covert sexual relationship with a patient's spouse. We conclude that a claim for professional negligence is not cognizable under the facts of this case, because a general practitioner's duty of care does not prohibit an extramarital affair with a patient's spouse. Although such conduct may be unethical, it does not provide a cause of action for negligence. Thus, we affirm.

At the relevant time, Walter Long (Patient) was married to Roseanne Long (Roseanne). Both were patients of Dr. Jonathan Ostroff. We will set forth the facts as the trial court described them:

[Patient] brought suit for professional negligence against [Dr. Ostroff], his family physician, based upon [Dr. Ostroff's] adulterous relationship with [Roseanne]. While serving as [Patient's] physician for six years (1992-1998), [Dr. Ostroff] began a sexual affair with [Roseanne] in September, 1998. [Patient] alleges [Dr. Ostroff] was negligent because during an office visit on October 27, 1998, where he was examined for chest pain, back pain, and anxiety [Dr. Ostroff] did not disclose his sexual relationship with [Roseanne]. We note [Rosanne] had previously expressed her intent to divorce [Patient]. In fact, five days prior to said office visit, [Patient] and [Roseanne] separated for the final time. They divorced five months later.

Dr. Ostroff and Roseanne are now married to each other. Patient alleges that during Dr. Ostroff's examination of Patient, Patient requested a referral to a mental health professional because of his marital problems. Patient does not argue that Dr. Ostroff's actual medical diagnosis was in any way negligent. . . .

Patient raises the following questions for our review:

1. Should Pennsylvania recognize a cause of action in medical malpractice when a physician harms his patient by having sexual relations with the patient's wife who also happens to be the physician's patient? . . . 4. Did the Philadelphia [County] Court of Common Pleas abuse its discretion when one judge found no cause of action for intentional infliction of emotional distress, but another judge of the same Court dismissed [Patient's] action on the basis that [Patient's] only valid cause of action might have been intentional infliction of emotional distress? 5. Should this Court permit an amendment to [Patient's] Complaint for a count of Intentional Infliction of Emotional Distress, a breach of fiduciary duty[,] and should this Court reinstate the punitive damages count which was dismissed without prejudice in the initial stages of the proceedings? . . .

We first consider whether a claim for medical malpractice is cognizable, as a matter of law, when a physician has an affair with his patient's spouse. Like the parties and trial court, we acknowledge that this is a novel issue in Pennsylvania. After careful analysis, we conclude that a claim for professional negligence cannot be sustained based upon a general practitioner having an affair with his patient's spouse, who is also a patient.

A medical malpractice claim is not cognizable unless the physician owes his patient a duty of care. Whether a physician owes a duty to his patients is a question of law. Upon review, we conclude that a general practitioner's duty of care does not prohibit an extramarital affair with a patient's spouse. For his contention that Dr. Ostroff owed him a duty of care not to engage in a sexual relationship with his wife, Patient relies heavily and solely on Mazza v. Huffaker . . . . The Mazza court found that psychiatrists have a duty not to engage in sexual relations with their patients' spouses. Even though Mazza is not binding, we also distinguish Mazza on two grounds.

First, in Mazza, the court took great care to enunciate why psychiatrists have a burdensome duty to maintain their patients' trust:

These basic duties apply and are even more stringent with psychiatrists, since a psychiatrist's patient reveals his innermost thoughts, feelings, worries, and concerns. Psychiatrists, therefore, have a strict duty not to breach the trusting relationship and must be very careful about what they say and how they influence patients. ****Especially in light of the intimate relationship between psychiatrist and patient, the psychiatrist's duty once the psychiatrist-patient relationship has been established extends beyond the hospital or consulting room and includes social situations. ****Covert sexual relations between a psychiatrist and a patient's wife, if discovered by the patient, would make it extremely difficult for the patient to establish ever again a necessary trusting relationship with any psychiatrist, would render previous treatment useless, and would do harm to the mental well-being of the patient.

Accordingly, we conclude that the Mazza decision, with its countless references to a psychiatrist's special duty, does not extend to general practitioners.

Second, when the North Carolina Court of Appeals decided Mazza, North Carolina law recognized claims for criminal conversation and alienation of affection. Criminal conversation occurs when the defendant has sexual intercourse with the plaintiff's spouse while the plaintiff and spouse are still married; it is an interference with "the fundamental right to exclusive sexual intercourse between spouses." Similarly, a claim for alienation of affection requires proof that defendant's "malicious acts" caused the loss of love and affection in the plaintiff's marriage. Accordingly, under North Carolina law, there are instances under which a person may prevail in a lawsuit against his or her spouse's paramour for the paramour's sexual relationship with the plaintiff's spouse. Hence, a cause of action for having a sexual relationship with the plaintiff's spouse would be consistent with North Carolina law. Pennsylvania, on the other hand, has abolished these tort claims. Therefore, Mazza is not persuasive; we find no duty. Order AFFIRMED.[32]

The trial court also distinguished the patient-physician and patient-psychiatrist relationships:

The special relationship between patient and psychiatrist is based upon "transference," used by psychiatrists to treat patients. Transference is described as: "a patient's emotional reaction to a therapist; generally applied to the projection of feelings, thoughts and wishes onto the analyst, who has come to represent some person from the patient's past. . . . Transference is crucial to the therapeutic process because the patient unconsciously attributes to the psychiatrist or analyst those feelings which he may have repressed towards his own parents." Lacking a therapist-patient relationship with either Walter or Roseanne Long, defendant's sexual conduct with plaintiff's estranged wife did not constitute malpractice under Pennsylvania law. . . . [33]

Linda J. Demaine took the view that the misconduct should not be treated differently in the two situations, arguing that "transference" is unnecessary because violation of trust in the physician is sufficient to causes harm to the patient, and that trust is important as well in the patient-physician relationship as the patient is equally dependent on the physician. In addition, some courts have recognized breach of fiduciary claims for other physician conduct not related to treatment, such as conflict of interest and misuse of confidential information.

32.   Long v. Ostroff, 854 A.2d 524 (Pa. Super. Ct. 2004), *appeal denied,* 871 A.2d 192 (Pa. 2005) (per curiam).
33.   Long v. Ostroff, 63 Pa. D. & C. 4th 444, 446 (Pa. Ct. Com. Pl. 2003), *aff'd,* 854 A.2d 524 (Pa. Super. Ct. 2004), *appeal denied,* 871 A.2d 192 (Pa. 2005) (per curiam).

Courts have also recognized the fact that psychological trauma may cause physical harm.[34]

— — — — — — — — — — -

Discussion Topics

a. Is the physician's behavior justified because the patient's marriage was already strained?

b. Do you agree with the court's evaluation of the patients' rights? Do you agree with the physicians' arguments?

c. How does the physician's affair with a patient's spouse affect the patient's health?

d. How does the discovery of the physician's affair with the patient's wife affect the patient's trust in physicians? Or the trust of people in physicians generally?

e. What are the various legal bases for suing a physician that has had an affair with the patient's spouse?

f. What are the various legal bases for suing a physician that has had an affair with the patient? Does it make a difference if the physician is a psychologist? Or if the patient is a drug addict?

— — — — — — — — — — -

c. Trustees

Trustees are required to earmark trust property. This rule aims at preventing harm to entrustors as well as chilling the trustees' temptations. Another reason for the rule is to prevent confusing trust property with the trustee's property. It protects potential creditors of the trustee from offering credit to the trustee on the basis of trust property that seems to be his own but is not. Earmarking the property notifies would-be creditors that they should not rely on the property in evaluating the trustee's creditworthiness. Further, the clear notice that the assets do not belong to the trustee but are held in trust protects the trust beneficiaries. It precludes the trustee's creditors from claiming trust property on the basis of being misled (or being holders in due course).[35]

In addition, the rule prevents trustees from manipulating the value of trust assets. For example, suppose trustees bought stock. Naturally, they do not know whether the price of the stock will rise or fall. They might leave the stock unmarked, wait, and allocate the stock to themselves if it appreciated, or allocate it to the trust if it depreciated. To nip such a temptation in the bud, the rule requires trustees to earmark the property. Unmarked property would therefore be attributed to the trustee (for better or worse).[36] Another, more subtle, purpose of this rule may be directed at trustees psychologically. If

---

34. Linda J. Demaine, *"Playing Doctor" with the Patient's Spouse: Alternative Conceptions of Health Professional Liability,* 14 VA. J. SOC. POL'Y & L. 308 (2007).
35. 2A AUSTIN W. SCOTT, THE LAW OF TRUSTS 509 (4th ed. 1987).
36. *Id.* at 508.

trustees are tempted to "borrow" trust assets ("just for a few days"), the earmark looks back at them to say: "Don't even think of it!" Earmarking creates in trustees a habit of recognizing that the entrusted assets are not theirs. Similarly, trustees may not commingle their assets with trust assets. However, efficiency plays a role in the rules. Lawyers who hold clients' assets, and banks acting as trustees, are allowed to commingle entrusted assets that belong to many entrustors, for efficiency reasons.

Often the trustors of wills leave for some beneficiaries, such as the wife, income through life (income beneficiaries). The wills then leave the remainder of the estate, after the death of the income beneficiaries, to other beneficiaries (remaindermen). This was the situation in *Russell v. Russell.*[37] In that case, the trustees were personally entitled to the trust assets after the death of the life beneficiaries. The trustees did not declare dividends on the stock that constituted the assets of the estate which they held in trust. Thus, the estate provided no income to the income beneficiaries and thereby enlarged the assets that the remaindermen-trustees would receive after the life beneficiaries died.

The court wrote:

In Rosencrans v. Fry, the will involved left testator's stock in a corporation to his wife and W. M. Fry, both directors of the company, as trustees of a trust estate which also included one-half of the testator's other real and personal property. The will provided that Fry could buy the stock from the trust at $25.00 per share during the existence of the trust which terminated on the testator's wife's death. The directors of the corporation were the testator, Mr. Rosencrans, Fry and an employee. The testator died in 1944 and his widow succeeded him as director. In 1949 Fry elected to exercise his option to buy. During the period the book value of the shares involved increased from $180,884.75 to $329,725.00 ($59.79 per share to $109). The shares in the trust were less than 50% and the others were held by about 50 investors. The increase in value (1944 to 1949) was due mainly to paying dividends less than annual earnings, which was a policy the testator had followed.... "Fry's performance of his duties as trustee must be appraised in conjunction with the propriety of his performance as a director of the company. The conflict of interest, if any, arising out of these duties was created not by Fry but by the testator, in accordance with whose wish Fry was elected president of the corporation and by whose will he was named co-trustee. His conduct must be evaluated in the light so given.

By the terms of the trust, the trustee may be permitted to do what, in the absence of such a provision in the trust instrument, would be a violation of his duty of loyalty.... The court below found Fry played a difficult role occasioned by the fiduciary and business responsibilities placed upon him by the testator but could not find that he acted 'with such unfairness as to prompt a court of conscience to charge him with breach of trust.' We have reached a like conclusion."[38]

[In another case described by the Rosencrans court, the trustees were reinstated after being removed.[39] The removal was based on the fact that the trustees acted under conflicting interests. The trustees were the sons of the testator. Each son owned stock in a corporation individually. They held "the rest of the stock as trustees for the benefit of their

37. Russell v. Russell, 427 S.W.2d 471 (Mo. 1968) (some citations omitted).
38. *Id.*
39. *In re* Gehl's Estate, 92 N.W.2d 372 (Wis. 1958).

three sisters for life, with remainder to the sisters' respective issue." The trustees acted as the directors of the corporation and throughout the period did not declare any dividends.] "The Will provided the stock could be held by the trustees whether or not it complied with the rules prescribed for the investment of trust funds, and the trustees could continue in the participation and conduct of any business in which the trust held an interest." [In that case the court wrote:] "The point of difference between the parties is whether the trustees should have caused the company to pay dividends when it made or makes profits or whether such profits should have been kept in the business for capital expansion and corporate purposes." The business was the operation of a farm. . . . "The conflict of interest between the trustees and the beneficiaries was created by the testator. He must have realized this in providing their actions should be without impeachment excepting for lack of good faith . . . . [Until] there is a showing that dividends could or should have been paid by the company under sound business practices and were arbitrarily withheld by the action of these trustees, they cannot be charged with misconduct in failing to vote as directors for the payment of dividends." It should be noted that the trustees in this case were not remaindermen of the trust shares. . . . [40]

[Comparing the two latter cases with the case at hand the Russell court held:] The Will in this case before us did not contain any provision authorizing retention of the stock of J.B. Russell, Inc., in the trust as was true in the [Gehl case]. . . . "In the absence of an express and sufficient authority therefor, the employment of trust property in trade or speculation, or in manufacturing, is a gross breach of trust on the part of the trustee, even though such investment is approved of by his own judgment, and is made with honest intent." "[Where] a testator leaves his estate in trust and the estate includes his interest in a business, whether conducted by him alone or by a firm of which he is a member, it is the duty of the trustee to withdraw the testator's property from the business, unless it is otherwise provided in the terms of the trust." Nevertheless the J. P. Russell Will presented the trustees a most difficult situation, due in a large part to the inadequate provisions of the Will. J.P. Russell, Inc., was a family corporation undoubtedly having no substantial market for such a minority interest. There is no evidence to show this interest could have been sold without great sacrifice of value. [The court concluded that the trustees and the trustors did not want to sell the business but rather to continue it.] . . .

[Thus, in all cases the will left a bequest to a life beneficiary and after the beneficiary died, to the remaindermen. In the cited cases the trustees occupied three postions: They were directors of the corporation that was the source of the income for the life beneficiary. If the corporation did not declare dividends, there was no income for the life beneficiary. The trustees were also trustees, subject to the provisions of the wills. In one case the will relieved them from legal constraints on investments. In others, the will did not. Hence the constraints applied. The third position of the trustees was as remaindermen. Not all the cases covered all these positions.]

[As to conflict of interest, the Russell court noted:] This leaves the issue of conflict of interest of the trustees in building corporate values they would receive as remaindermen instead of paying more liberal dividends. As to this, we agree with the trial court there is no basis for waiver or estoppel because it seems clear that Marlowe [one of the income beneficiaries who was also a trustee] accepted and acted on the statement as to his rights to income given him by the attorney for the trustees (apparently also attorney for the corporation) which did not properly consider the situation actually presented. He did not voluntarily surrender a known right as to reasonable dividends and the trustee's position as to corporate dividend policy was not shown to have been based or induced by any action,

---

40.   Russell v. Russell, 427 S.W.2d 471 (Mo. 1968) at 476.

representation or promise of his. No doubt, [the other trustees] too acted at least partially on the statement of their attorney as to Marlowe's rights to income but nevertheless acted in a way that would benefit them as remaindermen. It may be significant that the first two annual dividends declared were more than any of the later ones. The amount of dividends the trustees should have paid presents an issue that must be determined on the basis of their duties as trustees as well as their duties as directors. They could not claim a conflict of interest created by the testator as in the cases cited because the testator never mentioned the corporation or said what they should do with it. However, as the trial court said: "[If] the trustees, each year, had paid out all of the earnings of the corporation in dividends, then the earnings in following years would not have been as large as they were . . . the earnings generally were used as operating capital." In this situation, since we consider plaintiff barred from claiming all profits on the basis of an illegal investment for the reasons hereinabove stated, and with the welfare of the corporation to be safeguarded, we do not consider it was the obligation of the trustees (also directors) to pay out every cent of earnings in dividends every year. . . . Our view is that the amount of profits to be retained for the essential needs of this corporation for reasonable financing of its operations and the reasonable amount to be paid out in dividends is a matter that should be shown by expert testimony of accountants and corporation executives. This testimony should be based on the actual conditions of this corporation in carrying on its business, maintaining its financial position, keeping its share of the business in the areas in which it operated and preserving its values for purchasing power considering inflation of prices of labor and materials. Anything more than that would be building values in the trustees' own interest rather than the interest of the corporation and the income beneficiary of the trust. The expert testimony should be based on the actual situation, experience and prospects of this corporation. Our conclusion is that there was substantial evidence to support the court's finding that the dividend policy of the trustees as directors was improper for trustees, depriving the income beneficiary of the amount he reasonably should have received as income from the trust in dividends and building up for themselves as remaindermen greater values in the corporation at his expense.[41]

Discussion Topics

a. A trustee seeks to sell some of the trust's real estate. He does not find a buyer at an adequate price. He is willing to purchase the property at a better price. Advise him.

b. If you were to prepare a will for a client who wished to leave his thriving business to his sons and comfortable income to his elderly wife until her death, how would you design the will in light of the *Russell* case and the cases cited there? Would it matter that the wife and the sons had disagreements from time to time?

c. Assume the same facts as in question a., except that the fiduciary is a director of a corporation. Advise him. If your advice differs from the advice to a trustee, or agent or a director, why does it?

d. The courts held that, if a testator established conflicts of interest in the will, it could protect the fiduciaries. Is this holding justified?

---

41.   Russell v. Russell, 427 S.W.2d 471 (Mo. 1968).

d. Lawyers and accountants

Lawyers experience various situations that pose conflicts of interest. Susan P. Shapiro conducted a study comparing lawyers to other fiduciary services (accounting, psychotherapy, medicine, journalism, academia). She asked such questions as: (1) how conflict of interest regulation is accomplished; (2) where rules are most likely to be followed; (3) what the incentives for compliance are; and (4) what the costs and consequences of compliance are.[42] Ms. Shapiro found that "the legal profession takes conflict of interest more seriously than many of the rest of us."

Rule 1.7 of the Model Rules of Professional Conduct guides most of the issues concerning lawyers' conflicts of interest.[43]

(a) A lawyer shall not represent a client if the representation of that client will be directly adverse to another client, unless:

(1) The lawyer reasonably believes the representation will not adversely affect the relationship with the other client; and

(2) Each client consents after consultation.

(b) A lawyer shall not represent a client if the representation of that client may be materially limited by the lawyer's responsibilities to another client or to a third person, or by the lawyer's own interests, unless:

(1) The lawyer reasonably believes the representation will not be adversely affected; and

(2) The client consents after consultation. When representation of multiple clients in a single matter is undertaken, the consultation shall include explanation of the implications of the common representation and the advantages and risks involved.[44]

According to Ms. Shapiro's study, "[v]irtually all" law firms will refuse "to represent two clients in litigation against one another."[45] But in complex litigation or representation of large financial institutions it may be difficult to identify all the parties, and that creates problems. Another question is whether lawyers should argue conflicting arguments in different cases. Are lawyers "hired guns"? This issue is subject to debate.

Ms. Shapiro notes that conflicts of interests increase with the size of the law firms or when they act in more than one role, such as acting as directors and legal advisers. She notes that potential conflicts arise when lawyers take on new clients, engagements, or colleagues, and that actual conflicts are common (especially with large firms) and costly. Therefore, firms "devote substantial resources to identify, avoid, and deal with conflicts." [46]

The following are two excerpts concerning law firm billings and competition:

---

42. Susan P. Shapiro, *Bushwhacking the Ethical High Road: Conflict of Interest in the Practice of Law and Real Life*, 28 LAW & SOC. INQUIRY 87 (2003).
43. MODEL RULES OF PROF'L CONDUCT R. 1.7 (2002).
44. *Id.*
45. Susan P. Shapiro, *Bushwhacking the Ethical High Road: Conflict of Interest in the Practice of Law and Real Life*, 28 LAW & SOC. INQUIRY 87, 101 (2003).
46. *Id.* at 162.

"Some lawyers defrauded their own clients by 'padding' their bills. In her 1999 study of lawyers of 'elite' firms, Lisa Lerman researched cases involving frauds of 'padding the bills and expenses.' She found almost no prosecution of such cases before 1989 and 36 such cases during the following ten years. Of course, this increase could indicate either more incidents or more prosecution. The sixteen cases that were studied in more detail involved persons who had privileged background, graduated from elite schools, and worked at a number of large law firms. They were accused of stealing over $100,000 over an average of five years. Collectively they stole about $16 million from clients. These lawyers were at the height of their careers, serving as managing partners, members of the firms' executive committees, or 'rainmakers.' The researcher noted that in many cases 'it is clear that their partners knew about and/or participated in the billing fraud.'[47] Two lawyers were found guilty of mail fraud. One was disbarred, and one was suspended for three years for padding clients' bills. Another lawyer was found to have breached his contract and committed fraud. Judgment against him amounted to $3,124,414.[48] Put differently, these instances may represent the corruption of private guarantors of trust in the financial sector."[49]

Scott Turow discussed the problems of billable hours in law firms. He noted that due to increased competition in the profession, large firms expect 2,000 to 2,200 billable hours per year from young lawyers, an increase from 1,750 to 1,800 in 1986. He argues that billing by the hour comes close to conflicting with Rule 1.5 of the ABA Model Rules of Professional Conduct, pertaining to fees,[50] and creates a conflict of interest under Rule 1.7, which defines a conflict of interest as when "there is a significant risk that the representation of one or more clients will be materially limited by . . . a personal interest of the lawyer."[51] Even if lawyers do not "intentionally stall a case," there is a problem of "temptation and appearances." Turow also notes that America often sees lawyers as "self-seeking, manipulative, and greedy" and, given this perception, asks whether the practice should continue.[52]

— — — — — — — — — — — -

Discussion Topic

Do you approve of lawyers' fees that are based on billable hours? For many years annual billable hours for associates were expected to be about 2000. In the past 20 years the number has been increasing,

---

47. *Id.* at 162.

48. Among the cases are United States v. Myerson, 18 F.3d 153 (2d Cir. 1994) (affirming the lower court's decision on mail fraud); *In re* Duker, 723 A.2d 410 (D.C. 1999) (William Duker disbarred after pleading guilty to mail fraud and related charges); Attorney Grievance Comm'n v. Hess, 722 A.2d 905 (Md. 1999) (Stanford Hess suspended 3 years for padding bills); Dresser Indus., Inc. v. Digges, No. JH-89-485, 1989 U.S. Dist. LEXIS 17396 (D. Md. Aug. 30, 1989) (awarding the plaintiff $3,124,414 in liquidated damages in case against former attorney, Edward S. Digges, Jr., for breach of contract and fraud).

49. TAMAR FRANKEL, TRUST AND HONESTY: AMERICA'S BUSINESS CULTURE AT A CROSSROAD 23 (2006).

50. MODEL RULES OF PROF'L CONDUCT R. 1.5(a) (2003) ("time and labor required" is only one of several nonexclusive factors to be considered in determining reasonableness of fee).

51. MODEL RULES OF PROF'L CONDUCT R. 1.7(a)(2) (2003).

52. Scott Turow, *The Billable Hour Must Die, in* RAISE THE BAR: REAL WORLD SOLUTIONS FOR A TROUBLED PROFESSION (Lawrence J. Fox ed., 2007) (summarized).

reaching in some firms 3000 hours. What in your opinion caused the incentives to increase the billable hours?

- - — — — — — — — — - -

The effects of competition among professionals[53]

Historically, professionals, such as lawyers and teachers, belonged to fraternities. They did not compete. Their institutions created roles that made them more interdependent. These institutions result in greater reciprocity and fairness and more trust among their members. This form of institution makes sense when all members of the fraternities aim at public service. Competition is the antithesis of such fraternities. Competition makes sense when each member serves his own interests and is therefore in conflicts with the aims of all other members of the group.

Advertising accompanies competition. Until 1977, lawyers were barred from advertising, and the states approved the prohibition. In *Bates v. State Bar of Arizona*,[54] the Supreme Court ruled that the ban was unconstitutional and permitted lawyers to advertise. First Amendment rights served as the basis for the decision to allow advertising. Advertising and competition could bring benefits. Advertising could offer more information to clients. Competition would reduce the professionals' fees. Market forces could discipline the lawyers' and doctors' transgressions, and empower clients and patients. These expectations did not materialize; the fruits of these changes were not so sweet. In the words of Justice O'Connor: "In one way or another, time will uncover the folly of the approach [of allowing lawyers' direct and targeted solicitation]."

The expected competition among the professionals did arrive, perhaps with unexpected fierceness, and seemed to bring the morals of the profession down to the level of the marketplace....

As lawyers moved to offering revenue-producing advice, lawyers were drawn to search in the gray areas of law and accounting. Discovering or creating loopholes through which clients could crawl would reduce the clients' costs and gain for the clients a competitive advantage, at least until the competitors discovered the same loopholes and used them too....

... Law is not a precise science. Attorneys could justify saying "no" to almost every new design of a business that has not been tested in court. In the 1980s, they developed a more flexible attitude. A lawyer might decline to approve a prohibited transaction but may help the client design an alternative. The alternative might be less profitable, but still profitable, with minimal risk of illegality as a new design presents. This trend, which started in the 1960s, reached much wider dimensions in the 1990s.

The search for "creative" transactions, financial assets and accounting became the order of the day. For example, the large accounting firms KPMG and Ernst & Young have put their energies into marketing "leveraged" tax law and tax shelters. The legal effect of these innovative arrangements was not ascertained. In KPMG, money was the main driver. The firm did not comply with the rule that it required it to register as the creators of tax shelters. As a partner in the firm wrote in his memorandum: "Penalties [for failure to register] would be no greater than $14,000 per $100,000 of [the firm's fees] ...." Breaking the law was factored into the cost of doing business and was indistinguishable from the cost of rent and office supplies....

---

53. The following passage is taken from TAMAR FRANKEL, TRUST AND HONESTY: AMERICA'S BUSINESS CULTURE AT A CROSSROAD 140-43 (2006) (footnotes omitted).
54. Bates v. State Bar of Arizona, 433 U.S. 350 (1977).

With the new marketplace environment in the legal profession, clients began to shop around, but not necessarily for lower fees. Sometimes they shopped for better revenue-producing legal opinions and transaction structures. Sometimes they shopped for skewed legal opinions that other lawyers refused to give. It is unclear whether the cost of legal services went down. There are lawyers who demanded part of the clients' revenues from creative advice, and the revenues of large law firms rose dramatically. In May 2004 the American Lawyer called the past 25 years "a golden age of growth" for law firms and noted that between 1987 and 2003 "revenues at the top 100 firms quintupled to $38 billion, while profits quadrupled to $13.5 billion."

Money became an objective of professional teaching. The American Bar Association, Section on Law Practice Management, offered a training seminar, advertised in a fax entitled: "Beyond the Billable Hour." It describes ways to make money in law practice, including publishing and selling books on the Web, developing a referral network, partner with Web Sites as a content provider, providing adjunct services to clients, and creating and selling "legal commodities." Everything in this advertising was focused on developing the law service as a business and viewing legal advice as a commodity for sale....

Competition did not seem to bring quality services either. As sales became the main value for some firms, marketing diverted the focus from quality performance. While "rainmakers" were traditionally rewarded more than those who "only" did the work, rainmakers were also performers, and usually had enormous experience and reputation.

Problem

An article in the *New York Times* discussed whether lawyers who write opinion letters that might be used to defraud investors have violated their fiduciary duty. In "pump and dump" fraud schemes, individuals create companies with no operations or assets, sell the companies' worthless stocks to gullible investors, and gain millions in profits. Although these stocks are not yet registered with the Securities and Exchange Commission ("SEC"), securities lawyers submit questionable opinion letters vouching that "the newly issued stock could be traded immediately, despite a general rule that bars such trading unless the shares are registered with the [SEC]."[55] The lawyer's legal opinion is therefore crucial to the success of the fraudulent conduct. In the past, the SEC has successfully brought civil actions against lawyers who profited from writing misleading opinion letters covering these unregistered shares. To date, no criminal cases or disqualifying cases have been brought against lawyers who wrote these opinion letters. It is doubtful whether such actions would be successful. Lawyers who write false opinions but do not trade the corporate shares involved will argue that their recommendation was in good faith as evidenced by the absence of personal financial interest in the sale of these unregistered stocks. Are these attorneys liable to the defrauded clients of the schemes?

Problem

Please comment on the following issue of accounting firms' charges:

55.   Floyd Norris, *Should S.E.C. Act Against Lawyers?*, N.Y. TIMES, May 4, 2007, at C1, LEXIS, News Library, Nyt File.

Four consulting and accounting firms (BearingPoint Inc., Booz Allen Hamilton Inc., Ernst & Young, and KPMG) settled with the Justice Department on charges for overbilling the government for travel expenses. "[T]he government alleged that the companies failed to disclose that they were receiving volume discounts and rebates from airlines, hotels, car rental companies and credit card companies on travel billed to government contracts." The firms allegedly "billed the government the full retail rate, never passing on the discounts of up to 40%," in violation of the contracts and government regulations. Each firm agreed to pay two to three times the estimated overbilling. A spokesman for BearingPoint, a part of KPMG at the relevant time, noted that it did not "create" the "program."[56]

- - - - - - - - - - -

Discussion Topics

a. "Silicon Valley law firms were among the first to experiment in 'equity billing,' the practice of taking stock in high-tech clients as a component of a law firm's compensation for rendering legal services." Is this arrangement similar to contingency fees that litigating lawyers receive as a percentage of the judgment they gain for the clients? What incentives are created by such an arrangement? Should lawyers be permitted to be paid with shares of start-up corporations?[57]

b. Is it OK for lawyers to receive a percentage of the profits from a particular deal that they have served? Does it matter whether the directors or CEO who hired the law firm need legal advice in connection with their positions in the deals as opposed to private matters? Does it matter if an insurance company pays the fees?

c. The *ABA Journal*, in July 2007, reported on the first public offering of shares by a law firm engaged in personal injury claims.[58] Ethics rule 5.4 prohibits lawyers from becoming partners with non-lawyers. Yet the projection is that law firms are going to bring in outside investors someday soon. What are the pros and cons for allowing equity investments in law firms? Can the objections be regulated to allow investments to benefit the law firms, and presumably their clients?

d. What about a lawyer dining with the judge, who is a longtime friend, with whom the lawyer went to law school? Does it matter whether at the dining date the lawyer has a case pending before the judge friend?

e. What about social or intimate relationships between lawyers who appear for opposing parties? After all, law firms cultivate relationships to drum up business. Do these relationships pose conflicts? If so, how

---

56. *Four Firms to Settle Charges of Overbilling the Government*, CONSULTING MAG., Jan. 4, 2006, http://www.consultingmag.com/articles/128/1/Four-Firms-to-Settle-Charges-of-Overbilling-the-Government/Four-Firms-to-Settle-Charges-of-Overbilling-the-Government.html.
57. *See* Poonam Puri, *Taking Stock of Taking Stock*, 87 CORNELL L. REV. 99, 102 (2001).
58. Jason Krause, *Selling Law on an Open Market*, A.B.A. J., July 2007, at 34, LEXIS, Aba Library, Abajnl File.

should these conflicts be controlled? Is a motion to disqualify a law firm from appearing in a case desirable or effective?

f. Are there any other preventive rules that you can think of? Are there any disadvantages to these preventive rules?

g. Where would you research to find out what kinds of rules would prevent or allow conflicts of interest?

_ _ _ _ _ _ _ _ _ _ _ _ _

e. Corporate executives

Many members of the public are angry at the compensation that corporate executives collect on the job, and after they leave the job (willingly by retirement, or unwillingly by termination). The amounts are astounding, and only a handful of film, artists, and sports stars manage to come close to reaping such profits. Regardless of the negative, envious and admiring attention to these amounts and the arguments they raised, compensation of CEOs is continuing to rise. Stock options may have contributed to the rise in compensation to executives not only when the market prices of the stock.

Historically, for example, in the 1930s, when a similar public outrage had arisen, the courts refused to adjudicate how much compensation is too much compensation and Congress resorted to disclosure and tax provisions to resolve the issue.[59] Currently, there are attempts to allow for a stronger direct or indirect involvement of the shareholders, but these have not been effective.

However, there is no indication that CEOs have lowered their compensation demands and expectations.

"Nothing, it seems, can put the brakes on runaway executive pay. I don't actually believe we have made any real progress—or very, very little," said Robert A. G. Monks, a longtime corporate governance advocate. "If we cannot effectively monitor and control what the principal executives are paid, we are kidding ourselves if we can control anything else."[60]

_ _ _ _ _ _ _ _ _ _ _ _ _

Discussion Topics

a. Why should executives not be treated like, and get paid as, movie stars do? Is there any difference between a Chief Executive Officer (CEO) that manages Microsoft and a popular movie star?

b. Are executives employees or do they have an entitlement in their positions? What are the different results if they are one or another?

c. Evaluate the proposal of Robert A. G. Monks' eight steps to evaluate and control executive compensation.

---

59.   Charles M. Elson, *Executive Overcompensation — A Board-Based Solution*, 34 B.C. L. REV. 937, 398 (1993).
60.   Eric Dash, *Compensation Experts Offer Ways to Help Curb Executive Salaries*, N.Y. TIMES, Dec. 30, 2006, at C1, LEXIS, News Library, Curnws File.

(1) Hire independent advisers that do not have "financial ties" to the companies.

(2) Research well the data comparing the executive compensation of comparable companies; i.e., first, start with companies in the same industry; next, compensation should depend on the "complexity of the job."

(3) Executive compensation should be linked to benchmarks of performance.

(4) "Review and negotiate" with the CEO.

(5) Do not promise "golden parachutes" or pay without performance.

(6) Examine possible large amounts under other headings, such as pension plans.

(7) "Let shareholders vote" on executive compensation.

(8) "Get money managers to vote" on executive compensation; they can be "[t]he biggest influence on executive compensation" but "frequently do not exercise an opposing vote."[61]

- - - - - - - - - - - -

Problem

When the stock market prices rose in late 2006, some of the CEOs and top management as well as some employees received over $50 million in one year. A CEO who retired would receive $180 million in ten years, that is an $18 million a year pension for ten years. Top management can collect over 3000% as compared to the pay of lower paid employees and about 1000% as compared to mid-level paid employees (e.g., $70,000 a year). How and under what criteria are such compensations approved? Who approves, and who should approve the compensation?

In the United States there is a strong belief that prices, including salaries and compensation, should be determined by the market and not by legislators, regulators or the courts. However, there are exceptions to this belief when the parties that pay the salaries, such as investors, for example, are too numerous and too weak to negotiate. In such cases, the law may impose on representatives of the shareholders the duty to determine management compensation, and set forth criteria and guidance for determining the compensation. For example, mutual fund advisers and managers may not charge "excessive fees" to mutual funds. Shareholders may bring derivative suits against advisers and managers on charging excessive fees.[62]

With respect to corporate top management, the power to determine the compensation is vested in the board of directors. However, if the board of directors is composed mainly of CEOs or retired CEOs, or people chosen by the CEO to sit on the board, or friends of the CEOs, it is unlikely that they will be inclined to hold that the compensation of

---

61. *Id.*
62. Investment Company Act of 1940, § 36(b), 15 U.S.C. § 80a-35(b) (2000).

their CEO is excessive. In addition, to protect themselves from shareholder claims, boards would usually engage consultants or executive recruiters to advise them with respect to the going rate for a proposed CEO or for their current CEO who is negotiating a new contract. Thus, notwithstanding the criticisms of the high compensation, CEOs' compensation for the year 2006 was very high. The criticisms since the year 2000 did not deter the rising compensation of the CEOs, which reached a peak in 2007. There are cases in which compensation of management has risen as a result of laying off thousands of employees, thus reducing the cost (at least for a short while) and increasing the profits, to which the compensation was tied.

Should there be any limit on the CEOs' compensation in the first place? After all, their negotiations with the board seem to be at arm's length, as two parties of equal bargaining power. The board can say: "No." However, if the negotiations are not at arm's length, how should the compensation be determined? Should we seek a formula to decide what is excessive compensation? In any event, who should decide what the terms of the CEOs' contracts and compensation should be?

f. Judges

When fiduciaries hold positions of power, such as judgeships or high government offices, issues of possible conflicts of interest may arise even if they do not actually exist. The issues may arise if the behavior of the fiduciaries can raise the impression or suspicion of conflicts of interest. For example, teachers who receive significant gifts from students or their parents before the teachers have graded the students' performance may put themselves in such a questionable light. A judge who is related to one of the parties or who dines with one of the parties during the trial or with their lawyers might give such an impression even if they did not mention the case at all. The actions are enough to raise doubts about the judge's independence and lack of bias.

The question arose whether a judge, who had invested in one or more companies that filed *amicus curiae* briefs in the case, should withdraw from sitting in judgment. The investments may have been made a long time ago, and the companies are interested in the issues as outsiders. This question arose in the case of the *City of Hope v. Genentech*.[63] The outcome in that case has been of interest to a number of very large corporations that filed *amicus curiae* briefs, such as Microsoft, Apple Computers, Disney, and eBay. There was a likelihood that some of the judges had invested in these companies. The question was whether the judges who have had such investments should have recused themselves and not sat in the case. The California Supreme

---

63.   City of Hope Nat'l Med. Ctr.v. Genentech, Inc., 20 Cal. Rptr. 3d 234 (Ct. App. 2004), *modified, reh'g denied*, No. B161549, 2004 Cal. App. LEXIS 1962 (Ct. App. Nov. 22, 2004), *review granted, depublished*, 24 Cal. Rptr. 3d 178, 105 P.3d 543 (Cal. 2005). *City of Hope* is an unpublished disposition issued before January 1, 2007, and as such may not be cited to Ninth Circuit courts except in certain limited circumstances. 9TH CIR. R. 36-3(C).

Court decided that the judges that had invested in these companies should not recuse themselves.

– – – – – – – – – – -

Discussion Topics

a. Do you think that the judge should have recused himself in this situation?

b. Would it make a difference to your decision if the judge had been a partner in the business that now filed an *amicus curiae* brief?

– – – – – – – – – – -

Problem

Jane is a broker representing John, who is interested in buying a home in the Town. Jane also represents Sad, who is interested in selling his home in Town. Jane did not tell John that Sad had to sell his home because of divorce proceedings and that he was strapped for cash. John and Sad negotiated the price of the house. After John discovered Sad's circumstances, he accused Jane of breach of her duty of loyalty because she did not tell him about Sad's situation. That information could have helped John to reduce the price of the house during the negotiations.

What was the relationship between Jane and John? Did Jane violate her duties to John?

Problem

The following story is drawn from a book by Michael Lewis: *Liar's Poker*:[64]

Michael Lewis was a salesman in an investment bank, Salomon Brothers. In 1986, one of the biggest priorities at Salomon was eighty-six million dollars' worth of bonds issued by Olympia & York. The bonds were owned by a major client of Salomon Brothers. O&Y bonds had no buyers in the market. The client was desperate to sell the bonds and not particularly knowledgeable about them, and would probably sell them cheaply. He even made a deal with Salomon Brothers that if the bank could sell the bonds, he would buy another large block of bonds. The combination of that promise and the sale of the bonds could net Salomon about two million dollars. So the salesmen were searching for a buyer. Michael thought that the bonds were worth something because they were collateralized by a Manhattan skyscraper owned by O&Y rather than by a guarantee of the company.

Michael finally found a potential buyer, a Frenchman, who fully trusted Michael. Michael knew that the Frenchman was a speculator and did not intend to keep the bonds for long. In order to protect the Frenchman, Michael asked Salomon Brothers to keep promoting these bonds so that the Frenchman would find a buyer at a higher price,

---

64.   MICHAEL M. LEWIS, LIAR'S POKER (1989). This material is drawn, with consent, from a paper by Quing Ye and Hang Yuen Leung in satisfaction of a seminar requirements on fiduciary law at Boston University Law School, Spring 2007. The paper is edited and abridged, and some of the footnotes were omitted.

within a short period of time. A partner of the firm assured Michael that his client would not be hurt. When discussing the deal, Michael told the Frenchman how a panicked client wanted to sell eighty-six million dollars' worth of bonds cheaply; that the bonds were out of fashion and undervalued; and that if the Frenchman bought the bonds and held them for a few months, a buyer in America might emerge. After considering the issue, the Frenchman bought all the bonds. However, contrary to Michael's anticipation, the bonds did not sell well in the market and no buyers could be found for them.[65]

- - - - - - - - - - -

Discussion Topics

a. Should Michael be liable to the Frenchman? How would you analyze the issue? What questions would you ask?

b. Would your opinion change if you were a regulator or a legislator, concerned with the financial system and not only with the just result among the parties?

c. "If you are going to commit fraud, you may need a good lawyer. In some cases, you have to have a lawyer to pull off the fraud at all." Two men who made millions by selling worthless securities were each sentenced to five years in prison. They were aided by "a legal opinion that the newly issued stock could be traded immediately, despite a general rule that bars such trading unless the shares are registered with the S.E.C." These legal opinions were instrumental to the perpetration of the fraud. Yet, the SEC has not brought many cases against lawyers that provided such letters. "Government action against lawyers who issue fake opinions but do not trade shares could be difficult, facing a defense that the lawyer acted in good faith even if the opinion was wrong. But such an action could serve as a deterrent to other lawyers tempted to make money by signing letters they know misstate the law."[66]

- - - - - - - - - - -

2. Proposed relaxation of the prohibition on conflicts of interest: From "sole interest" of the entrustors to "best interest" of the entrustors

Currently, if a fiduciary does not act in the "sole interest" of the entrustor, the trustee's action is voidable at the election of the entrustor. The entrustor may keep the beneficial activities and reject the activities that are not beneficial. If the fiduciary did not act in the sole interest of the entrustor, the entrustor may sue for violation of fiduciary duties. All the entrustor has to show is that the fiduciary did not act in the sole interest of the entrustor. In such a case, the entrustor may reject even a transaction that is in his best interest. If, for example, the entrustor finds that even though the transaction is

---

65. *Id.*
66. Floyd Norris, *Should S.E.C. Act Against Lawyers?*, N.Y. TIMES, May 4, 2007, at C1, LEXIS, News Library, Nyt File.

beneficial to him, it is very beneficial to the trustee, the entrustor may, for envy, anger, animosity, or assumption that the personal benefit is insufficient, avoid the transaction.

It has been argued that the "sole interest" guide to fiduciary's duties should be substituted by a "best interest" guide.[67] "[A] transaction prudently undertaken to advance the best interest of the beneficiaries best serves the purpose of the duty of loyalty, even if the trustee also does or might derive some benefit. A transaction in which there has been conflict or overlap of interest should be sustained if the trustee can prove that the transaction was prudently undertaken in the best interest of the beneficiaries. In such a case, inquiry into the merits is better than 'no further inquiry.'"[68]

The argument is that the "best interest" measure would modernize the rule. First, the current fact-finding procedures are more effective. Therefore, the chances of concealment by the trustee are lower.[69] Besides, in some situations, the "sole interest rule" can harm entrustors. In addition, the banking trustees have been "professionalized," presumably rendering today's trustees more reliable and trustworthy than in the past. In light of the great success of institutional trustees, conflicted institutional and corporate trustees should be permitted to defend their actions by showing good and prudent actions even if they benefit from these actions.[70] In fact, courts did not strictly adhere to the "sole benefit" rule anyway, as they allowed trustees to ask for judicial approval of conflicts of interest transactions.[71] In these situations the courts look to the "best interests" of the entrustors. The article notes that the rules of the Comptroller of the Currency that regulate bank trust departments allow banks to engage in some conflict of interest under certain circumstances.

Therefore, the "best interest" proposition is to amend trust law and make it more similar to corporate law, which has evolved far more lenient rules with respect to fiduciary conflict of interest. The new rules should allow "overlapping interests" as follows:

(1) The trustee is under a duty to administer the trust in the best interest of the beneficiaries.

(2) A trustee who does not administer the trust in the sole interest of the beneficiaries is presumed not to have administered it in their best interest. The trustee may rebut the presumption by showing that a transaction not in the sole interest of the beneficiaries was prudently undertaken in the best interest of the beneficiaries. . . . The trustee asserting a best interest defense would bear the burden of proving it, echoing practice under the advance-approval doctrine and under those versions of the corporate rule that assign the

---

67.   John H. Langbein, *Questioning the Trust Law Duty of Loyalty: Sole Interest or Best Interest?* 114 YALE L.J. 929 (2005) (abridged and footnotes omitted).
68.   *Id.* at 932.
69.   *Id.*
70.   *Id.* at 990.
71.   *Id.* at 933.

burden of justifying fairness to the conflicted director who failed to seek and obtain advance approval.[72]

— — — — — — — — — — — -

Discussion Topics

a. What are the legal implications of changing trust rules to resemble corporate rules?

b. What effect would that analogy have on the operations of trusts and the powers and discretion of the trustees?

c. Do you agree with the "best interest" proposal? Is it important? What does it change in practice?

d. Do you think that the entrustor would sue the trustee for breach of the "sole benefit" rule? When will he sue? How relevant is the fact that evidence of breach of the duty of loyalty is easier to find and expose today than in the past (assuming that this is so)? Why is this change important to banks and perhaps other institutional trustees?

e. Generally, corporate statutes did not relax the prohibition on conflicts of interest. Statutes do, however, allow a corporate director or CEO or other corporate executives to disclose their conflicts to the boards of directors, and then, after receiving full information about the proposed transaction, a majority of the disinterested directors may approve and thereby "sanitize" the conflict of interest transaction. Should the same process apply to trustees and beneficiaries?[73]

f. How should the interests of the entrustor and fiduciary be balanced? How should the law avoid subverting their incentives to interact long term?

— — — — — — — — — — — -

3. Are there exceptions to the strict prohibition of conflicts of interest?

Under the common law, there are two main exceptions to the prohibition on conflicts of interest. The first exception is permission by legislation or regulations to engage in a transaction that involves a conflict of interest or violates preventive fiduciary duties. The second exception is by the informed and free consent of the entrustor that allows the fiduciary to engage in such transaction. The exception is treated in the following examples of statutory regulations concerning conflicts of interest. The second is treated in the following Chapter Four.

a. Statutory permission of limited conflicts of interest by money managers

In interpreting section 28(e) of the Securities Exchange Act of 1934, the Securities and Exchange Commission noted:

---

72.   *Id.* at 982.

73.   For a response to Langbein's article, *see* Melanie B. Leslie, *In Defense of the No Further Inquiry Rule: A Response to Professor John Langbein*, 47 WM. & MARY L. REV. 541 (2005).

Fiduciary principles require money managers to seek the best execution [of securities transactions] for client trades, and limit money managers from using client assets for their own benefit. Use of client commissions to pay for research and brokerage services presents money managers with significant conflicts of interest, and may give incentives for managers to disregard their best execution obligations when directing orders to obtain client commission services as well as to trade client securities inappropriately in order to earn credits for client commission services. Recognizing the value of research in managing client accounts, however, Congress enacted Section 28(e) of the Exchange Act to provide a safe harbor that protects money managers from liability for a breach of fiduciary duty solely on the basis that they paid more than the lowest commission rate in order to receive "brokerage and research services" provided by a broker-dealer, if the managers determined in good faith that the amount of the commission was reasonable in relation to the value of the brokerage and research services received.[74]

— — — — — — — — — — —

Discussion Topics

a. What precisely is the conflict of interest that Congress permitted?

b. Is a breach of promise not to steal entrusted property different from a rule that prohibits stealing the property?

c. Is it accurate to say that a stockbroker who charges a client more than is customary is not a fiduciary with respect to the charge? Under what conditions might the stockbroker be or not be a fiduciary?

d. What is the impact of section 28(e)?

— — — — — — — — — — —

Problem

The United States government allocated about $100 million to help the Kingdom of Rosko by moving Rosko's economy from a government-planned economy to a market economy. The best economists in the United States were drawn to participate in the project. Joe Brilliant, an economist, and his wife Jorjina, an expert in establishing and managing mutual funds, visited and worked in Rosko for a number of years, and so did their assistant, their assistant. Jorjina established the first mutual fund in Rosko and invested significant amounts of her customers' money in that fund. Their assistant invested $50,000 in his father's name. The fund did very well and gained about $700 million in two years. When the facts became known, the United States government sued Brilliant, his wife and their assistant. Have any of these persons done anything wrong?[75]

b. Regulatory permission of limited conflicts of interest for banks

Banks are strictly regulated and their powers are spelled out in the law and regulations. Among their powers, banks have long been

---

74.   Commission Guidance Regarding Client Commission Practices Under Section 28(e) of the Securities Exchange Act of 1934, Exchange Act Release No. 54,165 (July 18, 2006), 71 Fed. Reg. 41,978, 41,978 (July 24, 2006) (interpretation; solicitation of comment) (footnotes omitted).

75.   *See* David McClintick, *How Harvard Lost Russia,* INSTITUTIONAL INVESTOR, Jan. 1, 2006, at 62(29), LEXIS, News Library, Asapii File.

authorized to offer trustee services. Thus, most banks have trust departments serving as trustees to large and small trusts.

Being in the trust business and banking business poses an inherent conflict of interest. The main task of banks and their regulators is to ensure that banks remain "safe and sound," able to repay their obligations, especially to demand depositors. The more profitable banks are, the better off the banking system will be.

To be sure, there are rules that limit the banks' profits, such as the rules that limit the amounts that banks may charge their customers for some services. For example, customers who use ATMs may not be charged more than a fixed number of dollars per transaction. Yet, these rules may also aim at bank "safety and soundness." Fierce competition or a public outcry might pose for banks a "reputational risk." Therefore, the limitations on the charges serve the purpose of protecting bank businesses.

Similarly, if banks misbehave as trustees, they might lose their trust business, or be fined heavily, and that would undermine their ability to repay deposits. "A reputational risk" may affect not only bank trust-business but also the depositors' trust in the bank. That may result in the depositors' "run" on the discredited bank. Mistrust might induce a mass withdrawal of deposits. A "run" on a particular bank can result in a run on other banks as well. Thus, concern about danger to banks' safety and soundness induces bank regulators to ensure that the banks behave as trusted trustees and regulate them accordingly.

As trustees, banks are regulated by the Comptroller of the Currency and sometimes by the courts. The Comptroller has relaxed for banks some of the stricter rules in trust law. While trust law requires trustees to segregate trust assets (mainly to protect the assets from claims by third parties), banks may pool trust assets into "common trust funds." Pooling allows the banks to manage small trusts more efficiently.[76] Similarly, when banks hold trust funds in cash as demand or time deposits, they may benefit by increasing their "free cash" which they can lend at higher interest. That option, however, creates a conflict of interest because the trust beneficiaries are interested in returns on trust assets. On the other hand, trust assets are sometimes held in cash, for example, when investments are sold and not yet reinvested. To prevent violations of the banks' duties as trustees, the rules of the Comptroller of the Currency allow the banks to hold trust funds in their deposit accounts. But that permission is provided for a limited period only and requires the banks to pay acceptable market interest rate on the trust assets' cash accounts.[77]

A more fruitful area for conflicts of interest opened for banks in 1996. In that year, Congress amended the law that had been on the books for years and permitted banks to engage in securities activities. These activities were prohibited to banks under the Glass-Steagall Act

---

76.   George G. Bogert, THE LAW OF TRUSTS AND TRUSTEES § 677 (rev. 2d ed. 2006).
77.   *Id.*

of 1933. Thus, after 1996, banks were allowed to manage mutual funds and distribute funds' securities to public investors. Banks then sought to convert common trust funds into mutual funds.

Conversion of common trust funds into mutual funds gave banks a number of benefits. First, conversion allowed banks to increase the assets under their management. Not only common trust funds, but also funds of other public investors can be pooled into the banks' mutual funds. A larger pool of assets to manage raised bank fees and reduced their costs by economies of scale.

Second, banks can use trust funds, which the banks control as trustees, to start new mutual funds. New mutual funds are not profitable to the promoters. So long as the amount of assets under management is small, the promoters experience a period of low gains or losses. These are inevitable in managing start-up small funds. The ability to establish a new fund with an immediate large amount from the common trust funds' captive assets gives banks a competitive advantage over mutual fund managers that do not have assets entirely under their control with which to start new funds. They must gain new investors, which involves time and money.

Third, banks can decide to invest trust assets in their own managed funds and not in funds managed by others, even if their own funds' performance is not the highest or the most suitable. Beneficiaries have no power to order the banks to invest in other mutual funds.

Fourth, banks can collect management fees as managers of the funds *and* as trustees (subject to some discount). Conversion of trust assets into mutual funds thus benefits the banks. To be sure, banks can show that conversion benefits the entrustors as well, for example, by greater diversification of trust assets and far more investment opportunities than were previously available.

If the rule that prohibits trustees from investing trust assets in their own enterprise allows banks to invest not in the "sole interests" but the "best interests" of entrustors, that would make it far easier to justify the conversion of common trust funds into mutual funds. First, specific laws may permit banks to engage in conflicts of interest transactions. Most importantly, there is a need for a theoretical basis for such conflicts. That is especially true in the case of trusts. Trust beneficiaries cannot fire the trustees, who are chosen by the trustor. Trustees can be removed by the courts only in very egregious cases. The only way the trust beneficiaries can avoid a relationship with the trustees is to refuse to receive the benefits from the trusts. If they do not accept the trust income or assets, they need not deal with the trustees. But that decision does not make much sense.

That is where the "best interest" theory enters the field. If a bank can show that diversification is greater in mutual funds than in trust funds—trust beneficiaries have received investments in their "best interest." The fact that the bank has benefited from the conversion is then less serious. The burden is shifted to the beneficiaries to show that mutual funds are not the best investments for them.

There is a serious question of whether the courts will engage in an evaluation of the "best interest of the beneficiaries." First, the "best interest" is based at least in part on an exchange—contract—and not on entrusted property which involves fiduciary duties. Further, even if changing the "sole benefit" to "best interest" of the entrustors does not change substantive law, it muddies the waters and alters perception. Banks can benefit so long as they can show benefit to the entrustors as well.

Second, one can still insist that nothing has changed when "sole interest" becomes "best interest." Even though "best interest" helps trustees to profit handsomely, it may be beneficial for the beneficiaries to pay the trustees more than before, if the beneficiaries get something in return. In addition, the beneficiaries would be asked to agree to this additional payment and the rules would be changed to permit the added pay. So it must be in the best interest of the beneficiaries to pay more, even though it is not clear what the benefit is.

Third, it is desirable to create a better and more relaxed theoretical atmosphere for conflicts of interest. This is done by deepening the perception that trust relationships are contracts. After all, trustees are entitled to fees—by contract. Trustees must follow the trust instrument, and that instrument, rather than being a condition of entrustment, becomes a contract.

Fourth, if trustees obtain the consent of the beneficiaries to raising bank charges, the consent is a contract. To be sure, trustees must provide beneficiaries with information before they give their consent. But that is far easier to water down than to fight a strict prohibition. Disclosure is flexible. Disclosure can be accompanied with noise, implications, inferences, and signals. Coming from the big bank that holds the beneficiaries' money, and the trust officer who is too busy to meet with a beneficiary of a small trust, such a beneficiary can be helpless. The consent of beneficiaries who have no choice but to have their money managed and controlled by the trustee is generally not difficult.

— — — — — — — — — — -

Discussion Topics

a. What is your position in this argument? Should "sole interest" be converted into "best interest"?

b. Who should decide what the best interests of the beneficiaries are? The beneficiaries? The bank? The courts? The regulators? The market?

— — — — — — — — — — -

c. Regulatory permission for limited conflicts in the area of pension funds

The Employee Retirement Income Security Act (ERISA) was passed in 1974. It required employers, who promise employees pensions upon retirement, to create a fund on which retirement will be drawn (or insurance annuities be bought). The establishment of pension funds brought issues concerning the fiduciary duties of their managers. The following are the provisions relating to the fiduciary duties of the fund managers. In year 2006, Congress passed a number of exemptions from the rules. The exemptions apply to "parties in interest" who were subject to the rules applicable to fiduciaries. We start with the fiduciary duties.

Employee Retirement Income Security Act (ERISA): § 1104. Fiduciary duties

(a) Prudent man standard of care.

(1) Subject to sections 1103(c) and (d), 1342, and 1344 of this title, a fiduciary shall discharge his duties with respect to a plan solely in the interest of the participants and beneficiaries and—

(A) for the exclusive purpose of:

(i) providing benefits to participants and their beneficiaries; and

(ii) defraying reasonable expenses of administering the plan;

(B) with the care, skill, prudence, and diligence under the circumstances then prevailing that a prudent man acting in a like capacity and familiar with such matters would use in the conduct of an enterprise of a like character and with like aims;

(C) by diversifying the investments of the plan so as to minimize the risk of large losses, unless under the circumstances it is clearly prudent not to do so; and

(D) in accordance with the documents and instruments governing the plan insofar as such documents and instruments are consistent with the provisions of this subchapter and subchapter III of this chapter.[78]

(c) Control over assets by participant or beneficiary.

(1) In the case of a pension plan which provides for individual accounts and permits a participant or beneficiary to exercise control over assets in his account, if a participant or beneficiary exercises control over the assets in his account (as determined under regulations of the Secretary)—

(A) such participant or beneficiary shall not be deemed to be a fiduciary by reason of such exercise, and

(B) no person who is otherwise a fiduciary shall be liable under this part for any loss, or by reason of any breach, which results from such participant's or beneficiary's exercise of control.

(2) In the case of a simple retirement account established pursuant to a qualified salary reduction arrangement under section 408(p) of title 26, a participant or beneficiary shall, for purposes of paragraph (1), be treated as exercising control over the assets in the account upon the earliest of—

---

78. The next subsections, which are not directly relevant to our discussion, provide: (2) In the case of an eligible individual account plan (as defined in section 1107(d)(3) of this title), the diversification requirement of paragraph (1)(C) and the prudence requirement (only to the extent that it requires diversification) of paragraph (1)(B) is not violated by acquisition or holding of qualifying employer real property or qualifying employer securities (as defined in section 11407(d)(4) and (5) of this title).

(b) Indicia of ownership of assets outside jurisdiction of district courts. Except as authorized by the Secretary by regulation, no fiduciary may maintain the indicia of ownership of any assets of a plan outside the jurisdiction of the district courts of the United States.

(A) an affirmative election among investment options with respect to the initial investment of any contribution,

(B) a rollover to any other simple retirement account or individual retirement plan, or

(C) one year after the simple retirement account is established.

No reports, other than those required under section 1021(g) of this title, shall be required with respect to a simple retirement account established pursuant to such a qualified salary reduction arrangement....[79]

In 2006, Congress amended ERISA to include, among other provisions, the following:

A blanket exemption from the party in interest restrictions for transactions that involve persons who are parties in interest solely by reason of providing services to a plan (or by reason of a relationship to such a service provider), provided only that the amount paid by the plan is equal to or less than, or the amount received by the plan is equal to or more than, "adequate consideration" (generally, fair market value);

An exemption permitting an investment manager to engage in discretionary cross trading of publicly traded securities, provided certain requirements are met;

An exemption making it clear that fiduciaries do not engage in prohibited transactions by using electronic trading networks;

An exemption facilitating foreign exchange transactions;

An exemption permitting block trades involving the assets of certain employee benefit plans;

A provision permitting correction of inadvertent prohibited transactions involving securities within 14 days after the transaction occurs, and for abatement of the prohibited transaction excise tax when such correction occurs; and

A new exemption from the ERISA bonding requirements for registered broker- dealers (and an increase from a maximum of $500,000 to a maximum of $1,000,000 per plan in the amount of bond required in the case of plans holding employer securities).

The new party in interest exemptions would apply to transactions occurring after the date of enactment, the bonding exemption would apply to plan years beginning after the date of enactment, and the increase in the maximum bond amount would apply for plan years beginning after 2007. The new rules regarding correction of prohibited

---

79.   Employee Retirement Income Security Act of 1974, 29 U.S.C. § 1104 (2000), *as amended by* Economic Growth and Tax Relief Reconciliation Act of 2001, Pub. L. No. 107-16, § 657(c)(1), 115 Stat. 38, 136. (3) In the case of a pension plan which makes a transfer to an individual retirement account or annuity of a designated trustee or issuer under section 401(a)(31)(B) of title 26, the participant or beneficiary shall, for purposes of paragraph (1), be treated as exercising control over the assets in the account or annuity upon—
(A) the earlier of—
(i) a rollover of all or a portion of the amount to another individual retirement account or annuity; or
(ii) one year after the transfer is made; or
(B) a transfer that is made in a manner consistent with guidance provided by the Secretary.

transactions would apply to any transaction the non-plan party involved discovers, or should have been discovered, after the date of enactment.[80]

_ _ _ _ _ _ _ _ _ _ -

Discussion Topics

a. What are the activities covered by the 2006 exemptions?

b. What are the reasons for the 2006 exemptions?

c. Are the exemptions justified?

_ _ _ _ _ _ _ _ _ -

d. Regulation of conflicts of interests under the Investment Company Act of 1940, § 80a-17

The Investment Company Act regulates mutual funds. These are entities, usually corporations or trusts, that issue securities to investors and invest in securities.[81] Affiliates of such investment companies include not only their board of directors but also their advisers, their portfolio managers and many other service givers that are necessary to maintain as well as companies and their investment operations. The Act provides a prohibition on various transactions between affiliates. Section 17(a) provides a prohibition on transactions between affiliates who act as principals (not agents) and the companies as well as the following exemption:

§ 80a-17. Transactions of certain affiliated persons and underwriters

(a) Prohibited transactions

It shall be unlawful for any affiliated person or promoter of or principal underwriter for a registered investment company (other than a company of the character described in section 80a-12(d)(3)(A) and (B) of this title), or any affiliated person of such a person, promoter, or principal underwriter, acting as principal—

(1) knowingly to sell any security or other property to such registered company or to any company controlled by such registered company, unless such sale involves solely (A) securities of which the buyer is the issuer, (B) securities of which the seller is the issuer and which are part of a general offering to the holders of a class of its securities, or (C) securities deposited with the trustee of a unit investment trust or periodic payment plan by the depositor thereof;

(2) knowingly to purchase from such registered company, or from any company controlled by such registered company, any security or other property (except securities of which the seller is the issuer);

(3) to borrow money or other property from such registered company or from any company controlled by such registered company (unless the borrower is controlled by the lender) except as permitted in section 80a-21(b) of this title; or

(4) to loan money or other property to such registered company, or to any company controlled by such registered company, in contravention of such rules, regulations, or orders as the Commission may, after consultation with and taking into

---

80. Pension Protection Act of 2006, Pub. L. No. 109-280, § 611, 2006 U.S.C.C.A.N. (120 Stat.) 780, 967-75 (2006) (to be codified at 26 U.S.C. §§ 4975(d)(18)-(22), (f)(9), (10), 29 U.S.C. §§ 1002(42), 1108(b)(15)-(19)).

81. Investment Company Act of 1940, § 3(a)(1), 15 U.S.C. § 80a-3(a)(1) (2000).

consideration the views of the Federal banking agencies (as defined in section 1813 of title 12), prescribe or issue consistent with the protection of investors.

(b)   Application for exemption of proposed transaction from certain restrictions

Notwithstanding subsection (a), any person may file with the Commission an application for an order exempting a proposed transaction of the applicant from one or more provisions of said subsection. The Commission shall grant such application and issue such order of exemption if evidence establishes that—

(1) the terms of the proposed transaction, including the consideration to be paid or received are reasonable and fair and do not involve overreaching on the part of any person concerned;

(2) the proposed transaction is consistent with the policy of each registered investment company concerned, as recited in its registration statement and reports filed under this subchapter; and

(3) the proposed transaction is consistent with the general purposes of this subchapter.[82]

e. New York Corporation law[83]

(a) No contract or other transaction between a corporation and one or more of its directors, or between a corporation and any other corporation, firm, association or other entity in which one or more of its directors are directors or officers, or have a substantial financial interest, shall be either void or voidable for this reason alone, or by reason alone that such director or directors are present at the meeting of the board, or of a committee thereof, which approves such contract or transaction, or that his or their votes are counted for such purpose:

(1) If the material facts as to such director's interest in such contract or transaction and as to any such common directorship, officership, or financial interest are disclosed in good faith or known to the board or committee, and the board or committee approves such contract or transaction by a vote sufficient for such purpose without counting the vote of such interest director

or

(2) If the material facts as to such director's interest in such contract or transaction and as to any such common directorship, officership or financial interest are disclosed in good faith or known to the shareholders entitled to vote thereon, and such contract or transaction is approved by vote of such shareholders.

– — — — — — — — — — -

Discussion Topics

a. How and why does § 17 of the Investment Company Act of 1940 differ from the prohibition on conflicts of interest under the New York corporate law?

b. Do you agree with the differentiation?

c. What are the justifications for the exceptions that you examined?

– — — — — — — — — — -

---

82.   Investment Company Act of 1940, § 17, 15 U.S.C. § 80a-17 (2000 & Supp. II 2002).
83.   N.Y. BUS. CORP. LAW § 713 (McKinney 2003).

C. Duty of Care

1. What are the principles of care?

A lawyer, physician, money manager or a director and officer of a corporation, who serve entrustors, must exercise care, in the sense of performing their services with care without negligence. Fiduciaries who purport to be experts must use their skills in performing their services. Fiduciary positions are not honorary positions. Regardless of whether or how much they are paid (if anything), fiduciaries must perform their services with care.

There is extensive literature on the meaning of "care." As to corporate directors, for example, the level of care is not avoiding negligence but avoiding gross negligence. Care may depend on the kind of "red flags" that the fiduciaries should have noticed but failed to notice. It might mean diligence related to the importance of a situation or transaction (e.g., sales of the corporation) and reasonable expectations of the parties. A physician may interrupt a conversation with a patient on receiving a "margin call" from his broker. The physician may even ask to be excused, and go to the bank to deposit more money lest the shares will be sold resulting in a loss. But a physician who receives a margin call during an operation may not leave the operating room to rush to the bank to make the deposit. A physician who did this in fact had his license revoked for life (even though the patient survived).[84]

The duty of care is more limited than the duty of loyalty. People can, and do, make mistakes. Even experts make mistakes. In hindsight, we are usually much smarter to point at these mistakes. In addition, it is the entrustors that chose their fiduciaries. The shareholders chose the directors, at least formally. The patients chose the physicians and the clients chose the lawyers. The students (or their parents) chose the schools and their teachers.

Intent to defraud or conflicts of interest is something else. These are rarely based on mistake. Therefore, even though the law regulates fiduciaries in the performance of their duties, courts limit their interference in the exercise of the fiduciaries' discretion. So long as their decisions are not tainted by conflict of interest and so long as they paid attention to the performance of their duties, fiduciaries are protected from legal liability, even if their decisions were mistaken.

The purpose of this section is not to evaluate and study in detail the literature on the duty of care. Rather it is to focus on the principles that may help determine the extent to which fiduciaries must perform with such care. Therefore the following principles are suggested. A fiduciary's duty of care depends on the reasonable expectations of the parties on the one hand, and the implications for the behavior of the fiduciary and similar fiduciaries in the future, on the other. If a

---

84.   Anne Barnard, *Board Says Surgery Halted for Bank Trip: Doctor Suspended for Leaving Patient*, BOSTON GLOBE, Aug. 8, 2002, at A1, LEXIS, News Library, Arcnws File.

fiduciary is engaged full time, the duty of care may be greater than the duty of a fiduciary that is serving part time. The following problem highlights a simple situation that happens so often. There is not enough time! There is not enough time to read a document carefully.

Problem

This is the story of agent Carl Poston, the Washington Redskins and Lavar Arrington. Agent Carl Poston and the Washington Redskins were working on a contract for Lavar Arrington. The parties had to close an agreement by 6 p.m.[85] Arrington argues that the deadline for this deal, worth $68 million over eight years, was necessary for the Redskins. They wanted to get the deal done by a certain time due to salary cap ramifications under the National Football League's collective bargaining agreement.[86] Once Arrington agreed to a contract with the Redskins, Poston, an agent for 17 years, perused the contract, made alterations, and returned the draft to the Redskins. The Redskins subsequently faxed the final version of the contract back to Poston, allegedly telling him they included all the salary and bonus figures. However, the contract did not include a $6.5 million roster bonus that was supposed to be included in the contract.[87] Poston did not catch this detail and Arrington signed the contract. The NFL Players Association accused Poston of certifying a contract he did not read.

"I guess when they sent that, there was deception involved from the start and I guess they were hoping to bank on that and they got away with it," Arrington said. "I had no reason to believe at that time that if you are going to give me an eight-year contract and you are going to sit there and rob me, but that's the type of organization it is," Arrington said. The league suspended Poston for two years on the ground that Poston did not read Arrington's contract. The client entrusted Poston with ensuring that everything about the contract was correct and that everything the team had told the client (and agent) were in the contract. As a certified agent of the National Football League, Poston should have been more careful as this is the duty he owes to the client.[88]

Arrington, on behalf of Poston, argued that there was a deadline crunch and that the Redskins waited until directly before the deadline to fax him the final version of the contract. Arrington asserts that the Redskins, in bad faith, left out the bonus, knowing that there was a chance Poston would not recognize this omission due to the deadline.[89]

---

85.   Nick Cafardo, *This Law Is on Agent's Side*, BOSTON GLOBE, June 18, 2006, at F14, LEXIS, News Library, Curnws File.
86.   Associated Press, *Arrington Rips Union on Eve of Testimony*, ESPN.COM, Dec. 6, 2006, http://sports.espn.go.com/espn/print?id= 2689062&type=story.
87.   *Id.*
88.   *Id.*
89.   *Id.*

_ _ _ _ _ _ _ _ _ _ _ -

Discussion Topics

a. Did Poston breach a fiduciary duty while acting as an agent for his client?

b. Did the team owe a duty to the agent and player, as Arrington seems implicitly to suggest?

c. Is the suspension of Poston justifiable? Taking into account the fact that there have been appeals, is the cost worth it? Does the benefit to society outweigh the costs? Is there any benefit to Arrington to having his agent suspended? Note that even though Poston was suspended Arrington did not recover his $6.5 million bonus. The suspension of Poston did not compensate for the omitted bonus. Instead, Arrington, and other high profile football players who had also enlisted Poston as their agent in contract negotiations, were deprived of an agent. Who benefited by the suspension? The suspension injured those who were in the midst of contract negotiations. Poston had been working out a deal between those players and their respective teams. With his suspension, the players had to find a new agent and begin negotiations all over again. Some players elect to pay their agents an hourly wage. Thus, the players lost all the money invested in Poston's hourly wage for their negotiations and had to pay a new agent an hourly wage to commence negotiations from the beginning.

d. Poston's client, Arrington, has asserted that Poston should not be suspended by the league as the player felt Poston did not do anything wrong. Arrington felt that it was his team, the Washington Redskins, that tried to sneak the terms in question by the agent. The Redskins and Poston were under a deadline and the Redskins faxed Poston the contract right before the deadline, which didn't allow the agent much time to read the contract. Thus, Arrington felt that the alteration in terms was not in good faith and that the Redskins were just taking advantage of the lack of time Poston would have to read the contract, due to the deadline. Should this factor be considered?

e. Assuming Poston owes a duty to Arrington, would a suspension of Poston against Arrington's wishes indicate that Poston owes a broader duty to the league? Should that duty weigh more heavily than the duty to the individual who is affected?

f. Is this relationship something that, as a society, we want protected? The policy is that we want to be able to trust that attorneys will do their jobs with no mistakes. We want to know that the attorney will not miss any detail. However, the attorney in this case was not acting out of malice. He simply was working under a lot of pressure due to the deadline and inadvertently missed some language in the contract (albeit a very costly piece).

g. Weigh the costs and benefits to our culture. Does it make a difference that Arrington testified at Poston's hearing that he didn't want Poston to get a suspension from the league?

h. What about the costs and benefits to each of the parties, to Arrington, the rest of the players, to Poston? And to the League?

- - - - - - - - - - -

2. To what extent is the duty of care related to the duty of loyalty?

Most people view the duty of care differently from the duty of loyalty. Most people do not accord to a breach of the duty of care the same wrongfulness as to a breach of the duty of loyalty. There are even some suggestions that a breach of the duty of care must involve bad faith, not merely the lack of good faith. Intent seems to be the most important difference between the two duties. Even a lawyer who is unprepared may be liable for a breach of the duty of care but the punishment is unlikely to be serious. But consider the following problem.

Problem

Foundering Corporation (FC) has business strategy problems and these problems are reflected in the corporate stock price, which is lower than the value of its assets. The corporation seems to be worth more dead than alive (the assets are worth more than the ongoing concern). The CEO of the corporation brings to the board an offer of a very large conglomerate to buy all the shares of the corporation for cash at a price about 30% higher than the market price. The offer is conditioned on a few days' acceptance. The board is composed of busy and smart reputable businesspersons. They are convinced that the price is a bargain for the shareholders and are concerned that the offeror will change its mind and withdraw. The board signs a merger agreement sight unseen, with terms uncertain except for the price. The board does not inquire about possible suitors at a higher price. The majority of the shareholders vote for the merger. Did the board perform its duty of care?

Problem

Susan Saab Fortney wrote:

"This lament captures the concern of attorneys who bemoan their liability exposure for the acts or omissions of their law partners. In the wake of the explosion of legal malpractice claims, attorneys are reappraising the risks of law firm practice. Until recently, the risks were largely covered by professional liability insurance. Still, as dramatized by the $ 41 million settlement paid by the New York-based firm of Kaye, Scholer, Fierman, Hayes and Hadler ..., even multimillion dollar insurance policies may be exhausted, leaving partners personally liable for malpractice claims."[90]

The government has sued lawyers and law firms for "failure to monitor" their colleagues. Law firms have established "peer reviews" but do not concede that lawyers are responsible for the misdeeds of their colleagues.

---

90.   Susan Saab Fortney, *Am I My Partner's Keeper? Peer Review in Law Firms*, 66 U. COLO. L. REV. 329 (1995).

Should lawyers be responsible for their partners' liabilities? Under what conditions should lawyers be liable for the misdeeds of their colleagues in the law firms? Under what conditions should the law firm as an entity be liable? How can both lawyers and their law firms protect themselves for liability in such cases?

3. What is the corporate directors' duty of care with respect to their corporations' legal activities?

Directors need not ferret out problems in the organization but may not ignore possible problems inherent in the particular business that reasonable persons would notice and react to. For example, managers of an explosive factory must make sure that the factory has sufficient and appropriate insurance coverage from explosions whereas the managers of a bank may focus more on the honesty of the employees and the security of the bank's safe.

In addition, directors may not ignore specific signals that something may be wrong. A government negative report and fines on particular patterns of employees' behavior, such as payment of bribes, must trigger steps to prevent such transgressions in the future, even if they produce significant profits. However, in large corporations, with a decentralized structure, directors may not be able to receive all the information of what is happening in the corporation. Nor may directors be able to establish in such a structure sufficient controls over disparate and dispersed employee population. These circumstances are taken into consideration when determining the directors' personal liabilities.

What is corporate directors' liability for the wrongs committed by the corporation under their stewardship? Put differently, to what extent does the duty of care require the directors to enforce the law of the land and prevent the commitment of legal violations by the corporation on whose board they sit? In the case of *In re Caremark International Inc. Derivative Litigation*,[91] the Delaware court offers guidelines on directors' liability for legal enforcement.

Caremark was a publicly held Delaware corporation that was listed on the New York Stock Exchange. Caremark was a spin off from another corporation and the practices that created the problem described below existed before it became independent. As the court explained:

> A substantial part of the revenues generated by Caremark's businesses is derived from third party payments, insurers, and Medicare and Medicaid reimbursement programs. The latter source of payments are subject to the terms of the Anti-Referral Payments Law ("ARPL") which prohibits health care providers from paying any form of remuneration to induce the referral of Medicare or Medicaid patients. From its inception, Caremark entered into a variety of agreements with hospitals, physicians, and health care providers for advice and services, as well as distribution agreements with drug manufacturers, as had its predecessor prior to 1992. Specifically, Caremark did have a practice of entering into

---

91. *In re* Caremark Int'l, Inc. Deriv. Litig., 698 A.2d 959 (Del. Ch. 1996) (footnotes and citations omitted).

contracts for services (e.g., consultation agreements and research grants) with physicians at least some of whom prescribed or recommended services or products that Caremark provided to Medicare recipients and other patients. Such contracts were not prohibited by the ARPL but they obviously raised a possibility of unlawful "kickbacks."

As early as 1989, Caremark's predecessor issued an internal "Guide to Contractual Relationships" ("Guide") to govern its employees in entering into contracts with physicians and hospitals. . . . Due to a scarcity of court decisions interpreting the ARPL, however, Caremark repeatedly publicly stated that there was uncertainty concerning Caremark's interpretation of the law.

To clarify the scope of the ARPL, the United States Department of Health and Human Services ("HHS") issued "safe harbor" regulations in July 1991 stating conditions under which financial relationships between health care service providers and patient referral sources, such as physicians, would not violate the ARPL. Caremark contends that the narrowly drawn regulations gave limited guidance as to the legality of many of the agreements used by Caremark that did not fall within the safe-harbor. . . .

In August 1991, the HHS Office of the Inspector General ("OIG") initiated an investigation of Caremark's predecessor. Caremark's predecessor was served with a subpoena requiring the production of documents, including contracts between Caremark's predecessor and physicians (Quality Service Agreements ("QSAs")). Under the QSAs, Caremark's predecessor appears to have paid physicians fees for monitoring patients under Caremark's predecessor's care, including Medicare and Medicaid recipients. Sometimes apparently those monitoring patients were referring physicians, which raised ARPL concerns.

In March 1992, the Department of Justice ("DOJ") joined the OIG investigation and separate investigations were commenced by several additional federal and state agencies. . . .

During the relevant period, Caremark had approximately 7,000 employees and ninety branch operations. It had a decentralized management structure. By May 1991, however, Caremark asserts that it had begun making attempts to centralize its management structure in order to increase supervision over its branch operations.

The first action taken by management, as a result of the initiation of the OIG investigation, was an announcement that as of October 1, 1991, Caremark's predecessor would no longer pay management fees to physicians for services to Medicare and Medicaid patients. Despite this decision, Caremark asserts that its management, pursuant to advice, did not believe that such payments were illegal under the existing laws and regulations.

During this period, Caremark's Board took several additional steps consistent with an effort to assure compliance with company policies concerning the ARPL and the contractual forms in the Guide. In April 1992, Caremark published a fourth revised version of its Guide apparently designed to assure that its agreements either complied with the ARPL and regulations or excluded Medicare and Medicaid patients altogether. In addition, in September 1992, Caremark instituted a policy requiring its regional officers, Zone Presidents, to approve each contractual relationship entered into by Caremark with a physician. . . .

Throughout the period of the government investigations, Caremark had an internal audit plan designed to assure compliance with business and ethics policies. . . . [O]n April 20, 1993, the Audit & Ethics Committee adopted a new internal audit charter requiring a comprehensive review of compliance policies and the compilation of an employee ethics handbook concerning such policies.

The Board appears to have been informed about this project and other efforts to assure compliance with the law. . . .

During 1993, Caremark took several additional steps which appear to have been aimed at increasing management supervision. These steps included new policies requiring local branch managers to secure home office approval for all disbursements under agreements with health care providers and to certify compliance with the ethics program. In addition, the chief financial officer was appointed to serve as Caremark's compliance officer. In 1994, a fifth revised Guide was published. . . .

On August 4, 1994, a federal grand jury in Minnesota issued a 47 page indictment charging Caremark, two of its officers (not the firm's chief officer), an individual who had been a sales employee of Genentech, Inc., and David R. Brown, a physician practicing in Minneapolis, with violating the ARPL over a lengthy period. According to the indictment, over $1.1 million had been paid to Brown to induce him to distribute Protropin, a human growth hormone drug marketed by Caremark. The substantial payments involved started, according to the allegations of the indictment, in 1986 and continued through 1993. Some payments were "in the guise of research grants", and others were "consulting agreements". The indictment charged, for example, that Dr. Brown performed virtually none of the consulting functions described in his 1991 agreement with Caremark, but was nevertheless neither required to return the money he had received nor precluded from receiving future funding from Caremark. In addition the indictment charged that Brown received from Caremark payments of staff and office expenses, including telephone answering services and fax rental expenses.

In reaction to the Minnesota Indictment and the subsequent filing of this and other derivative actions in 1994, the Board met and was informed by management that the investigation had resulted in an indictment; Caremark denied any wrongdoing relating to the indictment and believed that the OIG investigation would have a favorable outcome. Management reiterated the grounds for its view that the contracts were in compliance with law.

Subsequently, five stockholder derivative actions were filed in this court and consolidated into this action. The original complaint, dated August 5, 1994, alleged, in relevant part, that Caremark's directors breached their duty of care by failing adequately to supervise the conduct of Caremark employees, or institute corrective measures, thereby exposing Caremark to fines and liability.

On September 21, 1994, a federal grand jury in Columbus, Ohio issued another indictment alleging that an Ohio physician had defrauded the Medicare program by requesting and receiving $134,600 in exchange for referrals of patients whose medical costs were in part reimbursed by Medicare in violation of the ARPL. Although unidentified at that time, Caremark was the health care provider who allegedly made such payments. The indictment also charged that the physician, Elliot Neufeld, D.O., was provided with the services of a registered nurse to work in his office at the expense of the infusion company [that belonged to Caremark], in addition to free office equipment.

An October 28, 1994 amended complaint in this action added allegations concerning the Ohio indictment as well as new allegations of over billing and inappropriate referral payments in connection with an action brought in Atlanta, *Booth v. Rankin.* Following a newspaper article report that federal investigators were expanding their inquiry to look at Caremark's referral practices in Michigan as well as allegations of fraudulent billing of insurers, a second amended complaint was filed in this action. The third, and final, amended complaint was filed on April 11, 1995, adding allegations that the federal indictments had caused Caremark to incur significant legal fees and forced it to sell its home infusion business at a loss.

After each complaint was filed, defendants filed a motion to dismiss. According to defendants, if a settlement had not been reached in this action, the case would have been dismissed on two grounds. First, they contend that the complaints fail to allege particularized facts sufficient to excuse the demand requirement under Delaware Chancery Court Rule 23.1. Second, defendants assert that plaintiffs had failed to state a cause of action due to the fact that Caremark's charter eliminates directors' personal liability for money damages, to the extent permitted by law. . . .

[The court held:]

The complaint charges the director defendants with breach of their duty of attention or care in connection with the on-going operation of the corporation's business. The claim is that the directors allowed a situation to develop and continue which exposed the corporation to enormous legal liability and that in so doing they violated a duty to be active monitors of corporate performance. The complaint thus does not charge either director self-dealing or the more difficult loyalty-type problems arising from cases of suspect director motivation, such as entrenchment or sale of control contexts. The theory here advanced is possibly the most difficult theory in corporation law upon which a plaintiff might hope to win a judgment. . . .

. . . Director liability for a breach of the duty to exercise appropriate attention may, in theory, arise in two distinct contexts. First, such liability may be said to follow *from a board decision* that results in a loss because that decision was ill advised or "negligent". Second, liability to the corporation for a loss may be said to arise from an *unconsidered failure of the board to act* in circumstances in which due attention would, arguably, have prevented the loss. The first class of cases will typically be subject to review under the director-protective business judgment rule, assuming the decision made was the product of a *process* that was *either* deliberately considered in good faith or was otherwise rational. What should be understood, but may not widely be understood by courts or commentators who are not often required to face such questions, is that compliance with a director's duty of care can never appropriately be judicially determined by reference to *the content of the board decision* that leads to a corporate loss, apart from consideration of the good faith or rationality of the process employed. That is, whether a judge or jury considering the matter after the fact, believes a decision substantively wrong, or degrees of wrong extending through "stupid" to "egregious" or "irrational", provides no ground for director liability, so long as the court determines that the process employed was either rational or employed in a *good faith* effort to advance corporate interests. To employ a different rule -- one that permitted an "objective" evaluation of the decision -- would expose directors to substantive second guessing by ill-equipped judges or juries, which would, in the long-run, be injurious to investor interests. Thus, the business judgment rule is process oriented and informed by a deep respect for all *good faith* board decisions.

Indeed, one wonders on what moral basis might shareholders attack a *good faith* business decision of a director as "unreasonable" or "irrational". Where a director *in fact exercises a good faith effort to be informed and to exercise appropriate judgment,* he or she should be deemed to satisfy fully the duty of attention. If the shareholders thought themselves entitled to some other quality of judgment than such a director produces in the good faith exercise of the powers of office, then the shareholders should have elected other directors. . . .

[The] core element of any corporate law duty of care inquiry [is]: whether there was good faith effort to be informed and exercise judgment. . . .

. . . The second class of cases in which director liability for inattention is theoretically possible entail circumstances in which a loss eventuates not from a decision but, from unconsidered inaction. Most of the decisions that a corporation, acting through its human agents, makes are, of course, not the subject of director attention. Legally, the board itself will be required only to authorize the most significant corporate acts or transactions:

mergers, changes in capital structure, fundamental changes in business, appointment and compensation of the CEO, etc. As the facts of this case graphically demonstrate, ordinary business decisions that are made by officers and employees deeper in the interior of the organization can, however, vitally affect the welfare of the corporation and its ability to achieve its various strategic and financial goals. . . .

In 1963, the Delaware Supreme Court in *Graham v. Allis-Chalmers Mfg. Co.,* addressed the question of potential liability of board members for losses experienced by the corporation as a result of the corporation having violated the anti-trust laws of the United States. There was no claim in that case that the directors knew about the behavior of subordinate employees of the corporation that had resulted in the liability. Rather, as in this case, the claim asserted was that the directors *ought to have known of it* and if they had known they would have been under a duty to bring the corporation into compliance with the law and thus save the corporation from the loss. The Delaware Supreme Court concluded that, under the facts as they appeared, there was no basis to find that the directors had breached a duty to be informed of the ongoing operations of the firm. In notably colorful terms, the court stated that "absent cause for suspicion there is no duty upon the directors to install and operate a corporate system of espionage to ferret out wrongdoing which they have no reason to suspect exists." The Court found that there were no grounds for suspicion in that case and, thus, concluded that the directors were blamelessly unaware of the conduct leading to the corporate liability.

How does one generalize this holding today? Can it be said today that, absent some ground giving rise to suspicion of violation of law, that corporate directors have no duty to assure that a corporate information gathering and reporting systems exists which represents a good faith attempt to provide senior management and the Board with information respecting material acts, events or conditions within the corporation, including compliance with applicable statutes and regulations? I certainly do not believe so. I doubt that such a broad generalization of the *Graham* holding would have been accepted by the Supreme Court in 1963. The case can be more narrowly interpreted as standing for the proposition that, absent grounds to suspect deception, neither corporate boards nor senior officers can be charged with wrongdoing simply for assuming the integrity of employees and the honesty of their dealings on the company's behalf.

A broader interpretation of *Graham v. Allis-Chalmers* -- that it means that a corporate board has no responsibility to assure that appropriate information and reporting systems are established by management -- would not, in any event, be accepted by the Delaware Supreme Court in 1996, in my opinion. In stating the basis for this view, I start with the recognition that in recent years the Delaware Supreme Court has made it clear -- especially in its jurisprudence concerning takeovers, from *Smith v. Van Gorkom* through *Paramount Communications v. QVC* -- the seriousness with which the corporation law views the role of the corporate board. Secondly, I note the elementary fact that relevant and timely *information* is an essential predicate for satisfaction of the board's supervisory and monitoring role under Section 141 of the Delaware General Corporation Law. Thirdly, I note the potential impact of the federal organizational sentencing guidelines on any business organization. Any rational person attempting in good faith to meet an organizational governance responsibility would be bound to take into account this development and the enhanced penalties and the opportunities for reduced sanctions that it offers. . . .

Obviously the level of detail that is appropriate for such an information system is a question of business judgment. And obviously too, no rationally designed information and reporting system will remove the possibility that the corporation will violate laws or regulations, or that senior officers or directors may nevertheless sometimes be misled or otherwise fail reasonably to detect acts material to the corporation's compliance with the law. But it is important that the board exercise a good faith judgment that the corporation's information and reporting system is in concept and design adequate to assure the board that appropriate information will come to its attention in a timely manner as a matter of ordinary operations, so that it may satisfy its responsibility.

Thus, I am of the view that a director's obligation includes a duty to attempt in good faith to assure that a corporate information and reporting system, which the board concludes is adequate, exists, and that failure to do so under some circumstances may, in theory at least, render a director liable for losses caused by non-compliance with applicable legal standards. I now turn to an analysis of the claims asserted with this concept of the directors duty of care, as a duty satisfied in part by assurance of adequate information flows to the board, in mind.[92]

*   *   *

In *Stone ex rel. AmSouth Bancorporation v. Ritter*,[93] the court reconsidered *Caremark*. An action was brought on AmSouth's behalf by William and Sandra Stone, who owned AmSouth common stock at all relevant times. AmSouth is a Delaware corporation with its principal offices in Alabama. AmSouth's subsidiary, AmSouth Bank, "operated about 600 commercial banking branches . . . throughout the southeastern United States."

In 2000, Louis D. Hamric, II and Victor G. Nance set up an illegal money-laundering scheme, using an AmSouth bank branch in Tennessee. The scheme was discovered in 2002, and Hamric and Nance were involved in several civil actions brought by defrauded investors. Hamric and Nance were indicted on federal money laundering charges, and both pled guilty. The government then began investigating AmSouth's involvement in the scheme. The investigation found that the bank employees had failed "to file 'Suspicious Activity Reports' ('SARs'), as required by the federal Bank Secrecy Act ('BSA') and various anti-money-laundering ('AML') regulations." "AmSouth and AmSouth bank paid $40 million in fines and $10 million in civil penalties."

[In dealing with the issue of "whether the complaint alleges facts sufficient to show that the defendant *directors* are potentially personally liable for the failure of non-director bank *employees* to file SARs" the court noted:] Delaware courts have recognized that "[m]ost of the decisions that a corporation, acting through its human agents, makes are, of course, not the subject of director attention." Consequently, directors are rarely held liable for employee failures.

For the plaintiffs' derivative complaint to withstand a motion to dismiss, "only a sustained or systematic failure of the board to exercise oversight-such as an utter failure to attempt to assure a reasonable information and reporting system exists-will establish the lack of good faith that is a necessary condition to liability." As the *Caremark* decision noted: Such a test of liability-lack of good faith as evidenced by sustained or systematic failure of a director to exercise reasonable oversight-is quite high. But, a demanding test of liability in the oversight context is probably beneficial to corporate shareholders as a class, as it is in the board decision context, since it makes board service by qualified persons more likely, while continuing to act as a stimulus to *good faith performance of duty* by such directors.

92. *Id.*
93. Stone ex rel. AmSouth Bancorporation v. Ritter, 911 A.2d 362 (Del. 2006).

The KPMG Report—which the plaintiffs explicitly incorporated by reference into their derivative complaint—refutes the assertion that the directors "never took the necessary steps . . . to ensure that a reasonable BSA compliance and reporting system existed." KPMG's findings reflect that the Board received and approved relevant policies and procedures, delegated to certain employees and departments the responsibility for filing SARs and monitoring compliance, and exercised oversight by relying on periodic reports from them. Although there ultimately may have been failures by employees to report deficiencies to the Board, there is no basis for an oversight claim seeking to hold the directors personally liable for such failures by the employees.

With the benefit of hindsight, the plaintiffs' complaint seeks to equate a bad outcome with bad faith. The lacuna in the plaintiffs' argument is a failure to recognize that the directors' good faith exercise of oversight responsibility may not invariably prevent employees from violating criminal laws, or from causing the corporation to incur significant financial liability, or both, . . . [in] this very case. In the absence of red flags, good faith in the context of oversight must be measured by the directors' actions "to assure a reasonable information and reporting system exists" and not by second-guessing after the occurrence of employee conduct that results in an unintended adverse outcome. Accordingly, we hold that the Court of Chancery properly applied *Caremark* and dismissed the plaintiffs' derivative complaint for failure to excuse demand by alleging particularized facts that created reason to doubt whether the directors had acted in good faith in exercising their oversight responsibilities.[94]

- - - - - - - - - - -

Discussion Topic

a. The corporate structure in Caremark Corporation was decentralized. Information about the salespersons and control over their activities were left to the heads of the lower units in the organization that shared the salespersons' incentives. The corporate structure is usually determined by its CEO and top management, but the board of directors has overall supervision and power over the structure. Should directors be liable if the corporate structure did not have sufficient controls over possible legal violations by the salespersons and that the board knew about this structural weakness to prevent violations, if not the actual violations by the employees? Is it likely that the courts will interfere and impose standards on corporate structure? Should the courts do so?

- - - - - - - - - - -

4. What is the lawyers' duty to prevent violations of fiduciary law by their clients?

The position of lawyers as "gatekeepers" against illegal activities on the one hand and as trusted advisers to clients on the other has long presented a difficult issue. That issue became prominent in the 1990s scandals, in which lawyers gave weak comfort letters to clients who in fact, had violated their fiduciary duties to entrustors. The letters indicated that the clients' activities were "not illegal" and contained reservations and generalities that were not absolutely clear.

---

94. *Id.*

Opinions as to the legitimacy of these opinions differ. For example, Steven L. Schwarcz suggested that lawyers should not be proactive enforcers of the clients' legal activities but should be reactive enforcers, after clear red flags marking illegal activities have been waving in the horizon.[95] He bases his analysis on costs and benefits. One could also suggest that the duties of the lawyer could depend on the degree to which others protect society and third parties. For example, in the court, the other party has its own lawyer, an independent judge presides and sometimes an independent jury determines the facts. In these cases, the duty of the lawyer to the client can be far higher than the duty to society and third parties. The lawyer may not facilitate perjury and even has the duty to prevent perjury but has no duty to protect the other party in the proceedings. In the case of negotiations among parties that are represented by lawyers, the duty to protect the other party to the negotiation is also very limited. But if, as in the case of preparation of a public distribution of securities, the lawyer represents the corporation (issuer) and the investors are not represented, the lawyer's duties may rise. And if the lawyer advises a client corporation and recognizes clear signs of misrepresentation, misappropriation of corporate assets or violations of the laws, then the lawyer's duty to attempt actively to prevent the wrongdoing or else to resign is much higher. Should the duty to enforce illegal client activities also depend on the scope of the lawyer's engagement?

Arthur B. Laby wrote: "[G]atekeeper is defined . . . as a person or firm that provides verification or certification services or that engages in monitoring activities to cabin illegal or inappropriate conduct in the capital markets."[96] Laby distinguishes between independent and dependent gatekeepers. Among the independent gatekeepers are auditors. Among the dependent gatekeepers are lawyers. Both types have easy, and sometimes invited, access to information that is not available to outsiders, including government enforcers. Both types have a function of a gatekeeper. So where is the difference? Dependence includes dependence on the clients, which tilts the scales against becoming more independent and preventing the client from coming close to "opening the gates" to forbidden actions. Why are auditors more independent than lawyers? "[Auditors] cannot be the clients' advocate[s]," and are discouraged by law from developing long term relationships.[97] Lawyers, on the other hand, are clients' advocates and not evaluators of the clients' actions.

---

95.   Steven L. Schwarcz, *Financial Information Failure and Lawyer Responsibility*, 31 IOWA J. CORP. L. 1097 (2006).
96.   Arthur B. Laby, *Differentiating Gatekeepers,* 1 BROOK. J. CORP. FIN. & COM. L. 119, 123 (2006).
97.   *Id.* at 124-125.

- - - - - - - - - - -

Discussion Topic

a. Assume that a lawyer advises management and during the discussion begins to suspect that the corporate books are doctored to show higher revenues than the corporation truly gains. The lawyer does not have clear proof that such violations are occurring, but there are signs of possible violations, when some materials are not forwarded and some awkward silences occur instead of clear answers. What should a lawyer do? What questions if any should the lawyer ask of the CFO or CEO? Should the lawyer approach the members of the board? Resign? Knock on the door of the SEC?

- - - - - - - - - - -

D. Is There a Fiduciary Duty to Public Policy?

1. Fiduciary duties increasingly include considerations of public affairs

Our view of fiduciary duties is based on the interests of the parties to the relationship. The interests of the public are not usually involved in a decision. However, it seems that increasingly, the courts do factor in the interests of the public. Courts might protect entrustors from public pressure. For example, the trustees of a public school had to sell the school's building. Towards the school, the trustees had a duty to sell trust property to the highest bidder. The duty prevented them from selling a public school building to a church at a lower cost. The duty was upheld "even though voters who attended a public meeting preferred to sell to the church."[98] The interests of the public school trust trumped the interests of the voters. There were other cases that involves issues of public interest as compared with breaches of fiduciary duties.[99]

Another example involves a director of a not for profit corporation who demanded to examine the corporate books and records in connection with suspected violations of fiduciary duties of the corporate personnel. The court held that a director was entitled to examine the corporate books and records.[100] A director was given access "to hospital records involving cancer experiments on patients," who consented to injections, but had not been "told that the injection was of cancer cells because the doctors did not wish to stir up any unnecessary anxieties in the patients. . . . [T]he Court of Appeals reversed the Appellate Division and reinstated the trial court's ruling [that the director was entitled to see the records]."[101] In another case in Erie County, a trial court required a director and manager of a business "to reimburse the

---

98. William E. Nelson, *The Law of Fiduciary Duty in New York, 1920-1980*, 53 SMU L. REV. 285, 307 (2000) (citing Ross v. Wilson, 127 N.E.2d 697 (N.Y. 1955)).

99. *Id.* at 308 (footnotes omitted) (citing cases).

100. *Id.* at 308-09 (footnotes omitted) (citing Hyman v. Jewish Chronic Disease Hosp., 206 N.E.2d 338 (N.Y. 1965)).

101. *Id.*

business for $ 800 in bribes paid to local officials to overlook violations of the Sunday closing laws."[102]

Courts were not consistent in all cases. They sometimes "opposed using concepts of fiduciary duty to attain desired public policies, even when the policies had been enacted legislatively."[103] In one case, the court protected corporate directors who decided to authorize the violation of antitrust laws. Today, the tendency is to allow fiduciaries to "opt against regulatory compliance if prospective profits seemed sufficiently high."[104] The "Court[s] refused to place the law of fiduciary duty in service of the regulatory state" at the expense of private trust arrangements. "[T]he law, at bottom, remained committed to insuring that private managers of private investments acted honestly and with due diligence."[105] Enforcement of the more restricted fiduciary law trumped enforcement of other laws.

2. Fiduciary duties based on the public's needs

As we shall see in Chapter Seven, courts may consider public needs when fashioning fiduciary duties of private organizations. For example, in *Greisman v. Newcomb Hospital,* the court factored into the duties of a hospital the community's needs and the near monopoly power of this private organization.[106] The plaintiff, a qualified physician, sought user privileges at a Newcomb Hospital in City of Vineland, near his home and practice. Newcomb Hospital was the only hospital in the area. The hospital denied the plaintiff the privilege on the sole ground that he graduated from a school that was not approved by the American Medical Association and was not a member of the County Medical Society. Many professional medical associations, however, accepted physicians with a background similar to that of the plaintiff. While Newcomb Hospital's by-laws contained the conditions of acceptance that excluded the plaintiff, the hospital did not have any specialized practices but rather accepted physicians that specialized in many areas. In light of these findings, the lower court determined that the by-laws of the Newcomb Hospital conflicted with the public policy of the State. Further, although Newcomb Hospital was a private hospital that could operate at its discretion, its position as the only hospital in the plaintiff's area and its special services concerning people's health imposed upon it certain duties when any other hospital was at least 100 miles away. The offer of the hospital to provide the plaintiff's patients services by its staff was not acceptable. Patients should have the right to choose their own physicians. The hospital was required to grant the plaintiff user privileges.

---

102. *Id.* at 311 (citing Kalmanash v. Smith, 51 N.E.2d 681, 688 (N.Y. 1943)).
103. *Id.* at 308-09.
104. *Id.* at 310-11 (citing cases).
105. *Id.* at 312 ("As a result, the law of fiduciary duty in 1980 did not differ greatly from what it had been in 1920.").
106. Greisman v. Newcomb Hosp., 192 A.2d 817 (N.J. 1963) (abridged and citations omitted).

E. What Are Other Fiduciary Duties?

As stated before, fiduciaries bear additional duties that derive from their main duties of loyalty and care. One duty, derived from the duty of loyalty, is the fiduciary's duty to follow the directives of entrustment with respect to the entrusted power or property. A second duty, that derives from the notion of entrustment, is the duty to disclose all relevant information with respect to the services and the entrusted property and exercise of entrusted power. A third duty requires the fiduciary to "account" for the entrusted assets and use of the entrusted power. A fourth duty is a prohibition on delegating the fiduciary services. Because fiduciary relationships are personal, the rule limits the extent to which fiduciaries may delegate their services to others.

1. Duty to follow the directives of entrustment with respect to the entrusted power or property

An agent may not exceed his authority to purchase an item for not more than a certain amount of dollars. A trustee may not invest trust property in assets which the trust instrument excluded. There are situations in which the law establishes limitations on the fiduciary's discretion. For example, the Investment Company Act of 1940 binds the manager of a mutual fund to the investment policies of the fund.[107] If the registration statement of the fund and its name indicate that the fund is investing in certain types of investments, such as "equities," the manager is bound to comply with the limitations.[108] Violations of the limits on the fiduciary's discretion are likely to result in prosecution by the Securities and Exchange Commission. Violations might also be subject to private rights of action by the shareholders, although this is less certain. Another example is a trustee bank that converts trust assets in cash and places them in as deposits for more than the allowed time. The purpose of such investment may be to cover its banking regulation needs, which would involve conflicts of interest. Otherwise, such an investment in deposits may simply be the result of forgetfulness of the managers, which would involve breach of duty of care.

2. Duty to disclose all relevant information with respect to the services and the entrusted property and exercise of entrusted power

The duty of the fiduciary to disclose information about the entrusted property or exercise of entrusted power is not limited to those situations in which the fiduciary was engaged in conflict of interest transactions or violated other rules. It is a duty to tell the entrustor how the fiduciary is providing the services and what happened to the entrustment, regardless of whether the entrustor asked for the information. The entrustor does not have to ask; the fiduciary must

---

107. Investment Company Act of 1940, § 13(a)(3), 15 U.S.C. § 80a-13(a)(3) (2000).
108. *Id.* (prohibiting deviation from industry concentration stated in registration statement); *id.* § 35(d), 15 U.S.C. § 80a-34(d) (2000) (prohibiting deceptive or misleading investment company names).

inform and report. However, the information must relate to the fiduciary's entrusted property or power.

Consider *Cotton v. Merrill Lynch, Pierce, Fenner & Smith, Inc.*:[109]

Plaintiffs' main allegation is that defendant handled the sale of plaintiffs' stock in United Energy Resources, Inc. ("United") shortly before Midcon Corporation ("Midcon") merged with United, causing the stock values to rise, and that defendant knew of the pending merger as financial adviser to both United and Midcon and did not disclose this information to plaintiffs. Plaintiffs therefore allege that defendant breached its fiduciary duty [presumably duty of loyalty and duty of care] to plaintiffs and defrauded them in connection with the sale of plaintiff's United stock in violation of the Securities Exchange Act. Defendant seeks dismissal . . . [arguing that the Plaintiffs] fail[] to state a cognizable legal theory under which plaintiffs can recover . . . .

The Magistrate also determines that plaintiffs have failed to show facts in support of their claim that defendant violated a duty owed to plaintiffs. Any confidential information about the United-Midcon merger which defendant's investment banking division might have had was its property. "Confidential information acquired or compiled by a corporation in the course and conduct of its business is a species of property to which the corporation has the exclusive right and benefit, and which a court of equity will protect . . . ." Disclosure of such information by an employee could have led to prosecution for violation of the federal mail and wire fraud statutes, which deal with any scheme to deprive another of money or property by means of false or fraudulent pretenses or promises. Defendant's employees had a fiduciary duty to protect the confidential information.

The courts have established that brokers have a primary obligation not to reveal inside information to clients for the clients' benefit in trading securities. In *In re Cady, Roberts & Co.*, . . . the court said "even if we assume the existence of conflicting fiduciary obligations, there can be no doubt which is primary here. . . . Clients may not expect of a broker the benefits of his inside information at the expense of the public generally."

The Supreme Court in *Basic Inc. v. Levinson* . . . found that the standard to measure whether an omitted fact is 'material' in a Rule 10b-5 action under the Securities Exchange Act of 1934 is whether 'there is a substantial likelihood that its disclosure would have been considered significant by a reasonable investor.' The Court notably said: 'To be actionable, of course, a statement must also be misleading. *Silence, absent a duty to disclose, is not misleading* under Rule 10b-5.' (Emphasis added.)

The Magistrate finds that plaintiffs have failed to show that defendant had a duty to ensure that information in its investment banking decision about the United-Midcon merger was passed on to its brokerage division for dissemination to brokerage clients involved in sales transactions, including a client who was a director and shareholder of one of the companies involved in the merger and could be expected to possess such information. Absent a duty to disclose, defendant's failure to give information was not misleading and thus was not actionable. . . .

The Magistrate finds that plaintiffs' complaint should be dismissed for failure to state any claims, because it appears beyond doubt that plaintiffs can prove no set of facts to support the claims which would entitle plaintiffs to relief. It is therefore recommended that defendant's Motion to Dismiss be granted. [The motion was subsequently granted.][110]

---

109. Cotton v. Merrill Lynch, Pierce, Fenner & Smith, Inc., 699 F. Supp. 251 (N.D. Okla. 1988) (some citations omitted) (The action was based on the Securities Exchange Act of 1934, 15 U.S.C. § 78j (2000), and Rule 10b-5, (2007) 17 C.F.R. § 240.10b-5).
110. *Id.*

- - - - - - - - - - - -

Discussion Topics

a. What was the nature of the information that the defendant had in this case? How is it related to the court's rationale for limiting the disclosure duty of the defendant?

b. Remember the source of the duty to inform the entrustor. Does the source and rationale of the duty support or contradict the result of this decision?

- - - - - - - - - - - -

3. Duty to account: "This is what I have done with your money"

A fiduciary, for example, a trustee, must account for the entrusted property. The accounting may not be sporadic or partial. It must be systematic, periodic and full, including the accounting at the termination of the relationship. But the accounting frequency must be reasonable. It need not be daily. Accounting involves disclosure. But it involves more than disclosure. It is not enough, however, for the fiduciary to send the information. If the fiduciary owes the entrustor money, then accounting means payment of the money due as well.

Thus, when an employee receives from the employer $100 and is told to buy groceries, he should come back with the groceries, a receipt for the groceries for which he paid $90 and the $10 change.

- - - - - - - - - - - -

Discussion Topics

a. What is the importance and impact of the duty to disclose and the duty to account? Can you distinguish between them? If the fiduciary relationship comes to a close, do both duties terminate?

b. Can the duty to account be modified by agreement? Can the duty to disclose be modified by agreement? What is the rationale in determining these questions?

- - - - - - - - - - - -

Problem

A husband and wife agreed on a settlement. The husband gave the wife information about all the assets of the family. She did not ask for the value of the assets and he did not volunteer the information. Later she discovered that some of the assets were far more valuable than she thought they were and sued him for the difference, Should the husband have disclosed to the wife not only the existence of the assets but also their value? [111] What if the husband gave the information but did not describe the property as community property?[112] What if the husband did not disclose information about the income from the community

---

111. RAFAEL CHODOS, THE LAW OF FIDUCIARY DUTIES 221 (2000) (citing Boeseke v. Boeseke, 519 P.2d 161 (Cal. 1974)).
112. *Id.* (citing Jorgensen v. Jorgensen, 193 P.2d 728 (Cal. 1948)).

property, which the husband and wife were operating together, or the interests of large corporations to buy the property?

4. Duty not to delegate fiduciary duties

Because fiduciary relationships are personal, there are limits on the extent to which fiduciaries may delegate their services to others. This does not mean that the fiduciaries cannot resort to the help of service givers in the performance of the fiduciaries' duties. Secretarial, research, and other such services are permissible. A board of directors may delegate to the CEO significant powers to operate the company, provided the board reserves the right to overrule the CEO, and to fire him (even though at a high cost of a significant pension). A trustee that transferred all trust duties to an attorney and enabled the attorney to deal with trust property without checking the operations of the trust property would be liable if the attorney had misappropriated part of the property.[113]

– – – – – – – – – – – -

Discussion Topic

a. Note that fiduciary relationships are personal. Suppose an employee has an employment agreement for 3 years. The employer loses trust in the employee. May the employer fire the employee? Under the common law, can the employee have a legal claim to be reinstated if he was unjustly fired? If you were the employee, would you make such a demand? If you were the employer's lawyer, would you recommend conceding to the demand? What would you recommend to resolve the issue? In your solution, what considerations would play a role?

– – – – – – – – – – – -

F. Chapter Review

The following excerpts provide an opportunity for reviewing our discussion about fiduciary duties as well as the effect of breach of fiduciary duties on the American financial system and its culture. They also relate back to the issue discussed in Chapter One: when and how do fiduciary duties arise?

1. Should American business be prohibited from competing by paying bribes to foreign officials to get the business?

The Foreign Corrupt Practices Act (FCPA) prohibits American companies from bribing foreign officials.[114] The exceptions provided by the Act cover gifts up to $10,000 and higher amounts, that were approved by the Department of Justice upon application and justification.

Arguably, this prohibition makes it difficult for American companies to compete with foreign firms that are not only allowed to

---

113. *Cf.* Gaver v. Early, 215 P. 394 (Cal. 1923) (imposing the liability on a guardian and attorney and charging compound interest from the time of the misappropriation).
114. Foreign Corrupt Practices Act, 15 U.S.C. §§ 78dd-1 et seq. (2000).

bribe but are also able to deduct the cost of bribes from their income taxes.[115]

"Two obvious but diametrically opposed policy approaches have the potential to place all nations on equal footing - convincing the rest of the world to ban extraterritorial payment of bribes or repealing the FCPA so that American companies can compete for foreign business by paying bribes as freely as companies in other countries do."[116] American companies will have an advantage if they can convince foreign countries to raise their standards because American companies have succeeded notwithstanding the preventive measures. Otherwise, "indeterminacy under the FCPA is a chilling effect on U.S. business activity abroad."[117] Yet many doubt the reception and adoption of FCPA by foreign nations.[118] A classified report compiled by U.S. intelligence agencies predicts that U.S. businesses will be seriously disadvantaged in bidding for $1 trillion in international capital projects against foreign companies that pay bribes.[119] Finally, even though America has established the FCPA, bribery in international business is still rampant.[120] It may well be that American companies are themselves violating the Act or that the Justice Department that has authority to allow American companies to bribe is generous in its permission to do so.

— — — — — — — — — —

Discussion Topics

a. What is the wrongful element in bribery?

b. If bribery were permitted, and if the briber could include the bribes in its books and records, would the objection to bribery be higher or lower?

c. Would you object to bribery by American companies if the bribe were allowed to be paid abroad only, but not in the United States?

d. What is the effect of requiring American companies that wish to pay bribes abroad to seek permission from the Justice Department?

---

115. Melissa Hurst, *Eliminating Bribery in Business Transactions*, 6 J. INT'L. L. & PRAC. 111 (1997).

116. Steven Salbu, *Bribery in the Global Market: A Critical Analysis of the Foreign Corrupt Practices Act,* 54 WASH. & LEE L. REV. 229, 256 (1997).

117. *Id.* at 270.

118. Beverley Earle, *The United States' Foreign Corrupt Practices Act and the OECD Anti-Bribery Recommendation: When Moral Suasion Won't Work, Try the Money Argument,* 14 DICK. J. INT'L L. 207, 209 (1996) (proponents of FCPA-approach are sometimes characterized as excessively idealistic and unrealistic, "the equivalent of Don Quixote tilting at windmills"); Stephen Muffler, *Proposing a Treaty on the Prevention of International Corrupt Payments: Cloning the Foreign Corrupt Practices Act Is Not the Answer,* 1 ILSA J. INT'L & COMP. L. 3, 15 (1995) (current attempts to develop multilateral agreement on FCPA-style legislation are likely to fail).

119. Robert S. Greenberger, *Foreigners Use Bribes to Beat U.S. Rivals in Many Deals, New Report Concludes,* WALL ST. J., Oct. 12, 1995, at A3.

120. *See generally* Stewart Toy et al., *From Corner Office to Corner Cell,* BUS. WK. INT'L ED., July 22, 1996, at 20.

e.   A trustee seeks to sell some of the trust's real estate. He does not find a buyer at an adequate price. He is willing to purchase the property at a better price. Advise him.

f.   Assume the same facts only the fiduciary is an agent. Advise him.

g.   Assume the same facts except the fiduciary is a director. Advise him. Why the different rules?

— — — — — — — — — — -

2.   Does the trust form help to circumvent the laws? If so, why is it allowed?

Consider the following article by Joel C. Dobris.

Joel C. Dobris discussed changes in the role and form of the trust.[121] Arguably a trust exists "for successive ownership, to avoid probate, to protect spendthrifts other than the grantor, to provide management for grantors who later become mentally incompetent, to save some taxes, and to obtain professional investment 'management.'" A lawyer might say that a trust exists for legitimate goals, such as taking care of an incompetent relative; a client might add that trusts are used to circumvent probate and taxation. Dobris argues that "there is an erosion of fiduciary responsibility in the trust world," especially with respect to creditors.[122]

— — — — — — — — — — -

Discussion Topics

a.   What are the underlying assumptions of each of the views described above?

b.   Which view of fiduciary law and which assumptions do you favor?

c.   What other circumvention of laws can you invent by the use of trusts? The form of trust was used to create "legal monopolies" until Congress passed antitrust laws prohibiting such use. What conclusions would you draw from the multi-use of trust law?

— — — — — — — — — — -

3.   Chapter review

As noted at the beginning of this Chapter, we separated two questions that are generally connected. The first question with which we dealt in Chapter Two is whether certain relationships are fiduciary. The second question with which we dealt in this Chapter Three is what fiduciary duties the relationships create. These two questions are usually related and treated together. Therefore, to review the materials in this Chapter, we return to Youngblood Hawke's story told at the end of Chapter Two. This story raises questions not only with respect to the existence of fiduciary relationships but also with respect to the duties

---

121.   Joel C. Dobris, *Changes in the Role and the Form of the Trust at the New Millennium, or, We Don't Have to Think of England Anymore,* 62 ALB. L. REV. 543 (1998).
122.   *Id.*

that are involved in the relationships. The following questions relate to the duties:

1. Suppose that Jean thought that the film would be bad, but wanted Lax's money?

2. Lax knew that the deal was not good for Mother but wanted to please his famous actress client?

3. Was it enough that Jean merely caused the situation to be what Mother wanted? Or should she have told Mother about Lax's offer? What would have been the results of such a disclosure?

4. Did Jean lie to Mother? Is this a good lie or a bad lie? Would this lie be differently judged if Jean had taken the money from Lax?

5. When should the law interfere to impose on Jean a duty to tell Mother or abstain from taking the money? In the contract model? In the fiduciary model? Or if Jean was an adviser to Mother?

6. Could Jean abstain from taking the money but not telling Mother about the offer? How different would it be if she took the money and donated it to build the museum?

7. If Jean told mother about Lax's offer, could Lax sue her if Mother dismissed him as her agent?

8. Was there anything wrong in Lax's offer to split his commission? Was anything wrong in his position as the agent of the actress?

Chapter Four
Default Rules in Fiduciary Law

A. Default Rules in Fiduciary Law

1. Can legal rules be default rules, subject to the parties' agreements?

Default rules can be viewed as rules that supply the terms that the parties omitted from their agreements. Therefore, default rules are efficient. However, default rules may help the parties to reach an agreement. After all, the very existence of default rules may signal the parties' inability to provide for contract terms. In addition, even though default rules are subject to the parties' final word, they can have a strong effect on the parties' behavior. By their very existence, legal rules influence the parties' negotiations. The rules signal community norm and culture, and the majority practices. Further, legal rules may indicate to the parties a presumably objective, third party, standard of behavior and serve as "tools of persuasion."[1]

In contrast to default rules, mandatory legal rules aim at fair results, but might prevent the parties from negotiating other terms, which may be more suitable to their situation. After all, regulators may not provide appropriate rules for every occasion. Referring to the Arab-Israeli conflict, Omar M. Dajani writes: "this tension between the desire to promote adherence to legal rules that represent collective standards of fairness, on the one hand, and the desire to support any deal that will bring a dispute to an end, on the other, has been particularly acute in peacemaking efforts."[2]

This distinction applies to fiduciary law as well. "Norms considered mandatory rules define a zone of lawfulness for negotiations, i.e., standards of procedural and substantive fairness that the parties may not lawfully contravene, even if they would prefer to do so. Norms not considered mandatory rules—i.e., default rules—may . . . help parties to define their bargaining zone[,] . . . allow parties to anticipate the contours of a legal remedy should negotiations fail, . . . [provide] the parties with objective standards for choosing among potential deals[,] [a]nd . . . help a court to fill in gaps that the parties intentionally or unintentionally failed to resolve."[3]

---

1.   Omar M. Dajani, *Shadow or Shade? The Roles of International Law in Palestinian-Israeli Peace Talks,* 32 YALE J. INT'L L. 61, 68-69 (2007).
2.   *Id.* at 70.

The status of fiduciary rules as default rules conflicts with fiduciary duties of loyalty and reliability. When fiduciaries wish to engage in conflict of interest transactions and seek their entrustors' consent, the entrustors must fend for themselves. Their right to rely on their fiduciaries must be eliminated. In fact, during the bargaining, the entire fiduciary relationship must be terminated and replaced by the relationship of contract.

Fiduciary law allows such termination of the relationship with respect to specified transactions only if the parties follow a specific procedure. This procedure is designed to ensure an effective transition from the fiduciary mode in which entrustors rely on their fiduciary, to a contract mode in which parties rely on themselves. That is why fiduciaries must put entrustors on notice that, in connection with the specified transaction, entrustors cannot rely on their fiduciaries. That is why entrustors must be capable of bargaining independently with their fiduciaries and have the capacity to enter into bargains. That is also why, to allow entrustors to make informed decisions, fiduciaries must provide them with information regarding the transaction, especially when the fiduciaries acquired this information in connection with the performance of their services to the entrustors. This procedure is, and should remain, mandatory.

In addition, circumstances exist where fiduciary duties are not waivable for reasons such as doubts about the quality of the entrustors' consent (especially when given by public entrustors such as shareholders), and the need to preserve institutions in society that are based on trust [without exceptions]. Further, non-waivable duties can be viewed as arising from the parties' agreement ex ante to limit their ability to contract around the fiduciaries' duties. Under these circumstances fiduciary rules should generally be mandatory and non-waivable.[4]

Mark J. Loewenstein offered an insight into the courts' decisions concerning entrustors' waiver of fiduciary rules. He notes that in cases where courts find a waiver unenforceable, generally "the underlying equities support the result, and broad language extolling the fiduciary nature of the parties' relationship is beside the point." Yet when the waiver is enforced, courts refer to "contractual freedom," when the underlying equities also support the result. Consequently, courts have adopted a "middle ground" where "judicial notions of fairness" are as important or more than fiduciary or contract principles. He advocates that "statutory drafters" avoid the "contractual freedom" adopted by Delaware's allowing parties in unincorporated business organizations to disclaim fiduciary duties, as courts have been reluctant to enforce it.[5]

2. Are default rules in fiduciary law justified?

Consider this excerpt:[6]

At first blush, fiduciary rules appear to be essentially mandatory rules, similar to criminal and many tort rules, aimed at deterring fiduciaries from violating their duties to

---

3.   *Id.*
4.   Tamar Frankel, *Fiduciary Duties as Default Rules*, 74 OR. L. REV. 1209, 1213-14 (1995) (footnotes omitted).
5.   Mark J. Loewenstein, *Fiduciary Duties and Unincorporated Business Entities: In Defense of the "Manifestly Unreasonable" Standard*, 41 TULSA L. REV. 411, 415 (2006).
6.   Tamar Frankel, *Fiduciary Duties as Default Rules*, 74 OR. L. REV. 1209, 1231-77 (1995) (footnotes omitted).

their entrustors. The timing and manner of articulating the rules support this first impression. The rules are varied, fact-specific, and developed at the adjudication stage, and that makes it more difficult for the parties to bargain around the rules. A closer examination, however, suggests that under certain circumstances fiduciary rules serve both as default terms for the parties and as deterrence against misbehavior.

There are good reasons for viewing fiduciary rules as default rules and for enforcing the parties' bargain around them. We should start with a presumption that rules are default rules. This presumption is based on our philosophy that people ought to be free to govern their relationship unless good reasons exist to impose mandatory rules on them. Default rules can be justified also as reducing the parties' costs of planning and transacting by providing a measure of uniformity and stability, and by filling gaps that the parties failed to address in their initial bargain. The rules are presumed to represent the terms to which most parties would agree had they negotiated the terms. If the particular parties wish to deviate from the default rules, they should be free to bargain around them. . . .

. . . A taking of property is a wrong if, and only if, the owner does not consent to the taking. Lack of the owner's consent constitutes an element of the wrong, be it larceny or a fiduciaries' misappropriation of entrusted property and power. Thus, fiduciaries accused of misappropriation can plead the entrustors' consent to the taking as a defense to liability for breach of a duty of loyalty.

. . . Boundaries

Part of the confusion and disagreement about bargains around fiduciary duties can be eliminated by distinguishing between (1) the regulation of the initial establishment of fiduciary relationships - ascertaining the fiduciaries' functions, and the powers with which they must be entrusted in order to perform these functions; and (2) the regulation of fiduciaries once they acquire the powers, designed to reduce the entrustors' risks from the relationship. . . .

[Once fiduciary relationships are established the rules of fiduciary law apply, unless the entrustors consent to changing the rules, and transform the relationship to a contract.]

In order to transform the fiduciary mode into a contract mode, four conditions must be met: (1) entrustors must receive notice of the proposed change in the mode of the relationship; (2) entrustors must receive full information about the proposed bargain; (3) the entrustors' consent should be clear and the bargain specific; (4) the proposed bargain must be fair and reasonable.

[In addition, the entrustor must be capable of independent will. In addition, there are some provisions, which the entrustor cannot waive.] . . .

Because entrustors are legally entitled to trust and rely on their fiduciaries, fiduciaries who seek waivers of their fiduciary duties must put entrustors on notice that the entrustors can no longer rely on them in the matter, and that the entrustors must assume full responsibility for defending their own interests. In their notice, fiduciaries must identify the proposed waiver of duties about which the parties will bargain. Notice may consist of words or actions. . . .

Fiduciaries must provide entrustors material information necessary for the entrustors to make an informed decision regarding the waiver. This is necessary because, in contrast to contract law, there is no assumption in fiduciary law that the parties' information about the proposed waiver or bargain is symmetrical. Asymmetrical information among the parties to a fiduciary relationship results both from the nature and from the purpose of the relationship. Fiduciaries possess far more information about their own activities. Entrustors and fiduciaries are not equally equipped to make a cost-benefit analysis of the contemplated change in their relationship. In reality, entrustors can seldom perform such an analysis because they lack accurate information to make it. Therefore, when the fiduciaries possess information in connection with the bargain, and especially if the information has come to them by virtue of their position as fiduciaries, the change of the relationship mode must be accompanied by the fiduciaries' disclosure of this information to the entrustors.

[In addition, the consent must be clear and the terms of the bargain must be specific.]

Whether entrustors receive something in return is less clear and depends on their ability to sever the umbilical cord with their fiduciaries, as well as on their bargaining capabilities. The requirement of clarity relates to the condition that the bargain be fair and reasonable. This condition, in turn, is grounded in a rationale, derived from contract law, suggesting that if the bargain is highly unfair and unreasonable, the consent of the disadvantaged party is highly suspect. Experience demonstrates that people rarely agree to terms that are unfair and unreasonable with respect to their interests. Because the bargain or waiver is more likely to be in the fiduciaries' interests, but less likely to be in the entrustors' interests, the consent, by entrustor's action or inaction, must be clear.

To ensure clarity, default rules should be as specific and precise as possible. Fiduciary duties of loyalty and care, however, are broad standard rules. Therefore, the bargain around these duties must carve out explicit and specific situations. . . . Overall, the courts are not likely to uphold bargaining around the broad duties of fiduciaries far in advance when the fiduciaries have substantial discretion over the entrustors' power or property. . . .

Even if above requirements are met, courts will generally not enforce an unfair or unreasonable bargain, but will require a showing that the transaction is fair and reasonable. . . . [T]his requirement . . . is often based on a general presumption that entrustors' consent to unfair or unreasonable terms is uninformed or not independent. Similar presumptions operate in other areas. Consents to tortious acts have been struck down because their substance indicated the likelihood that they were not voluntary.

A second reason for doubting the voluntariness of an apparent consent to an unfair transaction could be a lingering suspicion that generally, when entrustors consent to waive fiduciary duties (especially if they do not receive value in return) the transformation to a contract mode from a fiduciary mode was not fully achieved. Entrustors, like all people, are not always quick to recognize role changes, and they may continue to rely on their fiduciaries, even if warned not to do so. Lack of fairness may also signal the absence of more or less equal bargaining power by the entrustor. When the parties are sophisticated, however, courts are likely to refrain from examining the content of the transactions and uphold consents, as tort cases have demonstrated.

A third reason for the requirement that the bargain between fiduciaries and their entrustors be fair and reasonable relates to the role of the courts. When the courts, rather than the entrustors, determine on the merits the validity of transactions made in conflict of interest or when the courts pass on the validity of waivers by representatives or surrogates of entrustors, the courts need such standards by which to make the judgments. If the entrustors themselves consent to bargain around fiduciary duties or waive them, the courts need not pass judgment on the substance of the transaction; they only examine the quality of the consent. Although entrustors are entitled to give their fiduciaries gifts, or consent to transactions on the basis of a whim, the entrustors' surrogates and the courts cannot make decisions without standards against which their decisions (to approve the transactions or the approval of other surrogates for the entrustors) will be tested.

It should be noted that even though the rules governing consents may be similar in contract and fiduciary laws, the burdens of proof regarding flawed consents differ. In contract law, the burden of proving that a transaction is unfair and unreasonable is on the party asserting that its consent to the transaction is unenforceable. In contrast, the burden of proving that the transaction in conflict of interest is fair and reasonable and therefore binding the entrustors is usually on the fiduciaries....

To bargain in the contract mode, entrustors must be capable of independent will. If their dependence on their fiduciaries is chronic, no bargain can be reached and no waiver of fiduciary duties will be recognized. For example, if entrustors who are minors or who act under the undue influence of the fiduciaries bargain around fiduciary rules, the bargains will be unenforceable. If the parties act under a mistake of fact the bargains also will be flawed. Further, courts generally will not enforce waivers that are so open-ended as to suggest either fraud or lack of informed or independent consent.

One may criticize this legal scheme of waivers as imposing on fiduciaries much of the cost of contracting around fiduciary rules. However, the costs are lower to the fiduciaries than to the entrustors because, notwithstanding the uncertainty about the rules, fiduciaries have better information about fiduciary law, about the cost (to them) of the rules that they wish to avoid, and about the transaction with respect to which they seek the waiver or consent of the entrustors. In addition, some rules reduce the fiduciaries' cost of obtaining consent. In some circumstances entrustors' silence or inaction after the fiduciaries' disclosures will be deemed binding and enforceable consents.

– – – – – – – – – – –

Discussion Topics

a. If the fiduciary law prohibition on conflict of interest can be eliminated by the consent of the entrustor, what prevents the fiduciary from asking the entrustor to sign consent to all future conflicts of interest in which the fiduciary will engage?

b. Once the fiduciary receives the consent of the entrustor to engage in a conflict of interest transaction, can the entrustor sue the fiduciary on violating his fiduciary duties?

c. Are there situations in which the entrustors' consent would not be binding? Where would you draw the line in such situations?

– – – – – – – – – – –

Another issue in connection with fiduciary rules as default rules is: which fiduciary rules are waivable. Consider this excerpt:[7]

[Professor Scott wrote:]

Even where the beneficiaries consent, the transaction is not like one between persons dealing with each other at arm's length, which can be set aside only for fraud, duress, undue influence, or mistake.

In a number of states there are statutes that expressly prohibit self-dealing by fiduciaries [and by] corporate fiduciaries....

Similarly, the Model Rules of Professional Conduct regulating lawyers do not permit lawyers to opt out of certain fiduciary duties ....

Denial of entrustors' waivers can be based on a variety of reasons [such as paternalistic protection, the objective of a level playing field for all fiduciaries and fundamental tenets of society]....

[Legal classifications are not usually viewed as default rules. The parties have a limited power to determine the legal classification of their relationships.]

---

7. Tamar Frankel, *Fiduciary Duties as Default Rules*, 74 OR. L. REV. 1209, 1231-77 (1995) (footnotes omitted).

Presently, the courts determine the class to which legal rules, particular activities, and relationships belong, taking into account what the parties intend to do, and sometimes how the parties perceive their relationship in legal terms. For example, if a trust instrument allows the trustee to do with the trust property as he wishes (e.g., give it away to whomever he wishes) and relieves him from accounting to the beneficiary, a court is likely to reclassify the relationship as a gift, notwithstanding the parties' use of the term "trust." If the broad waiver of fiduciary duties is part of the original agreement creating the trust, the court may avoid the trust as inchoate, because the agreement is not sufficiently instructive to the fiduciary. The trust will be dissolved, and the assets will revert to the estate of the trustor....

To some extent courts allow the parties to establish the law that governs their agreements, arbitration, and judicial settlement. Even so, the final decision on legal classification is with the courts, and for good reason. Allowing the parties to determine the categories of laws that apply to their relationship would undermine the enforceability of mandatory rules....

When public and private fiduciaries are required to perform the same services, the power of public fiduciaries will be greater because public entrustors are less able to control their fiduciaries or give informed and deliberate consent to conflict of interest transactions. Therefore, to protect public entrustors we can either find reliable consent surrogates for them, or make mandatory the rules governing public fiduciaries....

1. Public fiduciaries are entrusted with relatively more power than private fiduciaries

a. Increased Power for Centralized Management

As compared to private fiduciaries, public fiduciaries that provide similar services have greater powers for a number of reasons. First, the function of public fiduciaries for numerous entrustors is often to provide centralized management, which requires limits on the entrustors' control over their fiduciaries in the day-to-day operations.

In the private fiduciary relationship of agency, principals use agents to enter into binding legal relationships with third parties (e.g., sell or buy stocks). To perform these functions, agents need power to bind their principals legally; often they need to be vested with either title or possession of the principal's property. These services, however, can be performed under the control of the principal without affecting any other entrustors. That is why the definition of an agent includes the principal's control in the performance of his fiduciary's functions.

An agent to many principals, such as corporate management, is not, and indeed cannot be, controlled by each shareholder in the performance of management's function. That is why shareholders are precluded from interfering in the day-to-day operations of the corporation....

Thus, at least in theory, agency is less risky to entrustor-principals than directorship is to entrustor-shareholders....

Second, in private fiduciary relationships the personal and varied needs of entrustors guide the services and limit the powers of the fiduciaries. Public fiduciaries offering mass-produced arrangements possess broader discretion to design their functions and the criteria guiding the performance of the services they offer entrustors.

There are counter arguments to the view that public fiduciaries possess more power than their private fiduciary counterparts. For one thing, when markets offer alternatives to the fiduciaries' services or opportunity to terminate the relationship through sale (e.g., of shares), public entrustors can terminate the relationship, and "discipline" public fiduciaries without the need for judicial regulation. Even if management was not regulated by fiduciary law, potentially raising the risk of corporate mismanagement, the price of the shares issued by their corporations is likely to be lower than the share price of similar enterprises whose management does not mismanage. Share prices will provide market evaluation of the risk of lower management duties. Management presumably will have an interest in maintaining or raising share prices, and will propose charter amendments that would reduce their fiduciary duties only to the extent that the share prices will not fall substantially. Prices will either constrain the reduction of management's accountability, or provide investors with an additional option of acquiring shares at lower prices denoting lower quality of management's accountability. This market-contract regime provides self-executing arrangements without the need for, and the costs of, judicial enforcement.

These arguments are faulty because they are based on a number of very questionable assumptions: (1) that shareholders and sophisticated investors can price the shares correctly by determining the risk of management's reduced or non-existent fiduciary duty; (2) that the level of management's dishonesty and lack of care will remain stable once it is relieved of accountability; (3) that when investors learn about management's lack of accountability and self-dealing, investors will not withdraw from the markets; and (4) that a rule under which people who control other people's money can bargain for freedom from accountability helps maintain efficient markets and is socially beneficial.

[I]t is very costly to establish shareholders' losses from mismanagement, even under the current legal regime. . . .

The force of market discipline is unclear. . . .

It is true that, to the extent entrustors hold liquid interests, they can terminate their relationship with their fiduciaries by selling the interests ("exit") rather than by removing the fiduciaries ("voice.") Recent corporate takeovers, institutional investors' activism, and activism of the independent directors of large corporations seem to suggest that other alternative mechanisms are at work to render corporate management more flexible and creative, less complacent, and more responsive to the changing environment. Arguably, that may be the reason why waivers of fiduciary duty of care have become more acceptable. Yet, in light of past experience, I venture to both predict that the courts will not, and suggest that they should not, relinquish their jurisdiction over fiduciaries in egregious cases, regardless of the parties' bargains or waivers of fiduciary duties in corporate statutes and charters, by shareholders or otherwise. Courts will react because the risks that such cases pose to our economic system are too great.

Most importantly, the ability of shareholders to terminate the relationship with their managements by selling their shares augments the public fiduciaries' power, as compared to that of fiduciaries in personal trust situations. When these shareholders terminate the relationship they do not recoup the entrusted property. That property remains in the hands of the fiduciaries, who then simply serve others who purchase the shares. If we compare corporate fiduciaries to other fiduciaries under the control of entrustors or courts, we will not see markets as disciplining corporate fiduciaries, but as ensuring their tenure. Shareholders' option to "exit" reduces judicial supervision and the incentives of entrustors to remove the fiduciaries, as they would in the case of private fiduciaries. Therefore, it is a mistake to view markets as justifying more lax fiduciary rules.

Third, the necessity to avoid deadlock and hold-outs through unanimous consent requirement produces a majority rule for entrustors. That rule can dilute the individual power of small entrustors (and increase the powers of larger ones) and in some cases augment the fiduciaries' powers by coalitions with concentrated majority or minority entrustors. . . .

a. Entrustors' Consent Is Weak and Indirect . . .

In the corporate setting, however, if the information about conflict of interest is incorporated into corporate charters that are not brought specifically to the attention of the shareholders, the shareholders do not make any decision based on this so-called disclosure, except if we believe that the share prices would represent the degree of public entrustors' decision. The apparent consent that numerous entrustors give to their public fiduciaries' conflict of interests is similar to the "social contract." It represents a theoretical model, not reality. That is why implicit in traditional corporate law is the recognition that shareholders cannot and do not give fully informed independent consent.

b. Surrogate Consenters Are Also Fiduciaries Requiring Supervision; Therefore, They Do Not Solve the Problem of Consent . . .

In a revolutionary step, the courts began to act as surrogates for the shareholders, which changed the substance of the default rules. Leaving the power to consent solely in the hands of the entrustors makes it harder for the fiduciaries to engage in conflict of interest transactions: entrustors can refuse to consent arbitrarily. If the courts (or other surrogates) exercise this function, they must adhere to standards; otherwise they are not accountable for their decisions. Therefore, courts established the standard of fairness, under which they approved conflict of interest transactions. The standard narrows the sphere of refusal to consent, and entitles corporate directors and officers to engage in conflict of interest transactions that are fair. . . .

c. An Exception: An Independent Government Agency as Surrogate for Consent

Another type of consenter is an independent administrative agency under a scheme that applies to fiduciaries of investment companies (mutual funds). This scheme has been in effect for more than fifty years and imposes on these fiduciaries strict prohibitory rules. . . .

Whether the cost of such government agency may exceed the benefits to the corporations and their shareholders is currently unknown. Maybe arbitrators, like the arbitrator in conflicts between broker dealers and their customers now in place, can serve as substitutes for judges. In any event, these routes should be explored to discover institutional arrangements in which consent to conflict of interest transactions can be more reliable. . . .

If we adopt the contractarian view, we will continue to recognize all fiduciary rules as default rules and give effect to broad consents of public entrustors regardless of how indirect or empty they are. I submit that as we continue to do so, we will produce two results. One is to eliminate fiduciary law altogether. The other is to create property rights in fiduciary positions, such as office.

A. Eliminating the Fiduciary Law

1. In Reality: Empty Consents Eliminate Fiduciary Law Altogether

We can recognize that by accepting empty consents of entrustors to fiduciaries' breach of duties of care or loyalty, we eliminate fiduciary law and reverse its default rules. Existing rules prohibit negligence and conflicts of interest actions unless permitted by entrustors or their surrogates; however, the contract regime would permit all negligence and conflict of interest actions unless explicitly prohibited by entrustors or their surrogates. While now, permission by entrustors must be limited to particular transactions, and should be independent and informed, under the contract regime permission can be open-ended and indirect, through surrogates and market mechanisms. Entrustors must expressly protect themselves by contracts - a bonanza to the legal profession - or else their fiduciaries can use the entrusted property for their own benefit. Presumably, unless the corporate charters so provide, shareholders will have no right to bring derivative suits (however limited they may become under increasing strictures).

There are already a number of examples of the contractarian trend. One new example concerns limited liability corporation statutes. Even though the driving force behind these corporate statutes is the avoidance of double taxation, the statutes allow incorporators to write their constitutive documents as contracts and to design the duties of their managers without regard to fiduciary law. If the documents contain waivers of fiduciary duties, the courts will be asked to determine whether the waivers will be disregarded and the duties will be superimposed on existing documents. Current developments in the law suggest that, while chanting the ancient rhetoric, we are beginning to grant public fiduciaries rights similar to those of squatters' adverse possession, without formally abrogating or creating property rights.

2. We Need a Legal Model of Trust Relationship

We should reject the view that all rules applicable to public fiduciaries are default rules, no matter how tenuous the "contract" bargain around these rules. If, as I suggest, the model of fiduciary law will be erased in the public fiduciary context, the cost to society will be quite high.

I believe that law should provide society with two models for financial and economic interactions: the model of fiduciary relationship representing trust and dependency; and the model of contract relationship representing mutual suspicion, "realistic" mistrust, and independence. These are, of course, theoretical models. Trust plays a role in contracts; self interest plays a role in fiduciary relationships. Yet, the contract model alone will not do. The trust model is important for a number of reasons.

First, pervasive mistrust impoverishes society; trust can bring rich rewards to society. Second, the very existence of a trust model constitutes a self-enforcing mechanism. It helps internalize the trustees' self-image as honest and respected persons. It calls for the trustees to live up to the public's expectations. Society's expectations of a public fiduciary offer a way to compel, even "discipline," public fiduciaries' behavior.

Third, this internalization is much like the moral interdependence theory of lawyer-client relationships. Recognizing that lawyers frequently collaborate with clients, not merely advise them at arms length, lawyers must accept some responsibility for the outcomes they achieve and thus internalize, at least in part, the moral dilemmas of their clients.

Fourth, the public trustee model influences other peoples' behavior. If society demands high standards of public fiduciaries, others will likely conform to similar standards. As a result, public fiduciaries, when choosing between honesty and self-gain, will strive to meet the articulated social standards, or at least, to avoid admitting failure and experiencing the associated shame. Thus, arguably, the very existence of a model of a fiduciary induces corporate managements to adhere to the duty of care and loyalty. In contrast, if entrustors and others habitually view fiduciaries as contract parties, they will also live down to the contract standard.

Fifth, the legal fiduciary model serves an important role, notwithstanding the possible internalization of other social norms by public fiduciaries. As one scholar suggested, a trust-based model of the firm must contain the traditional fiduciary duties because business relationships that require a balance of self-interest and trustworthiness are potentially unstable over time. Contract alone cannot fill this stabilizing role because the parties are unable ex ante to identify ex post problems that arise from absence of reciprocal treatment. Societal and corporate normative standards bolster a commitment to honor other persons' interests. Furthermore, by adopting norms as law, these norms are communicated to the large number of persons within society's sub-units, and the legal enforcement of these norms complements informal sanctions, such as social disapproval and refusal to deal with violators. The discipline of management arises not only from public fiduciaries' fear of external punishment, but perhaps more so from the fiduciaries' internalization of the expectations of society (or the corporation).

Sixth, the trust model can serve as a "decentralized" lawmaking, absorbing and enacting social custom. Such lawmaking develops by applying community norms to determine fault and liability, for example, by having established the community's consensus about what its members ought to do. When actors internalize these norms, a completely decentralized legal system is in place, which in theory dispenses with the need for state law and enforcement. Ample evidence supports the notion that informal sanctions to enforce accepted norms are often more important than state enforcement of these norms.

Seventh, informal sanctions to enforce accepted norms are usually effective when the same parties engage in continuing relationships. The promise of gains from future transactions, reciprocal treatment ("tit-for-tat"), the threat of termination of the relationship ("exit") and internalization of the norms of behavior, all strengthen informal enforcement of trustworthiness today. In the corporate context, however, management deal mostly with numerous and changing shareholders. In such a context, self-imposed efficient or mutually advantageous norms will be practiced less frequently. Shareholders cannot effectively reciprocate by terminating the relationship without incurring high costs and facing free-rider problems. Therefore, managements internalize the norms of behavior only partially, and informal enforcement as to management falls short of the optimal level. In the corporate context, optimal deterrence demands supplementing informal sanctions with legal sanctions. The appropriate role of the state, then, would be to draw on efficient social norms and elevate them to the level of law. Stricter mandatory rules on public fiduciaries would foster such internalization and protect against the instability of trust relationship over time.

Eighth, if the trust model did not exist, and if entrustors viewed their fiduciaries "realistically" and needed to verify the fiduciaries' trustworthiness, entrustors would (1) expand the monitoring of their fiduciaries at higher costs and reduced benefits from the relationship; (2) withdraw into the "do it themselves" mode, reducing specialization in services that require a high level of investment and bring benefits to society; and (3) abandon the activity altogether - for example, cease to invest in mutual funds. If the activity is beneficial, the losses to society as well as to individuals could be substantial.

2. Creating Property Rights in Office

Another result of recognizing empty entrustors' consents is to create property rights in directorships and offices for management. The contractarian regime is bound to produce this new type of property in a public office. In fact, such property rights existed in the past, and were slowly terminated with the emergence of democracy. Unlike private fiduciary relationships, corporations mirror political institutions that started with the rulers as the owners of the realm. Office constituted a species of property that could be bequeathed, sold, delegated and given as a gift. With the development of democracy the status of the rulers changed to that of trustees, holding the power of government in trust for the people. The power to rule was shorn of all its ownership features: the power could not be bequeathed, delegated, sold and given as a gift. Rulers were not allowed to benefit from the power except by specified and authorized compensation. These principles apply to corporate management. Thus, if the rules governing public fiduciaries are default rules that can be changed by imaginary and unreal consents, we will return to the ancient property rights of office.

By itself, this conclusion does not mean that the trend is bad. After all, if obtaining consent from public entrustors is costly and they themselves are not willing to bear the costs of having their voices heard, management should be allowed to acquire limited property rights in their office, similar to squatters' rights based on adverse possession. Yet, I suggest that awarding management such property rights, whether formally or in fact, is generally not a good idea.

First, this kind of a property right does not produce the desirable incentives that we expect property rights to produce. Rather, such a right in office produces the kind of incentives that bureaucracies possess, and that centralized management economies have demonstrated to be less productive and less competitive. Our concept of ownership vests control in those who take the residual risks (and residual gains) because we believe that those who take the residual risk from economic resources are the most suitable to set the optimal level of risk for the use of these resources: not so low as to produce gains to pay only the creditors and not so high so as to leave assets to pay only the creditors. Thus, if control without residual risk passes to corporate management (though with some residual gains), management's decisions will not be optimally efficient.

Arguably, as compared to small shareholders, management should be entitled to some propriety rights. Even though small shareholders contribute risk capital to the enterprise, they (1) lose less than each member of management when the corporation experiences losses, and (2) contribute less than management members to the success of the company. Even though members of management have not contributed substantial amounts of risk capital to the enterprise, they have in many cases contributed their talents and lives to the enterprise and made it a success. Thus, it is a misnomer to call small shareholders owners of the enterprise. They should be cast as "lenders of risk capital," and management as holding substantial powers and rights of the owners.

For political and doctrinal reasons, neither the legislatures nor courts will explicitly rearrange the ownership package. The arguments for such division of risks, benefits and control undermines our concept of ownership, and also opens the door to claims by other contributors of labor to ownership rights in the enterprise. In our system, labor is not entitled to control the means of production by virtue of its contribution, and the power of management to control the enterprise is legitimized on the basis of representing the corporation and its shareholders, not on the basis of its contribution to the growth and success of the corporation. Those who provide service (as fiduciaries or employees or independent contractors, or any other type of relationship) no matter how extensively their fortunes are linked to the enterprise, and how deep their commitment to the enterprise is, cannot become owners by virtue of these factors. Commitment to the enterprise demonstrates loyalty that would suggest lax rather than strict rules, but does not "buy" additional entitlements at the expense of the owners of the enterprise.

Second, a realistic view of public fiduciaries may justify the laxity of corporate law as compared with private fiduciary law by the simple fact that those who own more property (private entrustors) command greater protection of their property, in terms of rules and judicial enforcement, than those who own little property (shareholders in publicly held corporations). This explanation might seem cynical, but is grounded in history when political and governmental powers were tied to property ownership. It was property owners who used and employed fiduciaries and who needed protection from fiduciaries' abuse of power. It was rich property owners who used fiduciaries to evade inheritance and tax laws; those who owned little property were not occupied with such problems. Thus, in the past and today the private entrustors are those large property owners who can employ and use particular fiduciaries. The small property owners are the public entrustors who seek the services of public fiduciaries. They have less clout under the legal system.

I do not find this realistic view a justification and reject it. The law ought to protect small owners as it does large owners, not only because the law should offer equal protection, but also because our economy is not built on the savings contributions of the very rich but on the savings contributions of the middle class. Even if protection of the small entrustor is more costly overall, such protection provides incentives that make society better off long-term.

Finally, at this point it seems clear that the main problem with public fiduciary law is the absence of a reliable entity to consent to conflict of interest transactions. The problem does not arise when fiduciaries "own" their office, so to speak. They may own a fiduciary business as independent contractors. The problem arises when fiduciaries acquire "squatters' rights" to entrusted powers or property through misappropriation because the owners find it too costly to protect their property from the fiduciaries' conversion, and there is no surrogate for the owners to consent or prevent the misappropriation. Regardless of whether public fiduciaries act as independent contractors, or employees or elected officials, the duties of loyalty and care apply to them and should be effectively enforced against them.

3. Make All Public Fiduciary Rules Mandatory

So long as public entrustors cannot give effective consent and we believe that legal fiduciary relationships are important, we should render all fiduciary rules mandatory, and simply ignore so-called consents of public entrustors. In any event, the courts should continue to superimpose fiduciary principles on whatever statutory or contractual arrangements are in place, and I hope will continue to view with great skepticism the intracorporate and external surrogate consenters now in place, until the culture that contractarian policies have nurtured will be overcome by a culture of trustworthiness and self limitation.

Conclusion

Fiduciary law and contract law are designed to address somewhat different problems. Fiduciary law is designed mainly to deter fiduciaries from misappropriating entrusted power and acting with lack of care. Similar to the crime of embezzlement and the torts of conversion and negligence, fiduciary law regulates the holders of power that belongs to entrustors. Contract law is designed to formalize and enforce mutual promises between parties. It regulates both parties equally. The main difference between the two systems revolves around the right of one party to rely on the other. Entrustors are entitled to rely on their fiduciaries to a greater extent than contracting parties are entitled to rely on each other.

There are good reasons for allowing the entrustors and their fiduciaries to bargain around fiduciary rules and for enforcing the entrustors' consent to waive the fiduciaries' duties. There are also good reasons for providing a special process for these bargains and waivers, different from the contract process. This process is necessary in order to transform the relationship from the fiduciary mode to a contract mode.

In addition, there are reasons to limit entrustors' ability to waive some of their rights. Although the limitations seem paternalistic, they can be justified by concerns that, "once badly burned," entrustors will refrain from entering fiduciary relationships, to the great detriment to society as a whole. Even though some fiduciaries will be scrupulously honest and careful, a sufficient number of bad experiences might convince entrustors to limit their fiduciary relationships rather than bear the costs of protecting themselves.

Our present economic and business system requires that entrustors enter into numerous fiduciary relationships. If they withdraw, the system on which our national financial and economic well-being is based is likely to disintegrate. The probability of such an occurrence may be low, but the harm from such disintegration may be devastating. To prevent such a disastrous result, fiduciary duties should be imposed and entrustors' waivers of such duties should be allowed only under well-defined circumstances, or prohibited altogether. In sum, fiduciary law is not, and should not be, contract.

Public fiduciaries are different from private fiduciaries because they usually are vested with more power and are subject to less constraint. Therefore, the requirements of the process of the entrustors' consent to conflicts of interest by such fiduciaries should be stricter. However, we have not found an efficient mechanism to effectuate this process. Neither have we found reliable surrogates to consent for the numerous entrustors.

We thus have two possible solutions. One is to impose all fiduciary rules as mandatory. This solution will preserve the legal trust model, without which an economy such as ours cannot exist long. Further, we should not abandon the search for effective surrogates, and reexamine possible models such as a government agency or private compulsory arbitrators, who are independent and knowledgeable business persons to act as surrogate consenters for public entrustors. The second solution is the contractarian solution. In essence, it eliminates fiduciary law altogether and vests some kind of property rights in office, property rights that we have abolished generations ago with the evolution of democracy. I reject this solution as extremely harmful to our society. In sum, the anti-contractarians have it.[8]

B. How to Evaluate the Entrustors' Consent?

Legislative rules and cases may require fiduciaries to disclose certain facts. The entrustors who then establish a relationship with the fiduciaries are presumed to have consented to the exceptions that the fiduciaries disclosed. Thus, for example, investment advisers are required to disclose to future entrustors-advisees any criminal record that they might have.[9] Among the facts that the adviser must disclose to potential clients are, for example, financial and disciplinary information, such as "[a] financial condition of the adviser that is reasonably likely to impair the ability of the adviser to meet contractual commitments to clients, if the adviser has discretionary authority (express or implied) or custody over such client's funds or securities, or requires prepayment of advisory fees of more than $ 500 from such client, 6 months or more in advance." In addition the adviser must disclose "a legal or disciplinary event that is material to an evaluation of the adviser's integrity or ability to meet contractual commitments to clients." There is a rebuttable presumption that the following events involving the adviser or one of its management persons, not resolved in the person's favor or reversed, suspended, or vacated, are "material": "[a] criminal or civil action in a court of competent jurisdiction in which the person— (i) Was convicted, pleaded guilty or nolo contendere ('no contest') to a felony or misdemeanor, or is the named subject of a pending criminal proceeding (any of the foregoing referred to hereafter as 'action'), and such action involved: an investment-related business; fraud, false statements, or omissions; wrongful taking of property; or bribery, forgery, counterfeiting, or extortion; (ii) Was found to have been involved in a violation of an investment-related statute or regulation; or (iii) Was the subject of any order, judgment, or decree permanently or temporarily enjoining the person from, or otherwise limiting the person from, engaging in any investment-related activity."

The rule further states that the information "shall be disclosed to clients promptly, and to prospective clients not less than 48 hours prior to entering into any written or oral investment advisory contract, or no later than the time of entering into such contract if the client has the

---

8.   *Id.*
9.   17 C.F.R. § 275.206(4)-4 (2006).

right to terminate the contract without penalty within five business days after entering into the contract."[10]

In *SEC v. Capital Gains Research Bureau, Inc.,*[11] the Supreme Court held that a fiduciary's advisory letter must disclose the adviser's scalping, that is, trading on the effect of the letter which might raise the price of recommended stock for a short time.

— — — — — — — — — — —

Discussion Topics

a. Which of the forms of default rules are more effective? Is it the form that requires active consent of the entrustor after being provided with information? Or is it the form that requires the provision of the information but no active consent by the entrustor? Under what circumstances would the regulators and the courts not require the active consent of the entrustors?

b. Do you agree with the analysis in the Frankel article? Is there a simpler way to protect entrustors and yet allow the fiduciaries to benefit from the entrustment?

c. Why should fiduciary rules be so protective of persons who are sophisticated and can protect themselves? Why should the rules be protective of people who could learn to fend for themselves but are too lazy to do so, or decide to use their time differently or follow the advice of others?

d. In *Smith v. Van Gorkom,*[12] the Delaware Supreme Court held that directors were negligent and violated their fiduciary duty of care. This decision raised great concern among corporate management. Delaware is the State in which about 50% of the large US corporations are registered. Hence, great pressure was exerted on the legislature to amend the law and avoid the result of this case in the future. Consequently, the legislature amended the Corporation Act and substituted a mandatory rule prohibiting violation of the duty of care with a default rule that could limit the remedy of damages against directors that violated the duty of care. Thereafter, the articles of associations of most if not all corporations were amended to introduce the limitation. All the states followed the Delaware version. Thus, Delaware's General Corporation Law, with certain exceptions, permits a corporation to include in its certificate "a provision eliminating or limiting the personal liability of a director to the corporation or its stockholders" for breach of the duty of care.[13] Charter option provisions such as these are controversial. For example, Professor Lucian Arye Bebchuk pointed out that costs of obtaining information prevent

---

10.   *Id.*
11.   SEC v. Capital Gains Research Bureau, Inc., 375 U.S. 180 (1963).
12.   Smith v. Van Gorkom, 488 A.2d 858 (Del. 1985).
13.   *See* DEL. CODE ANN. tit. 8, § 102(b)(7) (2001). *See also* MODEL BUS. CORP. ACT § 2.02(b)(4) (2005) (allowing for exculpation of directors in an even broader range of circumstances).

shareholders from understanding the impact of provisions in corporate charters that decrease shareholder value.[14]

What was the effect of this amendment? What alternative solutions were available to the legislature?

e. Consider the Enron Corporation case. The directors in that case waived the constraints of Enron's code of ethics and allowed management to benefit from dealing with the corporation. One of the executives gained about $30 million within a short period, and the transactions themselves impoverished the corporation and defrauded investors. If the directors slept at the helm, and let the management of the corporation literally loot it, should the shareholders sue the directors for damages notwithstanding the fact that they were not liable for damages under the articles of association permitted by the default section?

f. Do you think that the shareholders' vote approving the change in the directors' duty of care constitutes consent by the shareholders? Did the shareholders consent to the substance of the waiver or did they consent to waive their rights to consent?

g. Assume that the agreement between an entrustor and his money manager provides that the entrustor waives the right to consent to a conflict of interest transaction. Should the court give effect to such a waiver? Does your answer depend on the circumstances in which the waiver was given, or on the entrustor's situation, or on other conditions?

h. To what extent should courts consider the balance of power between the entrustors and the fiduciaries in determining the extent of fiduciary duties, for example, of a trustee or a corporate director?

— — — — — — — — — — — — —

1. What is the weight of entrustors' power in negotiating with fiduciaries?

According to Robert S. Adler and Elliot M. Silverstein, "[n]egotiation power depends less on the other side's strength than on one's own needs, fears, and available options." Negotiating parties generally seek greater power, to enhance the outcome. Negotiation skills also play a role when there are power disparities. Oddly, a large power disparity may make it unlikely for the more powerful party to obtain a favorable outcome; under the "power paradox": "the harder you make it for them to say no, the harder you make it for them to say yes." In addition, the power dynamic can be influenced by information about the other party's "intentions, strength, or vulnerabilities" or its "perception of the power dynamic." [15]

---

14. Lucian Arye Bebchuk, *Limiting Contractual Freedom in Corporate Law: The Desirable Constraints on Charter Amendments,* 102 HARV. L. REV. 1820, 1836-37 (1989).
15. Robert S. Adler & Elliot M. Silverstein, *When David Meets Goliath: Dealing with Power Differentials in Negotiations,* 5 HARV. NEGOT. L. REV. 1 (2000), LEXIS, Lawrev Library, Hrvnlr File (LEXIS summary).

- - - - - - - - - - - -

Discussion Topics

a. Assume that an adviser publishes an advisory letter to subscribers. The letter discloses the fact that the adviser has a conflict of interest because the adviser is involved in a transaction of a corporation whose stock the adviser recommends. The subscribers do not answer or express their agreement. What is the default rule in such a case?

b. Would you reach the same conclusion if the fact that the adviser described above was involved in the transaction of a corporation whose stock the adviser recommends is known since it was reported in the media?

c. Would the same disclosure be sufficient in a face to face discussion between the adviser and the client if the client did not react?

d. Do you think that is it a good idea to allow any conflict of interest actions by fiduciaries that manage other people's money? Is that possible?

- - - - - - - - - - - -

2. Consent by government: The Investment Company Act of 1940, § 80a-17: Transactions of certain affiliated persons and underwriters[16]

(a) Prohibited transactions

It shall be unlawful for any affiliated person or promoter of or principal underwriter for a registered investment company (other than a company of the character described in section 80a-12(d)(3)(A) and (B) of this title), or any affiliated person of such a person, promoter, or principal underwriter, acting as principal—

(1) knowingly to sell any security or other property to such registered company or

to any company controlled by such registered company, unless such sale involves solely (A) securities of which the buyer is the issuer, (B) securities of which the seller is the issuer and which are part of a general offering to the holders of a class of its securities, or (C) securities deposited with the trustee of a unit investment trust or periodic payment plan by the depositor thereof;

(2) knowingly to purchase from such registered company, or from any

company controlled by such registered company, any security or other property (except securities of which the seller is the issuer);

(3) to borrow money or other property from such registered company or from any

company controlled by such registered company (unless the borrower is controlled by the lender) except as permitted in section 80a-21(b) of this title; or

(4) to loan money or other property to such registered company, or to any

company controlled by such registered company, in contravention of such rules, regulations, or orders as the Commission may, after consultation with and taking into consideration the views of the Federal banking agencies (as defined in section 1813 of title 12), prescribe or issue consistent with the protection of investors.

(b) Application for exemption of proposed transaction from certain restrictions

Notwithstanding subsection (a), any person may file with the Commission an application for an order exempting a proposed transaction of the applicant from one or more

---

16.   Investment Company Act of 1940, 15 U.S.C. § 80a-17(a), (b) (2000).

provisions of said subsection. The Commission shall grant such application and issue such order of exemption if evidence establishes that—

(1) the terms of the proposed transaction, including the consideration to be paid or received are reasonable and fair and do not involve overreaching on the part of any person concerned;

(2) the proposed transaction is consistent with the policy of each registered investment company concerned, as recited in its registration statement and reports filed under this subchapter; and

(3) the proposed transaction is consistent with the general purposes of this subchapter.[17]

3. Consent by representatives of the entrustors: Let us view the New York corporate law[18]

(a) No contract or other transaction between a corporation and one or more of its directors, or between a corporation and any other corporation, firm, association or other entity in which one or more of its directors are directors or officers, or have a substantial financial interest, shall be either void or voidable for this reason alone, or by reason alone that such director or directors are present at the meeting of the board, or of a committee thereof, which approves such contract or transaction, or that his or their votes are counted for such purpose:

(1) If the material facts as to such director's interest in such contract or transaction and as to any such common directorship, officership, or financial interest are disclosed in good faith or known to the board or committee, and the board or committee approves such contract or transaction by a vote sufficient for such purpose without counting the vote of such interest director

or

(2) If the material facts as to such director's interest in such contract or transaction and as to any such common directorship, officership or financial interest are disclosed in good faith or known to the shareholders entitled to vote thereon, and such contract or transaction is approved by vote of such shareholders.

– – – – – – – – – – –

Discussion Topics

a. How and why does § 17 of the Investment Company Act of 1940 differ from the prohibition on conflicts of interest under the New York corporate law?

b. Do you agree with the differentiation?

– – – – – – – – – –

4. Views from Australia: on the effect of consent on fiduciary duties

The Federal Court of Australia dealt with the duties of Citigroup Global Markets Australia Pty Limited (Citigroup). As discussed in Chapter Two, the Federal Court held Citigroup is not a fiduciary to its client Toll because the parties agreed in the "mandate letter" that Citigroup would not act as fiduciary but as an "independent contractor."[19] The court did focus on the issue of whether the parties agreed to the status of Citigroup, and discussed the shaping of

---

17. Investment Company Act of 1940, § 17, 15 U.S.C. § 80a-17 (2000 & Supp. II 2002).
18. N.Y. BUS. CORP. LAW § 713 (McKinney 2003).

fiduciary duties, the relationship between the duties, the status of fiduciaries, and the meaning of Toll's informed consent. The Court wrote:

An Adviser May Have Fiduciary Obligations

Lehane J observed that advisers may, and often do, have fiduciary obligations.

A fiduciary relationship arises between a financial adviser and its client where the adviser holds itself out as an expert on financial matters and undertakes to perform a financial advisory role for the client.

The same principle will usually apply to financial advisers and corporate advisers. Each will owe fiduciary obligations to the client because each undertakes to act in the client's interests and not solely in its own interests. This is consistent with the principle stated by Mason J.

A person may be in a fiduciary relationship as to some aspects of the relationship but not others. Thus, a bank which gives its customers financial advice in the course of a transaction that includes an advance of money to the client may be in a fiduciary relationship with the client in its role as adviser. The bank may be expected to act in its own interests in ensuring the security for the loan but it will undertake fiduciary obligations to the client if it creates an expectation that it will advise in the customer's interests on the wisdom of the investment.

Vulnerability of the client is one of the indicia of the fiduciary relationship. But this would appear to flow from the special opportunity of the adviser to abuse the expectation of loyalty.

The Scope of the Fiduciary Obligations

The subject matter over which any fiduciary obligations will extend must be determined by the character of the venture or undertaking. This is to be ascertained from the terms of the agreement and the course of dealing between the parties.

The scope of the fiduciary duties will vary and is to be determined according to the nature of the relationship and the facts of the case.

The distinguishing or over-riding duty of a fiduciary is the obligation of undivided loyalty.

In Australia, the duty of loyalty is proscriptive rather than prescriptive in nature.

This duty embodies "the twin themes" of preventing undisclosed conflict of duty and interest (or of duty and duty), and of prohibiting misuse of the fiduciary position. . . .

"The distinguishing obligation of a fiduciary is the obligation of loyalty. The principal is entitled to the single-minded loyalty of his fiduciary. This core liability has several facets. A fiduciary must act in good faith; he must not make a profit out of his trust; he must not place himself in a position where his duty and his interest may conflict; he may not act for his own benefit or the benefit of a third person without the informed consent of his principal. This is not intended to be an exhaustive list, but it is sufficient to indicate the nature of fiduciary obligations. They are the defining characteristics of the fiduciary. As Dr. Finn pointed out in his classic work Fiduciary Obligations (1977), p. 2, he is not subject to fiduciary obligations because he is a fiduciary; it is because he is subject to them that he is a fiduciary."

Informed Consent

A person occupying a fiduciary position will be absolved from liability for what would otherwise be a breach of duty by obtaining a fully informed consent.

---

19.   Australian Sec. & Inv. Comm'n v. Citigroup Global Markets Australia Pty. Ltd., [2007] FCA 963 (June 28, 2007) (some citations omitted).

There is no precise formula for determining whether fully informed consent has been given; it will be a question of fact in all the circumstances of each case.

In order to be exonerated, a fiduciary must give full and frank disclosure of all material facts. Consent need not be given expressly; it may be implied in all the circumstances.

The sufficiency of disclosure may depend on the sophistication and intelligence of the person to whom disclosure is required to be made.

A Special Instance of Conflict

The authorities which deal with time charging by solicitors reveal a special instance where a solicitor has a conflict between his or her own interest in earning fees, and the duty to the client. A central question in these proceedings is whether the principles stated in the authorities on solicitors apply where the alleged fiduciary relationship is not one of the established categories.

A solicitor who wishes to enter into a time charging costs agreement with the client must make full disclosure to the client of all the implications of such an agreement.

This principle applies whether or not the costs agreement is made before the solicitor is instructed. The reason given in those authorities for the proposition that the solicitor must make full disclosure even before the contract of retainer is that the fiduciary relationship may arise before the solicitor is actually retained.

Mahoney JA said . . . that fiduciary obligations, including full disclosure, exist not only in the carrying out of an agreement already made between a solicitor and client "but also in respect of the making of it."

Mr Walker submitted that this observation by Mahoney JA indicates that the disclosure obligation applies to the making of a contract where a person who would otherwise be in a fiduciary relationship seeks to exclude fiduciary obligations in the terms of the contract.

However, I do not consider that this submission provides an answer to the conundrum presented by the apparent exclusion of the fiduciary relationship in the present case. There are two reasons for this.

First, the authorities dealing with solicitors' costs agreements have, as their foundation, the Court's inherent jurisdiction over solicitors and the fiduciary nature of the solicitor and client relationship as an established fiduciary category.

Indeed, . . . Mahoney JA specifically pointed out that a solicitor is in a fiduciary position vis-à-vis the client and/or in a position of influence. Hence the need for the solicitor to give the client advice that would enable a proper understanding of the operation and effect of a time based costs agreement.

This points to a limitation of the principle to those who fall within an established category of fiduciary relationship or, at very least, to those who carry fiduciary obligations before the execution of the contract.

The second reason why the principle is not applicable in the present proceedings is that ASIC's case was that the fiduciary relationship between Citigroup and Toll arose from the mandate letter. ASIC specifically eschewed any suggestion that the fiduciary relationship arose prior to the execution of the mandate letter on 8 August 2005.

It follows that there is no place in these proceedings for the application of the principle that a person who is already subject to fiduciary obligations must obtain the client's fully informed consent to the exclusion or modification of those obligations.

Chinese Walls

A favoured technique for dealing with conflicts of interest which arise from the carrying on of business by large financial institutions is the use of Chinese walls. They are widely used by institutions in Australia, the United Kingdom, the United States and Canada.

Chinese walls are a means of restricting the flow of information between different departments of the same organisation.

Lord Millett described Chinese walls as a technique for "managing" conflicts of interest. The use of this word is significant because it suggests that Chinese walls do not eliminate conflicts; they are no more than a technique for managing conflicts of interests which continue to exist.

Indeed, this is a distinction which is recognised in s 912A(1)(aa) of the *Corporations Act*. It imposes a duty upon a financial services licensee to have in place adequate arrangements for "the management of conflicts of interest". The statutory requirement is to be contrasted with the duty in equity of a fiduciary to eliminate or avoid conflicts. Of course, one way of managing conflicts would be to eliminate them but s 912A(1)(aa) does not require a licensee to take that step.

Support for the proposition that Chinese walls do not eliminate conflicts may be found in the *Law Commission Consultation Paper*. . . .

The duty of a fiduciary is one of undivided loyalty. The "no conflict" rule is based on practical considerations and recognises that the fiduciary's over-riding duty may be swayed by a conflicting interest. The existence of a Chinese wall cannot, of itself, overcome the prohibition against a fiduciary acting at the same time both for and against the same client. . . .

However, . . . a financial conglomerate may obtain protection against any allegation of breach of the duty of loyalty if the client consents to the company carrying on business using Chinese walls as part of its organisational structure. The extent of the duty of loyalty would then be determined according to the contractual arrangements between the parties.

The scope of any duty, and the extent to which the existence of Chinese walls may protect against an allegation of breach would be determined not only by the express terms of the contract but also by any implied terms.

Cases dealing with claims brought by former clients of solicitors and accountants to restrain the firm from acting against it show a willingness by the courts to accept the concept of Chinese walls as a means of quarantining information within the firm.

The relief sought in those cases turned upon the question of whether there was a risk of disclosure or misuse of confidential information. Lord Millett said . . . that there is no rule of law that Chinese walls are insufficient to eliminate the risk of disclosure but the Court should restrain the firm from acting unless satisfied that effective measures have been taken to prevent disclosure.

Thus, the question of whether Chinese walls are effective will be a question of fact in each case, although Lord Millett emphasised that the wall must be "an established part of the organisational structure", not created *ad hoc*. The same approach must be taken in determining whether Chinese walls constitute adequate arrangements for the management of conflicts of interest within s 912(1)(aa) of the *Corporations Act*.

Lord Millett drew upon the observations in the *Law Commission Consultation Paper* to illustrate the type of organisational arrangements which would ordinarily be effective. These are:

— the physical separation of departments to insulate them from each other;
— an educational programme, normally recurring, to emphasise the importance of not improperly or inadvertently divulging confidential information;
— strict and carefully defined procedures for dealing with situations where it is thought the wall should be crossed, and the maintaining of proper records where this occurs;
— monitoring by compliance officers of the effectiveness of the Chinese wall;
— disciplinary sanctions where there has been a breach of the wall.

Nevertheless, warnings have been sounded in other authorities about the risk of leakage through Chinese walls.

... it is not realistic to place reliance on such arrangements in relation to people with opportunities for daily contact over long periods, as wordless communication can take place inadvertently and without explicit expression, by attitudes, facial expression or even by avoiding people one is accustomed to see, even by people who sincerely intend to conform to control." ...

The decision of a Full Court in *ABCOS v Jones,* on which ASIC relied, does not support its argument. *ABCOS v Jones* was a case where a fiduciary, who was involved in a professional capacity in the establishment of a thoroughbred horse-breeding venture, sought to limit the extent of his fiduciary duty to give advice in respect of certain matters. It was not a case involving a contractual acknowledgment that there was no fiduciary relationship. It was held that that clause was ineffective in the absence of informed consent, however I do not consider that this case is authority for the general proposition asserted by ASIC. In my view, the case was one which was decided on its own facts.

It follows in my view that, with the exception of ASIC's first proposition, the eleven propositions put forward by ASIC do not apply to these proceedings. I do not consider that Citigroup was bound to obtain Toll's informed consent to the exclusion of the fiduciary relationship." ....

I do not need to deal with this issue because I have found that Citigroup was not obliged to obtain Toll's informed consent to the insertion in the mandate letter of the clause excluding a fiduciary relationship. Nevertheless, I will consider the issue briefly.

Citigroup relied on the Custodian & Nominee Appointments which were executed before and after the execution of the mandate letter on 8 August 2005. A form of appointment was executed by Toll Transport on 17 June 2005. It was re-executed by Toll Holdings, in the same terms, on 18 August 2005. Both of these forms of appointment contained express disclosures permitting Citigroup to trade on its own account in securities which it had been instructed to acquire on behalf of Toll.

It is true that the Custodian & Nominee Appointment and the mandate letter formed integral parts of the overall contractual relationship between Toll and Citigroup. However, it seems to me that the mandate letter expanded Citigroup's retainer and laid down the contractual terms which applied to Citigroup's particular role as an adviser on the Patrick takeover.

I accept, as ASIC submitted, that informed consent may be express or implied. But I do not consider, as Citigroup submitted, that if consent was necessary for the exclusion of the fiduciary relationship in the mandate letter, it was to be found in the Custodian & Nominee Appointment. In my view, the consent which was given to the principal trading and conflicts of interest in relation to the more limited retainer did not amount to an implied consent to an exclusion of the fiduciary relationship in the expanded retainer of the mandate letter.

This seems to me to follow from the approach taken in *ABCOS v Jones,* although that case turned on its own facts. Of course, all the facts and circumstances must be considered to see whether fully informed consent is to be implied. But consent given in the context of a limited retainer will not necessarily imply consent where the scope of the retainer is subsequently extended. Nevertheless, the question of informed consent has to be considered in light of Mr Chatfield's evidence, and in particular, the concessions he made in cross-examination.

Citigroup did not obtain Toll's express consent to trade on its own account in the context of its advisory role in the Patrick takeover, but in my view informed consent is to be implied from Toll's knowledge of Citigroup's structure and method of operations. Toll's experience and "core competency" in mergers and acquisitions must also be taken into account in determining this question.

Although Mr Chatfield would have preferred Citigroup not to trade on its own behalf, he knew that Citigroup was a large financial conglomerate which did not act exclusively for Toll. He also knew that Citigroup had a proprietary trading desk which could operate for the benefit of Citigroup so long as knowledge of Toll's confidential information did not leak to the proprietary traders.

It is true that Mr Chatfield did not turn his mind to the question of whether Citigroup would suspend its proprietary trading during the period of the mandate, but the effect of his evidence was that he accepted that Citigroup could trade for third parties or for itself, so long as it did not use Toll's confidential information.

Moreover, Mr Chatfield did not believe that Citigroup had any obligation to inform Toll if it engaged in proprietary trading, so long as there was no possibility of Citigroup using Toll's confidential information.

I do not consider that the circumstances of the present case are identical with those of *Kelly v Cooper* where the Privy Council held that there was to be implied in a contract with a real estate agent, a term that the agent was free to act for other principals selling similar properties. Such a term was implied because the practice is notorious and it would otherwise be impossible for the estate agents to perform their ordinary business functions. In my opinion, there is nothing in the relationship of investment banker/financial advisor and client which requires a conclusion that it is an inherent part of the business of investment banking for the banker to engage in trading in its client's target's shares. But, in my opinion, in the particular circumstances of this case, for the reasons given above, Toll had sufficient knowledge of the real possibility of proprietary trading by Citigroup to amount to informed consent.

C. Chapter Review

What would be the consequences of allowing people to waive any protection they might have under fiduciary law? Is there a rationale which would enable courts to follow the principle that all fiduciary duties are waivable, and yet strike down some waivers while upholding others? Where would courts find the principles that would enable them to reach such results? Compare and contrast the approach of the courts in Australia and the U.S. Are they different in announced principles? Or are they in truth different only in application? Which would you prefer?

Chapter Five
Fiduciaries as Arbitrators and Intermediaries

Introduction. Fiduciaries are often placed in the position of arbitrators among entrustors. Sometimes, the fiduciaries' posture involves a whiff of their own conflicting interests as well. Other times, they act merely to attempt to shield themselves from liability. Even so, the arbitrator's posture poses a difficult dilemma for fiduciaries. How should they mediate among conflicting claims of entrustors to whom the fiduciaries owe duties of loyalty and care? This dilemma is the focus of our discussion in this chapter. The question is: How should fiduciaries resolve the issues to reach a decision without violating the law and ethical behavior?

One guide that fiduciaries ought to follow is to clarify the various rights of the conflicted entrustors. In some situations, when these rights seem conflicting, they may not be. A careful examination of the rights of the contending parties can help deal with the demands of each entrustor. After all, entrustors are not entitled to demand that their fiduciaries would violate the law or the rights of others (so long as the entrustors have been informed or made aware about the rights of others).

The second guide for fiduciaries in the arbitrators' situation is an understanding of their own role. Often the role of the fiduciaries is to determine and execute an action under certain conditions that are spelled out or that are implied in the fiduciary's position.

A third and less comforting position is a situation in which the fiduciaries face a conflict among two entrustors with no guidelines from the directives of the entrustment on what to do. In such a case the fiduciaries may attempt to envision what the parties would have agreed upon had they been asked. Better still, the fiduciaries might resort to general principles of law and precedent, such as maximizing the fairness to each party, and the impact of the fiduciaries' decisions on the parties, as well as the general legal or financial implications. We examine and evaluate each of these guides.

A. Two Guides for Directors

In *Zahn v. Transamerica Corporation,* the role of the fiduciaries was to determine and execute an action under certain conditions that were spelled out in the corporate documents.[1] The directors of the company, Axton-Fisher, were nominees (appointees) of the majority shareholder—Transamerica Corporation. The financial structure of

Axton-Fisher was a bit complicated. The structure consisted of (1) preferred stock, which entitled the holders to a fixed amount plus a fixed interest rate, and to priority in the event of the corporation's bankruptcy. Then came (2) Class A shares, which had priority over Class B as follows. Class A shares entitled the holders to a fixed dividend, and an equal share as Class B of any additional dividend. Upon liquidation of the corporation Class A shares were entitled to receive "twice as much per share" of the value of the remaining assets as compared to Class B shares. Then came (3) Class B shares. They were entitled to vote unless Class A shares did not receive their dividends, in which case Class A and Class B shares had equal voting rights.

At this point the structure of the corporation becomes more complicated. The terms of Class A shares included the following conditions: The corporations' directors had the power to "call" Class A shares, and pay them the face amount of the shares, plus dividend due, if any. Within 60 days from the date of the call by the directors, however, they have a choice. They can accept the money. Or they can choose to convert each of their shares into one Class B share at a fixed price (which is the face amount of the shares).

What was the purpose of these provisions? We recognize that Class A shares have significant rights as compared to Class B Shares. They could be considered "expensive" capital especially for Class B shareholders. Presumably, the directors were expected to exercise their power to call Class A shares when the company is successful and could raise money on less onerous terms. It could sell Class B shares in the market to pay off Class A, or borrow at lower cost than these shares. That was the directors' duty to Class B shareholders. They should give Class A shareholders the option to convert to Class B shares, presumably at a price that was lower than the market price. That was the directors' duty to Class A shareholders.

But then came an unexpected twist. While the company was losing money, and owed Class A shares about $80 per share in face amount and arrears in dividend payments, the corporation's main asset was tobacco. During the Second World War the value of the tobacco rocketed. That presented a temptation for the majority shareholder— Transamerica Corporation. So long as Axton-Fisher was not liquidated the company was sitting on a pot of gold that none of the shareholders could reach. But if the corporation sold the tobacco, it would be awash with cash, and upon its dissolution it would distribute its assets to the shareholders. However, if it simply dissolved while owing Class A money, the corporation would have to pay Class A shareholders twice the amount that Class B shareholders would receive. There was, however, another option. The directors could call Class A shareholders and offer them $80. Had Class A shareholders known about the imminent dissolution of the company, they would have waited for the

---

1.   Zahn v. Transamerica Corp., 162 F.2d 36 (3d Cir. 1947).

dissolution and collected twice the amount that Class B would collect. If they were "called," however, and knew about the impending dissolution, they could convert their shares and receive not the $80 due but more—an equal share with the controlling majority of class B shareholders.

The directors were mostly employees of Transamerica Corporation that was Class B's controlling shareholder (as well as owner of some Class A shares). They followed the directives of Transamerica. The directors called Class A shares, and offered to pay the face amount and arrears (approximately $80). The directors knew that the corporation held valuable tobacco and of the plan to sell it and dissolve the company. Being beholden to their employer—the majority Class B shareholder—they did not disclose to the Class A shareholders the probability that the tobacco will be sold and the value of the tobacco and the possible dissolution of the company. These facts were not public knowledge. Most Class A shareholders were happy to receive the $80. They did not convert into Class B shares which would have netted them more.

The court held that the directors breached their fiduciary duties to the Class A shareholders. The question was what should Class A shareholders receive? Class A shareholders demanded double the amount of Class B shareholders. After all, the company was dissolved. The court did not grant them that. The majority shareholder had no duty to dissolve the company on these conditions. The directors could indeed "call" Class A. In this case would choose to convert to Class B shares.

That is what the court awarded them. Class A shareholders were awarded an equal amount as Class B shareholders (not double the amount), based on the assumption that had the Class A shareholders known of the plan to liquidate the company and the value of the tobacco, and had they known that the directors would not dissolve the corporation and allow them to collect double the Class B shareholders, they would have converted their shares to Class B shares.

There are a number of theories about the nature of corporations. One view of a corporation is that its owners are the shareholders, and that the directors are their representatives, who manage the corporation on their behalf. "This principal-agent model, in turn, has given rise to two recurring themes in the literature: First, that the central economic problem addressed by corporation law is reducing 'agency costs' by keeping directors and managers faithful to shareholders' interests; and second, that the primary goal of the public corporation is—or ought to be—maximizing shareholders' wealth."[2]

Another view is that all relationships within corporations and their various actors are contracts running from all actors to all actors. There is also a vision of the corporation as a "team." The guiding model of this

---

2.   Margaret M. Blair & Lynn A. Stout, *A Team Production Theory of Corporate Law*, 85 VA. L. REV. 247, 248-49 (1999).

view is the way corporations operate to achieve the goals of their business. This model leads to allowing the directors and officers of the corporation to consider the interests of members of the team. And there are those who argue that the directors should broaden their considerations to the community and the country's economy generally.[3] Depending on the views of the corporation, directors might find it necessary to establish priorities. It seems that they may consider other parties' interests, but a high priority in their decision still lies with the interests of the shareholders. If they show a decision that prioritized the shareholders' interests they have met their duties. In addition, in a conflict between two groups of shareholders, the interests of the majority are likely to guide the directors, so long as both majority and minority are treated equally.[4] After all, there is no justification for treating the minority better than the majority.

- - - - - - - - - - -

Discussion Topics

a. Consider *Zahn v. Transamerica,* discussed above. Which theory fits the decision?

b. What would be the decision if another theory were applied?

- - - - - - - - - - -

B. Trustees of Private Trusts as Mediators or Arbitrators

One conflict among trust beneficiaries arises when the trust has two types of beneficiaries: income beneficiaries and remaindermen. The income beneficiary is entitled to the income from trust investment. The remaindermen are entitled to the capital, once the income beneficiary dies. Usually income beneficiaries are wives of the trustor and remaindermen can be the children or charitable institutions and alike.

Suppose the trust requires the trustee to invest the assets in such a way as to create income for the trustor's wife after his death and after her death to pay the rest to his children. If the trustee invests the assets in more risky assets, he may provide the wife with higher benefits while risking the payment to the remaindermen, the children. Conversely, if the trustee invests the assets in a very conservative manner, the wife will receive little and the children may be assured of more. What should guide the trustee in making investments? Would it matter if the husband and wife during his lifetime lived in luxury or in modest conditions? Would it matter that the children are of age and can earn a living? What if the couple was estranged and lived separately?

Another type of conflict arose in *Rippey v. Denver United States National Bank,*[5] when some of the beneficiaries fought for the controlling shares of a newspaper while the other beneficiaries fought to realize the highest price for the share, and did not care who controlled the enterprise. In that case, the bank trustee sided with the

---

3.   *Id.*
4.   Sinclair Oil Corp. v. Levien, 280 A.2d 717 (Del. 1971).
5.   Rippey v. Denver United States Nat'l Bank, 273 F. Supp. 718, 723 (D. Colo. 1967).

daughter of the trustor that sought control of the paper against an "outsider" who was ready to pay a far higher price for the shares. The court held that the trustee bank failed in its duty to maximize the price for the controlling shares. The bank trustee had no business in siding with the daughter of the deceased. The court recognized that the bank was under pressure of "persuasion" by the daughter and representatives of the newspaper staff, but not coerced. Therefore, undue influence over the bank was not proven. The allegation of a conspiracy between the bank and the daughter was not proven. But the disregard of the higher potential offer was proven.

The court held:

1. The first duty of a fiduciary is to protect the interests of its beneficiaries. In selling an asset of the trust he must make every reasonable effort to sell at the best price obtainable. It is a violation of the fiduciary duty to sell at a private sale to one purchaser to the exclusion of another known interested purchaser who would foreseeably pay more. The Bank's failure to make any effort to contact Mr. Newhouse [the outside bidder for control of the newspaper] and its determined effort to sell to Miss Bonfils [the daughter of the deceased] without regard to consequences, which determination is evidenced by the exclusive shareholders' agreement together with its other actions which were designed to complete the sale without either contacting Mr. Newhouse or affording opportunity for Newhouse to make an offer, constituted a breach of trust.

2. The appropriate remedy is surcharge, rather than rescission. The plaintiffs have stated a preference for the remedy of rescission and resale.... [But the] request has been alternative.... Furthermore, the measure of relief which the plaintiffs are entitled to have in this type of breach is the difference between the sale price and the price which would have been obtained if the Bank had conducted a non-restricted sale. This measure can be best realized by awarding damages. If plaintiffs are correct in their predictions that Mr. Newhouse [potential buyer] would pay as much as $1,000.00 per share the trust would obtain a measure far in excess of that provided by law in the type of breach of trust here presented (non-fraudulent).

3. As noted above the proper measure of recovery in circumstances like the present is out of pocket loss as of the time of sale. There is substantial evidence that Mr. Newhouse would have paid the sum of $450.00 per share for the Agnes Reid Tammen shares if he had been given the opportunity to purchase them. Therefore, plaintiffs are entitled to recover for and on behalf of the Trust the sum of $150.00 per share the same being the difference between the $300.00 purchase price and the sum which probably would have been obtained had the Bank carried out its fiduciary duty.

4. Mr. Newhouse is not a party to this suit although his presence as a possible bidder has enhanced the sale price of the shares in question. He does not have any rights in this case either legal or equitable. Therefore, in fashioning the appropriate remedy and measure of recovery we cannot properly consider the interests which he seeks to advance. He alone would probably gain an advantage from the grant of rescission. This is not and cannot be a factor in our decision.[6]

[On the issue of breach of trust by the bank the court noted:]

We emphasize that this is not a self-dealing case, such as is often encountered in this area of the law. Thus the trustee Bank has not sought monetary benefit from extrinsically fraudulent acts or from acts which were beyond the authority granted in the will. Here the

---

6.   *Id.* at 734-35.

trustee had the legal power to sell at private sale and hence the alleged breach of trust arises, according to plaintiffs, from the failure of the trustee to exercise good judgment in conducting the sale and from its failure to act fairly and to follow accepted trust practices in seeking a sale which would yield the maximum price....

... The trustee may not subject his trust property to hazards which a man dealing with his own property might consider warranted if to do so would create danger to the trust estate.

We have examined the will to ascertain whether this general standard was modified....

The trustee is not authorized to exercise unlimited or absolute discretion in making a sale of trust property. Therefore, it cannot be said that it was intended that the trustee could operate beyond the bounds of prudent judgment or that he could act unreasonably. But even if the instrument had contained language granting absolute and uncontrolled discretion, it would not follow that the trustee could act recklessly or in *willful* abuse of discretion. In the instant case the action of the Bank in failing to test the market or to make a move toward [the potential interested party] created not a simple risk of injury and damage to the trust, but rather in our mind a high degree of probability that the interests of the beneficiaries would be damaged. Consequently even a grant of absolute discretion in the will would not have protected the Bank in this case. Nor can it be said that the grant of authority to sell at private sale increases the authority of the Bank or excuses it from exercising reasonable diligence. The same can be said of the authorization to sell without advertisement or notice. These powers assume that reasonable methods will be employed. Furthermore, the authorization to sell without consulting the beneficiaries does not modify the standard of care even though the trust regulates the information which the trustee must give. The trustee is not as a result of this excused from communicating information to the beneficiary which would permit him to enforce his rights under the trust or to prevent a breach of trust. Finally, the authorization to determine the price at which the property will be sold does not have the effect of allowing the trustee to sell at a price less than the best price obtainable. He must use reasonable diligence and judgment in selling trust property, and cannot expose the trust to a high degree of hazard of loss.

There are two exculpatory clauses in Article XV of the will which the Bank contends frees it from liability.... [However, one provision did] not limit the trustee liability for even negligence[.]...

The other clause goes further but it does not expressly apply to the misfeasance of a trustee in conducting a sale....

The Bank would have us broadly interpret this to apply to each and every act of the trustees. Plaintiffs argue that it should not be applied beyond the particular setting in which it appears. The intention of the decedent is not clear and the clause is not one in any event which commends itself to a court of equity whereby extensive or expansive application is invited. Our disposition is to hold that it was not intended to and does not excuse negligent conduct of a trustee in relationship to a sale....

The obligation of the trustee to exercise prudence is a species of his duty of loyalty to the beneficiaries. He owes his allegiance to the beneficiaries first. Other considerations are secondary. The accepted standard is declared in the famous opinion of the late Mr. Justice (then Judge) Cardozo in *Meinhard v. Salmon*[.] ... The Bank directors - (special committee members) made the error throughout the negotiations and the consummation of the sale that ordinary business mores governed. All of their testimony at the trial proceeded on the assumption that the practical standards of business conduct which they were accustomed to observe in their various enterprises were adequate in the present fiduciary sale. This, of course, is not the law. That which appears over-all practical is not sufficient in the trust area of the law. The courts do not now and never have allowed a compromise with this fundamental principle of loyalty.

As previously noted, the Bank had somewhat of a conflict in that it owed loyalty to Miss Bonfils in connection with the F. G. Bonfils Trust and also owed loyalty to the beneficiaries of the Tammen Trust. This was a difficult dilemma. This of itself does not however appear to be the factor which caused it to favor Miss Bonfils. Nor do we believe that the Bank was overpowered by the Post management group. And it does not appear that the factor of personal friendships (of directors) was the prevailing element. It seems more likely that the personality of Miss Bonfils who has been an important and benevolent figure on the Denver scene together with reluctance to disturb the status quo explains the unreasonable Bank actions.

It is, of course, obvious that a fiduciary cannot allow personal motives to interfere with the discharge of its fiduciary duties. It cannot favor the interests of third persons and subordinate the interests of its beneficiaries as it did here and this duty is not modified by the provision of Article IV of the will which allows the trustees to enter into stockholder agreements limiting the sale of stock when such agreements would, in the sole judgment of the trustee, "promote the best interest of said company or companies and the beneficiaries in this Article named, and procure the best price for said stock in the event of the sale thereof." While this provision allowed the trustee to consider the interests of the Post, it did not empower it to disregard the interests of its beneficiaries. In any kind of balancing of interests under this clause the beneficiaries' interests must prevail. . . .

[The court questioned the justification of the bank's creation of a restrictive contract which allowed it to ignore the potential buyer.]

In summary the reasons advanced for preferring the Bonfils group are not convincing and appear to be in the nature of afterthought. . . .

. . . One reason which the Bank does not mention and which probably entered into the Bank's thinking and that is that they had decided to favor Miss Bonfils and on that basis it was impractical and unconscionable to contact [the potential buyer] knowing that he had little or no chance to buy the stock. This, of course, goes back to the impropriety of making such a decision. We are of the opinion that the reasons given are after the fact rationalizatons [sic]. They are not convincing.

The law is clear that the Trustee's duty of loyalty and of reasonable care dictate that he must seek to obtain the best price obtainable for the property which he is selling. . . .

We are aware that the duty to seek competition is but an application of the broader "prudent man" rule and that there will be variations depending on the circumstances. The Bank urges that the peculiar facts of the case at bar fully justify their decision not to seek competitive bidding. . . .

It is true as the Bank contends that [some] cases generally uphold the decision of the trustee to sell to a particular purchaser. However, the circumstances in each of these cases are quite different from the circumstances that are here presented in that in every one of them except [one] there was not an available purchaser who was ignored as in the present case. . . .

. . . We have concluded that even without this the Bank's conduct was culpable.[7]

Problem

John, Bob and Penny Smith were the children of Caleb Smith who died in 1969 and left them a lumberyard business, Smith's Lumber. Most of the estate consisted of shares of the corporation that owned

---

7.   *Id.* at 735-42 (footnotes and citations omitted).

Smith's Lumber. Caleb Smith left the shares of Smith's Lumber in equal shares to the two sons, John and Bob, who were operating the corporation. He left Penny the dividends to be distributed by Smith's Lumber. John and Bob operated the business and never declared a dividend. Neither did Smith's Lumber ever declare dividends in Caleb's life. From 1969 to 1996, the two sons operated the business, paid themselves salaries but never paid a dividend. So Penny got nothing. When she demanded payment, her brothers told her that the business required reinvestment and they did not have enough funds to spare.

Note that in *Dodge v. Ford Motor Company,*[8] the court held that the directors of a corporation have the discretion with respect to the declaration and amount of dividends the corporation would pay shareholders, subject to avoiding conflicts of interest and subject to a plan to reinvest the assets for the benefit of the corporation. Penny sues John and Bob for dividends under her father's will.

– – – – – – – – – – -

Discussion Topics

a. How should Penny argue her case? What facts should she assert and have to prove?

b. What would the brothers argue?

c. Which law would apply to the case?

d. What should be the court's decision?

– – – – – – – – – – -

Problem

Immense Bank is a publicly held corporation held by more than a million shareholders. Immense Bank has a trust department that manages trust funds of over $1 billion and fiduciaries that number more than 10,000. These trust funds are pooled and invested together in what is called "common trust funds." These funds are regulated by the Comptroller of the Currency's Rule 9.18. Until recently, Immense Bank was not allowed to be an adviser to mutual funds and manage mutual funds. Since 1996, it has been allowed to do so. Now the Bank has the opportunity to convert the common trust funds into mutual funds by liquidating the common trust funds and transferring the proceeds to buy for each trust shares in its mutual fund. One of the reasons for the conversion is that the Bank can then offer the mutual fund shares to non-trust funds. The other is that, because the regulatory systems differ, the Bank can collect more charges through mutual funds than through the common trust funds. The beneficiaries have no power over the trustee Bank. However, before the Bank can convert the trust funds into mutual funds, the Bank would notify the beneficiaries and ask for their consent.

---

8.   Dodge v. Ford Motor Co., 170 N.W. 668 (Mich. 1919).

- - - - - - - - - - - -

Discussion Topics

a. To whom does Bank owe a fiduciary duty? To its shareholders or to the trust beneficiaries?

b. If the bank owes a fiduciary to both, is the Bank allowed to increase the profits of the bank at the expense of the beneficiaries?

c. If the bank is not allowed to increase its profits, what directives would you give the bank management?

- - - - - - - - - - - -

Discussion Topics

a. An attorney receives two cases. One involves $5,000; the other—$500,000. Both cases deal with similar issues requiring a similar investment of time. May the attorney use the research done on one case to prepare the other? How should the attorney allocate expenses and fees?

b. A trustee agrees with a money market fund to invest trust funds and receives part of the fees, which the fund would charge. The trust investment would be more or less similar to that of the fund, but the trustee would benefit by this arrangement. How should the parties effectuate the deal?

c. Suppose the majority shareholder is not interested in dividends because he has sufficient income and falls into a high tax-paying bracket, but the minority shareholder is in a different position and needs the dividends. Should the directors declare a dividend? What if the majority shareholder plans to force the minority shareholder to sell his stock at a lower price and the directors decide not to pay any dividends? In many cases, the non-payment of dividends will reduce the market value of the minority's stock especially if there is a "thin" market for the shares and buyers would depend on a constant payment of dividends. If the rule is fair treatment of all shareholders, how should the directors decide the issues?

d. Does fair treatment mean equal treatment?

- - - - - - - - - - - -

C. Duty to the Public and to the Professional Community

In *Pinsker v. Pacific Coast Society of Orthodontists,* the court examined an issue that we have met before, that is, the fiduciary duties of an organization that has the power to accept or reject professionals.[9] In this case, the petitioner was an orthodontist. The court observed that, because of the social importance of these fiduciaries' services their organization owes expanded duties that are not limited to their self-interests. That means that the organizations of these service givers are fiduciaries not only to their members but to the public as well. The organizations must take the public's needs and interests into

---

9. Pinsker v. Pac. Coast Soc'y of Orthodontists, 526 P.2d 253 (Cal. 1974).

consideration in making decisions on whether to admit or reject applicants. The balancing consideration would require the organizations to reject unqualified applicants but to accept qualified applicants even if they do not meet the educational or other conditions of the association. These conditions cannot be final without considering the interests of the public.

A similar permission (although not a requirement) to consider the interests of communities has appeared in the context of corporate law. A number of jurisdictions allowed the directors of corporations to consider in their decisions about the future of the corporations (and takeover proposals) the interests of the communities. That enabled the directors to deny and fight against proposed takeovers which might have benefited the shareholders but harmed at least short-term the communities around which the corporate enterprises were located.[10] The fact that the directors may have had identity of interest with the community would not in this case pose a shadow of conflicts of interest on their decision. Not everyone agrees with this approach, however. In addition to questioning the economic wisdom of the policy, such a permission to consider the communities undermines the accountability of the directors to the shareholders. The issue is far from clear and the debate continues.

D. When Physicians Recognize Incompetent or Unethical Colleagues

With very few exceptions, people are not required to avoid negligent behavior by others. Fiduciaries, however, may be subject to such duties. E. Haavi Morreim has argued that physicians have a responsibility to expose unethical or incompetent colleagues.[11] The physician should assess the colleague's performance according to a number of criteria: quality of performance and moral wrong. On the quality side, there are a number of degrees. The accident may be entirely unanticipated (e.g., a sudden power failure). The physician cannot be responsible for such an accident. Or the accident may be due to a reasonable decision that was very unlikely to turn out badly, but did, such as administering a medicine to a patient with no history of allergic reaction to this drug. In that case, however, the physician could have tested the patient's propensity to allergy, but if there were no reasons to do that the physician need not have done that. Further, there are cases in which the balance between benefits and risks of treatment are unclear. These may be subject to disagreement among

---

10.   Lawrence E. Mitchell, *A Theoretical and Practical Framework for Enforcing Corporate Constituency Statutes,* 70 TEX. L. REV. 579 (1992).
11.   E. Haavi Morreim, *Am I My Brother's Warden? Responding to the Unethical or Incompetent Colleague,* HASTINGS CENTER REP., May 1993, at 19, LEXIS, News Library, Arcnews File. For the question of whether one physician owes a duty to act in light of the incompetence of another, *see* Frances H. Miller, *Doctors in the Executive Suite: Should the U.S. and U.K. Be Putting M.D. Licensure at Risk for Shortfalls in Institutional Quality of Care?,* 31 J. HEALTH L. 217 (1998) (a story of an incompetent surgeon who had a horrendous history of death during surgery yet was not removed for many years, and the issue of the duties of his superiors who managed the hospital).

good physicians. In such a case, the physician may have acted with care.

If a physician made a poor but not horribly bad judgment or exercised questionable skill, such as not recognizing something obvious on an X-ray, the behavior shows questionable skills, and the failure of care is more serious. The most serious case is an outrageous violation of required care, such as operating on the wrong leg.

A fundamental distinction should be made between accidents due to ignorance or even insensitivity and deliberate and morally wrong actions. A physician should consider to what extent the colleague's conduct violated accepted ethical standards of medicine and the medical community. These violations may be intrinsically wrong, regardless of the likelihood of harm, such as misuse of placebos or lying to a patient. But in less egregious situations, the harm must be weighed as well.

In responding to a colleague, the physician should first determine the nature of the problem. If the problem is ignorance, the response is education. If the problem is misguided ethics, the response may be moral education. If the problem is a morally wrong conduct, the response may be retribution.

If unsure of another physician's competence, a physician should discuss the matter with other trusted colleagues, without violating the physician's anonymity, and apprise colleagues of the situation. But in no case may a physician ignore the problem, or pass the problem on by recommending the colleague to another employer.

Initially it may be best for the physician to act alone. But sometimes it may be appropriate to seek help from a colleague. Some situations may require a formal group action. In the latter case, the physician must consider which group to address (e.g., a hospital committee). More serious misconduct should be reported to medical boards and/or legal authorities. In general, the author suggests that the profession should move from a "punitive approach" to a "continuous improvement" approach, except for very incompetent or unethical physicians.[12]

- - - - - - - - - - - -

Discussion Topics

a. What is your opinion of the issues described above: (i) as the patient who became an invalid and whose life was shortened by a negligent performance of a physician's operation? (ii) as a physician who is the physician's colleague? (iii) as the head of the physicians' association in which the physician works? (iv) as the lawyer for the patient?

b. Under what circumstances would you care about the degree of malfeasance of the physician?

---

12.   E. Haavi Morreim, *Am I My Brother's Warden? Responding to the Unethical or Incompetent Colleague*, HASTINGS CENTER REP., May 1993, at 19, LEXIS, News Library, Arcnews File.

c. What duties should the law impose on the colleague who discovered the negligence or incompetence of another colleague?

— - — — — — — — — — - -

E. Employee Whistle-Blowers and Fiduciary Duties

Employees who uncover or are aware of violations of the law in their organizations are not required to "blow the whistle" and report to the authorities unless they are coerced into taking part in the illegal activities. But employees perform a public service if they do inform the authorities of such illegal activities. After all, employees are more likely to have the information and the evidence, or know where it can be found. This knowledge is very valuable especially in large corporations.

"The usefulness of private arrangements and legal rules for the maintenance and promotion of social and economic relationships depends, in great part, on their effective enforcement. Enforcement, however, is not possible unless violations are first detected. It therefore seems critical to consider the ability and motivation of legal actors to monitor each other's behavior." [13]

At the same time, whistle-blowing is not necessarily without problems. First, an employee that holds or has access to insider information is in almost all cases a fiduciary to whom the information is entrusted. Knowing about illegal activities, the employee faces conflicting duties. One is to the employer. The other is to society.

Assume the following facts.

The US division of a diversified global manufacturing company based in London has been losing money over the past fiscal year. Rumors are rampant US operations may be shut down. Alice and Bob are data analysts in the finance department for US operations and are responsible for consolidating data from all US operations. The organization has recently been restructured so that product lines report to global product leadership while country leaders report to regional leadership. These changes have not been well-received by the workforce. Besides significantly increasing the number of reports that Alice and Bob's group need to generate, the matrix structure has created confusion as to who is ultimately responsible for making key business decisions. It seems that everything is being decided by committee.

The finance team is finding that that they spend hours each day reformatting the same data to meet the needs of the various leadership channels. Moreover, when Bob and Alice request sales and inventory data from multiple sites around the country, the local analysts are beginning to resist turning over their data. They let Alice and Bob know their requests are getting ridiculous, especially since they no longer formally report to them. This is causing tension among the finance analysts since the data they now require to do their job is coming from field operations that are not accountable to them.

Several members of the finance team, including Bob and Alice, have been letting their managers know that the situation is becoming untenable. However, they have not been given much encouragement that the situation will improve anytime soon.

---

13.   Saul Levmore, *Monitors and Freeriders in Commercial and Corporate Settings*, 92 YALE L.J. 49, 49 (1982).

Then things came to a boiling point. After submitting a consolidated US sales report, Bob was asked by London to find more revenue from a specific division. A lengthy series of often heated discussions ensued where Bob tried to enlist the support of Kim, his direct supervisor, to convince London that there wasn't any additional data that wasn't already in his report and there was no way he could "find" more revenue. Kim was not able to provide any support and in fact, told Bob to clear his plate of other work so as to devote the necessary time to meet London's request. Data world-wide, from analysts like Bob, is being consolidated in London to prepare for the annual financial statements.

After a week or so, the urgency seemed to suddenly dissipate and the requests stopped. Alice asked Bob what had happened but he didn't want to talk about it. Alice began to suspect that Bob had made some questionable decisions on how to account for certain items in order to meet the requests for greater revenue. When she asks him about it, he vehemently denies it and shows her the reports. She can't find any fault with them but her instincts tell her there's a problem somewhere.

Alice requests a meeting with Marc, the head of the department. When she arrives, Marc immediately starts talking about their lack of staffing. Marc lets her know in no uncertain terms that she, Kim, and Bob are going to have to work even harder to keep up with the demands from the main office. Alice isn't even given the chance to frame her concern before Marc rushes her out of the office so he won't be late for a meeting.

At lunch, Alice tells Carole, a colleague in the training department, about her difficulties with Marc and her concerns about Bob. Carole points out a tent card on the lunch room table that publicizes the new company helpline. Carole suggests Alice call to register her concerns, but Alice says she doubts the helpline is truly anonymous. She's certain Marc will hear about it if she calls.

Don and Elsa, data analysts in Alice's group, join Alice and Carole at lunch, and Alice fills them in. Unlike Carole, they recommend that Alice keep her suspicions and her conflict with Marc to herself. If Bob is indeed running inaccurate reports and he's fired, it won't change anything for the company but their work load will increase. And if the compliance department hears of the situation, the whole team might get a new set of procedures which would require more training, more time and even more resistance from the field offices.[14]

－ － － － － － － － － -

Discussion Topics

a. Can the CFO rely on data being generated from the field?

b. What factors encourage and discourage both the reporting of accurate data as well as the reporting of concerns of inaccurate data being relied on higher up in the organization?

c. What are preventative steps that could be taken?

d. What are the fiduciary duties of an employee that suspects or discovers wrongful actions in the employer's operations? Is disclosure of these wrongful acts a violation of the employee's fiduciary duties?

－ － － － － － － － － -

---

14. David Gebler, Culture Risk Case Study (2007) (Draft) (on file with author). Reproduced with the author's permission.

F. Chapter Review

How can fiduciaries that owe duties to numerous parties with different interests determine any issue that concerns both beneficiaries? Should the fiduciaries determine in advance who would have the priority among the fiduciaries? Or what principles the fiduciaries should use to determine the priority? Or should the fiduciaries determine the principles by which they would prefer the interests of one group of beneficiaries over another? Or should they avoid this line of analysis and reach their decision by analyzing the wishes of those who established the fiduciary relationships in the first place, be they the trustees, the patients, or the promoters of the corporation?

Chapter Six
Why View Fiduciary Law as a Separate Category?

A. Should Categories Matter?

1. Humans need to categorize information

"Categories are important, efficient, and inevitable. Unlike computers, our brain is unable to store and remember many details. Humans need to organize details, and usually do so in related groups and hierarchies. For this reason, theories, paradigms, categories and classifications as well as professional disciplines are crucial to memory and understanding. Not surprisingly, categories of a discipline have been referred to as 'a table of contents.'"[1] We cannot do without categories because we cannot find the items we need in unorganized data, and we cannot organize data without categories. A category is a heading under which we file related legal data; it is the key to the book of rules that applies to a particular relationship.

Studies have shown that humans retain memory in a top-down fashion. The brain organizes related details in categories. We can search for an item by resorting to the heading of the category. We also search for details by a bottom-up movement, when we combine details. An explanation between bottom-up and top-down categorization is instructive. "[T]op-down" processing relies on prior experience. It is distinguished from "bottom-up" (data-driven) processing which govern "memory-based effects that clearly go beyond those implicated in immediate perception, effects of elaboration, question answering, comprehension of complex passages, etc."[2]

---

1.   Tamar Frankel & Joshua Getzler, *Fiduciary Law* (Draft) (on file with the author) (citing Fulvio Cortese et al., *Back to Government? The Pluralistic Deficit in the Decisionmaking Processes and Before the Courts*, 12 IND. J. GLOBAL LEG. STUD. 409, 409 (2005); John Henry Schlegel, *From High in the Paper Tower, an Essay on von Humboldt's University*, 52 BUFFALO L. REV. 865, 881 (2004) ("disciplines . . . provide useful categories and clearly, thought is impossible without categories")). For the definition of category, *see* MERRIAM-WEBSTER'S COLLEGIATE DICTIONARY 180 (10th ed. 1999) ("any of several fundamental and distinct classes to which entities or concepts belong;" "a division within a system of classification"). To classify is defined as "to assign . . . to a category." *Id.* at 212.
2.   *Id.* (citing Marcia K. Johnson & William Hirst, *MEM: Memory Subsystems as Processes, in* THEORIES OF MEMORY 241, 260 (Alan F. Collins et al. eds., 1993)) (stating that "top-down" processing relies on prior experience; distinguishing from "bottom-up" (data-driven) processing; stating that top-down processes "govern memory-based effects that clearly go beyond those implicated in immediate perception, effects of elaboration, question answering, comprehension of complex passages, etc.") (citation omitted).

It seems that bottom-up categories are case-based and experience-based generalizations. In United States law, categories "are often generated by events, not by scholars, and can always be abolished by those same events."[3] One author suggested that categories "should be tentative, relational, and unstable," but that in law, "abstraction and 'frozen' categories are the norm."[4] The emphasis on a bottom-up generalization may be responsible for the method by which American lawyers and judges often reason from analogy.[5] This method is distinguished in law from disciplines that rely on "top-down" theories.[6]

Top-down categories are based on generalizations under which details or cases are grouped. Perhaps one difference between the United States and the United Kingdom on one hand, and the European Community laws' ways of thinking on the other hand, is derived from this distinction. Generally, United States law is organized in a "bottom-up" method and United Kingdom law is organized to a greater extent in a "top-down" method, while the European Union law is organized almost uniformly in a "top-down" method.

The grouping of items in the brain is instructive. Items can belong to more than one category. For example, fruit is a category, and so is color. If we search for apple, we search in the fruit category. But if our search is more refined, seeking a red apple, then we resort to the category of fruit as well as to the category of color to find our red apple.

Categories can signal the objectives and values of those who establish the categories and those who search for information. Categories can tell us about the frequency with which we focus on certain concepts or ways of behavior. The more often the concepts and ways of behavior are discussed and used, the more entrenched is the category that contains them. In contrast, "[w]hen meanings are distinct, distributions must be autonomous."[7]

The way categories are named has a similar effect. In our example, if searchers care only or mainly for fruit rather than color, a general category of fruit would suffice. If the searchers care about any color, the general category of color would suffice. The more searchers value the combined apple and red, the more they use the combined item, the more likely the searchers will resort to the two categories. If the value and use of the combination is truly great, searchers might create a special category for red apple as distinct from fruits in general and color in general. In sum, categories demonstrate a form of organizing

---

3.   Edward L. Rubin, *Law and the Methology of Law*, 1997 Wis. L. Rev. 521, 536 (1997).

4.   Ruth Colker, *Abortion and Violence*, 1 Wm. & Mary J. of Women & L. 93, 97 (1994).

5.   Cass R. Sunstein, *On Analogical Reasoning*, 106 Harv. L. Rev. 741, 746 (1993).

6.   William S. Blatt, *Interpretive Communities: The Missing Element in Statutory Interpretation*, 95 Nw. U. L. Rev. 629, 643 (2001). *See also* George M. Cohen, Comment, *Posnerian Jurisprudence and Economic Analysis of Law:* The View from the Bench, 133 U. Pa. L. Rev. 1117, 1164 (1985) (contrasting top-down approach of economics with bottom-up approach of jurisprudence).

7.   Michael Walzer, Spheres of Justice: A Defense of Pluralism and Equality 10 (1983).

information as well as the value and importance that we assign to particular items and names.

2. Legal categories

Because one of the main objectives of the law is to address social problems, legal categories are focused on problems and their reduction or elimination. Combining legal categories may create internal conflicts among objectives and details. For example, a contract would view the entrustment of property as an exchange in which the rights to the property are vested in the fiduciary in exchange for a promise or an obligation to act in a certain way, including the return of the property after the service is completed. That view assimilates a fiduciary trust relationship to a debt. If the property is not returned in violation of the promise, contract remedies will apply. A classification of the relationship as fiduciary will continue to treat the property in the hands of the fiduciary as the entrustor's property. A violation of fiduciary duties will be deemed embezzlement and a breach of trust; a worse kind of theft. Fiduciary law addresses certain human relationships that affect society. If the law is earmarked as a separate category, the importance of the problems it addresses is highlighted. If the problems are devalued and considered unimportant, no category of fiduciary law need arise.

Legal categories are crucial to a smooth functioning law, especially in a society with a complex economy, diverse business relationships and numerous rules that govern them. Categories reduce our information costs of determining applicable law. They facilitate a multi-tier analysis. We determine first which category applies to a relationship and then draw on the rules in the category, thereby narrowing the choices of applicable rules and remedies. A category provides a general description of the rules it contains, in terms of their substance, type (coercive or permissive) and number. For example, the contract category contains few prohibitory and mandatory rules and fewer default rules. The parties must specify most of the rules that govern their relationship. In contrast, the fiduciary category contains more prohibitory and mandatory rules and a substantial number of default rules.

Categories signify what legal enforcement and remedies are available to parties in a particular relationship, for example, by generally defining the role of the courts and extent of their discretion in interfering in the parties' relationship. Thus, courts exercise greater self-restraint in interfering in contracts than they do in interfering in fiduciary relationships.

Further, categories paint an image of the relationship they govern (e.g., contract v. fiduciary). For example, in contract, parties are warned to take care of themselves. In fiduciary relationships, parties are assured of a legal right to rely on the honesty of the other party to the relationship. Thus, categories reduce peoples' information costs in finding the law.

3. Who has the power to categorize relationships?

Under our current system, while parties can agree on any lawful terms in their relationships, they do not determine the legal category of their relationship. The power to categorize a relationship (i.e., whether it is partnership or contract, loan, agency or trust) vests in the courts and the legislatures, regardless of how the parties characterized it.[8] For example, even if a party specifies in its contract that it is not a fiduciary, a court can determine that it is a fiduciary.

Arguably, fiduciary rules are default rules. Therefore, if the parties "contract out" of fiduciary rules, they contract out of the fiduciary category and thereby change the legal classification of their relationship. Yet, that is not necessarily valid. The courts have the last word as far as legal reclassifying of relationships go. Some hybrid relationships may be classified as sales and contracts, notwithstanding even the use of the word "trust" by the parties.[9]

There are reasons for limiting the parties' ability to classify their relationships. The parties' categories may result in disorganized legal material and lack of uniformity. Further, if parties' ability to classify their relationship is not limited, the legal system would be designed in accordance with the parties' interests rather than the interest of developing a coherent legal system as a whole. Some people might applaud this result; others may lament it. Before taking such a drastic change in our jurisprudence, however, its consequences should be further studied.

4. Placing the transaction into the right category

In *Martin v. Peyton,*[10] discussed earlier in Chapter Two, the issue before the courts was whether the parties' arrangement framed as a loan was in fact a partnership:

In the spring of 1921 the firm of K. N. & K. found itself in financial difficulties. John R. Hall was one of the partners. He was a friend of Mr. Peyton. From him he obtained the loan of almost $ 500,000 of Liberty bonds, which K. N. & K. might use as collateral to secure bank advances. This, however, was not sufficient. The firm and its members had engaged in unwise speculations, and it was deeply involved. Mr. Hall was also intimately acquainted

---

8.   Courts may consider the parties' view of the legal category that governs their relationship, and in most cases the category is non-controversial. However, in borderline cases, the courts overrule the parties' view and classify the relationship in light of the actual terms and sometimes the behavior of the parties.

9.   *See, e.g.,* Banco Espanol de Credito v. Security Pac. Nat'l Bank, 973 F.2d 51, 53 (2d Cir. 1992); First Citizens Fed. Sav. & Loan Ass'n v. Worthen Bank & Trust Co., N.A., 919 F.2d 510 (9th Cir. 1990) (agreement by the lead bank to hold notes and any collateral in trust for the participants who bought parts of the loans, did not in and by itself result in a fiduciary relationship. The relationship here will not be inferred "absent unequivocal contractual language similar to that discussed in [another case]"); Corestates Bank, N.A. v. Signet Bank, 1996 U.S. Dist. LEXIS 12673 (E.D. Pa. Aug. 23, 1996) (sale of loan participations. Contract allocated the risk of fraud involving the loans to the buyers. The assignment was without recourse and the buyers of the participations provided a warranty that relieved the lead bank of liability). For a further discussion *see* 2 TAMAR FRANKEL, SECURITIZATION § 18.3 (2d ed. 2006). For a discussion of whether courts should defer to parties' legal classification of their relationship, *see* Tamar Frankel, *Fiduciary Duties as Default Rules,* 74 OR. L. REV. 1209, 1246-51 (1995).

10.   Martin v. Peyton, 158 N.E. 77 (N.Y. 1927) (citations omitted).

with George W. Perkins, Jr., and with Edward W. Freeman. He also knew Mrs. Peyton and Mrs. Perkins and Mrs. Freeman. All were anxious to help him. He, therefore, representing K. N. & K., entered into negotiations with them. While they were pending a proposition was made that Mr. Peyton, Mr. Perkins and Mr. Freeman or some of them should become partners. It met a decided refusal. Finally an agreement was reached. It is expressed in three documents, executed on the same day, all a part of the one transaction. They were drawn with care and are unambiguous. We shall refer to them as "the agreement," "the indenture" and "the option."

We have no doubt as to their general purpose. The respondents were to loan K. N. & K. $ 2,500,000 worth of liquid securities, which were to be returned to them on or before April 15, 1923. The firm might hypothecate them to secure loans totalling (sic) $ 2,000,000, using the proceeds as its business necessities required. To insure respondents against loss K. N. & K. were to turn over to them a large number of their own securities which may have been valuable, but which were of so speculative a nature that they could not be used as collateral for bank loans. In compensation for the loan the respondents were to receive 40 per cent of the profits of the firm until the return was made, not exceeding, however, $ 500,000 and not less than $ 100,000. Merely because the transaction involved the transfer of securities and not of cash does not prevent its being a loan . . . . The respondents also were given an option to join the firm if they or any of them expressed a desire to do so before June 4, 1923.

Many other detailed agreements are contained in the papers. Are they such as may be properly inserted to protect the lenders? Or do they go further? Whatever their purpose, did they in truth associate the respondents with the firm so that they and it together thereafter carried on as co-owners a business for profit? The answer depends upon an analysis of these various provisions.

As representing the lenders, Mr. Peyton and Mr. Freeman are called "trustees." The loaned securities when used as collateral are not to be mingled with other securities of K. N. & K., and the trustees at all times are to be kept informed of all transactions affecting them. To them shall be paid all dividends and income accruing therefrom. They may also substitute for any of the securities loaned securities of equal value. With their consent the firm may sell any of its securities held by the respondents, the proceeds to go, however, to the trustees. In other similar ways the trustees may deal with these same securities, but the securities loaned shall always be sufficient in value to permit of their hypothecation for $ 2,000,000. If they rise in price the excess may be withdrawn by the defendants. If they fall they shall make good the deficiency.

So far there is no hint that the transaction is not a loan of securities with a provision for compensation. Later a somewhat closer connection with the firm appears. Until the securities are returned the directing management of the firm is to be in the hands of John R. Hall, and his life is to be insured for $ 1,000,000, and the policies are to be assigned as further collateral security to the trustees. These requirements are not unnatural. Hall was the one known and trusted by the defendants. Their acquaintance with the other members of the firm was of the slightest. These others had brought an old and established business to the verge of bankruptcy. As the respondents knew, they also had engaged in unsafe speculation. The respondents were about to loan $ 2,500,000 of good securities. As collateral they were to receive others of problematical value. What they required seems but ordinary caution. Nor does it imply an association in the business.

The trustees are to be kept advised as to the conduct of the business and consulted as to important matters. They may inspect the firm books and are entitled to any information they think important. Finally they may veto any business they think highly speculative or injurious. Again we hold this but a proper precaution to safeguard the loan. The trustees may not initiate any transaction as a partner may do. They may not bind the firm by any action of their own. Under the circumstances the safety of the loan depended upon the business success of K. N. & K. This success was likely to be compromised by the inclination of its members to engage in speculation. No longer, if the respondents were to be protected, should it be allowed. The trustees, therefore, might prohibit it, and that their prohibition might be effective, information was to be furnished them. Not dissimilar agreements have been held proper to guard the interests of the lender.

As further security each member of K. N. & K. is to assign to the trustees their interest in the firm. No loan by the firm to any member is permitted and the amount each may draw is fixed. No other distribution of profits is to be made. So that realized profits may be calculated the existing capital is stated to be $ 700,000, and profits are to be realized as promptly as good business practice will permit. In case the trustees think this is not done, the question is left to them and to Mr. Hall, and if they differ then to an arbitrator. There is no obligation that the firm shall continue the business. It may dissolve at any time. Again we conclude there is nothing here not properly adapted to secure the interest of the respondents as lenders. If their compensation is dependent on a percentage of the profits still provision must be made to define what these profits shall be.

The "indenture" is substantially a mortgage of the collateral delivered by K. N. & K. to the trustees to secure the performance of the "agreement." It certainly does not strengthen the claim that the respondents were partners.

Finally we have the "option." It permits the respondents or any of them or their assignees or nominees to enter the firm at a later date if they desire to do so by buying 50 per cent or less of the interests therein of all or any of the members at a stated price. Or a corporation may, if the respondents and the members agree, be formed in place of the firm. Meanwhile, apparently with the design of protecting the firm business against improper or ill-judged action which might render the option valueless, each member of the firm is to place his resignation in the hands of Mr. Hall. If at any time he and the trustees agree that such resignation should be accepted, that member shall then retire, receiving the value of his interest calculated as of the date of such retirement.

This last provision is somewhat unusual, yet it is not enough in itself to show that on June 4, 1921, a present partnership was created nor taking these various papers as a whole do we reach such a result. It is quite true that even if one or two or three like provisions contained in such a contract do not require this conclusion, yet it is also true that when taken together a point may come where stipulations immaterial separately cover so wide a field that we should hold a partnership exists. As in other branches of the law a question of degree is often the determining factor. Here that point has not been reached. The judgment appealed from should be affirmed, with costs.[11]

- - — — — — — — — — -

Discussion Topics

a. Why did the lenders call themselves trustees? Assuming they aimed at getting as much information as possible about the firm's activities and control over the securities they were lending, what advantage did they gain in the position of a trustee? Could they gain the same information as lenders? If the lenders were trustees, who are fiduciaries, why did the court hold that they were not partners and not fiduciaries? What is the difference between (i) holding a security

---

11.   *Id.*

interest in an asset (as a lender); (ii) owning the assets as owner; and (iii) owning an asset as a trustee?

b. Why does the court emphasize that there was "no obligation that the firm shall continue the business. It may dissolve at any time"?

c. The court makes it clear that it is not enough for the parties to state that no partnership has been created by the contract. Why not? At the same time, the court suggests that such a statement is nonetheless a fact to be considered. Why? What are the implications of your conclusions to the understanding of the legal system? Should the parties rather than the courts determine the issue of classification? May parties write a contract and state: "This agreement shall be governed by the law of contracts and not by fiduciary law"?

d. If the firm K. N. & K were in a solid financial condition, would the court have come to a different conclusion?

e. Examine the nature of the actors. What do you think of their behavior? Did Hall behave correctly? To whom was he more committed? How would another trustee have behaved? Why did the lenders not seek another "trustee"?

f. What was the role of personal trust in this case? Suppose the parties were strangers to each other. How would the transaction be accomplished?

– – – – – – – – – – – -

5. When do legal categories arise?

Legal categories would be created, for example, to bunch together fairly defined situations and objectives. The more specific or clear the subject matter is, the easier it would be to categorize it. Thus, it is easier to combine contracts, which can be defined by about five features, than to combine fiduciary relationships, which take about eight features or more to define.

However, there are a number of reasons to treat fiduciary law as a distinct body of law.[12] One reason is the growing importance of fiduciary relations in our society. A second reason is that this treatment will help provide a better method for developing fiduciary law than the present methods do. Courts currently examine existing prototypes, such as agency, trust, or bailment that are defined as fiduciary. Then, courts create rules for new fiduciary relations by drawing analogies with these prototypes. I maintain such a method of developing fiduciary law is unsatisfactory. A new approach is necessary in order to provide a better analytical framework for the law.

Traditionally, the courts have developed fiduciary law by defining various relations as fiduciary and designing rules for these relations. The definitions describe the arrangements that the parties establish and bring before the courts. For example, a trust is defined as a

---

12.   Tamar Frankel, *Fiduciary Law*, 71 CAL. L. REV. 795, 804-07 (1983) (abridged and footnotes omitted).

fiduciary relation in which property is transferred to the trustee. The trustee is free from the beneficiaries' control, and the beneficiaries consent is not necessary to establish the relation. Similarly, agency is defined as a consensual arrangement under which one party acts on behalf of another, subject to the other's control.

This method of developing the law was adequate in the past because new types of fiduciaries were recognized gradually over the centuries. The "use" emerged during the twelfth and thirteenth centuries in England, and the trust developed over the fourteenth through seventeenth centuries. Partnerships appeared in the sixteenth century, and evolved into joint stock companies and corporations. Emancipated servants and employees emerged from domestic relations law to become agents and factors. It was therefore sufficient to describe an arrangement, call it fiduciary, and decide on appropriate rules.

As the number of relations similar to existing fiduciary relations increased, the courts began to analogize the new relations to the established fiduciary prototypes, and to apply the rules of the prototypes to the new relations. Corporate law, for example, frequently analogizes directors to trustees, agents, and managing partners. But such analogies are uninstructive, because the courts do not explain why some similarities between directors and trustees are relevant and others not. Furthermore, analogies are not helpful in solving specific problems that new situations pose, because the rules that apply to the old prototypes do not necessarily respond to the problems posed by the new ones.

In addition, the courts are inconsistent in choosing their analogies. One decision, for example, held that directors are trustees, and applied trust rules against self-dealing to them. But, in order to avoid applying trust law's strict liability for unauthorized unintentional acts to the directors, the court then proceeded to hold that those directors were not trustees.

The inappropriateness of such analogies is illustrated by the courts' treatment of the removal of corporate directors from office, a treatment that essentially blends trust and agency rules and applies the concoction to corporate directors. Under trust law, a beneficiary cannot remove the trustee without proving in court that the trustee is incapacitated or has a substantial conflict of interest. Each party in an agency relation, however, may terminate the relation at will, even if the result is a breach of contractual obligations. These rules fit the purpose and structure of each relation. A trustee is chosen by the trustor, and must be able to manage the trust assets independently of the beneficiary's control. In contrast, an agent is chosen by the principal, and is subject to the principal's control.

Corporate directors do not fall squarely into the category of either trustee or agent. Just as trustees are free from the interference of beneficiaries, corporate directors should be able to manage without the frequent interference of shareholders. But directors are elected by the shareholders, just as principals choose their agents. Therefore, the shareholders should be able to terminate the directors' tenure in the appropriate circumstances.

Consequently, the courts designed a process to permit shareholders to remove directors that applies a combination of trust removal procedures and agency rules. A director's removal superficially resembles that of a trustee because both contain elements present in a judicial proceeding; a director must be given notice of the charges against him and must have an opportunity to be heard. The power to terminate the relation, however, is vested not in the courts but in the shareholders, the "principals" under the agency model. The courts further adjusted the rules by providing a "mixed" standard for removal that was neither the trust law standard of incapacity or conflict, nor the agency law standard of arbitrary termination. Instead, corporate directors can be removed by the shareholders only for cause, but the standard of cause—some wrong or injury to the corporation that need not amount to a legal wrong or an incapacity to act—is less strict than that applied to trustees.

This removal process is cumbersome and inappropriate. The trust model for termination is flawed because the shareholders of a publicly held corporation are not a suitable functional equivalent of a judicial tribunal. Consequently, a number of legislatures authorized removal of directors by a majority of shareholders without cause. But this agency model for termination is also flawed, because allowing the majority of shareholders to remove the directors at will can needlessly disrupt the centralized management services that directors are supposed to provide. Thus, in publicly held corporations, this procedure is rarely used to remove a director during his term, with or without cause. Instead, directors are usually terminated informally (consent), through a takeover (a market mechanism), or in the election process (by a proxy fight).

Courts have also used analogies based on functional similarities between various fiduciary relations. For example, both agents and union officials "represent" another party, principals and employees respectively. Thus, an analogy to this function has led at least one commentator to apply agency law to union officials.

These examples illustrate how mechanical analogies to the features of prototypical fiduciary relations result in rules that are confusing and inappropriate. A more useful approach to fashioning fiduciary law would begin with the general reason for legal intervention in fiduciary relations, namely, the nature and severity of the problem that the law is designed to solve.

- - - - - - - - - - - -

Discussion Topics

a. Why is fiduciary law an elusive category, and why is it important to recognize it as a category? Should not a category of trust, partnership, corporation, agency, etc. suffice?

b. How can one categorize fiduciary law as contract, or as tort?

c. Is the desire to simplify categories justified in this case? Would it work?

d. What are the benefits and disadvantages of providing specific rules to govern fiduciaries' behavior?

e. Why should fiduciaries be subject to restrictions that lower their ability to gain even though the activities do not harm the entrustors?

– – — — — — — — — — — -

B. Contract Law v. Fiduciary Law

1. The drive to re-categorize

In recent years innovative legal scholars have adopted a view of fiduciary relationships as contracts. Thus, contractarians define corporations as criss-crossing contracts among the different actors, including shareholders and management, and propose to reclassify partnership relationships as contracts, switching to the language and jurisprudence of contract.[13]

Judge Posner, an advocate of the contractarian view of fiduciary duties, expresses this view in the dissenting opinion in *Jordan v. Duff & Phelps, Inc.*[14]

The Judge described the facts of the case:

A corporate employee at will quit, owning shares that he had agreed to sell back to the corporation at book value. The agreement was explicit that his status as a shareholder conferred no job rights on him. Nevertheless the court holds that the corporation had, as a matter of law, a duty, enforceable by proceedings under Rule 10b-5 of the Securities Exchange Act, to volunteer to the employee information about the corporation's prospects that might have led him to change his mind about quitting, although as an employee at will he had no right to change his mind. I disagree with this holding. The terms of the stockholder agreement show that there was no duty of disclosure, and since there was no duty there was no violation of Rule 10b-5.

The plaintiff, a young man named Jordan, had gone to work for Duff and Phelps as a financial analyst. He had no employment contract; he was an employee at will. As a junior executive he was permitted to buy modest quantities of stock in the company, which was (and is) closely held. He agreed that if he left the company, whether voluntarily or involuntarily, he would sell back his stock at its book value on the December 31 preceding or coinciding with the end of his employment.

After working for Duff and Phelps for six and a half years Jordan had accumulated about one percent of the company's stock. His stock had a book value on December 31, 1983, of $23,000 (I round all dollar figures to the nearest $1,000). Earlier in 1983 Jordan had decided to leave Chicago because his mother, who also lived in Chicago, didn't get along with his wife. After Duff and Phelps declined to move him to its only other office (Cleveland), he began to explore the possibility of leaving the firm. On November 11, 1983, he accepted a job in Houston, Texas, at a substantially higher salary than his salary at Duff and Phelps ($110,000 versus $67,000). On November 14 he told Hansen, the chief executive officer of Duff and Phelps, that he was quitting, and on November 16 handed him a letter of

---

13.   Tamar Frankel, *Fiduciary Duties as Default Rules*, 74 OR. L. REV. 1209, 1209-11 (1995) (edited, footnotes omitted).

14.   Jordan v. Duff & Phelps, Inc., 815 F.2d 429, 444-52 (7th Cir. 1987) (Posner, J., dissenting).

resignation. At Jordan's request, Hansen agreed that the resignation would not take effect till the end of the year, so that Jordan would get a higher price for his stock. Both men believed that the book value of the stock would be higher on December 31, 1983, than it had been on December 31, 1982, the relevant date if Jordan's resignation took effect before the end of the year.

Hansen did not reveal to Jordan that in the summer he and Jeffries (the other principal officer of Duff and Phelps) had negotiated with some executives at Security Pacific Corporation to sell Duff and Phelps to Security Pacific for $50 million; that had the deal gone through Jordan's stock would have been worth $640,000 rather than $23,000; that the deal had been nixed in August by higher levels of Security Pacific's management; but that the episode had so encouraged Hansen that at a meeting of the board of directors of Duff and Phelps on November 14 (just before Jordan came to him with the news that he was leaving) he had sought and obtained authority to make active efforts to sell the company.

Negotiations between Duff and Phelps and Security Pacific resumed in December. On December 30, Jordan, who knew nothing of the negotiations, delivered his shares to Duff and Phelps, as his agreement with the company required him to do. The resumed negotiations were successful, and resulted in an announcement in January (1984) that Security Pacific would buy Duff and Phelps for $50 million, contingent on regulatory approval. Shortly afterward Duff and Phelps sent Jordan a check for $23,000 in payment for his stock. Rather than cash the check Jordan brought this suit, seeking damages equal to the value of his stock if he hadn't quit Duff and Phelps and if the deal with Security Pacific went through. It didn't go through. It collapsed the following January when the Federal Reserve Board refused to approve it except on conditions that Security Pacific found too onerous. Jordan amended his complaint, dropping the claim for damages and asking instead for rescission of the sale of his stock to Duff and Phelps. Almost a year later, Duff and Phelps reorganized, and its shareholders exchanged their stock for a combination of cash, notes, and pension rights that Jordan believes to be worth about $40 million.

Rule 10b-5 forbids "fraud or deceit" in the sale or purchase of corporate securities. Jordan does not argue that Duff and Phelps made any misleading statements. He makes nothing of the fact that when he told Hansen he was quitting, Hansen said that the firm had a good potential for growth and that Jordan's shares would rise in value if he stayed. The target of the complaint is not misrepresentation or even misleading half-truths; it is Hansen's omission to tell Jordan that he should think twice about quitting since the company might soon be sold at a price that would increase the value of Jordan's stock almost 30-fold. The statement that Hansen failed to make may have been material, since it might have caused Jordan to change his mind about resigning. I say "may have been material" rather than "was material" because Hansen need not have allowed Jordan to change his mind about resigning. But I shall pass this point and assume materiality, in order to reach the more fundamental question, which is duty. "One who fails to disclose material information prior to the consummation of a transaction commits fraud only when he is under a duty to do so."

We should ask why liability for failing to disclose, as distinct from liability for outright misrepresentation, depends on proof of duty. The reason is that information is a valuable commodity, and its production is discouraged if the producer must share it with the whole world. Hence an inventor is not required to blurt out his secrets, and a skilled investor is not required to disclose the results of his research and insights before he is able to profit from them. But one who makes a contract, express or implied, to disclose information to another acts wrongfully if he then withholds the information. The question is whether Duff and Phelps made an undertaking, and therefore assumed a duty, to disclose to any stockholding employee who announced his resignation information regarding the prospects for a profitable sale of the company.

My brethren find such a duty implicit in the fiduciary relationship between a closely held corporation and its shareholders. By this approach, what should be the beginning of analysis becomes its end. A publicly held corporation is a fiduciary of its shareholders, too; yet if Duff and Phelps had been publicly held it would have had no duty to tell Jordan about the company's prospects of being sold. This is the "price and structure" rule, which this circuit adopted in *Flamm v. Eberstad* -- rightly so, in my opinion. Thus the mere existence of a fiduciary relationship between a corporation and its shareholders does not require disclosure of material information to the shareholders. A further inquiry is necessary, and here must focus on the particulars of Jordan's relationship with Duff and Phelps.

The cases do not establish an automatic duty to disclose, even on the part of closely held corporations, though they are not sheltered by the "price and structure" rule. *Kohler v. Kohler Co.* says that the duty "must be fashioned case by case as particular facts dictate." The court found no duty in that case. *Michaels v. Michaels* did find a duty, and it is the case most like the present one factually, because it involved a shareholder who, like Jordan, was also an employee. But his status as a shareholder, unlike Jordan's, was not contingent on his remaining an employee. The contingent nature of Jordan's status as a shareholder has a twofold significance. First, it raises a question about the applicability of the majority's rule requiring disclosure "in the course of negotiating to purchase stock." One may doubt whether there was any real negotiation in this case, for once Jordan resigned he was contractually obligated to sell back his stock at a predetermined price. Second, and more important, the contingent nature of Jordan's status as a shareholder negates the existence of a right to be informed and hence a duty to disclose. This point is central to my dissent and has now to be explained.

Jordan's deal with Duff and Phelps required him to surrender his stock at book value if he left the company. It didn't matter whether he quit or was fired, retired or died; the agreement is explicit on these matters. My brethren hypothesize "implicit parts of the relations between Duff & Phelps and its employees." But those relations are totally defined by (1) the absence of an employment contract, which made Jordan an employee at will; (2) the shareholder agreement, which has no "implicit parts" that bear on Duff and Phelps' duty to Jordan, and explicitly ties his rights as a shareholder to his status as an employee at will; (3) a provision in the stock purchase agreement between Jordan and Duff and Phelps (signed at the same time as the shareholder agreement) that "nothing herein contained shall confer on the Employee any right to be continued in the employment of the Corporation." There is no occasion to speculate about "the implicit understanding" between Jordan and Duff and Phelps. The parties left nothing to the judicial imagination. The effect of the shareholder and stock purchase agreements (which for simplicity I shall treat as a single "stockholder agreement"), against a background of employment at will, was to strip Jordan of any contractual protection against what happened to him, and indeed against worse that might have happened to him. Duff and Phelps points out that it would not have had to let Jordan withdraw his resignation had he gotten wind of the negotiations with Security Pacific and wanted to withdraw it. On November 14 Hansen could have said to Jordan, "I accept your resignation effective today; we hope to sell Duff and Phelps for $50 million but have no desire to see you participate in the resulting bonanza. You will receive the paltry book value of your shares as of December 31, 1982." The "nothing herein contained" provision in the stockholder agreement shows that this tactic is permitted. Equally, on November 14, at the board meeting before Hansen knew that Jordan wanted to quit, the board could have decided to fire Jordan in order to increase the value of the deal with Security Pacific to the remaining shareholders.

These possibilities eliminate any inference that the stockholder agreement obligated Duff and Phelps to inform Jordan about the company's prospects. Under the agreement, if Duff and Phelps didn't want to give him the benefit of the information all it had to do to escape any possible liability was to give Jordan the information and then fire him. This case is just like *Villada v. Merrill Lynch, Pierce, Fenner & Smith Inc.*, and the court's words are strikingly apropos:

It seems to us an extraordinary proposition that a defendant can be charged with fraud by its mere neglect to tell a plaintiff facts which might have enabled the plaintiff to persuade defendant to refrain from taking certain action concededly within its own absolute discretion. Such a contention seems particularly absurd on the facts before us. Let us suppose that Merrill Lynch, having failed to dissuade plaintiff from deserting it for Bache, had told him "Well, you'll be sorry because we're going public and the stock you hold will become much more valuable;" and the plaintiff had responded "O.K. in that case I'll wait around until you go public and then desert you for Bache." It seems to us that Merrill Lynch would have been well within its rights if it had -- and probably would have -- exercised its option forthwith and told plaintiff to find such solace as he could in whatever employee stock option plan Bache might offer him.

My brethren correctly observe that, "[B]ecause the fiduciary duty is a standby or off-the-rack guess about what parties would agree to if they dickered about the subject explicitly, parties may contract with greater specificity for other arrangements." But, they add, "we need not decide how far contracts can redefine obligations to disclose. Jordan was an employee at will; he signed no contract." It is true that he signed no contract of employment, but he signed a stockholder agreement that defined his rights as a shareholder "with greater specificity." The agreement entitled Duff and Phelps to terminate Jordan as shareholder, subject only to a duty to buy back his shares at book value. The arrangement that resulted (call it "shareholder at will") is incompatible with an inference that Duff and Phelps undertook to keep him abreast of developments affecting the value of the firm.

The majority states that "the absence of explicit clauses counsels caution in creating implicit exceptions to the general fiduciary duty." A similar caution was not evident when this circuit in *Flamm* adopted the "price and structure" rule. That rule allows a publicly held corporation to withhold material information from its shareholders until a corporate transaction is firmed up. Its premise is that the shareholders are compensated for being kept in ignorance, by the prospect of greater gains than if the information were disclosed. Ignorance will cause some shareholders to sell their shares before the transaction takes place, and thus to be losers after the fact; but on average the winners will outnumber the losers; so the shareholders can be assumed to have consented in advance to surrender their right to be informed. The grounds for an inference that Jordan surrendered his right to be informed are stronger. His stockholder agreement, read in light of his status as an employee at will (a status the agreement emphatically declined to modify), waived either explicitly or by implication every pertinent right he might otherwise have had, except to the book value of his shares on the December 31 preceding or coinciding with the end of his employment. Since the company had a right to deprive him of any participation in the profits from a sale of the company, a duty to reveal to him information about the value of the company would have been empty. If Hansen had wanted Jordan to stay he would have told him about the rosy prospects for selling Duff and Phelps. Evidently Hansen didn't care whether Jordan stayed or not, so he didn't tell him. He could have fired him, or told him and then fired him -- possibilities that make my brethren's statement that Jordan "could have remained at Duff & Phelps" highly ambiguous.

Since receipt of the information would have conferred no right on Jordan to benefit from the information, how can the parties be thought to have intended Duff and Phelps to have an enforceable duty to disclose the information to him? There is no duty to give shareholders information that they have no right to benefit from. By signing the stockholder agreement Jordan gave Duff and Phelps in effect an option (as in Nye) to buy back his stock at any time at a fixed price. The grant of the option denied Jordan the right to profit from any information that the company might have about its prospects but prefer not to give him. If Hansen had known of the rule of law that my brethren adopt today, he could have avoided liability simply by telling Jordan that, come what may, December 30 would be Jordan's last day working for Duff and Phelps. Failure to disclose would be immaterial because Jordan could not act on the disclosure. Only because Hansen failed to make Jordan's resignation effective immediately (a generous gesture, which we have given Hansen cause to regret), as he could have done without violating any contractual obligation, is he held to have violated a duty of disclosure.

The case would be different if Jordan had had an employment contract or if he had had the right to retain his stock after ceasing to be an employee. Then a right to information about the prospects of the company would have been meaningful. Such a right is not meaningful when the employee has no right to act on it. That was Jordan's position. The company could have told him everything yet still have prevented him from benefiting from the information, by firing him.

Was Jordan a fool to have become a shareholder of Duff and Phelps on such disadvantageous terms as I believe he agreed to? (If so, that might be a reason for doubting whether those were the real terms.) He was not. Few business executives in this country have contractual entitlements to earnings, bonuses, or even retention of their jobs. They would rather take their chances on their employer's good will and interest in reputation, and on their own bargaining power and value to the firm, than pay for contract rights that are difficult and costly to enforce. If Jordan had had greater rights as a shareholder he would have had a lower salary; when he went to work for a new employer in Houston and received no stock rights he got a higher salary.

I go further: Jordan was protected by Duff and Phelps' own self-interest from being exploited. The principal asset of a service company such as Duff and Phelps is good will. It is a product largely of its employees' efforts and skills. If Jordan were a particularly valuable employee, so that the firm would be worth less without him, Hansen, desiring as he did to sell the firm for the highest possible price, would have told him about the prospects for selling the company. If Jordan was not a particularly valuable employee -- if his departure would not reduce the value of the firm -- there was no reason why he should participate in the profits from the sale of the firm, unless perhaps he had once been a particularly valuable employee but had ceased to be so. That possibility might, but did not, lead him to negotiate for an employment contract, or for stock rights that would outlast his employment. By the type of agreement that he made with Duff and Phelps, Jordan gambled that he was and would continue to be such a good employee that he would be encouraged to stay long enough to profit from the firm's growth. The relationship that the parties created aligned their respective self-interests better than the legal protections that the court devises today.

My brethren are well aware that Duff and Phelps faced market constraints against exploiting its employee shareholders, but seem to believe that this implies that the company also assumed contractual duties. Businessmen, however, are less enthusiastic about contractual duties than lawyers are, so it is incorrect to infer from the existence of market constraints against exploitation that the parties also imposed a contractual duty against exploitation. Contractual obligation is a source of uncertainty and cost, and is therefore an expensive way of backstopping market forces. That is why employment at will is such a common form of employment relationship. It is strange to infer that firms invariably assume a legal obligation not to do what is not in their self-interest to do, and stranger to suppose -- in the face of an explicit disclaimer -- that by "allow[ing] employees to time their departures to obtain the maximum advantage from their stock," Duff and Phelps obligated itself to allow them to do this.

Having earlier in its opinion tried to get mileage out of the fact that Jordan "signed no [employment] contract," the majority later tries to get additional mileage from the observation that employment at will is a "contractual relation." This is the kind of legal half-truth that should make us thankful that our opinions are not subject to Rule 10b-5. Employment at will is a voluntary relationship, and thus contractual in the sense in which the word contract is used in the expression "freedom of contract." And the relationship can provide a framework for contracting: if Duff and Phelps had not paid Jordan his agreed-on wage after he had earned it, he could have sued the company for breach of contract. But the only element of employment at will that is relevant to this case is that employment at will is terminable at will, meaning that the employer can fire the employee without worrying about legal sanctions and likewise the employee can quit without worrying about them. Freedom of contract includes freedom not to contract.

The distinction between the underlying "at will" relationship and the separate contracts that may grow out of it is well stated in *Nat Nal Service Stations, Inc. v. Wolf*:

> The agreement alleged here was clearly one at will and for no definite or specific time . . . It is clear from the complaint and affidavit that neither party obligated itself to do anything. Unless and until plaintiff had offered to place an order for gasoline and the defendants had accepted such offer and filled the order, only then did there come into existence a legal obligation, viz., the obligation of defendants to pay the agreed discount.

My brethren say that *Coleman v. Graybar Electric Co.* holds that employment at will is subject to an implied duty not to be opportunistic; actually *Coleman* rests on the distinction articulated in *Wolf*. "The appellant does not challenge, but concedes, the right of the defendant to discharge him at any time, but asserts that nevertheless should it do so without cause it was impliedly obligated to pay the plaintiff the *commissions earned by him* up until the time of discharge." Coleman had a contractual right to be paid at the agreed-upon rate for work done. Jordan had no contractual right that he would have been deprived of by being fired. His only relevant contractual right was to sell back his shares at book value.

The majority's view that "the silence of the parties" is an invitation to judges to "imply other terms -- those we [judges] are confident the parties would have bargained for if they had signed a written agreement" is doubly gratuitous. The parties did not want their relationship dragged into court and there made over by judges. And the parties were not silent. The stockholder agreement provides that Jordan's rights under it do not give him any employment tenure.

The inroads that the majority opinion makes on freedom of contract are not justified by its quotation from my academic writings concerning the purpose of contract law (which presupposes an agreement that the parties regard as legally enforceable) or by the possibility that corporations will exploit their junior executives, which may well be the least urgent problem facing our nation. The majority's statement that "one term implied in every written contract and therefore, we suppose, every unwritten one, is that neither party will try to take opportunistic advantage of the other" confuses the underlying rationale of contract law with the actual requirements of that law, and is anyway irrelevant since the parties decided not to subject the relevant parts of their relationship to the law of contracts and not to give Jordan any contractual protections against being fired. There was no "implied pledge to avoid opportunistic conduct" any more than there were "implicit parts of the relations" giving rise to contractual obligations. . . . "The common law doctrine that an employer may discharge an employee-at-will for any reason or for no reason is still the law in Illinois, except for when the discharge violates a clearly mandated public policy." "The rule in this state is that an employment at will relationship can be terminated for 'a good reason, a bad reason, or no reason at all.'" "Where discharge was for the purpose of avoiding a benefit [that] the employer was not obligated to provide" (this case precisely), it still is not actionable. And of course Jordan was not fired.

And if Duff and Phelps had fired Jordan (or refused to let him withdraw his resignation), this would not necessarily have been opportunistic. One might equally well say (in the spirit of *Villada*) that by trying to stick around merely to participate in an unexpectedly lucrative sale of Duff and Phelps, Jordan would have been the opportunist. The majority says that "understandably Duff & Phelps did not want a viper in its nest, a disgruntled employee remaining only in the hope of appreciation of his stock." I call that "viper" an opportunist.

The majority cites *Rao v. Rao,* which held, applying Illinois law, that a restrictive covenant that by its terms became effective if the employee was discharged "for any reason" was unenforceable because the employee in question had been discharged in bad faith. That decision provides very weak support for the majority's position in this case. The employee, Hari, had a contract with Mohan Corporation which entitled him, on completing four years of service, to obtain 50 percent of Mohan for $1. Ten days before the four years were up, Hari was fired -- precisely so that he would not obtain the 50 percent interest. This court did not suggest that the divestment of Hari was a breach of contract or otherwise unlawful; he apparently had made no such argument. All the court held was that Mohan could not enforce the restrictive covenant. The primary reason was that the covenant was too restrictive, and therefore contrary to public policy. Restrictive covenants are disfavored, and the bad faith displayed by Mohan was an additional reason against enforcing this one.

The issue of Duff and Phelps' duty to Jordan is a little more complicated than I have portrayed it. A resolution passed at the November 14 meeting of Duff and Phelps' board of directors provided that any employee who was terminated involuntarily could retain his stock for up to five years. If treated as an amendment to Jordan's stockholder agreement, the resolution would have prevented Duff and Phelps from forcing him to give up his stock by converting his voluntary termination into an involuntary one. There is a question, however, whether the resolution was effective without all the shareholders' consent. Moreover, another provision of the same resolution weakens Jordan's position: "If an employee voluntarily resigns (or gives notice of resignation) from the Corporation, the employee shall sell to the Corporation and the Corporation shall buy all of the Corporation's common stock then owned by the employee at book value." Jordan gave notice of resignation on November 14; and, under the resolution, having given notice he was obligated to sell his stock back to the company at book value.

I would understand, though might not agree, if the majority thought that the issue whether Duff and Phelps had a duty to disclose is unclear enough to warrant a trial. I cannot understand its holding that the duty exists as a matter of law. If, as appears, the holding is that just because Jordan was a shareholder Duff and Phelps had a duty to disclose material information to him, it is inconsistent with the basic premise of the "price and structure" rule (that premise being that a corporation isn't always required to disclose to its shareholders inside information regarding the prospects for selling the corporation), with the proposition seemingly endorsed by the majority that a duty of disclosure can be waived by its beneficiary, with the even more fundamental proposition that duty is a function of circumstances, and with the terms of the stockholder agreement in this case and of the employment relationship to which that agreement was expressly linked. If the holding is, instead, that the duty to disclose wells up from the complex of implied parts of relations, implied understandings, implied pledges, usual practices, and other particulars of the relationship between the parties (that is, if the discussion of these things in the majority opinion is anything more than rebuttal of this dissent), then I do not see how the duty can be thought a matter of law, to be imposed by this court without the benefit of a jury's or a trial judge's findings. I have a similar doubt whether characterizing the dealings between Hansen and Jordan as "negotiations" within the meaning of the rule announced today is a question of law rather than fact.

Although my principal disagreement is with the majority's holding about duty to disclose, I also have reservations about the majority's discussion of causation and damages. The majority is rightly troubled by the issue of causation. If Hansen had made full disclosure to Jordan, what would have happened? Would Jordan have tried to snatch back his resignation? Would Hansen have let him? (He wouldn't have had to.) Would Jordan's wife have let him? The case on remand will be a soap opera. The majority believes that the issue of causation can be elided by computing damages as follows: ask an investment banker to estimate the value of shares in Duff and Phelps on December 31, 1983, given what Hansen knew on that day; then subtract (1) the book value of the shares plus (2) the difference between Jordan's salary at Duff and Phelps and his higher salary at the Houston firm to which he switched. For illustrative purposes only, the court assumes that the investment banker would find that there was a one-third chance of no sale, a one-third chance of the sale to Security Pacific, and a one-third chance of the reorganization made after the deal with Security Pacific fell through.

I have three reservations about this approach:

(1) The book value of Jordan's shares shouldn't be subtracted from the award of damages. Jordan never received that book value. He didn't cash Duff and Phelps' check for $23,000 in 1984 when he received it, and it is too late to cash it now.

(2) My brethren say they need not choose between "rescissionary damages" and "market damages," because these are the same thing in this case. They are not; for if the proper measure of damages is compensation rather than restitution, the emotional cost to Jordan of remaining in Chicago must be monetized and subtracted from the award of damages. It is a cost that he avoided by going to Houston; hence it is a benefit that Hansen conferred on him by failing to disclose the information about the firm's prospects.

(3) Also, if market damages are the correct measure, Duff and Phelps must be permitted to show that the difference between Jordan's salary from it and from his new employer in Houston was a net benefit to him, rather than merely compensation for giving up a right to buy stock in the new employer. Only if it was the latter would his new, higher salary fairly estimate a cost that Duff and Phelps saved by his departure.

Finally, I do not share the majority's hope that its suggested method of determining damages will answer the question of causation. That question (would Jordan have stayed with Duff and Phelps if he had known what Hansen knew?) depends not on the valuation of the firm by an investment bank (though that valuation may be relevant) but on the answers to the following questions:

(1) What value would Jordan have placed on the shares, if he had known what Hansen knew? He is not an investment bank.

(2) What was Jordan's attitude toward taking risks?

(3) How would Jordan have traded off his estimate of the value of his shares -- a value he could not have realized immediately even if he had remained with Duff and Phelps -- against the higher salary he was to receive in Houston and against freedom from domestic conflict?

(4) Would Hansen have let Jordan rescind his resignation?

(5) If so, would Jordan still have been working for Duff and Phelps two years later, when the firm was reorganized?

(6) In this connection, how would Jordan have reacted to the collapse of the Security Pacific deal? Would this have precipitated his departure?

The larger the estimated value of Duff and Phelps when Jordan resigned, the less likely it is that he would have resigned. But that is different from saying, as the majority does, that estimating that value "appears to kill two birds with one stone," the second bird being the issue of causation. The basis of this statement is the majority's unduly sanguine assumption that "the probability of Jordan's remaining tracks the probabilities of these different outcomes. . . ." The majority believes that since Jordan presumably would have left Duff and Phelps if but only if he saw no prospect of a sale of the company, the hypothesized one-third probability of no sale is the probability he would have left. Using the court's figures, this would knock Jordan's damages down to $192,000.

If this is what the court is doing, it is breaking with the tradition of expressing causation in either-or terms, and I applaud its boldness. Only it is using the wrong formula for the relevant probability. The probability that Jordan would have stayed if Duff and Phelps had fulfilled its duty of disclosure is not the probability that an investment bank would assign to Duff and Phelp's being sold or reorganized; it is a function of the six factors that I have listed.[15]

Part of the court's majority decision is as follows:

Employment creates occasions for opportunism. A firm may fire an employee the day before his pension vests, or a salesman the day before a large commission becomes payable. Cases of this sort may present difficult questions about the reasons for the decision (was it opportunism, or was it a decline in the employee's performance?). The difficulties of separating opportunistic conduct from honest differences of opinion about an employee's performance on the job may lead firms and their employees to transact on terms that keep such disputes out of court -- which employment at will usually does. But no one . . . doubts that an *avowedly* opportunistic discharge is a breach of contract, although the employment is at-will. The element of good faith dealing implied in a contract "is not an enforceable legal duty to be nice or to behave decently in a general way." It is not a version of the Golden Rule, to regard the interests of one's contracting partner the same way you regard your own. An employer may be thoughtless, nasty, and mistaken. Avowedly opportunistic conduct has been treated differently, however.

The stock component in Jordan's package induced him to stick around and work well. Such an inducement is effective only if the employee reaps the rewards of success as well as the penalties of failure. We do not suppose for a second that if Jordan had not resigned on November 16, the firm could have fired him on January 9 with a little note saying: "Dear Mr. Jordan: There will be a lucrative merger tomorrow. You have been a wonderful employee, but in order to keep the proceeds of the merger for ourselves, we are letting you go, effective this instant. Here is the $23,000 for your shares." Had the firm fired Jordan for this stated reason, it would have broken an implied pledge to avoid opportunistic conduct. It may well be that Duff & Phelps could have fired Jordan without the slightest judicial inquiry; it does not follow that an opportunistic discharge would have allowed Duff & Phelps to cash out the stock on the eve of its appreciation. . . . So, here, an opportunistic discharge would not necessarily allow Duff & Phelps to buy back the stock. As a result, Jordan's employment

---

15. *Id.* (citations omitted) (Posner, J. dissenting).

at will, the essential ingredient of our colleague's argument that Jordan waived the duty to disclose, does not establish that the firm had no duties concerning the stock.

The timing of the sale and the materiality of the information Duff & Phelps withheld on November 16 are for the jury to determine. . . . REVERSED AND REMANDED.[16]

Frank H. Easterbrook and Daniel R. Fischel wrote an article advocating the contractual approach.[17] Roberta Romano wrote a response.[18]

In the response, Romano notes theories of fiduciary law other than the contractual approach. Some theories rely on unequal information. Some theories are property-based, and appear to be compatible with the contractual approach. Romano states that some property-based relations (e.g., trustee-beneficiary, manager-stockholder) involve greater fiduciary duties than some other relations (e.g., manager-debtholder, franchisor-franchisee, majority-minority stockholder), and "expertise in handling the property in trust could provide the rationale for imposing a higher level of duty." Some relations are regulated by statute, as the Employee Retirement Income Security Act of 1974 regulates some aspects of the pension relationship, as it may be easier to create obligations than to leave them to the common law.

Romano also distinguished among types of fiduciary relations. Relations where market forces are not strong (e.g., guardian-ward, union leader-union member, "and, to a lesser extent," attorney-client (as "lawsuit claims cannot be sold")) involve more stringent obligations than relations where there are strong market forces (e.g., manager-shareholder, broker-investor, manager-debtholder, majority-minority shareholder), as markets provide incentives that protect the principals. High transaction costs may also require stronger obligations. It is not clear whether, in the multiple principal context, the duty of loyalty should be more strict, or more difficult to enforce, In addition, fiduciaries who receive incentive or contingent compensation (e.g., managers, some attorneys) should be subject to weaker duties than others (e.g., trustees, guardians, union leaders).[19]

On reclassification of fiduciary relations as contracts, consider this excerpt:[20]

This reclassification has far-reaching practical implications for fiduciaries and for those they serve (entrustors). Behind it lurk drastic and fundamental changes in the current law and a substantial reduction in entrustors' protection such that fiduciary duties would be grounded in express or implied provisions of the agreements among the parties and enforced as contract obligations. This reclassification reverses traditional default rules.

---

16.   *Id.* at 438-39, 443 (citations omitted).
17.   Frank H. Easterbrook & Daniel R. Fischel, *Contract and Fiduciary Duty,* 36 J.L. & ECON. 425 (1993).
18.   Roberta Romano, *Comment on Easterbrook and Fischel, "Contract and Fiduciary Duty,"* 36 J.L. & ECON. 447 (1993).
19.   *Id.* (footnotes omitted).
20.   Tamar Frankel, *Fiduciary Duties as Default Rules,* 74 OR. L. REV. 1209, 1210-1211 (1995) (footnotes omitted).

Under current law, fiduciaries owe entrustors both a duty of care—to act carefully and not negligently—and a duty of loyalty—to perform their services in the interest of their entrustors and not in conflict of interest. In most cases fiduciaries can be relieved of these duties only if entrustors expressly or impliedly waive these duties; in some cases the duties are non-waivable.

Under contract law fiduciaries would be permitted to act negligently and in conflict of interest, unless expressly or impliedly prohibited from doing so, or if they fulfill certain conditions, such as disclosure. Further, courts would exercise less discretion in fashioning fiduciary duties. Rules regulating fiduciaries would be far more specific and dependent on the terms of the arrangement among the parties.

Some contractarians do not go so far as to completely eliminate fiduciary law. They are willing to recognize fiduciary duties but would impose the contract regime to allow entrustors to waive duties owed to them. These waivers would be enforced like the waiver or bargaining around of contract obligations.

The consequences of reclassifying fiduciary law as contract law are not necessarily ordained and do not logically follow the contractarian approach. We could, after all, import fiduciary rules into contract law and view them as regulating special types of contracts. Yet, in terms of both psychological fact and organization of the law, a name is important and reclassification can be treacherous. When we blur the distinctions between fiduciary and contract relationships, calling them by the same name, we tend to disregard the reasons for the different rules that govern them. Having forgotten these reasons, we are proposing seriously flawed rules that could come back to haunt us.[21]

During the past 25 years there developed a theoretical struggle among lawyers and judges on the status of fiduciary law category as such. Academics led the way and offered many theories. For example, one academic questions whether "the fiduciary duty of good faith" is actually "the implied covenant of good faith and fair dealing in a fiduciary setting." Courts do not agree on whether this is "a distinct fiduciary duty." The Delaware Supreme Court takes the position that it is; however, subsequent Delaware cases speak of "the ability of limited partnership or LLC agreements to replace fiduciary duties with contractual alternatives," suggesting that "the contractual duty of good faith is not qualitatively different" in the limited partnership/LLC context from the duty in an ordinary contract.[22]

Henry N. Butler and Larry E. Ribstein argue that, in the context of the corporation, the relationship among shareholders and management is essentially contractual.[23] They demonstrate the market and contractual mechanisms that govern the relationships among the actors within the corporate organization and argue that the critics do not appreciate the mechanisms that align the interests of management with the interests of the shareholders and thereby protect the shareholders from corporate misdeeds. They also argue that fiduciary duties and remedies are part of this protection. Parties may contract

---

21. *Id.*
22. Andrew S. Gold, *On the Elimination of Fiduciary Duties: A Theory of Good Faith for Unincorporated Firms*, 41 WAKE FOREST L. REV. 123 (2006), LEXIS, Lawrev Library, Wakelr File (LEXIS summary).
23. Henry N. Butler & Larry E. Ribstein, *Opting Out of Fiduciary Duties: A Response to the Anti-Contractarians*, 65 WASH. L. REV. 1 (1990).

for fiduciary remedies where market constraints are inadequate, and where "securities markets adequately discipline contractual choices, shareholders should be permitted to opt out of these rules."

In the opinion of these authors, the market price of corporate shares will "provide[] pressure toward development of optimal contract terms, including the optimal reliance on legal constraints such as fiduciary duties," and contract terms allowing or permitting amendment should be enforceable "since market forces constrain both the scope of the amendment power in the initial contract and the amendment process itself." And even if there are deficiencies in the markets, they doubt the efficiency of mandatory terms.[24]

The different views of trust law are demonstrated in academic writing. Analyzing the functions served by trust law, two other academics ask: (1) whether the essentials of contract and agency law could serve these functions, and (2) whether trust law provides additional benefits to corporations law. Consequently, they used different names for settlor, trustee and beneficiary unless the law of trusts clearly applies in the situation, i.e., "we are clearly talking about a situation in which the law of trusts applies." One view of trust is that "even if the trustee . . . specifically pledges trust property as security for credit extended to the trustee by a third party creditor who is unaware that the property is held in trust, the creditor will not be permitted to enforce his security interest in the trust property." Yet another academic argues that this view is mistaken and that, in contrast, we should view trust law as a branch of contract law, as the agreement between the settler and the trustee is essentially a third party beneficiary contract.[25]

2. There are economic-based theories and reasons for viewing fiduciary law as part of contract law

Courts that side with the contractarian group do not necessarily base their decisions by re-categorizing the relationships or the law. Yet, their rationales and results of their decisions speak louder than the categorization would. For example, a judge states that investors in a mutual fund should not complain if their adviser-fiduciary charges them the market price for brokerage transactions, even though the adviser was supposed to charge them "cost" and paid the broker only a third of the amount charged the fund. The violation of the adviser's fiduciary duty remains without a remedy.[26] Academics that know better than to call fiduciary relationships contracts have nicknamed these relationships "contractarian" and then proceeded to chip off the

---

24.   *Id.* at 6-7.
25.   Professors Henry Hansmann and Ugo Mattei suggest that the laws of agency and contract could substitute for trust law. *See* Henry Hansmann & Ugo Mattei, *The Functions of Trust Law: A Comparative Legal and Economic Analysis,* 73 N.Y.U. L. Rev. 434, 434, 439, 455, 469, 470 (1998).
26.   Tamar Frankel, *The Seventh Circuit Decision in Wsol v. Fiduciary Management Associates and the Amendment to Rule 12b-1,* INV. LAW., Aug. 2004, at 11.

protective rules against conflicting interests, thereby classifying them under the same name.

As one commentator remarked: Fiduciary duties were developed by the Church acting against markets and commercialism. Fiduciary duty rules "are vestiges of partnership law's medieval religious origins, and are ill-suited to the modern, secular business world," and were not "founded on their inherent practical value." Instead, "fiduciary duties between partners should be default provisions amendable by partnership agreements."[27]

Another commentator disagreed: The law of partners and alike, he asserted, "is transforming the duty of loyalty into a contractarian construct." [28] This transformation is based on "doctrinal confusion, outworn economics, and weak policy," and "[i]f anything, the duty of loyalty needs to be strengthened." "Contractarianism ignores externalities, assumes perfect bargaining within a static analytic framework, and slights transaction costs and institutional analysis."[29]

The Role of Self-Interest. Parties to a business interaction have both an identity of interest and a conflict of interest. The identity of interest relates to closing the transaction. Presumably, both desire to interact. For example, both the seller and buyer of an item desire to conclude the transaction of the sale and purchase. However, each desires to obtain conditions that are beneficial to it. Some of the conditions are gained at the expense of the other party. For example, while the buyer desires to buy at the lowest price and the seller to sell at the highest price, they may also value the item differently. In addition, the circumstances of the parties may differ. Some sellers are under greater pressure to sell for need of cash; some buyers are under greater pressure to buy, for need of the item. The motivations and circumstances of each party differ and may change even as they negotiate the transaction. Price and market conditions are only some of the important conditions to a sale.

These conflicts and potential conflicts render crucial the reliability of the parties. After the deal is made but the exchange is not completed, the buyer may find the item for sale at a lower price, or the seller may find a buyer at a higher price. The importance of the fundamental conditions is increased because we recognize the actual and potential conflicts among the parties, and the temptation that they face to violate these conditions. Similarly, an agent and his principal have an identity of interest and a conflict of interest. Both are interested in entering the relationship. However, the agent may be interested in the highest pay and lowest amount of effort; the principal may be interested in just the reverse.

---

27.   Dennis J. Callahan, *Medieval Church Norms and Fiduciary Duties in Partnership*, 26 Cardozo L. Rev. 215, 218 (2004).
28.   Reza Dibadj, *The Misguided Transformation of Loyalty Into Contract*, 41 Tulsa L. Rev. 451, 452 (2006) (footnotes omitted).
29.   *Id.* at 452, 470.

The Role of Self-Help. Some transactions lend themselves to self-help. Simultaneous exchanges reduce if not eliminate the condition of keeping one's word. The fundamental condition of telling the truth is of no value to parties that can easily verify the facts necessary to execute the transaction. In some cases, one party may be sufficiently strong to withhold the performance of its promises until the other party has performed its promises. In other cases, a party does not contribute information and makes no statements. It offers the items "as is," and the buyer is willing to absorb the costs of verification, perhaps because the relatively lower price reflects these costs. Under these conditions self-help pays and there is no need for legal interference.

3. What is the debate about?

If one pauses to think about this highly theoretical legal debate, one finds the underlying motivation for the arguments. First and foremost, contract would relieve fiduciaries of certain duties, which will be discussed below. That is, those who are entrusted with other people's money or power will be free of some of restrictive rules, such as the duty to act solely for the benefit of the entrustors. It will be fine if these fiduciaries act for the best benefit of the entrustors and could benefit themselves or others, with certain softer requirements. Thus, the result of re-categorizing fiduciaries as contract parties leads to educating entrustors and requiring them to fend for themselves. They might then combine to create a counter power to those who control their property or have fiduciary power. That, at least, is the road to which this contract/market category leads. With this model emerges the invisible hand of the market instead of the visible hand of government. Not everyone is enthused with this vision. If management controls and entrustors unite to gain counter power, the individual entrustors must have an agent and that agent will control their fate. If those managers are freed from controls by the courts or Congress or other mechanisms, then the model that might emerge is what some call "managerial capitalism." There will be a new type of property, denoting not owners but those who control money or power entrusted to them by other people—the multitudes.

— — — — — — — — — — -

Discussion Topics

a. Do you agree that the results of reducing the legal controls over fiduciaries would be to expose entrustors to greater risk of abuse of trust?

b. What other results from these relaxed controls do you envision?

c. What are the benefits of relaxed controls over fiduciaries? Assume that a CEO of a corporation would worry less about being sued, what are the advantages to this reduced worry?

d. When lawyers sue on behalf of a corporation, they negotiate a multimillion-dollar settlement for one million shareholders. Assume that 30% of the settlement money is paid to the lawyers. Each of the million shareholders receives $2.63 per share. Does this type of enforcing control over fiduciaries make sense? What if the fiduciaries are scientists who work for a very prestigious Health Foundation and also consult for pharmaceutical companies that need the Foundation's approval or recommendation of new drugs? The scientists would not be inclined to work for the Foundation if they could not collect the hefty fees from the companies. Do you believe in all the assertions above? Do you view the situation as satisfactory? If not, how would you remedy it? Would the conversion of fiduciary duties to contract duties help to remedy your concerns?

e. Where does the reclassification of fiduciary law come from? What disciplines affect the movement to reclassify? Is it economics, business, social science? Does culture have something to do with this movement to reclassify?

f. Comment on the following: When sophisticated parties include in their agreements a broad but unambiguous clause in which the sophisticated entrustor clearly agrees that it cannot rely on its fiduciary, the Delaware Supreme Court will likely assume that "they said what they meant and meant what they said."[30]

– – – – – – – – – – – –

4. The mantle of contract has enveloped corporate law

Professor Lewis A. Kornhauser wrote that the "nexus of contracts" model of the corporation has become popular.[31] However, neither it nor a trust model is ideal.

One problem with the trust model is that a number of parties act as trustee and beneficiary; i.e., managers, directors, and majority shareholders act as trustees; and not only the shareholders but the corporate assets may be deemed the beneficiary. The trust model uses the same duties of loyalty and care, while a contract model allows greater flexibility to fit the relationships.

In addition, the trust model determines the trustee's obligations by the beneficiary's interests, and the beneficiary or its interests may not be correctly defined.

There are difficulties as well with the contract model, as the "agreement" "is generally unwritten, frequently ambiguous or contradictory and often not an agreement"; instead, the approach "constructs" an agreement. The default rule "that the parties would have chosen the term that maximized joint wealth" may not reach the terms the parties would have chosen, and the underlying conditions of "full information" and "costless contracting" may not reflect the situation at the time of the contract.

Joint wealth maximization is not always the appropriate guide to construction for four reasons: (1) parties may have objectives other than wealth; (2) a party may be interested in its own wealth and not

---

30. MBIA Ins. Corp v. Royal Indem. Co., 426 F.3d 204, 218 (Del. 2005).
31. Lewis A. Kornhauser, *The Nexus of Contracts Approach to Corporations: A Comment on Easterbrook and Fischel*, 89 COLUM. L. REV. 1449 (1989).

joint wealth; (3) actors (e.g., shareholders) may disagree on the plan for joint wealth; and (4) joint wealth maximization will ignore contract terms that do not maximize wealth.

In addition, there are two definitions of "ideal contract": the "complete contingent claims" contract which covers "each possible state of the world," and the "full information and costless contracting" contract. The two definitions are not identical, and the parties may not have full information.[32]

5. Is contract a promise? What is the difference?

The argument in contract law highlights the distinction between contract and trust.

Wallace K. Lightsey criticizes the "promise model" of contract law.[33] Some scholars adopt the "promise model" of contract, that contracts are a "subset of promises." One scholar who adopts this model also adopts the "promise principle," that promises are legally binding; another scholar who adopts the model theorizes that there is no obligation without harm to the promisee if the promise is not kept or unjust enrichment of the promisor.

However, Lightsey adopts the "exchange model"; i.e., that contract is "the relationship that exists and develops among parties who have made a commitment to a future exchange." Lightsey demonstrates that contract law developed from the exchange relationship, citing both Roman law and English common law.

Unlike the promise model, the "exchange-relationship model views contractual relationships as flexible, adaptable, and capable of incorporating rights and obligations from sources other than the promises of the parties." Lightsey notes the rigidity of the promise model, under which "[c]ontractual rights and obligations are rigidly defined by the promises of the contracting parties, and trust between the parties is confined to the explicit terms of the promises." He contrasts it to the exchange-relationship model, which "seeks to heighten the interaction between contract and community. It underscores the flexibility and porosity of contractual obligation, stresses mutual dependence and cooperation between contracting parties, protects and encourages intense personal involvement."[34]

6. Similarities of fiduciary law and contract law

Similarities. Those who advocate the termination of fiduciary law as an independent legal category and its absorption into the law of contract point to the fact that both relationships are "consensual" and "voluntary." It should be noted, however, that it is the fiduciary that must consent and voluntarily accept the service. Beneficiaries of a trust, for example, do not choose the trustees; it is the trustor that has

32. *Id.*
33. Wallace K. Lightsey, *A Critique of the Promise Model of Contract,* 26 WM. & MARY L. REV. 45 (1984).
34. *Id.*

chosen the trustee. Nonetheless, in many cases, such as agency and partnership and patient-physician or client-lawyer relationships, the relationship is consensual on both sides, and both can terminate the relationship, subject to some contractual constraints.

What are the main duties of contract law? Contract law duties can be listed as two. Each party must tell the truth when asked and perform its promises according to its undertaking in the contract. An added duty is for each party to deal fairly with the other party. For example, a party may not take steps that would make it hard or impossible to perform its promises.[35]

What are the main duties in fiduciary law? A fiduciary must also tell the truth but the fiduciary need not be asked. The fiduciary must account for actions and offer the entrustor information when faced with conflict of interest. Here the shoe is on the other foot. It is doubtful whether an entrustor can effectively waive the right to truthful information.

Like the contract party, an entrustor must meet any obligations and perform any promises. With respect to entrusted property and power, a fiduciary must act for the benefit of the entrustor. No such duty exists in contract law. With respect to services in relationship to entrusted property and sometimes in general, the fiduciary must perform the services with care. A contract party is less bound by such a duty.

With respect to entrusted property and power, fiduciary relationships are drawn from property law. That is why the entrustor has the right to follow and reclaim entrusted property from anyone except from a buyer of the property for who gave value for the property and had no notice of the trust imposed on the property. Contract duties are promise-based. As compared to contract law, the creation of new forms of property rights is more limited.

The judicial approach to contract also differs. Judges are far more inclined to follow the terms of contracts and less inclined to create a contract among the parties. Fiduciary duties are judge-made, based on the interpretation and evaluation of the parties' terms by the judges. Even today, after the onslaught of contractarianism on fiduciary law, and the search for what the parties would have agreed upon had they known about the new circumstances that resulted in conflict, the presumed agreements are broader and result in judge-made rules.

Fiduciary law remedies differ from contract remedies. Breach of duty by fiduciaries can result in damages. However, to the best of my knowledge, there is (still?) no recognition of "efficient breach" of fiduciary obligations.[36] In addition, the duties involve accounting relating to entrusted property and power, as well as accounting for profits from breach of fiduciary duties and misuse of

---

35. 17A Am. Jur. 2d *Contracts* § 370.
36. A. MITCHELL POLINSKY, AN INTRODUCTION TO LAW AND ECONOMICS 31-34 (2d ed. 1989).

entrusted property. Finally, unlike contract law, there is a punitive damages award for breach of fiduciary duties in egregious cases. In that respect, fiduciary law abuts the law of torts.

Fiduciary law is often framed and phrased in terms of morality and ethics. A fiduciary is recognized as someone who must control the temptation to take what is not his even when there are no police around. In contrast, contract is recognized as a deal in which each party is allowed or perhaps encouraged to fend for itself and tend to its own interests.

_ _ _ _ _ _ _ _ _ _ -

Discussion Topics

a. Where do you stand in the debate of contract v. fiduciary law, and what arguments do you espouse for your position?

b. Which one of the arguments above do you find more plausible?

c. What criteria are most important to you or would you put them in lines of priorities?

d. Is a moral behavior and a trustworthy behavior entirely altruistic?

_ _ _ _ _ _ _ _ _ _ -

C. The Tort Connection

1. Torts are civil wrongs[37]

Consider the following situation: A man is driving along an empty suburban street on a clear day. There is no traffic in either direction. His cell phone rings. He reaches into his pocket, temporarily letting go of the wheel. As he scrounges around, trying to separate the buzzing cell phone from his loose change, he accidentally presses his foot hard down on the gas pedal. The car spins out of control. It drives up onto the sidewalk and rams into a parked car sitting in a nearby driveway of a nearby house. Both cars are destroyed. Thankfully, the man suffered no injuries since he was wearing his seat belt. But there are now big bills to be paid. The first is for the car totaled in the driveway. The second is for the car being driven by the man. Who should pay?

Any diligent law student should immediately recognize that this is a fairly basic tort scenario. Tort law is a foundational legal subject because its rules guide the way individuals within a society are able to protect their property from others. In this respect, tort is both related to and the opposite of contract law. In contract law, parties voluntarily enter into a relationship for an exchange of goods or services. The basis of contract law is consent between the parties to contract for a certain exchange. Conversely, the basis of tort law is a lack of consent. Two or more parties are suddenly forced to deal with each other, damage is caused, but there was no consent. There was no contract. The injuries

---

37. Torts are civil wrongs: This material is drawn, with consent, from a paper by Judah Skiff in satisfaction of a seminar requirements on fiduciary law at Boston University Law School, Spring 2007. The paper is edited and abridged, and some of the footnotes were omitted.

caused by torts occur either accidentally, as in the case of negligence, or on purpose as some kind of intentional tort like battery.

Because the crashing car incident is an example of negligent driving our instincts tell us that the negligent driver should pay. The question is why? What informs this sense? How do we articulate that instinct? Would you take a couple of moments and try to articulate why the negligent driver should pay for causing the car accident. Think beyond the basic, simple answer of "it was his fault." Of course it was his fault. Go beyond that. Why do we make people at fault pay for the damage they cause? What type of societal incentives does it create/not create? What type of behavior does it encourage/discourage? Now expand the inquiry: how are the laws of tort and fiduciary related? What types of connections can you see between them? What, philosophically, do they share in common?

Answering the basic question of why we hold people at fault financially responsible for their wrongs is not as simple as it appears. The simplest answer works according to the following syllogism: The man was driving poorly, he crashed his car into someone else's car; therefore, he should pay for the damage to both cars. How much should he pay? He should pay the cost of fixing the cars. Now let's complicate the hypothetical. Let's say the car he damaged was a piece of junk and the owner was ready to turn it in for about one thousand dollars. And let's say, the cost of fixing the car, because it is so old, and because it has so many parts that are faulty, would be well over one thousand dollars. An easy answer would be: "the negligent driver should pay according to the damage he caused. However, let's say that amount of money is not enough to fix the car. And on and on and on . . . ." We could continue to complicate this hypothetical and others, subject of a tort law class. However, we need to settle on a price, or a method of determining a price that is satisfactory to all parties and society as a whole. After all, the rules and damages imposed by judges in a common law system, such as ours, are rules, which will apply to everyone.

The contemporary tort law scholarship that draws on economic theories and focuses on economic incentives that accompany tort decisions and the imposition of damages provides a useful lens for understanding tort law. It introduces a critical language that helps understand fiduciary law. Imagine that the two car owners discussed in the scenario above were able to meet before to the accident. If they were able to foresee the accident they might discuss this accident. Imagine they were negotiating: the negligent driver says to the owner of the car, "If I drove my car negligently and crash it into your car while it is parked in your driveway, how much do you think I should pay you for that?" In other words, one answer to the question is: "the tortfeasor pays damages based on what the parties would have agreed had they been able to contract in advance in the assumed circumstances of the accidence." This view of tort law attempts to figure out what the parties would have decided had they been armed with proper foresight. That is before the parties know who will drive negligently and who will be hurt. In addition, would the parties then agree that driving negligently is a bad thing and that the negligent driver should be punished?

Does this conflate tort law too closely with contracts? Does this view sell tort law short, stripping it of its independence as a body of law? Or does this make a great deal of sense? After all, there are going to be a certain number of accidents in any society, and tort law, under this economic analysis, seeks to create a meaningful and workable method of dealing with these disputes. Regardless of where we come out, we recognize that most tort rules are default rules. In other words, they are rules, which come into play when the parties have not figured out in advance what should happen. Yet, who should decide what the default rules should be? This question can be modified with a moral qualifier: "does tort law impose damages based on what the parties should have agreed to, had they been given an opportunity to negotiate in advance? If so, again, who decides? Judges? Juries?"

Tort rules, like fiduciary rules, function as default rules. However, they only work as default rules in a theoretical sense. Some rules, unlike traditional default rules, cannot be negotiated away. For example, assume that you go to skate on a roller skating rink. There is a big sign on the front door: "Skate At Your Own Risk." The skating rink management could still, probably, be held liable if they negligently maintain the skating rink, for example, if there is a big hole in the wood on their skating floor. What the law and economics theorists challenge us to do is to think of default rules as substitutes for contract. In other words, we try to imagine what the parties would have or should have agreed to had they had the chance to do so in advance. As we shall see in the next Chapter, fiduciary law rules have a similar flavor. Tort damages are not always limited to mere restitution, that is, simply paying for the damage caused. When a tort is egregious, the tortfeasor can be charged with punitive damages—money punishment. Thus two threads bind fiduciary law with tort. Not all rules are default rules, waivable by the parties. And not all money damages are limited to restitution. In egregious cases, they are higher—punitive.

2. What is the message that both tort and fiduciary send through punitive damages?

In this Chapter, we are exploring the ways in which fiduciary rules are similar to tort rules. When a breach of fiduciary duties involves egregious behavior, the court or jury can award the plaintiff punitive damages, as it would in the case of a tort. In *City of Hope v. Genentech*[38] discussed below, the jury awarded the plaintiff punitive damages in the amount of $200 million. That is because the jury found that the defendant did not merely make innocent mistakes but

---

38. City of Hope Nat'l Med. Ctr.v. Genentech, Inc., 20 Cal. Rptr. 3d 234 (Ct. App. 2004), *modified, reh'g denied,* No. B161549, 2004 Cal. App. LEXIS 1962 (Ct. App. Nov. 22, 2004), *review granted, depublished,* 24 Cal. Rptr. 3d 178, 105 P.3d 543 (Cal. 2005). *City of Hope* is an unpublished disposition issued before January 1, 2007, and as such may not be cited to Ninth Circuit courts except in certain limited circumstances. 9TH CIR. R. 36-3(C).

intentionally attempted to deprive the inventors of the money due to them, and did not disclose to the inventors the true facts.

City of Hope v. Genentech[39] focuses on the classification of an agreement among the parties. The story is as follows:

While they were working for City of Hope in the mid-1970's, [Dr. Arthur] Riggs and [Dr. Keiichi] Itakura achieved a breakthrough in biotechnology by inventing a way to genetically engineer human proteins. At about the same time, Dr. Herbert Boyer (Boyer) and a businessman named Robert Swanson (Swanson) joined forces to form a venture to exploit biotechnology. Boyer, who had worked with Riggs and Itakura in the past, called Riggs and proposed that they collaborate together on a project to make bacteria produce human insulin. Riggs was amenable. . . .

On May 18, 1976, Swanson sent City of Hope a letter proposing that Genentech provide City of Hope with approximately $ 300,000 over a two-year period to "complete the synthesis of genes coding for somatostatin and insulin." [Genentech offered the inventors a royalty 1 ½%, the inventors demanded 3% and the parties settled for 2%, and Genentech will be the owner of the patent.] . . .

On August 28, 1980, Swanson sent a letter to City of Hope's executive director that stated: "Our agreement of August 1976 currently calls for Genentech to pay City of Hope a two percent royalty on net sales by it or *its licensees* on polypeptide products: [¶] 1. The manufacture of which employs DNA synthesized by City of Hope under the Agreement or replications of that DNA; and [¶] 2. Which following five years from signing of the Agreement are covered by one or more patents accruing from Genentech's funding of research at City of Hope." Swanson proposed that Genentech pay City of Hope $ 400,000 in exchange for reducing the royalty obligation to one percent and delaying it to 1985.

City of Hope rejected Swanson's offer. [He did not disclose to City of Hope that he was negotiating a license for $100 million.] . . .

[In October, 1986, City of Hope attempted to get a list from Genentech of third party licenses related to the methods of genetic engineering provided by City of Hope. They were unsuccessful, after several letters and meetings. Genentech's patent lawyer finally showed City of Hope's lawyer files about the application for patent 362 and any documents relevant to the agreement, but not files for unrelated third party licenses.] . . .

Genentech obtained 11 United States patents and over a 100 [sic] foreign patents with Riggs and Itakura named as the inventors.

By practicing the Riggs-Itakura patents, Genentech was able to manufacture human growth hormone and generate $ 2.9 billion in sales. Also, Genentech licensed the Riggs-Itakura patents to third parties, including but not limited to: Eli Lilly, KabiGen, Hoffman-La Roche, Monsanto, Boehringer-Ingelheim, Mitsubishi Chemical Industries (Mitsubishi), SmithKline Beechum (SmithKline), Cambridge Biotech, Chiron, Delca Biotechnology, E. Merck, Life Technologies, Repligen, Research and Diagnostic Systems, Sandoz, Seragen, Shionogi, Sunnery, Takeda Chemical Industries (Takeda), and Wyeth-Ayerst.

City of Hope received $ 72 million under Article 6.02 from Genentech's sales of human growth hormone. Also, pursuant to Article 6.08, City of Hope received $ 133 million from Eli Lilly's licensed sales and $ 97 million from KabiGen's licensed sales. However, City of Hope never received royalties with respect to any of the other licenses.

[After Genentech settled a patent infringement suit against Eli Lilly, Genentech stated that they did not need to give City of Hope any of the settlement because Eli Lilly was not

---

39.   *Id.*

using City of Hope DNA. City of Hope responded that the DNA use requirement did not apply. Genentech and City of Hope eventually settled.] . . .

Genentech sued Novo Nordisk for infringing the Riggs-Itakura patents. [The parties settled.] After deducting expenses, City of Hope's 2 percent share would have been $ 181,817. Despite a demand by City of Hope under Article 7.02, Genentech refused to share any part of the settlement. . . .

Believing it had been wrongfully deprived of royalties from various licenses and the Novo Nordisk settlement, City of Hope sued Genentech for declaratory relief, breach of contract, breach of the implied covenant of good faith and breach of fiduciary duty. City of Hope sought compensatory and punitive damages. . . .

[II. Breach of Fiduciary Duty] . . .

B. Genentech owed City of Hope a fiduciary duty. . . .

[Genentech argued that it owed no fiduciary duty to City of Hope.]

. . . There is no need to belabor the point. Under the facts of this case, the parties had a confidential relationship and Genentech had a fiduciary obligation to treat City of Hope with the utmost good faith.

C. Genentech breached its fiduciary duty.

Genentech does not dispute that it failed to disclose various licenses and pay royalties on those licenses. Rather, it contends that it did not breach any fiduciary duty so long as it was adhering to an erroneous but legally tenable interpretation of the agreement. In essence, Genentech would have us hold that even if it followed an interpretation it knew was contrary to what the parties intended and agreed upon, it could not be held liable so long as that interpretation was objectively sustainable under the law. [The cases that Genentech cites do not aid it.] None of them allows a party to profit from a legally tenable contract interpretation when the party knows that the agreement has a wholly different meaning. In any event, it would be antithetical to the very nature of the obligations imposed on fiduciaries for us to hold that a fiduciary could act in the manner suggested by Genentech.

To the extent Genentech contends that its interpretation of the agreement was held in good faith, that contention fails. The jury's finding of fraud or malice demonstrates that it believed that Genentech acted in bad faith. . . .

[The Court of Appeals awarded City of Hope $300 million in damages and $200 in punitive damages. Punitive damages cannot be awarded for a breach of contract, but can be awarded in the case of a breach of fiduciary duties, under the circumstances described in this case. Hence the importance of the finding of fiduciary relationships. As the court noted:]

Genentech contends that if there was a breach of fiduciary duty, it was the failure to report licenses and properly account for royalties. But any injury, Genentech posits, flowed strictly from the nonpayment of royalties, which only gave rise to contract damages. We disagree. Where, as here, the nonpayment violated "a duty independent of the contract arising from principles of tort law" . . . , it gave rise to contract and tort liability. Moreover, Genentech's failure to report the licenses and properly account for royalties prevented City of Hope from asserting its contractual right for an accounting and to receive payment. This additional breach enabled Genentech to withhold royalties to which it had no rightful claim and helped precipitate the damages.[40]

40. *Id.*

— — — — — — — — — — -

Discussion Topics

a. If you prepared the case on behalf of City of Hope, what is the most important fact or set of facts that determined in this case the award of punitive damages? If you prepared the case on behalf of Genentech on this point, what witnesses would you seek? On what would you focus your cross-examination?

b. How would the issue be resolved by an economic analysis? Imagine that Genentech was able to discuss with the plaintiff the possibility that it would make "innocent mistakes." How much money would the plaintiff demand?

c. Do you think the decision in *Genentech* matches that demand? Now add to that the intentional attempt to deprive the investors of what was due to them. Does $200 million sound right?

— — — — — — — — — — -

Consider fiduciary duties outside the context of corporate directors or trustees. Think about the types of fiduciary responsibilities that can arise in everyday life in other situations. It might be difficult to think about corporate directors or managers handling investor money similarly to someone man who negligently drives a car. But fiduciary duties in the current environment might extend to situations beyond corporate directors and trustees.

In *Vai v. Bank of America National Trust and Savings Association,* the Supreme Court of California imposed fiduciary duties on a spouse in connection with community property even as the couple was in divorce proceedings.[41] The court held:

> The fiduciary relationship arising from our community property system is not that of a trustee and beneficiary of an express trust. A trustee has no interest in the assets of the trust and may not assume a position in conflict with the interest of the beneficiaries. Each spouse, however, has a half interest in the community property and upon division of such property the spouses are in a position adverse to each other. Moreover, the liability of a husband for management and spending of community assets is markedly dissimilar to those of a trustee of an express trust.
>
> The fiduciary relationship between spouses arises from the confidential relationship between them and from the control that one spouse exercises over the community property. When a confidential relationship exists the spouses are held to a very high degree of fiduciary duty and no spouse will be permitted to gain any advantage from the trust and confidence placed in him or her by the other. Even when the confidential relationship is destroyed by dispute between the spouses, as the court found was the case between plaintiff and Mr. Vai, the spouse controlling the community property still owes a fiduciary duty to the other spouse. This duty, however, is analogous to the duty, not of a trustee to a beneficiary, but of one partner to another during the dissolution of a partnership.[42]

Here the court recognizes that certain trust law issues apply in the marital context. Corporate fiduciary responsibilities were developed in

---

41.   Vai v. Bank of America National Trust & Savings Ass'n, 56 Cal.2d 329, 15 Cal. Rptr. 71, 364 P.2d 247 (1961) (citations omitted).
42.   *Id.* at 349 (citations omitted).

large part from the fiduciary framework, which applied to trust law. Groups—corporate directors and trustees—were charged with making other people's money productive. So too, in this case, are spouses in community property states.

This decision notes another similarity between fiduciary law and tort law. That is "control." However, in tort law, the concept of control plays an introductory role: the negligent driver had control over the way he drove the car. He drove the car negligently; therefore, he must be held responsible. Tort law seeks to hold liable the person who was in the best position to prevent the accident from happening. According to that theory, it will encourage the people who are in a position to prevent accidents to be more careful. Therefore, in tort law, control should be seen as a threshold concept. In fiduciary law control by the fiduciary is part of the ongoing analysis.

– – – – – – – – – – – –

Discussion Topics

a. Should the *Genentech–City of Hope* relationship be governed by contract law or fiduciary law?

b. What are the implications of distinctions in the classification?

– – – – – – – – – – – –

D. Viewing Relationships Through Different Lenses

Robert H. Sitkoff views the prohibition on conflicts of interests through the lens of economic theory of agency costs,[43] that is, roughly translated, the cost of conflicts of interest by fiduciaries. The theory and the economic jargon was applied to corporate laws but rarely discussed in terms of private express trusts. Yet, the problem, he notes, is the same. It is the "separation of ownership and control" which is the main feature of a private trust. Sitkoff "develops an agency costs theory of trust law as organizational law, here focusing on donative private trusts. The analysis should be amenable to extension in future work to commercial and charitable trusts."

In a standard trust, the settler (S) "in effect contracts with the trustee" (T) so that T will manage assets "in the best interests of the beneficiaries" (B1, B2, or the Bs). T could be considered the agent of both S and B1/B2. There are two sources of agency costs; the S/T relationship (where T does not act in the way S would) and the T/Bs relationship (where T does not act in the way Bs would; analogous to the relationship between management and shareholders). Sitkoff states that the law should minimize these costs "but only to the extent that doing so is consistent with the ex ante instructions of [S]." The law generally takes this approach.

Sitkoff concludes that this approach "not only helps to advance the ongoing debate over whether trust law is closer to property law or

---

43. Robert H. Sitkoff, *An Agency Costs Theory of Trust Law*, 89 CORNELL L. REV. 621 (2004).

contract law, but also, and more importantly, . . . provides a rich positive and normative framework for further economic analysis of trust law."[44]

— — — — — — — — — — -

Discussion Topics

a. The Sitkoff article looks to the roots of the economic foundation of trust law. Do you think this is a useful way for understanding fiduciary law?

b. What are the differences between fiduciary law and trust law? Trusts are vehicles for testamentary transfer. They are a way to pass wealth from one generation to the next, or one person to the next, in a more efficient manner than, say, intestacy or wills. In that sense, they are the most private of legal vehicles. They are more intimate than contracts because they do not involve arm's length bargaining. Portions of the above article suggest that trusts create little more than third-party beneficiary rights in the beneficiaries of a trust. Is this a good way to think about them? Or should they be seen as private vehicles for transferring wealth?

The issue has powerful implications for the role of the fiduciary. Traditionally, the administrator of a trust is a fiduciary for the settlor. It is true that third party contract rights are created for the beneficiaries. However, perhaps a more compassionate way to look at a trust is as a settlor who is trying to help the beneficiaries in some way. The trustee is as the caretaker or guardian of that trust. The trustee is the one charged with making that trust productive. Trust law separates legal and equitable title. In that sense, it is a derivative of property law, because those basic property concepts and legal rights are directly wound up in the creation and administration of any type of trust. But there is a human element. Understanding trust law simply in terms of economics, simply in terms of legal roles may, in fact, weaken the sense for which the trust was initially created.

c. Is it appropriate to apply an economic analysis of law framework to understanding fiduciary duties within the context of trust law? Is it appropriate to use the lens of efficiency to examine one of the most private aspects of the legal system? And if so, what is the appropriate way to understand the role that an economic analysis should play?

— — — — — — — — — — -

Washington Steel Corp. v. TW Corp. discusses the issue of whether there are limits "on a commercial bank which wishes to advance funds to one client in order to facilitate that client's takeover of another of the bank's clients":[45]

On January 15, 1974, Washington executed a credit agreement with Pittsburgh National Bank, Chemical, and Morgan Guaranty Trust Company, pursuant to which the

---

44. *Id.*
45. Washington Steel Corp. v. TW Corp., 602 F.2d 594 (3d Cir. 1979) (footnotes and citations omitted).

banks agreed to lend Washington up to $ 10,000,000. Pittsburgh National was the lead bank in that transaction, agreeing to advance 55% of the funds. The credit agreement identified Pittsburgh National as "agent" of the lenders for purposes of the loan. Chemical agreed to advance 22.5% of the funds, or an amount up to $ 2,250,000. Morgan Guaranty made a similar commitment.

In connection with its participation in the loan to Washington, Chemical received certain information from Washington, some of which was non-public in nature. This information included a May, 1973 Study produced by Washington, providing cash flow and earnings projections for Washington through 1982. In addition, Washington supplied Chemical with quarterly statements of its financial affairs as well as a year-end statement dated December 28, 1978 for the fiscal year ending September 30, 1978.

Besides participating as one of three banks lending money to Washington, Chemical also served as one of two registrars for its common stock. Its function as registrar was to ensure that no more than the authorized number of Washington shares of stock were issued.

Over the years, Chemical has also been the lead bank in loans to Talley. In January, 1979, Talley decided to endeavor to acquire Washington. On or about January 13, 1979, Talley spoke to Paul Fitzgerald, a Vice President at Chemical. Fitzgerald was the principal Chemical liaison to Talley, having worked on four or five Talley loan agreements during the prior seven years. At that time Talley discussed a possible acquisition of an unnamed company. Two days later, on January 15, Fitzgerald met with Talley representatives at the offices of Chemical's legal counsel. A discussion was held as to whether Chemical might participate in financing Talley's proposed acquisition of Washington, which was for the first time identified as the proposed acquisition target. An attorney for Talley indicated a belief that Chemical had an ongoing business relationship with Washington. As noted above, this relationship included an outstanding loan agreement and Chemical's service as a registrar for Washington stock.

Later in the day of January 15, Fitzgerald and other members of the Chemical Corporate Banking Department discussed in greater detail the possibility of financing the proposed acquisition. . . . At the conclusion of the meeting, a senior officer of the Chemical Corporate Banking Division made a policy decision that the Bank was not precluded from participating in the proposed loan, assuming that the loan was justified from the standpoint of Talley's creditworthiness. . . .

. . . Concluding that the company was a favorable credit risk, senior credit officials approved the loan commitment [to Talley. Soon thereafter Talley proposed a merger with Washington, and upon refusal of the board of directors increased the price it was offering for Washington shares.] . . .

. . . On February 5, 1979, Washington brought the instant suit in the United States District Court for the Western District of Pennsylvania . . . (2) that Chemical had violated its fiduciary duty to Washington in that it had allegedly misused confidential information obtained from Washington in deciding to finance the tender offer. Washington sought an injunction to foreclose the tender offer. . . .

. . . On February 16, the court preliminarily enjoined Chemical from participating in the loan to Talley, although it did not enjoin the tender offer. The court found that, prior to the arrangement with Talley, Chemical "was the agent of the Plaintiff Washington Steel and was purporting to advance the several corporate purposes of Plaintiff Washington Steel at all relevant times, and in particular said Chemical Bank was the transfer agent of Plaintiff Washington Steel." Moreover, the trial court determined, "Chemical Bank was entrusted with comprehensive, confidential financial information" which "was relevant and pertinent to the formulation of the plan (to take over Washington)" as well as "any proposed financing arrangement" on Chemical's part. In view of Chemical's role as "transfer agent" (registrar) for Washington, as well as its receipt of confidential information, the court found that Chemical "was acting as agent for . . . Washington . . . and . . . was charged with the responsibility of advancing the best welfare and corporate interests of . . . Washington . . . ." Chemical thus "had a duty not to act adversely to the interests of . . . Washington," a duty which it breached by participating in a loan to Talley which would ultimately result in the "take over and control (of) all of . . . Washington Steel's assets . . . ." Characterizing Chemical's participation in the Talley loan as "egregious and unethical conduct," the trial court preliminarily enjoined Chemical from further involvement in the loan to Talley. . . .

V. THE MERITS

The trial court granted the preliminary injunction on the ground that Chemical had violated a common law fiduciary duty to Washington. While the court's opinion did not make clear its precise origins or nature, Washington urges two possible theories in support of such a duty. First, it maintains that Chemical, by receiving confidential information in connection with its loan to Washington, impliedly assumed a duty not to act on behalf of another company whose purpose was to "subvert . . . Washington Steel's . . . capital development program . . . ." Second, Washington urges that even if there is no such Per se rule which forbids a bank in Chemical's position from advancing the efforts of one client to merge with another, nonetheless there is a duty, which Chemical violated, not to misuse confidential information supplied by the target company.

A. The Per Se Fiduciary Duty

The trial court ruled that, as a matter of law, Chemical "had a duty not to act adversely to the interests of Plaintiff Washington Steel under the circumstances. . . ." As noted above, the court seemed to derive this duty from Chemical's role as a registrar of Washington stock as well as from its receipt of information supplied by Washington in connection with a commercial loan. On appeal Washington does not rely on Chemical's role as registrar in urging a Per se fiduciary duty. Rather, it contends that, having entrusted Chemical with the May, 1973 Study projecting future earnings as well as periodic financial reports, Washington reasonably expected Chemical to take no actions adverse to the continued viability of the Company. Whatever expectations it may have entertained, however, we cannot fairly imply a duty whose sweep is as broad and whose restrictions are as severe as that urged by Washington. . . .

. . . To imply a common law fiduciary duty of banks not to deal with competitors of their borrowers, or even just potential acquirers of those borrowers, could wreak havoc with the availability of funding for capital ventures. Companies seeking to insulate themselves from takeovers, or even from ordinary competition, could simply arrange for a series of loans from most of the major banks, supplying those banks with the requisite non-public information. Under the Per se rule urged by Washington, the banks would thereby be foreclosed from financing competitors and potential acquirers of the borrowing firms "[tending to impose a burden] on the free flow of bank financing and the ability which a bank now has to deal with customers who may have adverse interests to other customers."

Moreover, even if the rule Washington proposes were sound public policy, it would hardly be the province of this court to say so in the context of this present litigation. First, establishing a Per se common law fiduciary duty of banks to their borrowers seems archetypically within the domain of legislative judgment. A legislature is best suited to consider the delicate financial issues at stake and strike the appropriate balance between sound economics on the one hand, and expectations of loyalty on the other. In addition, even were we to presume to venture into this area, we would be reluctant to do so as a matter of state common law, as the trial court apparently did and as Washington urges on appeal. Given the need for uniform rules in an area so vital to our national economy as banking, any state common law rule that we might imply would likely give way to the preemptive force of federal law. . . . In addition, the Comptroller of the Currency has recently proposed a regulation for national banks which suggests ways of restricting the use of confidential information obtained from one client on behalf of another. These developments evince a concern at the national level with the issues raised by Washington. Any common law fiduciary duty which we might imply would, in all probability, have to yield to whatever national policies might emerge from these deliberations.

Accordingly, we reject the contention that Chemical, having received confidential information from Washington in connection with its participation in a loan to that company, was necessarily precluded from financing the efforts of Talley to merge with Washington.

B. The Misuse of Confidential Information

Besides urging a Per se rule of fiduciary duty, Washington supports the preliminary injunction on the theory that Chemical allegedly misused Washington's confidential information in arranging the loan to Talley. We note at the outset that the trial court did not make an express finding that such misuse occurred. Rather, the order and accompanying recitals seem to suggest that the mere receipt by Chemical of confidential information is, without more, a sufficient basis for enjoining its participation in the loan to Talley. . . .

. . . Washington has not contended, and the trial court did not hold, that Chemical relayed any confidences to Talley. Count 3 of appellee's complaint, on the basis of which the preliminary injunction issued, charges Chemical with liability for using confidential information obtained from Washington Steel in connection with its Own decision to participate in the loan to Talley. Washington reiterates that position on appeal. Accordingly, we have no occasion at this time to decide whether a bank which actually provides one client with confidential information obtained from and concerning another client may be enjoined from financing the former client's takeover of the latter.

We turn, therefore, to the remaining questions, whether the Chemical officers in evaluating the loan to Talley used confidential information obtained from Washington, and, if so, whether such use was ground for a preliminary injunction. Washington contends that Chemical should be deemed to have used the information, offering two arguments in support of this position. First, it urges that we adopt a presumption of such use because, given Talley's allegedly weak financial picture, Chemical officers would have had particularly strong reasons to inquire into Washington's financial position and thus to avail themselves of confidential information supplied by Washington. Second, Washington claims that actual use of information did occur, in that Mr. Roach the Chemical officer in charge of the Washington Steel account said nothing at the January 15, 1979 meeting at which the loan to Talley was discussed. . . . [T]he other officers could have inferred that the target was a wise investment. Washington asserts, finally, that Chemical's use of this confidential information in making its own decision on the Talley loan was unlawful.

We do not accept Washington's contentions. [Barring evidence of improper use, the court refused to assume such use by the bank merely on the basis of the weak position of Talley and the strong financial position of Washington. The evidence suggested otherwise.] Chemical was "eminently familiar with Talley," having "done business with them for years." Chemical performed a "worse-case" analysis of Talley's ability to repay the loan. That analysis convinced Chemical of Talley's ability to cover its debt service. In performing that analysis, Chemical considered only Washington's current dividend payout; it made no assumptions about a change in Washington's dividend rate.

. . . Roach [the bank's employee] said nothing at the meeting beyond the fact that there was a loan relationship with Washington and that he did not know what Washington's reaction to the Talley offer would be. Moreover, Mr. Fitzgerald testified that his staff was instructed not to talk to anyone who worked on the Washington account, nor was it to look at any files kept on the target company. Fitzgerald himself had no access to Washington files. Indeed, both Roach and his assistant John Watkins submitted affidavits stating that they had personally secured all of the Washington files and kept them out of the possible sight of those persons working on the Talley loan. Thus we do not share appellee's view that Chemical used the Washington information in deciding to make the loan to Talley.

But assuming, arguendo, that such use occurred, we reject for a more fundamental reason Washington's contention. We do not believe that a bank violates any duty it may owe to one of its borrowers when it uses information received from that borrower in deciding whether or not to make a loan to another prospective borrower. First, like the Per se rule adopted by the trial court and discussed above, the promulgation of a rule restricting the dissemination of confidential information within the loan department of a bank is neither the proper province of a court nor an appropriate subject for state law adjudication. More critically, the adoption of such a rule would make unwise banking policy. To prohibit a bank from considering all available information in making its own loan decisions might engender one or both of two undesirable outcomes. First, it might force banks to go blindly into loan transactions, arguably violating its duties to its own depositors. Alternatively, such a rule might discourage banks from lending money to any company which expresses an interest in purchasing shares of stock of another of the bank's customers. The adverse implication of this result for the free flow of funds is precisely the reason why we rejected the Per se rule urged by Washington. Bank credit is, after all, the largest part, by far, of the national money supply.

Of course, we intimate no view on whether a bank may be foreclosed from disseminating confidential information to a Separate bank department, such as the trust department, whose function it is to recommend particular investments to its clients. Such dissemination of insider information arguably might violate Section 10(b) of the Securities and Exchange Act of 1934 and the S.E.C.'s rule 10b-5. So, too, might the dissemination of such information to the acquiring company itself. Neither of these issues, however, is presented in this appeal. We deal solely with dissemination within the commercial loan department. That is another matter entirely. In making loans, unless it is to take imprudent risks with the funds on deposit with the bank, the commercial loan department must be free to make full use of the information available to it. If, for example, a competitor of a borrower seeks a loan for a purpose which the loan department knows, from information in its files supplied by that borrower, is preordained to failure, it should hardly be permitted, let alone required, to ignore the information, finance a foolhardy venture, and write off a bad loan. Thus, we hold only that the use within that loan department of information received from one borrower, in evaluating a loan to another borrower, does not, without more, state a cause of action against the bank. . . .

. . . While the legal theories pressed on this appeal do not support that restraint, we note that the trial court has not yet ruled on Washington's allegations of Talley's liability under the Williams Act. Liability under those sections might have foreclosed Talley from effecting the actual takeover once the loan from Chemical was finalized. As a result, certain of the costs allegedly incurred by Talley because of the erroneously issued preliminary injunction specifically, the inability to consummate the takeover might have been incurred anyway. The extent of Talley's recovery on the bond must therefore await a final resolution of those outstanding issues. Accordingly, the case is remanded for further proceedings not inconsistent with this opinion.[46]

---

46.   *Id.*

- — — — — — — — — — - -

Discussion Topics

a. Do you agree with this decision? Although this case occurred twenty-five years ago, many of the issues remain current. Today people and corporations lend and borrow money through bank syndicates. Notes are sold on exchanges and to private buyers. Borrowers may not even know who owns their debt at any given time. The challenge for fiduciary law is to create a workable framework within this fluid environment. If anyone owning financial interest in a particular corporation were precluded from acting against it, the financial markets could come to a standstill. That is simply not a practical solution.

b. What about the economic questions implicit in the dilemma? How can the law create and protect this complicated set of incentives? (1) Providing incentives for creating businesses and consequently jobs and generate wealth. That results in the need for borrowing. (2) Providing incentives for entities, such as banks, to lend money. Historically, banks were the main, perhaps the only, source of institutional lending. However, today, there are many other types of financial institutions engaged in the business of making loans. Their interests should be protected as well.

What happens when those two interests are at odds, and a lender plans to assist someone in taking over the borrower? Lenders are not fiduciaries to their borrowers. And borrowers are not fiduciaries to their lenders, unless they are in bankruptcy. Therefore, on the face of it, there does not appear to be a problem. However, what if a lender obtains confidential information about a borrower?

c. Does the mere possession of confidential information render the holder of the information a fiduciary? If we use the economic analysis described above, what would the parties have agreed upon had they known the facts as they emerged? How would the borrower have reacted to the possible financing of its takeover by the lending bank?

d. Assume that a mailman regularly makes deliveries to the home of a hedge fund manager and, in the course of his work, discovers that the manager is planning to buy a huge block of stock in a public corporation, an event that would send the price of the stock up. Does the mailman owe a fiduciary duty to anyone?

e. Assume that the mailman is not liable as a trader in insider information,[47] but note that peering into someone's mail is a felony or at least a misdemeanor. Why does the law interfere by criminal law in these circumstances and not in the case of the bank?

f. In the context of borrowers and lenders, as discussed in the case above, what is the value of private information? If lenders are free to

---

47.   Securities and Exchange Commission Rule 10b-5, 17 C.F.R. § 240.10b-5 (2007).

use private information to the detriment of their debtors should that information be considered private nonetheless?

g. Is the issue in the case above classified as contract law? Should a creditor be able to contract with a borrower in a way that would allow the lender to act against that borrower's interests or prevent the lender from doing that? Thinking in those terms inevitably leads to a discussion about relative power of the parties. A lender might likely have much more bargaining power than a small borrower, but not in the case of large corporations to whom the bank caters. A borrower might be so desperate as to contract away almost anything. Against that backdrop, do we still need fiduciary laws to protect the borrower? If the borrower does not need such protection, is there still the issue of protecting the market? In other words, is it good or bad for the market to give lenders the dominant upper hand? Or perhaps we should distinguish and design two rules depending on the bargaining position of the parties?

— — — — — — — — — — — — -

In the case of *Warsofsky v. Sherman*, a bill in equity was brought to impose a constructive trust on four parcels of land.[48] [Although we will study about constructive trust in more detail later, note here that a constructive trust is a remedy imposed on persons who wrongfully hold property, requiring these persons to transfer the property to the rightful owners.] The title to the parcels had been conveyed to a Milford bank. The plaintiff wished to buy back for $10,000 these parcels that the defendant, through breach of a fiduciary relation, had wrongfully acquired and retained in the name of his wife, the other defendant. The court below dismissed the bill. The following is the decision of the appeal:

The plaintiff's father held in his own name or in that of his wife four parcels of real estate in Millis upon which a Milford bank held mortgages. The father was aged, infirm, and blind and was unable to comply any longer with the terms of the mortgages. As a result of a conference between the officials of the bank and the plaintiff's father and his family, all these premises were conveyed to the bank on March 12, 1940, and releases were given to the bank. At the time these conveyances were made there was a discussion to the effect that, if the plaintiff's father or the plaintiff subsequently became able to carry the property, the bank would reconvey the property. The plaintiff thereafter, acting as the nominee of his father, conferred from time to time with an official of the bank with reference to acquiring the property. Sometime in November, 1940, it became apparent that the plaintiff would be drafted into the army and he increased his efforts to secure the property before he entered the service. On or about November 1, 1940, he was told the terms and conditions upon which he could purchase the property from the Milford bank. From all the evidence, the inference is plain that he was justified in understanding, as he did, that the bank was willing to convey these parcels for $10,000. The plaintiff, in an endeavor to secure financial aid to enable him to purchase the property, orally applied on or about the middle of November, 1940, for a loan from a cooperative bank. He was referred by the treasurer of this bank to one Smith, a director and member of the security committee, with whom he discussed his

---

48.   Warsofsky v. Sherman, 93 N.E.2d 612 (Mass. 1950) (citations omitted).

request for a loan. Acting on Smith's advice, he conferred on the same day with . . . the defendant. He told the defendant that he desired to discuss a matter in strict confidence with him as a director and member of the security committee of the cooperative bank, that Smith had sent him to the defendant, and that he wanted to secure a loan of $10,000 from the bank. He then told the defendant where the property was, gave him the details as to income and expenditures, and stated that he wanted to get the property back. The defendant replied that the proposition seemed to be a good one. The defendant understood that the information was given to him in confidence as a director and member of the security committee of the cooperative bank, and he received the information in that capacity and solely for the purpose of enabling himself and other officials of the bank to determine whether the security warranted the granting of the loan. It is apparent that the judge did not believe the testimony of the defendant and his witnesses that the defendant knew that the property was for sale and that he had negotiated for its purchase long prior to the time the plaintiff testified he had consulted him. In this there was no error of law. We find that he did not know the property was for sale until so informed by the plaintiff, and that within about two days thereafter he offered to buy and the Milford bank voted to sell it to him for $10,000. The defendant acquired title in the name of his wife on December 9, 1940. The property was worth more than the purchase price.

. . . [T]he trial judge ruled that there was not sufficient basis to establish a fiduciary relationship. . . .

Doubtless, there are many familiar and well recognized forms of fiduciary relationships such as attorney and client, trustee and beneficiary, physician and patient, business partners, promoters or directors and a corporation, and employer and employee. The relationship is not confined, however, to these and similar situations, for the circumstances which may create a fiduciary relationship are so varied that it would be unwise to attempt the formulation of any comprehensive definition that could be uniformly applied in every case. There is jurisdiction in equity to prevent, by means of the remedial device of a constructive trust, unjust enrichment arising out of a breach of a fiduciary relation. The existence of the relationship in any particular case is to be determined by the facts established. . . . "Wherever two persons stand in such a relation that, while it continues, confidence is necessarily reposed by one, and the influence which naturally grows out of that confidence is possessed by the other, and this confidence is abused, or the influence is exerted to obtain an advantage at the expense of the confiding party, the person so availing himself of his position will not be permitted to retain the advantage, although the transaction could not have been impeached if no such confidential relation had existed." . . .

The plaintiff was not seeking any loan from the defendant but desired a loan from the cooperative bank, and was dealing with the defendant only in his capacity as an official of the bank. [To secure a loan the plaintiff] was required to file a written application and to furnish the bank with such information concerning the property he contemplated purchasing as was necessary and adequate to enable the security committee to pass on the loan, which could not be granted unless it was approved by at least two members of the committee. The information given by the plaintiff to the defendant was furnished in confidence . . . in order to enable the defendant and other members of the committee to whom he might convey the information to determine whether the loan should be granted. It was to be used for no other purpose, and the defendant, impliedly at least, understood the terms upon which the information was given and voluntarily undertook to comply with those terms. He stood in a fiduciary relation toward the plaintiff with reference to the matters disclosed. We are confirmed in this view by various other circumstances involved in the conference between the plaintiff and the defendant. Cooperative banks deal largely with persons of small or moderate means to aid them in accumulating savings, and an important branch of their activity is to assist those who are willing to help themselves acquire homes by a plan of monthly payments for interest on the loan and a reduction of the principal. Those who desire to purchase a home do not ordinarily possess any considerable property, and it becomes important for a cooperative bank to have all the material details of the property intended to be offered as collateral security in order to decide whether it is of sufficient value to justify the granting of the loan. If the information furnished by the applicant for a loan is to be seized upon immediately by the bank official to whom it is given and if by virtue of the information he can purchase the property behind the back of the applicant, then public confidence in such institutions will be seriously impaired if not utterly destroyed. In any event, an applicant for a loan ought not to be subjected to such risks. A bank official to whom an application for a loan is made must act fairly and impartially toward the bank and toward the applicant. He is prohibited from deriving any personal gain at the expense of the applicant or to the detriment of the bank, and he is subject to a penalty if he requests or receives any fee, commission, or gift for or on account of a loan.

Members of a security committee acquiring confidential information by virtue of their official position cannot use that information for their own personal gain as against the bank. It is true that the defendant was not employed by the plaintiff, but it is plain that, in accepting the information confidentially conveyed, he voluntarily undertook to use it solely for the purpose for which it was given, and that he could not properly derive any personal gain from carrying out his undertaking any more than he could if he were an employee in like circumstances.

The instant case is distinguishable from [a case in which no confidential information was conveyed to the defendants]. The relation between the parties in [another case] was that of mortgagor and mortgagee, which is not a fiduciary relation except in the actual conduct of the power of sale.

We do not think it material that no written application for a loan from the cooperative bank was made by the plaintiff. As we have already said, no loan could have been granted in the absence of a written application, but the absence of such an application does not absolve the defendant from the consequences of his own wrongdoing especially where, as here, the filing of a written application when the plaintiff got around to it would have been an idle gesture, for the plaintiff had then been prevented from purchasing the property from the Milford bank.

The final decree is reversed and a new decree is to be entered with costs requiring the defendants to convey the property to the plaintiff upon the payment of $10,000 increased or diminished as will be shown by an accounting of the profits and expenses to the date of the new final decree. So ordered.[49]

Note another view of fiduciary law by Andrew S. Gold. Gold questions whether "the fiduciary duty of good faith" is actually "the implied covenant of good faith and fair dealing in a fiduciary setting," noting that courts do not agree on whether this is "a distinct fiduciary duty." The Delaware Supreme Court takes the position that it is; however, subsequent Delaware cases speak of "the ability of limited partnership or LLC agreements to replace fiduciary duties with contractual alternatives," suggesting that "the contractual duty of good

---

49.   *Id.*

faith is not qualitatively different" in the limited partnership/LLC context from the duty in an ordinary contract.[50]

– – – – – – – – – –

Discussion Topics

a. Compare and distinguish *Warsofsky v. Sherman* with *Washington Steel Corp. v. TW Corp.* Do the identities of the parties play a role?

b. Does it make a difference that one case dealt with an individual and the other with a corporation? Or that one dealt with trust law and the other with corporate law? Or are the principles too similar to distinguish? If so, what are the implications for having those rules apply with such uniformity to such a diverse number of legal actors?

– – – – – – – – – –

E. Chapter Review

Having read this Chapter, is fiduciary law a separate legal category? Is it contract law? A sub-category of contract? A contractual duty of good faith? A tort? Or should we care?

---

50.   Andrew S. Gold, *On the Elimination of Fiduciary Duties: A Theory of Good Faith for Unincorporated Firms*, 41 WAKE FOREST L. REV. 123 (2006), LEXIS, Lawrev Library, Wakelr File (LEXIS summary).

Chapter Seven
Judicial Discretion and Remedies

This Chapter consists of two related subjects. The first is the extent to which the courts use their discretion to recognize fiduciary relationships and shape fiduciary duties. We have covered materials that demonstrated some courts' "activism" and other courts' "conservatism." Here we view the exercise of the courts' discretion to factor in concerns about public interests. In addition, we discuss the limitations that the courts impose on their use of discretion in recognition of the fiduciaries' expertise and the fact that the entrustors have chosen them.

The second part of this Chapter deals with remedies for breach of fiduciary duties. We have covered materials that dealt with these remedies. Now we return to focus on them in greater length. The types of remedies and their very existence reflect the place of fiduciary law in the law generally and indicate their "legality" and importance.

Like the following Chapters in this book, this Chapter offers an opportunity to review the materials that were presented in the earlier Chapters and relate them to the courts' discretion and to the remedies that they mete out for violations of fiduciary law.

Judicial discretion. The roles of courts in fiduciary law can be viewed in different ways. In one view the courts are more intrusive into fiduciary relationships than they are in respect to contract relationships. In another view, courts are not more intrusive but offer more default rules in fiduciary relationships because the parties' relationships are more open-ended and usually also long-term. After all, the parties cannot establish all terms in fiduciary relationships in advance. Therefore, the courts seem to be more intrusive by providing default "contract" rules. In fact, courts merely offer the terms that the parties would have established for themselves, had they been asked. Regardless of how we view the courts' exercise of their discretion, courts are more active in designing and producing rules of fiduciary law (mostly default rules).

As our previous discussions have shown, the courts determine the nature of the parties' relationships and (barring the entrustors' explicit consent to the contrary) design the rules and the remedies for the breach of these rules. "Even when the courts defer to the parties' limitations on judicial intervention in their relations, the courts always examine whether the entrustor's consent was informed and independent, thus reserving a measure of judicial review. For example, a court may defer to a trustor's appointment of a family member as trustee even when the latter has a conflict of interest, because the trustor is probably in a better position to evaluate the wisdom of the appointment. But when a conflict of interest arises in circumstances that the trustor could not have anticipated, or if the appointed trustee in fact abuses his trust, the court's confidence in the trustor's judgment may weaken, and the court might then remove the trustee."[1]

Further, by declaring a relationship to be fiduciary, the courts shift to the entrustors the beneficial ownership in the subject matter property or power. The shift of the property entitlement enables the courts to award fiduciary law remedies against fiduciary wrongdoers who obtained property legally. By declaring the wrongdoers "constructive trustees," courts can order the fiduciary to revert the beneficial (and legal) ownership of the property to the wronged party. "Constructive trustees" are not true trustees, who accepted their position and duties as such. Declaring persons "constructive trustees" is a method by which courts can impose on wrongdoers the kind of remedies that are imposed on fiduciaries that breached their duties *as if the wrongdoers* were trustees that breached their fiduciary duties.

In addition, the classification of a person as a fiduciary helps entrustors enforce their fiduciaries' promises and duties. "First, the classification strengthens the constraints on the use of delegated power. If the beneficial ownership does not 'belong' to the fiduciary, the fiduciary can deal with the property only according to the terms of the delegation of power and for the entrustor's benefit. Second, if the ownership of the property 'belongs' to the entrustor, he can seek the court's intervention not only when the relation ends, but also at any time during the relation when the fiduciary abuses his power. The courts thus assume the authority to supervise the fiduciary in the use of his delegated power throughout the relation. . . . [In addition,] the [constructive] trust technique provides the vehicle for the judicial creation of *in personam* property rights by which one person (the fiduciary) can be excluded from the use of a certain bundle of property rights even though the exclusion does not affect anyone else."[2]

A. Judicial Use of Discretion

1. Factoring in public interest

Greisman v. Newcomb Hospital demonstrates a judicial approach to fashioning fiduciary duties and remedies.[3] In this case the court factored into the duties of a private organization third party interests, such as the community's needs and the near monopoly power of the private organization. The plaintiff, a qualified physician, sought user privileges at a Newcomb Hospital in City of Vineland, near his home

---

1.   Tamar Frankel, *Fiduciary Law,* 71 CAL. L. REV. 795, 822 (1983) (footnotes omitted).
2.   *Id.* at 828-29.
3.   Greisman v. Newcomb Hosp., 192 A.2d 817 (N.J. 1963) (abridged and citations omitted).

and practice. Newcomb Hospital was the only one in the area. The Hospital denied the plaintiff the privilege on the sole ground that he graduated from a school that was not approved by the American Medical Association and was not a member of the County Medical Society. Many professional medical associations, however, accepted physicians whose backgrounds were similar to that of the plaintiff. While Newcomb Hospital's by-laws contained the conditions of acceptance, which excluded the plaintiff, the hospital did not have any specialized practices but rather accepted physicians that specialized in many areas. In light of these findings, the lower court determined that the by-laws of the Newcomb Hospital conflicted with the public policy of the State. Further, although Newcomb Hospital was a private hospital that could operate at its discretion, its position as the only hospital in the plaintiff's area where any other hospital was at least 100 miles away, and its special services concerning people's health imposed upon it certain duties.

The *Greisman* court referred to another case which held that a hospital's power of exclusion was to "be viewed judicially as a fiduciary power to be exercised in reasonable and lawful manner for the advancement of the interests of the medical profession and the public generally," regardless of the fact that the hospital was a private organization.[4] The *Greisman* court's views of its role in the development of fiduciary law are instructive:

> The persistent movement of the common law towards satisfying the needs of the times is soundly marked by gradualness. Its step by step process affords the light of continual experience to guide its future course. When courts originally declined to scrutinize admission practices of membership associations they were dealing with social clubs, religious organizations and fraternal associations. Here the policies against judicial intervention were strong and there were no significant countervailing policies. When the courts were later called upon to deal with trade and professional associations exercising virtually monopolistic control, different factors were involved. . . . [Where a case involves] sufficiently compelling factual and policy considerations, judicial relief will be available to compel admission to membership. . . ."

> [In a precedent case, the court held that] the Medical Society's authority to pass on membership applications by licensed physicians is a power which is fiduciary in nature, to be exercised accordingly, and it held that, under the evidence presented, [the physician] was entitled to admission despite the Society's requirement of four years' study at a school approved by the American Medical Association. [In this case, as in a precedent case,] similar policy considerations apply with equal strength and call for, a declaration that the hospital's power to pass on staff membership applications is a fiduciary power, and a holding that Dr. Greisman is entitled to have his application evaluated on its own individual merits without regard to the bylaw requirement rejected by the Law Division. . . .

> [The court emphasized that both the patients and the physician should have access to the hospital. The hospital staff is no substitute for their own physician.] . . . In this day there should be no hesitancy in rejecting as arbitrary, the stand that a doctor of osteopathy, though fully licensed by State authority and reputably engaged in the general practice of medicine and as the local school and plant physician, is nonetheless automatically, and

---

4.   *Id.* at 823 (citing Falcone v. Middlesex County Med. Soc'y, 34 N.J. 582, 597 (1961)).

without individual evaluation, to be considered unfit for staff membership at the only available hospital in the rather populous metropolitan area where he resides and practices. The public interest and considerations of fairness and justness point unerringly away from the hospital's position and we agree fully with the Law Division's judgment rejecting it....

... [H]ospitals are operated not for private ends but for the benefit of the public, and that their existence is for the purpose of faithfully furnishing facilities to the members of the medical profession in aid of their service to the public. They must recognize that their powers, particularly those relating to the selection of staff members, are powers in trust which are always to be dealt with as such. While reasonable and constructive exercises of judgment should be honored, courts would indeed be remiss if they declined to intervene where, as here, the powers were invoked at the threshold to preclude an application for staff membership, not because of any lack of individual merit, but for a reason unrelated to sound hospital standards and not in furtherance of the common good.[5]

Discussion Topics

a. Why did the court choose fiduciary law to resolve the case? What did it want to achieve? Could it achieve the same result by another theory?

b. Suppose the Hospital refused an applicant's admission on evidence that the applicant was a confirmed alcoholic or had been sentenced to prison for assault. Would the court have interfered in the decision? If so, on what grounds?

c. Could you describe the principles that guided the judicial discretion in this case?

2. Judicial self-limitation
a. The general principle

In *Oakland Raiders v. National Football League*[6] the limits on the courts' intervention in the decisions of managers were considered:

A member club of a professional football league sued defendants, the league and its commissioner, alleging that defendants breached their fiduciary duty to the club. The club claimed that it was discriminated against and treated unfavorably as compared with the other member clubs, thereby placing it at a competitive disadvantage. The trial court granted summary adjudication in favor of defendants.

The Court of Appeal affirmed. The court held that neither defendant stood in a fiduciary relationship with the club. The relationship between the club, on the one hand, and the league and the commissioner, on the other hand, was not one under which a fiduciary relationship existed as a matter of law. There was no merit to the club's claim for breach of fiduciary duty arising out of a joint venture. Although the member clubs shared revenues, they did not share profits or losses. There was no fiduciary relationship between defendants and the club arising either as a result of agreement or by operation of law. The breadth of the commissioner's powers delineated in the league's constitution plainly showed that there were numerous and varied potential circumstances in which the commissioner could be required to act against the best interests of the club. The trial court properly concluded that it was barred by the abstention doctrine from resolving the

---

5.   *Id.*
6.   Oakland Raiders v. Nat'l Football League, 32 Cal. Rptr. 3d 266 (Ct. App. 2005) (citations and footnote omitted).

dispute between the club and defendants. The trial court also properly rejected the club's additional claims, both because they were not pleaded, and because they were without merit as a matter of law. . . .

The Raiders contends that the trial court also erred by concluding that it was required to abstain from this intra-association dispute . . . . It argues that the court's decision was based on an unwarranted expansion of the abstention doctrine. The Supreme Court in *California Dental* (the Raiders asserts) "held that courts should not interfere in 'intra-association disputes' concerning whether certain conduct breaches an association's bylaws unless that conduct 'plainly contravenes' the association's bylaws." Stated otherwise, the abstention doctrine applies only to intra-association disputes that involve the association's bylaws. Because the Raiders claims are not ones that concern the interpretation of NFL bylaws (the Raiders argues), the abstention doctrine does not apply.

We disagree. The abstention doctrine as enunciated by the Supreme Court in *California Dental* applies to the Raiders claim here. Thus, even were there triable issues as to the existence of a fiduciary relationship between defendants and the Raiders -- and, as we have concluded in part III, ante, there were none -- summary adjudication of this claim under the abstention doctrine of *California Dental* was nonetheless proper.

The Raiders argument represents a second attempt to convince this court that abstention under *California Dental* applies only to a narrow range of intra-association disputes. In Oakland Raiders, we rejected the Raiders assertion that *California Dental* applies only in the narrow context of a dispute following "judicial review of the decision of a neutral quasi-judicial body" established by the association. In our rejection of the Raiders contention there, we held that "[t]o the contrary, the case language [of *California Dental*] applies broadly."

In this appeal, the Raiders asserts that the abstention doctrine, as enunciated by the Supreme Court in *California Dental*, is limited to disputes involving voluntary associations' noncompliance with their own bylaws. Once again, the Raiders -- in this second appeal -- misconstrues *California Dental*.

In *California Dental*, the state dental society expelled a member dentist after hearing, concluding that he had violated both its code of ethics and those of the national society of which the state society was a constituent. The national society reversed the expulsion after the dentist appealed; in doing so, it did not consider whether the dentist had violated the state society's code of ethics. Because the national society's bylaws permitted constituents to have higher ethical standards --which was the case in this instance -- the trial court granted the state society's petition for writ of mandate, ordering the national society to rehear the dentist's appeal by considering the state society's higher standards. The Supreme Court affirmed.

The Supreme Court commenced its analysis by acknowledging that the terms of a voluntary association's constitution and bylaws prescribe the rights and duties of its members. The court then stated: "In many disputes in which such rights and duties are at issue, however, the courts may decline to exercise jurisdiction. Their determination not to intervene reflects their judgment that the resulting burdens on the judiciary outweigh the interests of the parties at stake. One concern in such cases is that judicial attempts to construe ritual or obscure rules and laws of private organizations may lead the courts into what Professor Chafee called the 'dismal swamp.' Another is with preserving the autonomy of such organizations that 'in adjudicating a challenge to the society's rule as arbitrary a court properly exercises only a limited role of review. As the Arizona Supreme Court observed in *Blende v. Maricopa County Medical Society*: "In making such an inquiry, the court must guard against unduly interfering with the Society's autonomy by substituting judicial judgment for that of the Society in an area where the competence of the court does not equal that of the Society. . . ."

The court went on to identify action that plainly contravenes the unambiguous language of an association's bylaws as a *particular instance* in which judicial intervention *would be appropriate,* i.e., because such action would constitute "an abuse of discretion, and a clear, unreasonable and arbitrary invasion of [the party's] private rights." Under those circumstances, if the action "plainly contravenes the [association's] bylaws . . . and if the burden on the courts and on the interest of the [association] in its autonomy do not outweigh the [member's] interests, it is appropriate for courts to exercise jurisdiction."

To reiterate, "the case language [of *California Dental*] applies broadly." As we also noted before, the Supreme Court in *California Dental* "affirmatively stated that it was applying general common law that governed disputes within private organizations." From our careful review of *California Dental,* we conclude that the abstention doctrine described by the Supreme Court was one that applies broadly to intra-association disputes, irrespective of whether the particular dispute concerns a claimed breach of association bylaws.

This conclusion is consistent with other cases that have followed *California Dental.* [abstention doctrine means that "[c]ourts must guard against unduly interfering with an organization's autonomy by substituting judicial judgment" for the organization's]; In *California Trial Lawyers,* the court found that the *California Dental* "policy of judicial restraint control[led]" to preclude judicial intervention in interpreting the bylaws of a voluntary association of attorneys that impacted the election of the association's president. In so holding, the court explained that "[t]his reluctance to intervene in internecine controversies, the resolution of which requires that an association's constitution, bylaws, or rules be construed, is premised on the principle that the judiciary should generally accede to any interpretation by an independent voluntary organization of its own rules which is not unreasonable or arbitrary."

In this instance, the trial court properly held that it was barred by the abstention doctrine from resolving the dispute between the Raiders and defendants. Ignoring for the moment that the Raiders breach of fiduciary duty claim is not viable as a matter of law, the underlying basis for the claim is not one for an asserted breach of the NFL constitution. The court correctly concluded--after a discussion in its order of each alleged act that the Raiders claimed constituted breaches of fiduciary duty--that the Raiders had not shown any evidence of a violation of a clear and unambiguous provision of the NFL constitution. Indeed, the Raiders admits that its claim is *"not for breach of the NFL's bylaws."* Further, the Raiders opposition to defendants' summary adjudication motion presented no facts that demonstrated " ' "an abuse of discretion, and a clear, unreasonable and arbitrary invasion of [the Raiders's] private rights." ' "

In short, the court correctly construed and applied the abstention doctrine of *California Dental.* We observe that the rationale of abstention from intra-association disputes applies with particular force in this instance. Given the unique and specialized nature of this association's business--the operation of a professional football league--there is significant danger that judicial intervention in such disputes will have the undesired and unintended effect of interfering with the League's autonomy in matters where the NFL and its commissioner have much greater competence and understanding than the courts. We note that other courts have expressed similar unwillingness to intervene in matters that involve the business operations of professional sports organizations. We decline to descend into "the 'dismal swamp'" of resolving complex matters involving professional football that are best left to the voluntary unincorporated association that is the NFL.[7]

b. Judicial self-limitation in regulating fiduciaries

The business judgment rule appears under different names but in all cases demonstrates the limitations that the courts impose on themselves in exercising their supervision of fiduciaries' decisions. Courts recognize that the fiduciaries were chosen by the entrustors and that the fiduciaries often have significant expertise. Therefore, the courts apply a "hands off" attitude to the fiduciaries' decisions, so long as there is no evidence that the fiduciaries have acted in violation of their fiduciary duties. The following case, *Bal Harbor Club, Inc. v. AVA Development, Inc.* (In re *Bal Harbor Club, Inc.*),[8] illustrates the exception to the judicial abstention approach.

The court held:

In this case, the bankruptcy court dismissed the debtor's Chapter 11 bankruptcy case for cause, pursuant to 11 U.S.C. § 1112(b), concluding that the debtor, in commencing the Chapter 11 proceeding, had abused the bankruptcy process. The district court affirmed on appeal, concluding that the bankruptcy court committed no error in its application of section 1112(b) to the facts before it. The debtor now appeals, contending that the bankruptcy court (and therefore the district court on appeal) failed to afford its decision the benefit of "the business judgment rule" in concluding that its filing of the Chapter 11 case abused the bankruptcy process. We find no error, and accordingly affirm. . . .

The debtor, the Bal Harbour Club, Inc. (the "Club"), is a not-for-profit Florida corporation that owns and operates a private social and yacht club in Bal Harbour, Florida. In 1993, the Club's Board of Governors (the "Board") decided to sell its oceanfront property, consisting of 5.5 acres. In June 1995, the Board found a buyer, AVA Development, Inc. ("AVA"), and agreed to sell the property to AVA for $ 34 million, conditioned on a favorable modification (for AVA) in the applicable zoning regulations. While AVA was pursuing such modification, Joseph Imbesi acquired control of the Club's Board, and immediately took steps to prevent AVA from acquiring the oceanfront property. To this end, the Board resolved that the Club file the instant Chapter 11 case, which it did on October 2, 1998. On October 15, 1998, AVA moved to dismiss the Club's petition pursuant to 11 U.S.C. § 1112(b)
. . . .

The bankruptcy court held an evidentiary hearing on AVA's motion. In a comprehensive order entered on January 12, 1999, the court granted the motion, finding that "the bankruptcy filing in this case was an improper use of the bankruptcy process and the Court." Evidence of such improper use included Imbesi's "purchase of proxies to influence" the selection of Board members; "the initiation of litigation to frustrate" AVA's acquisition of the oceanfront property; the "'highjacking' of the Debtor by replacing the Board through the use of 'phony' loans"; and "the borrowing of $ 1.145 million dollars, without agreeing to any terms of repayment or an interest rate, from a person holding the control of an insider [i.e., Imbesi or a company he controlled,] in a last minute rush in order to gain a strategic advantage over another interested party." . . .

II.

The Club argues that the bankruptcy court abused its discretion in reaching the decision to dismiss the appeal because it misapplied the law. The error consisted of the court's failure to give the Club the benefit of the "business judgment rule." The case the

7.　*Id.*
8.　Bal Harbor Club, Inc. v. AVA Dev., Inc. (*In re* Bal Harbor Club, Inc.), 316 F.3d 1192 (11th Cir. 2003) (some footnotes omitted) (citations omitted).

Club cites for the rule is *FDIC v. Stahl,* which states that "'the [business judgment rule] is a policy of judicial restraint born of the recognition that directors are, in most cases, more qualified to make business decisions than are judges.' In this light, the [rule] may be viewed as a method of preventing a factfinder, in hindsight, from second guessing the decisions of directors." As the Club properly points out, "under the business judgment rule, courts presume that directors have acted in good faith. A court will not call upon a director to account for his action in the absence of a showing of abuse of discretion, fraud, bad faith, or illegality."

The Club says that the bankruptcy court should have presumed that it filed and was going to prosecute its Chapter 11 petition in good faith, and that the court erred in failing to give it the benefit of that presumption. The problem with the Club's position is that in the litigation of a motion brought under section 1112(b) to dismiss a Chapter 11 petition - which is what the bankruptcy court had before it - the movant, AVA, had the burden of proof. In short, the Club did not need a presumption. Moreover, a presumption is a procedural device that aids a party having the burden of proof in establishing a point - as to which his adversary has possession of the critical evidence.[9] In the situation here, the Board possessed all of the evidence concerning its reasons for filing the instant petition. . . . In using the word "presumption" or "presumed" in articulating the business judgment rule, the courts have not intended to create a presumption in the classical procedural sense - as a vehicle that puts the burden of going forward with the evidence on the party without the burden of proof. Rather, the courts are merely expressing the substantive rule of director liability. As the panel in Stahl expressed it, "directors are protected by the [business judgment rule under Florida law], no matter how poor their business judgment, unless they acted fraudulently, illegally, oppressively, or in bad faith. Said differently, so long as due care was exercised, the [rule] protects a 'good director' (one who did not act fraudulently, illegally, oppressively, or in bad faith) who made an honest error or mistake in judgment, but not a 'bad director' (one who acted fraudulently, illegally, oppressively, or in bad faith) who made a bad decision."

The question before the bankruptcy judge was a question the business judgment rule envisions - whether the Board acted in bad faith when it filed the instant petition. AVA had the burden of proof on that issue, and, as the bankruptcy court's findings indicate, it fully satisfied that burden. Section 1112(b) authorized the court to dismiss the petition on a finding that it had been filed in bad faith, for the purpose of abusing the judicial process and the reorganization afforded by Chapter 11. In sum, the bankruptcy court did not misapply the law in reaching its decision. The court's decision is therefore due to be upheld. We uphold it by affirming the judgment of the district court. AFFIRMED.[10]

The Broker-Dealer-Adviser-Seller. The multiple roles of actors, especially in the financial area, make economic sense. However, these multiple roles can raise difficult legal issues when the actors' relationships with others combine contractual and fiduciary relationships. Broker-dealers offer a telling example. Brokers are agents and therefore fiduciaries. They represent and find, for client buyers or sellers, their counterparties. In the securities markets brokers execute the transactions among these parties. Brokers are

---

9.   . . . A presumption is invoked when a party's adversary possesses evidence that is essential to the claim (or affirmative defense) but is, as a practical matter, unavailable to all but the adversary." . . .

10.   Bal Harbor Club, Inc. v. AVA Dev., Inc. (*In re* Bal Harbor Club, Inc.), 316 F.3d 1192 (11th Cir. 2003) (some footnotes omitted) (citations omitted).

entrusted with the buyers' or sellers' assets or cash and are fiduciaries with respect to these entrusted assets and cash. As discussed in Chapter Three, pages 91-92, they perform multiple functions which pose difficult issues in fiduciary law.

— — — — — — — — — — -

Discussion Topics

a. Compare the court's analysis with the analysis of the author of the article. Which approach is more acceptable to you?

b. As a dues-paying union member, and a member of the Republican Party, what would be your position if the union used your dues to support the Democratic Party?

c. Compare the *Greisman, Oakland Raiders, and Bal Harbor* cases you just read. How did the courts' approach to its own discretion differ and why?

d. In corporate law, the courts have established a "business judgment rule" to guide their intervention in corporate affairs. Under the rule, the court will concede to the decisions of the board of directors even if mistaken, so long as there was no evidence of violations of the duty of loyalty (conflicts of interests) and no violation of the duty of care (insufficient and reasonable attention). Should the business judgment rule in the context of corporate business decisions apply to the courts' evaluation of union's activities? In what contexts should the courts exercise more discretion and intrusion on the unions' leadership decisions?

— — — — — — — — — — -

c. Judicial self-limitation under contract law

The courts' attitude and exercise of discretion under contract law differs in emphasis and approach from their exercise of judicial discretion in the context of fiduciary law. In contract law, the parties determine most of the terms of their relationship. Courts do not interfere unless the contract terms suggest fraud or undue influence. "'Hard bargains,' as unfair as they might be, are likely to survive attack in the courts. The attitude is a 'too bad' attitude, a 'you should have been more careful' attitude. Under the fiduciary regime, the beneficiaries, such as the investors or the patients, are more protected from unfair treatment. By definition, the dependent party to a fiduciary relationship is less able to protect itself. Therefore, the courts assume that the dependent trusting party would not have agreed to an unfair behavior of the fiduciary, and attribute these results to the relationship with the fiduciary."[11]

---

11.   TAMAR FRANKEL, TRUST AND HONESTY: AMERICA'S BUSINESS CULTURE AT A CROSSROAD 130 (2006) (*citing* RESTATEMENT (SECOND) OF CONTRACTS § 208 cmt. d (1981); *accord,* U.C.C. § 2-302 cmt. n.1 (2003); SAMUEL WILLISTON, 3 WILLISTON ON CONTRACTS 3:383-386 (Richard A. Lord ed., 4th ed. 1990); RESTATEMENT (THIRD) OF TRUSTS § 2 cmt. b (2003); 1 Austin W. Scott & William F. Fratcher, The Law of Trusts 43 (4th ed. 1987)); *see* Tamar Frankel, *Fiduciary Duties as Default Rules,* 74 Or. L. Rev. 1209, 1212 (1995).

A rationale for the courts' non-interference could be that contract parties are able to specify the terms of their relationships while the parties to a fiduciary relationship cannot. By definition, the terms of fiduciary relationships cannot be thus specified in detail. The less able a party is to specify the terms of the relationship with another, the more likely the courts may interfere in the bargain and establish what they consider to be fair and equitable terms.

– – – – – – – – – – –

Discussion Topics

Assume that a very sophisticated and knowledgeable jeweler bought jewels from another and found the delivered jewels to be faulty. The buyer argues that the faults are not up to the standard of the marketplace. The seller argues that the faults are not excluded specifically in the contract, and therefore, the delivered jewels meet the contract's requirements.

a. What are the factual and legal questions, which the court should entertain?

b. How different, if at all, would judicial interference be if the buyer was the entrustor and the seller was the trustee?

– – – – – – – – – – –

Remedies on Breach of Fiduciary Duties. Remedies for violation of fiduciary duties vary, depending on the circumstances. While the confidential relation principle was applied to certain corporate employees, different remedies based on different facts were sought.

In the E. I. Du Pont de Nemours Powder Company case, [for example,] the use of the company's trade secrets by a former employee was enjoined.[12] In the Essex Trust Company case,[13] a newspaper reporter who learned by eavesdropping that his employer wished to renew the lease of the property in which its business was being conducted secretly acquired the lease for himself and was held to be a constructive trustee. The information acquired and used by the employee had no connection with his duties as a newspaper reporter. "When, therefore, a person 'in a confidential or fiduciary position, in breach of his duty, uses his knowledge to make a profit for himself, he is accountable for such profit....'"[14]

A similar decision followed in *General Instrument Corporate Securities Litigation,*[15] where the court dealt with this issue, affirming *Brophy v. Cities Serv. Co.* The court wrote: "in equity, when breach of a confidential relation by an employee is relied on and an accounting for any resulting profits is sought, loss to the corporation need not be charged in the complaint."[16]

---

12.   E.I. Du Pont de Nemours Powder Co. v. Masland, 244 U.S. 100 (1917).
13.   Essex Trust Co. v. Enwright, 102 N.E. 441 (Mass. 1913).
14.   Brophy v. Cities Serv. Co, 70 A.2d 5 (Del. Ch. 1949) (footnotes added) (citations omitted).
15.   *In re* Gen. Instrument Corp. Sec. Litig., No. 96 C 1129, 2000 U.S. Dist. LEXIS 17082 (N.D. Ill. Nov. 21, 2000).
16.   *Id.* at *6.

The multiple remedies available to a plaintiff on breach of fiduciary duties are described in the following case:

In *Henderson v. Axiam, Inc.*, the president had been hired to help turn the corporation into a more profitable venture.[17] The president hired his wife as treasurer of the corporation and began to manipulate the corporation's finances to his benefit. He obtained bridge loans and convertible notes for the corporation. When the corporation bought out a major shareholder's stock, he secretly retained some of the stock for himself. He brought in the former director in order to gain more control. The president formed separate corporations and secretly transferred the corporation's unpatented inventions to the new corporations. He then attempted to move the corporation's headquarters. Plaintiffs sued for injunctive and declaratory relief. Defendants filed a counterclaim against the former director. The court found that the president and treasurer committed multiple breaches of their fiduciary obligations and wasted corporate assets but did not disregard the corporate entity. The court also found that the former director had breached his duty and that plaintiffs were entitled to recover legal fees.[18]

The court wrote:

In determining the appropriate remedy to resolve dissension in a closely held corporation, a court must consider the reasonable expectations of the aggrieved shareholders and the best interests of the corporation.

There is no adequate remedy at law to compensate the shareholders for the Holts' conduct. Under the Holts' control, Axiam has been looted of much value. Only an order restoring the balance between the shareholders, removing the Holts from their position of control, and securing the return of Axiam's intellectual property and its development can adequately remedy the wrongs committed by defendants....

Whether a prevailing plaintiff...is entitled to attorneys fees is a matter of discretion for the judge. "[The minority stockholder's right of action is his legal remedy against corporate mismanagement as well as] a powerful deterrent to greedy corporate management generally. And this prophylactic aspect of suits of this kind has been held to warrant a liberal attitude in awarding fees."...

It is both fitting and just that the ... plaintiffs be reimbursed for their attorneys fees and costs incurred in this action. Their efforts have resulted in benefits to Axiam and all its shareholders....

[P]laintiff shareholders seek a declaratory judgment that Axiam, not Holt, owns the SuperStack technology and any other technology related to Axiam's business developed by Holt while he was an officer or director of Axiam. Under G.L.c. 231, § 1, this Court is empowered to "make binding declarations of right, duty, status and other legal relations sought thereby, either before or after a breach or violation thereof has occurred in any case in which an actual controversy has arisen and is specifically set forth in the pleadings and whether any consequential judgment or relief is or could be claimed at law in equity or not ..."

---

17. Henderson v. Axiam, Inc., No. 96-2572-D, 1999 Mass. Super. LEXIS 580 (Mass. Super. Ct. June 22, 1999).
18. *Id.*

Declaratory relief is appropriate where: 1) an actual controversy has arisen in the case presented; 2) the plaintiffs have an interest therein; and 3) and the granting of declaratory relief will terminate the controversy. These three requirements are met here. There is an actual controversy between the shareholders, who assert that Axiam owns the SuperStack technology, and Holt, who asserts, somewhat inconsistently, that he owns it and that it does not exist. The shareholders have an obvious interest in confirming Axiam's ownership rights in its technology, since that technology constitutes Axiam's principal asset. Moreover, the shareholders are bringing this suit in a representative capacity to vindicate the interests of the corporation with respect to its technology. Axiam clearly has an interest in protecting its own technology. Finally, granting this relief will terminate the controversy and remove the uncertainty as to the ownership rights of the SuperStack technology....

... [T]he shareholders are entitled to a declaration that Axiam owns the SuperStack technology and any derivative of that technology.

The shareholders are also entitled to a declaration that Axiam owns all technology developed or under development at Axiam during the period of Holt's employment based on Holt's status as a fiduciary of Axiam....

As a director, officer and significant stockholder of Axiam, Holt stands in a fiduciary relationship with the corporation. Accordingly, any rights he may claim to have in any inventions related to Axiam's business developed while he was an Axiam fiduciary belong to the corporation.

... Violations of G.L.c. 93A.... [B]oth the convertible noteholders and the bridge loan lenders contend that Axiam--under the Holts' domination and control--violated G.L.c. 93A, § 11. The bridge loan lenders allege that Holt's refusal to permit Axiam to repay the bridge loans constitutes an unfair and deceptive act. The basis for the convertible noteholders' c. 93A claim is Holt's failure to seek patent protection and his attempt to divert the intellectual property of Axiam, their security under the Security Agreement, to his new corporation and move it to California to impair their legal rights.... [B]oth seek to recover their damages and attorneys fees and costs, trebled, against the Holts personally.

As detailed throughout, under the widely-cited "rascality test," Holt's course of conduct appears to be the paradigm 93A violation, having attained a level "that would raise an eyebrow of someone inured to the rough and tumble world of commerce." Similarly, his actions "reek with the rancid flavor of unfairness."...

Acts are "unfair or deceptive" if they fall "within at least the penumbra of some common-law, statutory, or other established concept of unfairness," or were "immoral, unethical, oppressive or unscrupulous," and resulted in "substantial injury to . . . other businessmen."... A breach of the implied covenant of good faith and fair dealing between parties to a contract may constitute an unfair or deceptive act for the purposes of chapter 93A....

... [A]n officer or director who engages in behavior violative of c. 93A is personally liable for that conduct.....

Holt's actions in refusing to allow Axiam to repay the demand obligations were unfair and deceptive.... Furthermore, Holt, who sought to punish the bridge loan lender plaintiffs, engaged in this unlawful conduct willfully and knowingly.

The bridge loan lenders seek recovery from Holt for the amount of their loans ($ 275,010 plus interest), trebled, and attorneys fees and costs. The Court shall award the bridge loan lenders attorneys fees and costs from Holt personally. However, the Court declines to award treble damages because the bridge loan lenders did not offer evidence quantifying the damages they suffered for the loss of the use of their money....

Holt's failure to seek patent protection for Axiam's SuperStack technology also constitutes an unfair act or practice.... Holt's reason for not seeking patent protection was to enable its transfer to another entity owned and controlled by him and his wife, thus allowing the technology to be exploited for their benefit.

Under c. 93A, § 11, a plaintiff may obtain an injunction if he has not suffered any loss of property or money "if it can be shown that the aforementioned unfair method of competition, act or practice may have the effect of causing such loss of money or property." Injunctive relief is appropriate here. In addition, the noteholder plaintiffs are entitled to recover their attorneys fees and costs from Holt. . . .

. . . [T]he shareholders allege that the Holts have improperly converted Axiam funds for their own personal use and enjoyment. One who intentionally and wrongfully exercises acts of ownership, control or dominion over personal property to which he has no right of possession at the time is liable for the tort of conversion. Moreover, "if the owner has not retaken the goods, he is entitled also to interest upon the value, to compensate him for the delay in obtaining redress."

Holt and Mrs. Holt used Axiam funds for their own personal benefit . . . . The evidence at trial establishes that at a minimum, the Holts converted $ 54,257.26 from Axiam. Accordingly, the plaintiff shareholders are entitled to recover for the corporation money damages equal to the amount converted, plus interest. . . .

. . . [T]he shareholders seek a full equitable accounting of Axiam's disbursements from July 1, 1995, until the present. Where an agent is charged with fraud and breach of fiduciary duty, a court may exercise its equitable jurisdiction to examine the entire account between the agent and principal. "The traditional equity remedy of an 'accounting,' . . . like other remedies of restitution, . . . requires one owing a fiduciary duty to pay to the beneficiary of that obligation--to 'disgorge'--money taken in derogation of that duty."

The Holts commingled Axiam funds with their own personal bank accounts. On numerous instances, they used Axiam funds to pay personal expenses. Accordingly, an order requiring a full accounting is appropriate. In conjunction with that order, the shareholders are also entitled to an order requiring the Holts to reimburse Axiam for any additional funds determined by the accounting to have been improperly diverted to their personal use and enjoyment.[19]

The remedy of constructive trust depends on the wrongful conduct of a defendant that results in unjust enrichment. If fiduciary relationships are viewed as relationships that arise from entrustment, then accounting is a by-product of fiduciary relationships. However, accounting for profits involves a further step. A fiduciary that profits from entrusted property or power in violation of a fiduciary duty is no more entitled to the profits than to the entrusted property or power. Therefore, even though the profits may be due to the fiduciary's efforts and talent, the profits do not belong to the fiduciary. In such a case a court may require the fiduciary to account to the entrustor for all illicit profits.

B. Constructive Trust and Resulting Trusts

1. Definitions and distinctions

Constructive trust is defined as follows:

Where, for any reason, the legal title to property is placed in one person under such circumstances as to make it inequitable for him to enjoy the beneficial interest, a trust will

---

19. Henderson v. Axiam, Inc., No. 96-2572-D, 1999 Mass. Super. LEXIS 580 (Mass. Super. Ct. June 22, 1999).

be implied in favor of the persons entitled thereto. This arises by construction of equity, independently of the intention of the parties. Equity will raise a constructive trust and compel restoration, where one through actual fraud, abuse of confidence reposed and accepted, or through other questionable means, gains something for himself which, in equity and good conscience, he should not be permitted to hold.[20]

The distinction between constructive trust, resulting trusts and express trust clarifies the nature of constructive trust. "A [resulting trust] arises where property is transferred under circumstances which give rise to an inference that the person who makes the transfer or causes it to be made does not intend the transferee to take the beneficial interest in the property . . . ." A common type of resulting trust arises "where the purchase price of the property is paid by one person and at his direction the vendor conveys the property to another person."[21]

The *Restatement (Second) of Trusts* distinguishes the resulting trust situation above from similar situations in which constructive trusts arise. In the resulting trust situation, the person furnishing the purchase price consents to both use of the money and the transfer to another. However, a constructive trust arises if that person did not consent to use of the money or did not consent to the other person receiving title. In addition, constructive trusts arise if fiduciaries purchases property with their own money and in their own name in violation of their fiduciary duty.[22]

Unlike express trusts and resulting trusts, a constructive trust is not based on intention but is remedial in nature and imposed by a court.[23] "A constructive trust is not a true trust; . . . and it does not impose extensive fiduciary duties on the trustee, but only the duty to make restitution."[24]

The beneficiary of a constructive trust may be entitled to specific enforcement of the constructive trust where there is an adequate remedy at law (*e.g.*, where the property is land or other unique property).[25] Specific enforcement may also be appropriate where the constructive trustee is insolvent.[26] In addition, specific enforcement is allowed if the property was obtained through abuse of a fiduciary

---

20.   Seventh Elect Church in Israel v. First Seattle Dexter Horton Nat'l Bank, 299 P. 359, 360 (Wash. 1931); *see also* RESTATEMENT (THIRD) OF TRUSTS § 1 cmt. e (2003); RESTATEMENT (FIRST) OF RESTITUTION § 160 (1935).
21.   Moses v. Moses, 53 A.2d 805, 807 (N.J. 1947); *see also* 2 RESTATEMENT (SECOND) OF TRUSTS 392 (1959). Other types of resulting trusts arise where an express trust "fails in whole or in part" or is "fully performed without exhausting the trust res." 53 A.2d at 807; *see also* 2 RESTATEMENT (SECOND) OF TRUSTS 323 (1959).
22.   2 RESTATEMENT (SECOND) OF TRUSTS 392 (1959).
23.   RESTATEMENT (THIRD) OF TRUSTS § 1 cmt. e (2003); RESTATEMENT (FIRST) OF RESTITUTION § 160 (1935). The *Restatement (Third) of Trusts* does not apply to constructive trusts (unless an express trust is involved). The *Restatement (First) of Restitution* applies instead. RESTATEMENT (THIRD) OF TRUSTS § 1 cmt. e (2003).
24.   United States v. Fontana, 528 F. Supp. 137, 143 (S.D.N.Y. 1981) (citing 5 SCOTT, TRUSTS § 462.4 (3d ed.)).
25.   RESTATEMENT (FIRST) OF RESTITUTION § 160 cmt. e (1935).
26.   *Id.* cmt. f.

relationship, regardless of whether there is an adequate remedy at law.[27]

One example of the imposition of a constructive trust is described in the following case:

In the case of *Simonds v. Simonds,* a decedent husband had promised in a separation agreement with his first wife to maintain insurance policies and name his first wife as the beneficiary.[28] However, at the time of the husband's death, no such policy existed. The first wife claimed a constructive trust on the proceeds of another insurance policy in which the beneficiary was the second wife of her former husband. The appellate court affirmed an order for partial summary judgment in favor of the first wife and the recognition of a constructive trust to the extent of $7,000 of insurance policies for her benefit.

The court found that the first wife, the plaintiff, was entitled to a constructive trust based on her equitable interest in the insurance policies of the second wife. At the time of the separation agreement, the decedent and the plaintiff remained in a fiduciary relationship. Because decedent and plaintiff were husband and wife, each had a duty of fairness in financial matters toward the other. Therefore, the first wife's equitable interest attached to all substituted insurance policies, whether the policies named the second wife or the daughter as beneficiary. At the time each substituted policy was issued, the decedent had an obligation to name the first wife a beneficiary. Without recognizing a constructive trust in favor of the plaintiff, the second wife would be unjustly enriched. Unjust enrichment did not require the performance of any wrongful act.[29]

2. When will constructive trust be awarded?

a. To impose constructive trust one needs more than a vague one-sided "understanding."

We visit *Yamins v. Zeitz,* in which the court considered a claim to impose a constructive trust on the defendant's lease.[30] The plaintiff and other members of his family owned a corporation, which controlled and managed several movie theaters in Fall River. Most of the theaters in Fall River were controlled by the plaintiff, except for Academy Theatre. Between 1922 and 1940, plaintiff leased the Academy Theatre and rarely operated it, essentially to prevent any competitor from operating the theater. In 1940, plaintiff failed to renew the lease, because a new theater was being constructed which would compete with plaintiff's theaters. When plaintiff's lease of the Academy Theatre expired, defendant, Zeitz, obtained a six-year lease of the Academy. Shortly after defendant leased the Academy Theatre, plaintiff managed

---

27. *Id.* cmt. e; *see also, e.g.,* Unicure, Inc. v. Thurman, 599 P.2d 925, 928 (Colo. Ct. App. 1979).
28. Simonds v. Simonds, 380 N.E.2d 189 (N.Y. 1978).
29. *Id.*
30. Yamins v. Zeitz, 76 N.E.2d 769 (Mass. 1948).

to lease the new Center Theatre, which rendered the Academy his only direct competitor. In September, 1940, the defendant assigned the Academy lease to plaintiff for the remainder of the lease and received from the plaintiff $6,375. Plaintiff told the defendant that he was acquiring the Academy to protect his investments in the other theaters in Fall River.

In this claim plaintiff alleged the parties' "understanding" that the plaintiff would be able to negotiate and obtain extensions and renewals of the Academy lease at the end of its six year term, and that defendant would in good faith do nothing to impair plaintiff's right to do that. Before the six year term was over, defendant secretly negotiated with the owner of the Academy Theatre a new lease, and began operating the theater. Upon discovery, plaintiff notified the defendant that unless the lease was assigned to the plaintiff, plaintiff would sue the defendant to obtain a constructive trust of the lease and for accounting of profits or damages. And he did.

The court held:

Manifestly the allegations of the bill do not establish an express trust, there being no allegation of any written instrument signed by the defendants .... And ... no agreement or valid contract is alleged in the bill, but only an oral understanding. If the bill is to stand against the demurrer, a trust must be found by implication of law. Equity will, of course, impose a trust without regard to the intention of the parties if, in order to avoid unjust enrichment, the person who holds the property should be charged with a duty to convey it to another. But this equitable relief is granted only where there has been either fraud in securing the property or violation of a fiduciary relation whether express or arising out of a confidential relationship. Such a relationship can arise where special trust or confidence is placed in one party by another. ... In the present case, however, the facts alleged are clearly insufficient to establish any fiduciary or confidential relationship between the plaintiff and the defendants arising out of the acquisition of the leasehold in question by the defendants or otherwise. Counsel for the plaintiff properly concedes that the mere relation of the assignor and the assignee of a lease does not, without more, give rise to a confidential relationship. We find nothing in the bill to show more. The allegations of the bill disclose that the defendants were competitors of the plaintiff and that that was why the plaintiff sought the assignment of the lease in question. It is not alleged that any confidential information was given to the defendants by the plaintiff. If the plaintiff did place confidence and trust in Zeitz, there is no allegation that Zeitz was aware thereof. A person cannot create obligations on the part of another by merely trusting the other. And in a business relationship even the existence of mutual respect and confidence does not make the relationship fiduciary. This is not affected by the allegation in the present bill of the "understanding" between the plaintiff and the defendants or either of them. Even though the plaintiff had engaged Zeitz to secure the new lease for him and Zeitz had secured it for himself, a constructive trust for the plaintiff would not arise. Any trust in such a case must arise solely from the oral agreement and is unenforceable because [the statute requires the trust to be in writing]. A mere understanding, such as that alleged in the bill before us, that the defendant assignor would permit the plaintiff assignee to obtain a renewal of the lease, in like manner would not give rise to any implied or constructive trust. [The court denied the remedy.][31]

---

31.   *Id.*

b. When can the right to the remedy of constructive trust be waived?

In the case of *Beatty v. Guggenheim Exploration Co.*, the court considered the waiver of the constructive trust remedy.[32] Beatty was a mining engineer and assistant manager of Guggenheim, under a five-year contract with the company. Under his contract, he was bound to "devote himself exclusively to the business of the defendant company, and not to accept, engage in or enter upon any other business or employment whatever, and not to become, either directly or indirectly, interested in or connected in any way with any business similar to that which the defendant company carried on."[33] Beatty explored some properties in which the company might have been interested. When the company did not show an interest in these properties, Beatty agreed to become a partner with the persons who offered to sell the properties (the partners). His agreement was made on condition that his employer will consent to his involvement in this deal. The dealing between Beatty and his partners involved two contracts. One contract promised Beatty certain payments. The other involved a deal with his employer-company. The court held that Beatty breached his duties to his employer. Beatty did not receive his share according to his second agreement with the partners, and sued them for it.

The court wrote:

The defendants [the partners] argue that the two contracts [the contract that involved Beatty's employer, and his contract with the partners] are inseparably united in scheme and execution. They say, therefore, that misconduct in respect of one [the contract in which the employer was involved] defeats recovery under the other [Beatty's contract with the partners]. But we think there is no such union as the argument assumes. The two transactions are clearly severable. . . . We held that [in one transaction Beatty breached his duty to his employer]. The payment [which he received on that basis] was subject to a constructive trust. Our decision went no farther. [The court distinguished the payment based on the second contract from payment on the first.] The amount due under each head is stated in the findings. Increase of the one had no tendency to swell the measure of the other [in violation of Beatty's duties to the employer]. Subsequent misconduct in another and distinct transaction does not work a forfeiture of rights already lawfully accrued.

There remains, however a question at once more important and more difficult. It is whether the plaintiff [Beatty] ever lawfully acquired a share in [the second contract], considered by itself. He had agreed with his employer that he would not become directly or indirectly interested in, or connected with, any person, partnership, or corporation engaged in any similar business. He had also agreed that none of the covenants or conditions of the contract should be "waived, modified, altered, or annulled" except by writing subscribed by the parties, who further covenanted that they would not "urge or claim any such waiver, alteration, modification, or amendment unless the same be evidenced by such writing." The finding is that the president and the general manager of the employer knew that plaintiff was interested in the Perry-Treadgold contract and consented thereto, but no written consent was found or proved. The question, therefore,

---

32. Beatty v. Guggenheim Exploration Co., 122 N.E. 378 (N.Y. 1919).
33. Beatty v. Guggenheim Exploration Co., 119 N.E. 575, 576 (N.Y. 1918), *modified,* 122 N.E. 378 (N.Y. 1919).

subdivides itself into two branches. One is whether the plaintiff, if he had purchased an interest in the claims without the consent of his employer, would be chargeable as a trustee; the other is whether consent not evidenced by a writing has varied the employer's rights. . . .

We think therefore, that aside from the special provisions of this contract, the agent became a trustee at the election of the principal. But the contract reinforces that conclusion. It is true that an agent or a partner who breaks a covenant not to engage in some other business does not, as a matter of course, become chargeable as a trustee for the profits of the forbidden venture. The agent may be discharged; the partnership may be dissolved; there may be an action for damages. But to raise a [constructive] trust there must be more. It is sometimes said that the profits of the forbidden venture must have been diverted from the business of the principal or the partnership. We think it may fairly be found that there was a diversion of profits here. But the test of diversion is not exhaustive. For most cases it may supply a working rule, but the rule is a phase or illustration of a principle still larger. A constructive trust is the formula through which the conscience of equity finds expression. When property has been acquired in such circumstances that the holder of the legal title may not in good conscience retain the beneficial interest equity converts him into a trustee. We think it would be against good conscience for the plaintiff to retain these profits unless his employer has consented. . . .

We conclude, therefore, that the plaintiff was chargeable as a trustee if the employer so elected. But the Appellate Division has found upon sufficient evidence that the employer consented to the investment [by Beatty]. The plaintiff [Beatty], when he associated himself with [the partners], reserved the privilege of withdrawal. The contract was that if the president or the general manager disapproved of his investment, then the payment which he had made, instead of being a purchase of a share in a joint enterprise, should be a loan to Perry personally. This is found by the trial judge as well as by the Appellate Division. The testimony is that, in that event, the loan was to be repaid in a reasonable time. The president and the general manager, with knowledge that the plaintiff had reserved this privilege of withdrawal, consented that the investment be retained. The question is whether the employer may now have the aid of a court of equity to impress upon the investment the quality of a constructive trust.

The question would answer itself if it were not for the covenant that there shall be no waiver or amendment not evidenced by a writing. The employer sets up this covenant to nullify its oral consent. The employee asserts that the covenant is nugatory. Those who make a contract may unmake it. The clause which forbids a change may be changed like any other. The prohibition of oral waiver may itself be waived. . . . The plaintiff had reserved the right to withdraw from the joint enterprise if his employer disapproved of it, and in that event to treat his advances as a loan. On the faith of the consent, he turned a loan into a purchase. It is too late, years afterwards, for the employer to cancel the consent, and insist that the purchase be turned back into a loan.

We hold, therefore, that the consent, though oral, gives protection to the agent, and acquits him of a breach of contract.[34]

Problem

On January 1, 2000, Baker asked Able for $100,000 in order to refurbish his shop and promised to return the money on January 2001. Baker gave Able a loan agreement and a note confirming his obligation to repay the money on that date. No other conditions were attached to

---

34.   Beatty v. Guggenheim Exploration Co., 122 N.E. 378 (N.Y. 1919).

the agreement. On February 1, 2000, Able noticed that Baker is not refurbishing his shop but instead had taken a year's travel around the world. Does Able have any legal means of preventing Baker from using the money for any other purpose but refurbishing the shop? What legal form can Able adopt to ensure that Baker uses the money for the sole purpose of refurbishing his shop?

C. Accounting for Profits

We have dealt with the case of *Brophy v. Cities Service Co.*[35] As a reminder: Thomas F. Kennedy, a defendant, was an executive and confidential secretary to an officer and director of Cities Service Co., the plaintiff. During Kennedy's employment at Cities Service Co., he acquired confidential knowledge that the company planned to buy back its own shares to raise the company's stock price. Based on this non-public insider knowledge, Kennedy purchased Cities Service Co. shares for his personal account before the company's stock was repurchased and sold them at a profit when Cities Service Co. share prices rose after the repurchase.

Cities Service Co. argued that Kennedy held the insider information as a fiduciary and sought to collect from him "all profits made by him [as a constructive trustee of the company] from the purchase and sale of [company] stock."[36] The court held that, "if an employee in the course of his employment acquires secret information relating to his employer's business, he occupies a position of trust and confidence toward it, analogous in most respects to that of a fiduciary, and must govern his actions accordingly."[37]

The relief sought against Kennedy is that he be directed to account as a constructive trustee for all profits made by him from the purchase and sale of such stock, and that he be adjudged liable to Cities Service Co. for the amount of such profits. Kennedy defended on the ground that Cities Service Co. did not appear to have suffered any losses by his purchase of the stock.

The court, however, held that, when a person in a fiduciary position uses entrusted information to make a profit for himself, he is accountable to repay the profit regardless of the company's actual loss. The court reasoned that, "[i]n equity, when the breach of a confidential relation by an employee is relied on and an accounting for any resulting profits is sought, loss to the corporation need not be charged in the complaint. [Furthermore,] public policy will not permit an employee occupying a position of trust and confidence toward his employer to abuse that relation to his own profit, regardless of whether his employer suffers a loss."[38]

---

35.   Brophy v. Cities Serv. Co, 70 A.2d 5 (Del. Ch. 1949) (citations omitted).
36.   *Id.* at 7.
37.   *Id.*
38.   *Id.* at 8.

1. Is accounting appropriate for determining restitution damages?

The question of whether the remedy of accounting is appropriate for determining the remedy of restitution damages demonstrates that the two remedies are very similar. Their origins, however, may differ. The issue of these remedies arises in *Bostic v. Goodnight.*[39] In that case, Goodnight and his wife Julie incorporated Goodnight Farms in February 2000. The farm's business objective was to "buy, grow and feed, and then resell matured cattle for a profit. In January 2001, Lindy and Shannon Bostic purchased a 50% interest in Goodnight Farms, and [the Goodnights] retained the remaining 50% interest in the corporation. Under the new ownership structure, each [of the four shareholders] assumed a management role in the operation of Goodnight Farms. . . . The shareholders' relationships soon soured. Due to disagreements regarding the management of the corporation and bookkeeping irregularities, the parties agreed to dissolve the corporation . . . on April 16, 2002. The dissolution was in process when, in early 2003, the Bostics sued the Goodnights alleging deceit, violation of federal and state securities acts, and breach of fiduciary duty and corporate waste—a . . . claim brought on behalf of Goodnight Farms. The Bostics requested monetary damages, including attorneys' fees and costs, and an equitable accounting of the [misappropriated] corporate funds."[40]

"The [District Court] found that Goodnight diverted $ 1,741,417.62 in corporate funds for his own benefit. Accordingly, the court ordered Goodnight to pay the Bostics their 50% share of the diverted amount: $ 870,708.81." However, the accounting that the plaintiff is entitled to is limited "to only those funds that Goodnight diverted from the corporation for his own benefit." The Bostics are entitled to an accounting because it is "essentially a calculation of restitution owed to the corporation by Goodnight based on his diversion of corporation funds for his own benefit."[41] In fact, the court traced the misappropriated money: from Goodnight to the corporation and upon its dissolution from the corporation to the Bostics. Thus, regardless of whether Goodnight was a fiduciary of the corporation, in which case he would have been charged with an accounting, he owed the corporation the misappropriated money in restitution as well.

— — — — — — — — — —

Discussion Topic

a. Under what circumstances would the distinction between restitution and accounting have made a difference?

— — — — — — — — — —

---

39. Bostic v. Goodnight, 443 F.3d 1044 (8th Cir. 2006).
40. *Id.* at 1046 (footnote omitted).
41   *Id.* at 1049.

2. Is accounting for profits appropriate on breach of contract?

Another case in which accounting was the subject of contention is *Snepp v. United States,*[42] discussed in Chapter Two. In that case, a former Central Intelligence Agency ("CIA") agent's employment contract contained an undertaking to refrain from publishing or disclosing any information about the agency without pre-clearance from the CIA. After retiring from the CIA, Snepp published a book without receiving prepublication approval from the CIA. The CIA sued on breach of the agreement and sought, but could not prove, damages. The majority held that Snepp breached his fiduciary duty to the CIA and awarded the CIA a constructive trust over all future profits from the book.

Justice Stevens, with whom Justice Brennan and Justice Marshall join, dissented. In their opinion, constructive trust was not justified. They distinguished between Snepp's fiduciary and contractual duties. That is, they implicitly distinguished between misappropriation by a fiduciary and breach of contract. Because the book that Snepp wrote did not contain any confidential, nonpublic information, Snepp did not breach his fiduciary duty to protect confidential information, but merely breached his contractual duty to obtain prepublication clearance. This breach does not deserve a constructive trust remedy. Further, Snepp has not gained any profits as a result of his breach of the duty to obtain prepublication clearance. If the Government is entitled to all of Snepp's profit earned from his own legitimate activity, the Government would be unjustly enriched.

The dissent wrote:

Snepp admittedly breached his duty to submit the manuscript of his book. . . for prepublication review. However, the Government has conceded that the book contains no classified, nonpublic material. Thus, by definition, the interest in confidentiality that Snepp's contract was designed to protect has not been compromised. Nevertheless, the Court today grants the Government unprecedented and drastic relief in the form of a constructive trust over the profits derived by Snepp from the sale of the book. . . .

The rule of law the Court announces today is not supported by statute, by the contract, or by the common law. Although Congress has enacted a number of criminal statutes punishing the unauthorized dissemination of certain types of classified information, it has not seen fit to authorize the constructive trust remedy the Court creates today. Nor does either of the contracts Snepp signed with the Agency provide for any such remedy in the event of a breach. The Court's *per curiam* opinion seems to suggest that its result is supported by a blend of the law of trusts and the law of contracts. But neither of these branches of the common law supports the imposition of a constructive trust under the circumstances of this case.

Plainly this is not a typical trust situation in which a settlor has conveyed legal title to certain assets to a trustee for the use and benefit of designated beneficiaries. Rather, it is an employment relationship in which the employee possesses fiduciary obligations arising out of his duty of loyalty to his employer. One of those obligations, long recognized by the

---

42. Snepp v. United States, 444 U.S. 507 (1980).

common law even in the absence of a written employment agreement, is the duty to protect confidential or "classified" information. If Snepp had breached that obligation, the common law would support the implication of a constructive trust upon the benefits derived from his misuse of confidential information.

But Snepp did not breach his duty to protect confidential information. Rather, he breached a contractual duty, imposed in aid of the basic duty to maintain confidentiality, to obtain prepublication clearance. In order to justify the imposition of a constructive trust, the majority attempts to equate this contractual duty with Snepp's duty not to disclose, labeling them both as "fiduciary." I find nothing in the common law to support such an approach.

Employment agreements often contain covenants designed to ensure in various ways that an employee fully complies with his duty not to disclose or misuse confidential information. One of the most common is a covenant not to compete. Contrary to the majority's approach in this case, the courts have not construed such covenants broadly simply because they support a basic fiduciary duty; nor have they granted sweeping remedies to enforce them. On the contrary, because such covenants are agreements in restraint of an individual's freedom of trade, they are enforceable only if they can survive scrutiny under the "rule of reason," [requiring] that the covenant be reasonably necessary to protect a legitimate interest of the employer (such as an interest in confidentiality), that the employer's interest not be outweighed by the public interest, and that the covenant not be of any longer duration or wider geographical scope than necessary to protect the employer's interest.

. . . Like an ordinary employer, the CIA has a vital interest in protecting certain types of information; at the same time, the CIA employee has a countervailing interest in preserving a wide range of work opportunities (including work as an author) and in protecting his First Amendment rights. The public interest lies in a proper accommodation that will preserve the intelligence mission of the Agency while not abridging the free flow of unclassified information. . . .

But even assuming that Snepp's covenant to submit to prepublication review should be enforced, the constructive trust imposed by the Court is not an appropriate remedy. If an employee has used his employer's confidential information for his own personal profit, a constructive trust over those profits is obviously an appropriate remedy because the profits are the direct result of the breach. But Snepp admittedly did not use confidential information in his book; nor were the profits from his book in any sense a product of his failure to submit the book for prepublication review. For, even if Snepp had submitted the book to the Agency for prepublication review, the Government's censorship authority would surely have been limited to the excision of classified material. In this case, then, it would have been obliged to clear the book for publication in precisely the same form as it now stands. [43] Thus, Snepp has not gained any profits as a result of his breach; the

43.   If he had submitted the book to the Agency and the Agency had refused to consent to the publication of certain material in it, Snepp could have obtained judicial review to determine whether the Agency was correct in considering the material classified. . . . It is noteworthy that the Court does not disagree with the Fourth Circuit's view in *Marchetti*, reiterated in *Snepp*, that a CIA employee has a First Amendment right to publish unclassified information. Thus, despite its reference in footnote 3 of its opinion to the Government's so-called compelling interest in protecting "the appearance of confidentiality," . . . and despite some ambiguity in the Court's reference to "detrimental" and "harmful" as opposed to "classified" information, . . . I do not understand the Court to imply that the Government could obtain an injunction against the publication of unclassified information.

Government, rather than Snepp, will be unjustly enriched if he is required to disgorge profits attributable entirely to his own legitimate activity.

. . . The Court states that publication of "unreviewed material" by a former CIA agent "can be detrimental to vital national interests even if the published information is unclassified.". . . It then seems to suggest that the injury in such cases stems from the Agency's inability to catch "harmful" but unclassified information before it is published. I do not believe, however, that the Agency has any authority to censor its employees' publication of unclassified information on the basis of its opinion that publication may be "detrimental to vital national interests" or otherwise "identified as harmful.". . . The CIA never attempted to assert such power over Snepp in either of the contracts he signed; rather, the Agency itself limited its censorship power to preventing the disclosure of "classified" information. Moreover, even if such a wide-ranging prior restraint would be good national security policy, I would have great difficulty reconciling it with the demands of the *First Amendment.*

The Court also relies to some extent on the Government's theory at trial that Snepp caused it harm by flouting his prepublication review obligation and thus making it appear that the CIA was powerless to prevent its agents from publishing any information they chose to publish, whether classified or not. The Government theorized that this appearance of weakness would discourage foreign governments from cooperating with the CIA because of a fear that their secrets might also be compromised. . . .

In any event, to the extent that the Government seeks to punish Snepp for the generalized harm he has caused by failing to submit to prepublication review and to deter others from following in his footsteps, punitive damages is, as the Court of Appeals held, clearly the preferable remedy "since a constructive trust depends on the concept of unjust enrichment rather than deterrence and punishment. . . ."

The uninhibited character of today's exercise in lawmaking is highlighted by the Court's disregard of two venerable principles that favor a more conservative approach to this case.

First, for centuries the English-speaking judiciary refused to grant equitable relief unless the plaintiff could show that his remedy at law was inadequate. Without waiting for an opportunity to appraise the adequacy of the punitive damages remedy in this case, the Court has jumped to the conclusion that equitable relief is necessary.

Second, and of greater importance, the Court seems unaware of the fact that its drastic new remedy has been fashioned to enforce a species of prior restraint on a citizen's right to criticize his government Inherent in this prior restraint is the risk that the reviewing agency will misuse its authority to delay the publication of a critical work or to persuade an author to modify the contents of his work beyond the demands of secrecy. The character of the covenant as a prior restraint on free speech surely imposes an especially heavy burden on the censor to justify the remedy it seeks. It would take more than the Court has written to persuade me that that burden has been met. I respectfully dissent.[44]

— — — — — — — — — — -

Discussion Topics

a. If the court in *Brophy* (against Kennedy) had adopted the dissent's view in *Snepp*, would the result in *Brophy* be different? On what grounds?

---

44. Snepp v. United States, 444 U.S. 507 (1980).

b. What is the theoretical justification for imposing on a disloyal fiduciary the accounting for profits as a remedy? Should accounting for profits be imposed on a fiduciary that violated the duty of care?

c. How would you approach the remedies in the following case, taking into consideration the cases cited as well? In *Clay v. Thomas*, the issue involved:

the effect of a sale of trust property by a trustee, under a will with the power of sale, to himself individually. . . .

. . . [T]he trustees are vested with the power to sell the property therein devised. . . .

[After a certain interval the parties negotiated the sale of the property which culminated in the purchase of the property by some of the trustees for $ 190,000.00 for the entire property.] . . .

Within less than three years after that purchase by the [trustees] they sold the [properties] for a total sum of about $ 490,000.00, which, as will be seen, was an increase of $ 300,000.00 above what they had paid for it.

This suit was filed by [beneficiaries against the trustees] seeking to charge the [trustees who purchased the property] with the . . . proportion of the profits which [the trustees] realized out of their purchase and sale of the trust property, upon the grounds that as trustees they had no right to sell to themselves individually the trust property. . . .

It will thus be seen that the precise question for determination is not the right of a trustee to purchase the trust property from the *cestui que trust,* but it is the right of the trustee to purchase the trust property from himself as such trustee. Generally speaking, unless modified by some peculiar facts, a trustee cannot purchase from himself the trust property free from the right of the *cestui que trust* [beneficiary] to either treat his purchase as a continuation of the trust [and view the money which the trustee collected as the trust property] or to adopt the subsequent disposition of the property by the trustee and to ask for an accounting of the profits realized by the trustee. . . .

"If persons having a confidential character were permitted to avail themselves of any knowledge acquired in that capacity, they might be induced to conceal their information and not to exercise it for the benefit of the persons relying on their integrity. The characters are inconsistent." . . .

. . . "As a general rule a party occupying a relation of trust or confidence to another is, in equity, bound to abstain from doing everything which can place him in a position inconsistent with the duty or trust such relation imposes upon him, or which has a tendency to interfere with the discharge of such duty. Upon this principle no one placed in a situation of trust or confidence in reference to the subject of a sale can be the purchaser, on his own account, of the property sold." . . .

. . . "The inquiry is not whether there was fraud in fact. In such a case the danger of yielding to the temptation is so imminent, and the security against discovery so great, that a court of equity, at the instance of the *cestui que trust* if he applies in a reasonable time, will set aside the sale as of course."

[In some special cases] a trustee, especially if he be one not vested with the power of sale, may be empowered by a court of equity to become a bidder at the sale of the trust property. But . . . where the trustee has full and complete authority from the creator of the trust to sell, [there seems to be no precedent for such court permission. . . .

Stripped of irrelevant matter, this is simply a case where trustees purchased from themselves the trust property, and, as we view the record, for an inadequate consideration. One of the remedies of the *cestui que trust* in such a case, recognized everywhere, is . . . [that]: "If the trustee has actually sold the estate, a *cestui que trust* may compel the trustee to pay him what he received above the original purchase price. If the *cestui que trust* adopt the sale by the trustee, he must submit to it altogether."

Here the trustees have sold the property, and the *cestui ques trust* are seeking to make them account for the profits. They clearly have the right to do so.

If it should be thought that the rule which we have applied is harsh, and in some cases apparently encroaches upon strict justice, it may be said in answer that there are many instances in the law where such seeming results occur. For instance, it would be a great disaster to a creditor holding a perfectly solvent note for a large sum, and to which there was no other defense, to be deprived of collecting it because his right to sue was barred by limitations; but no sympathetic condolences on the part of the court could give relief. We must administer the law as we find it. Indeed, there would be a more defendable incentive to give relief if possible to the one whose cause of action was barred than to a trustee in a case like the one we have here. The condition of the former was produced by mere lapse of time, arbitrarily fixed by the legislature, and non-action by the creditor during that time, which may have in part been caused by innocent oversight. The trustee, however, has no such palliating circumstances in his favor. He is forbidden to profit by trading for or trafficking with the trust property, thus arraying self-interest against that standard of good faith which the law exacts and demands of the trustee for the protection of the confiding *cestui que trust*. The doctrine is founded upon the principle that the strong must be honest and the weak must be protected.

. . . The court should therefore ascertain the amount of money actually collected by the trustees from the sale which they made, and the amount, if any, which is yet due, and deduct from the amount of these sums the expenses, if any, which the trustees incurred in effecting the sale, or in perfecting titles, also the amount of taxes which they may have paid after their purchase of the trust property, and allow such sums as a credit upon the purchase price with interest, and adjudge in favor of the plaintiffs. Wherefore, the judgment is reversed, with directions to proceed in accordance with this opinion.[45]

d. Would contract law allow the plaintiff beneficiary to prevail? Was the plaintiff beneficiary's consent faulty because it was "procedurally unconscionable"? Was the consent substantively unconscionable, even if the procedure that was used to obtain the consent was fair?

In *Roberts v. Sears, Roebuck & Co.*,[46] which we studied in Chapter Two, the court considered whether a plaintiff could collect the defendant's past profits from a misappropriated patent. The plaintiff invented a new type of socket wrench during his off-duty hours while employed by defendant, a department store. After successfully applying for a patent, the plaintiff revealed his invention to his manager and was encouraged to submit his idea to defendant. After positive reports on the invention's sales, defendant misrepresented the value of the invention to the plaintiff in order to procure the assignment of the plaintiff's patent rights.

In a jury trial, the defendant was found guilty of fraud, breach of confidential relationship, and negligent misrepresentation. On the remedy issue, the plaintiff demanded both the past profits that the

45. Clay v. Thomas, 198 S.W. 762 (Ky. 1917) (citations omitted).
46. Roberts v. Sears, Roebuck & Co., 573 F.2d 976 (7th Cir. 1978) (footnotes and citations omitted).

plaintiff had collected from the patent as well as the return of the patent. The defendant argued that the plaintiff had to choose between the past profit awarded by the jury and the return of the patent and that the plaintiff's acceptance of the jury award precluded him from seeking an equitable remedy.

The court held that sending the case to the jury with an instruction to determine past profits did not bar the plaintiff from seeking rescission of his assignment to the plaintiff and the recovery of his patent. The court found that the plaintiff did not have to elect which profits to be awarded, because rescission and a return of the patent would not constitute a double recovery, and there would be no factual inconsistency between the remedies:

> Having determined that the district court is not bound by the rigid requirements of Illinois law on election of remedies, there remains the question whether plaintiff can still pursue his equitable remedies under the facts of this case. We conclude that the district court correctly decided not to disturb the jury's monetary award, but that the court erred in not considering whether rescission of the contract and return of plaintiff's patent were appropriate.
>
> The general rule as to when an election is necessary is that "a certain state of facts relied on as the basis of a certain remedy is inconsistent with, and repugnant to, another certain state of facts relied on as the basis of another remedy." Here, the jury was instructed that plaintiff could receive profits for Counts I and II, fraud and breach of a confidential relationship. Apparently dissatisfied with the size of the jury verdict, plaintiff sought in a post-trial motion to have the court reconsider the evidence and award relief based on essentially the same standard the jury used. To have granted plaintiff's request would have been completely unfair to [defendant]. It might have been better for the court to require the plaintiff to elect his remedy expressly prior to instructing the jury, but plaintiff did not object to the court's procedure, and therefore, must have been satisfied to let the jury determine the appropriate award. Having let the case go to the jury without getting the issue clarified, plaintiff should not be heard to complain about the outcome of that procedure.
>
> With regard to an election between the profits awarded by the jury and return of the patent based on rescission, however, we see no basis for invoking the election of remedies doctrine. Based on the jury instruction, plaintiff will receive one million dollars as the measure of *past* profits earned by [defendant] up to the time of trial. That award, however, is not inconsistent with return of the patent so that plaintiff can receive the *future* benefits of the patent that Sears fraudulently acquired. There will be neither a double recovery nor a factual inconsistency between these remedies. Therefore, we conclude that going to the jury under a past profits instruction did not bar plaintiff from seeking rescission and thereby possibly recovering his patent. Whether rescission is appropriate, however, is an issue that should be decided in the first instance by the district court.[47]

D. Equitable Remedies

Doctrinally, the source of the remedies on violations of fiduciary obligation is equity, because fiduciary obligations originated in equity. "As Equity evolved, concrete rules in many instances it clarifies . . . an earlier and imprecise vocabulary. The term 'fiduciary' itself was

---

47.   Roberts v. Sears, Roebuck & Co., 573 F.2d 976 (7th Cir. 1978) (footnotes and citations omitted).

adopted to apply to situations falling short of 'trusts,' but in which one person was nonetheless obliged to act *like* a trustee."[48]

Corporate law adopted fiduciary principles that derived from trust law. However, corporations are different from trusts. Corporate managers have the power to direct corporate use of assets but do not have the legal ownership of the assets.[49] Further, corporate managers have more discretion to deal with corporate assets than trustees do because the objectives of corporations are open-ended, while those of trusts are usually more specific and can be described in the trust documents.[50]

1. When are equitable remedies awarded?

In *Watson v. Button*,[51] the plaintiff, a stockholder, and the defendant, general manager and director of the corporation, jointly owned all of the stock in a corporation. The defendant sold all his stock to third parties (buyers). Upon the sale the defendant secured a discharge from any future claims against him in favor of the corporation. After the sale, the plaintiff (the remaining stockholder) discovered that before the date of the sale, the defendant had misappropriated corporate funds. This misappropriation caused both the defendant and the plaintiff to be jointly responsible for $68,000 in corporate liabilities. The court awarded the plaintiff a judgment for the entire misappropriated amount: "Suits against directors for violations of fiduciary duties are equitable in nature. It is unlikely that the Oregon courts would allow a director to misappropriate funds and leave those injured without a remedy."[52]

- — — — — — — — — — -

Discussion Topics

a. In *Watson v. Button,* had the case not been in equity, what would have been the judgment? If the seller of the shares was not a fiduciary of the corporation, either because he was a controlling shareholder or a director, would the seller of the shares have kept the price of the shares? Why did equity interfere here?

b. How easy was it for the buyers of the shares to find out whether the defendant had misappropriated corporate funds? Should not the buyers be responsible to the plaintiff for the plaintiff's liabilities?

c. If the plaintiff had examined and evaluated the corporate books (without the misappropriated assets) and paid the appropriate price,

---

48. Deborah DeMott, *Beyond Metaphor: An Analysis of Fiduciary Obligation,* 1988 DUKE L. J. 879, 880 (1988).
49. *Id.*
50. *Id.* at 880-81.
51. Watson v. Button, 235 F.2d 235 (9th Cir. 1956).
52. *Id.* at 237.

why should he receive additional amounts for which he did not bargain?

– – – – – – – – – – – – – –

2. The relationship between restitution and unjust enrichment

Restitution can be viewed as a remedy for the wrong of unjust enrichment. But if unjust enrichment is not a wrong but a remedy, then, to justify restitution, something else must be a wrong, such as a breach of fiduciary duty, to justify restitution.

Ripley v. International Railways of Central America & United Fruit Co. is instructive.[53] In that case, International Railways of Central America ("Irca") provided transportation for United Fruit Company's ("United") banana import and export business in Guatemala. The court noted that "United was in practical control of Irca at least after the creation of the voting trust in 1928, and [therefore] stood in a fiduciary relationship to Irca as respects the latter's minority shareholders insofar as concerned business transactions between Irca and United or its subsidiary."[54] The minority shareholders of Irca claimed that United breached its fiduciary duties by obtaining below-the-market freight rates for its own advantage. The plaintiff sought to recover the difference between the contracted freight rate and the fair and reasonable transportation cost.

Based on the unjust enrichment principle, the court granted restitution to the plaintiff in the amount equal to the difference between the amount United paid Irca and the fair market value of the services. The lower freight charge was void of consideration. United received the favorable price solely because of its leverage and control of Irca.

The court wrote: "Considered as divisible [from the main clauses of the contract], the effect of the rate agreements is similar to any situation where the fiduciary has received and retained property or services at less than [market] value. It has to pay the difference, and the result is not different merely because the rate transaction has taken the form of a contract. The obligations of the fiduciary cannot be escaped merely by making a contract with the *cestui*, nor is rescission necessary (if the rate contracts are divisible) since the *cestui* has received nothing under them belonging to the fiduciary which it is bound to give up."[55]

---

53.   Ripley v. Int'l Rys. of Cent. Am., 171 N.E.2d 443 (N.Y. 1960).
54.   *Id.* at 444.
55.   *Id.* at 448.

- - - - - - - - - - - -

Discussion Topic

What are the practical and theoretical distinctions between restitution, accounting, and unjust enrichment?

- - - - - - - - - - - -

E. Entrustor's Right to a Jury Trial

A plaintiff who seeks equitable remedies is not entitled to a jury trial. A plaintiff who seeks legal remedies is. Does a plaintiff who seeks equity remedies as well as legal remedies have a right to a jury trial? A jury trial is often strategically important when the plaintiff relies on facts with which the jury may strongly identify.

This issue was considered in *Dairy Queen, Inc. v. Wood.*[56] In that case, the plaintiff, Dairy Queen, sued defendant, Wood, for breaching its contract to pay $150,000 for the exclusive use of the "DAIRY QUEEN" trademark. Dairy Queen sought: "(1) temporary and permanent injunctions to restrain [the defendant] from any future use of or dealing in the franchise or trademark, (2) an accounting to determine the exact amount of money owing by [the defendant] and a judgment for that amount, and (c) an injunction pending accounting to prevent [the defendant] from collecting any money from Dairy Queen stores."[57]

The district court held that the plaintiff lost its right to a legal claim when it received equitable relief. On appeal, the court reversed the district court's decision: "[W]here both legal and equitable issues are presented in a single case, 'only under the most imperative circumstances . . . can the right to a jury trial of legal issues be lost through prior determination of equitable claims. . . . A jury, under proper instructions from the court, could readily determine the recovery, if any, to be had here, whether the theory finally settled upon is that of breach of contract [legal remedy], that of trademark infringement [equitable remedy], or any combination of the two."[58] The right to trial by jury is a constitutional right. It is not always determined and dependent on the remedy sought in the pleadings.

In *Pereira v. Farace*, the court discussed the right to trial by jury in cases of a breach of fiduciary duty:[59]

Until 2000, Trace was a privately-held Delaware corporation headquartered in Manhattan. . . .

---

56. Dairy Queen, Inc. v. Wood, 369 U.S. 469 (1962) (plaintiffs, a corporation's shareholders, convertible noteholders, and bridge loan lenders, filed an action seeking injunctive and declaratory relief, an accounting, and damages for injury to the corporation caused by various breaches of contract and fiduciary duty, conversion, and unfair practices by defendants, the corporation, its president and treasurer. Defendants filed a counterclaim for breach of fiduciary duty against a former director).

57. *Id.* at 475.

58. *Id.* at 472-73, 479.

59. Pereira v. Farace, 413 F.3d 330 (2d Cir. 2005), *cert. denied,* 126 S. Ct. 2286 (2006) (citations omitted).

Marshall Cogan helped to form Trace in 1974. Since that time, he has been Trace's majority shareholder, chairman of the board of directors ("Board"), and the company's chief executive officer ("CEO"). Although Cogan's conduct lies at the heart of this case, he is not a party to this appeal. [The company was driven into bankruptcy and Cogan was sued by the Trustee in bankruptcy. Cogan was] found liable by the district court for $44.4 million [for various unauthorized loans, gifts, and salary increases]. He then settled with the Trustee.

[Defendants Farace, Marcus, Smith, and Winters were all officers or board members at Trace up through 1999.] . . .

At the core of this appeal are several transactions which effectively exhausted Trace's capital, driving Trace into bankruptcy. . . .

In July 1999, Trace filed for reorganization under Chapter 11 of the Bankruptcy Code in the United States Bankruptcy Court for the Southern District of New York. At the time, Trace's liabilities exceeded its assets by $121 million. . . .

On January 24, 2000, the Bankruptcy Court converted Trace's Chapter 11 reorganization into a Chapter 7 liquidation. John Pereira was appointed as trustee [for the corporation in the bankruptcy proceedings]. . . .

Pereira's complaint alleged that: (1) all Trace's officers and directors had breached their fiduciary duties to Trace under Delaware common law (Count IV); and (2) all the directors had violated Delaware General Corporation Law §§ 160 and 174(a), which prohibit the payment of dividends while the corporation is insolvent or which will render it insolvent, or the redemption of stock when a corporation's capital is impaired or which will impair the corporate capital (Count V).

According to the complaint, Trace had been insolvent since 1995; therefore the directors and officers owed fiduciary duties to Trace's creditors as well as to its stockholders. The Trustee sought damages for: (1) Cogan's unauthorized borrowing of over $13 million from Trace; (2) Cogan's unauthorized loans and gifts to other insiders; (3) Cogan's excessive compensation; (4) Cogan's unilateral renewal of his employment agreement; (5) payment of dividends without Board approval and at a time when Trace's capital was impaired; (6) a $3 million redemption of Trace preferred stock when capital was impaired; and (7) use of over $1 million in corporate funds for Cogan's birthday party.

Prior to trial, defendants demanded a jury trial on Counts IV and V. The Trustee responded that he was seeking the equitable remedy of restitution on Counts IV and V (despite his request for compensatory damages in the complaint). . . .

[The court wrote:]

Although Rule 2 of the Federal Rules of Civil Procedure grandly proclaims that "[t]here shall be one form of action to be known as 'civil action' " thereby causing the merger of law and equity, the distinction "retains its viability" today. By preserving the right to a jury trial only in "suits at common law," the Seventh Amendment of the United States Constitution perpetuates the law/equity dichotomy. U.S. Const. amend. VII. Indeed, the phrase "suits at common law" refers to "suits in which legal rights [are] to be ascertained and determined, in contradistinction to those where equitable rights alone [are] recognized and equitable remedies [are] administered." Therefore, despite the near universal merger of law and equity effectuated by Federal Rule of Civil Procedure 2, trial by jury remains today "the sword in the bed that prevents the complete union of law and equity."

The right to trial by jury has long been an important protection in the civil law of this country. According to the Founding Fathers, the right served as "an important bulwark against tyranny and corruption." As then-Justice Rehnquist reminded us: "Trial by a jury of laymen rather than by the sovereign's judges was important to the founders because juries represent the layman's common sense, the 'passional elements in our nature,' and thus keep the administration of law in accord with the wishes and feelings of the community."

In deciding whether a particular action is a suit at law that triggers this important protection, we are instructed to apply the two-step test set forth in *Granfinanciera*. First, we ask "whether the action would have been deemed legal or equitable in 18th century England." *Second*, "we examine the remedy sought and determine whether it is legal or equitable in nature." We then "balance the two, giving greater weight to the latter." . . .

After three decades of grappling with the law versus equity analysis, the late Justice William Brennan threw up his hands. He had wearied of "rattling through dusty attics of ancient writs" and suggested that Seventh Amendment jurisprudence should sever its dependence on historical analogies to English common law as it existed in 1791. However much we may sympathize with his position, Justice Brennan's suggestion has gone unheeded, and thus, we are left to scour through the "dusty attics" ourselves.

Count IV, brought pursuant to Delaware common law, alleges a claim for breach of fiduciary duty. Count V, which seeks damages against Farace and Marcus for allowing payment of dividends while Trace's capital was impaired, is a claim for breach of Delaware General Corporation Law § 174(a). Nevertheless, Count V is analogous to a breach of fiduciary duty claim, and was properly treated as such by the district court.

In analyzing Counts IV and V, the district court concluded that "the general rule is that 'actions for breach of fiduciary duty, historically speaking, are almost uniformly actions "in equity"—carrying with them no right to trial by jury.' " The court thus believed that the first step of the *Granfinanciera* test tilted in favor of denying defendants a jury trial.

We accept the district court's statement that as a "general rule" breach of fiduciary duty claims were historically within the jurisdiction of the equity courts. Defendants emphasize, however, that this was and is only a general rule. They contend that under *Ross v. Bernhard*, "the *Seventh Amendment* question depends on the *nature of the issue* to be tried rather than the character of the overall action."

Applying the "nature of the issues" test, defendants maintain that the issues in Counts IV and V are negligence-based because Delaware applies a "gross negligence" standard to breach of fiduciary duty claims. Because negligence is historically a legal claim, defendants assert they are entitled to a jury trial under the *Seventh Amendment*.

Judge Sweet rejected this argument. He cautioned that defendants' interpretation of *Ross* would effectively permit every breach of fiduciary duty claim to be recast as an action at law such that "parties seemingly would be entitled to a jury trial on any and all breach of fiduciary duty claims."

We agree with Judge Sweet that defendants mischaracterize the holding of *Ross*. In *Ross*, shareholders brought a . . . suit against corporate directors, alleging breach of fiduciary duty, breach of contract, and gross negligence. Although shareholder . . . claims had been traditionally heard in equity, the Supreme Court found a right to a jury trial because plaintiff's claims presented legal issues-breach of contract and negligence. Despite defendants' claim that *Ross* requires us to break the Trustee's breach of fiduciary duty claim into its most elemental parts, *Ross* merely requires courts to look beyond the procedural vehicle of a shareholders . . . suit to the possible legal nature of the corporation's underlying claims.

We decline, therefore, to adopt defendants' expansive interpretation of *Ross*. Accordingly, we hold that Counts IV and V would have been equitable in 18th century England and thus that step one of *Granfinanciera* weighs against a jury trial. . . .

The second step of the *Granfinanciera* test focuses on the nature of the relief sought. It calls upon us to decide whether the "type of relief [sought] was available in equity courts as a general rule." This step is accorded "greater weight" than the first, and, as such, is the "more important" step.

In his prayer for relief, the Trustee sought "compensatory damages," which is, of course, the classic form of *legal* relief. The district court, however, "looked beyond [the Trustee's] characterization [as] to what the claim for relief actually [was]." The district court then went on to determine that the Trustee had, in fact, *actually* "limited his relief to restitution," which is equitable in nature. In so doing the district court concluded that "the fact that the officers and directors never personally possessed any of the disputed funds [does] not militate that the relief [is] not equitable."

On appeal, defendants challenge the court's characterization of the relief as equitable. They emphasize that, because they never possessed the funds in question and thus were not unjustly enriched, the remedy sought against them cannot be considered equitable. Rather, according to defendants, the remedy sought was legal and thus they were entitled to a jury trial. We agree. . . .

. . . [T]he Supreme Court's decision in *Great-West Life & Annuity Insurance Company v. Knudson* reconfigured the legal landscape of restitution. In *Great-West,* the Supreme Court stated that, "for restitution to lie in equity, the action generally must seek not to impose personal liability on the defendant, but to restore to the plaintiff particular funds or property *in the defendant's possession*.". . .

The Trustee contends that the holding of *Great-West* is inapplicable here because *Great-West* involved only non-fiduciary defendants. In *Callery,* the Tenth Circuit rejected this same argument. That court found that, while the "distinction made in Strom . . . based on the status of the defendant as a fiduciary . . . may have been compelling before *Great-West,* [it is] not so now."

Like our sister circuits, we are compelled to read *Great-West* as broadly as it is written. Nor can we ignore the Supreme Court's inclusion of footnote 2, highlighting a single exception to its rule that a defendant must possess the funds at issue for the remedy of equitable restitution to lie against him.

Finally, Justice Ginsburg's dissent in *Great-West* offers further guidance by pointing out that restitution is measured by a defendant's "unjust gain, rather than [by a plaintiff's] loss." It is undeniable here that the Trustee seeks only to recover funds attributable to Trace's loss, not the director's unjust gain.

We thus hold that the district court improperly characterized the Trustee's damages as restitution. Plaintiff's claim is for compensatory damages--a legal claim. Because we afford "greater weight" to *Granfinanciera's* second step than to its first, we conclude that defendants were entitled to a jury trial on the Trustee's breach of fiduciary duty claims and we remand for that purpose.[60]

F. Restitution

Restitution was mentioned throughout this Chapter as well as in the previous Chapters. It is a close relative to accounting and in some cases to constructive trust. One of the distinctive features of restitution is its origin. It is a remedy for contract violations.

As Professor E. Allan Farnsworth noted,[61] in a contract relationship, the promisor may have violated his promise while the promisee may have benefited the promisor, for example, by paying for goods in advance. In such a case the court may award the promisee (who paid) an amount that would deprive the promisor of his benefit,

---

60. *Id.*
61. 1 E. ALLAN FARNSWORTH, FARNSWORTH ON CONTRACTS § 2.1, at 77; 3 *id.* § 12.20, at 329-32 (3d ed. 2004) (footnotes omitted).

even if the damages would be higher than the amount that the promisee lost. In addition, restitution would likely be awarded if the promise involved other than money. In *Bush v. Canfield*, the buyer advanced $5,000 of the $14,000 price for flour. Even though the market price of the flour fell, the seller failed to deliver. The buyer claimed restitution of the advance payment of $5,000. The defendant argued that the recovery should be only for the difference between the amount of money advanced ($5,000) and the fall in price of the flour ($3,000). After all, the buyer could buy the flour in the market cheaper. The court held: "The defendant has violated his contract; and it is not for him to say, that if he had fulfilled it, the plaintiffs would have sustained a great loss, and that this ought to be deducted from the money advanced."[62] In sum, the defendant cannot benefit from his breach of contract. The grant of specific restitution, however, is not equitable but in law. The same remedy would apply when the benefit to the party that breached the contract was other than money.

— — — — — — — — — — -

Discussion Topic

Suppose a builder contracts to build a building for an owner for $1,000,000. The builder spends $500,000, which is lost if the house is not built, and stops building because the owner repudiates the contract. "[I]f the builder cannot prove with sufficient certainty how much it would have cost to finish the job, and therefore cannot establish lost profit, the builder can still recover the $500,000 spent." What is the rationale for this result? What if the owner proves that the builder's cost to complete the building would be $600,000, ending with a loss? Is there a reason to ignore the negative "profit" term?[63]

— — — — — — — — — — -

G. Specific Performance

Specific performance is not a likely remedy for violations of fiduciary duties. "An injunction for specific performance is equitable relief that is available when legal relief is, for some reason, inadequate." Sometimes the property is unique, such as a Picasso painting. No amount of money can compensate for lack of delivery. The same approach applies to land, but less to personal property.[64] Because generally fiduciary relationships involve services, and because the relationships are based on trust, an entrustor would not seek the remedy of specific performance against the fiduciary the entrustor does not trust. In addition, courts are unlikely to grant an injunction requiring a fiduciary to continue serving the entrustor because of the difficulty of enforcing the injunction.

---

62.   3 *id.* § 12.20, at 329-31 (quoting Bush v. Canfield, 2 Conn. 485, 488 (1818)).
63.   *Id.* at 331-32.
64.   RANDY E. BARNETT, CONTRACTS: CASES AND DOCTRINE 183 (3d ed. 2003).

H. Liability of Transferee of Entrusted Property

An important benefit of fiduciary relationships is the ability of a fiduciary to deal as owner with entrusted property and power. This ability allows the fiduciary to perform services more efficiently and shelters innocent third parties from the claims of the entrustors. The rule protects buyers of entrusted property that paid reasonable value for the property and had no notice of the facts that the property was entrusted and that the seller was a fiduciary. Such buyers are entitled to maintain the bargain.

However, buyers are not sheltered if they are aware of the fact that the property is entrusted property. The following is a discussion of the buyer's rights and liabilities in such a case.

> [I]t has long been settled that when a trustee in breach of his fiduciary duty to the beneficiaries transfers trust property to a third person, the third person takes the property subject to the trust, unless he has purchased the property for value and without notice of the fiduciary's breach of duty. The trustee or beneficiaries may then maintain an action for restitution of the property (if not already disposed of) or disgorgement of proceeds (if already disposed of), and disgorgement of the third person's profits derived therefrom.[65]

– – – – – – – – – – – –

Discussion Topics

a. Art, trustee, sells property in breach of trust to Barb. Barb has notice of the breach. Art misappropriates the amount received for the property. Barb sells the property to Curt, who purchased for value and without notice of the breach. Identify those the beneficiary can sue and for what? [66]

b. Art, trustee, sells property in breach of trust to Barb. Barb has notice of the breach. Art misappropriates the amount received for the property. Barb sells the property to Curt. The proceeds from the sale to Curt are unavailable (i.e., Barb has disposed of the proceeds or they otherwise cannot be reached). What are the beneficiary's remedies?[67]

c. Art, trustee, sells property in breach of trust to Barb. Barb has notice (but not knowledge) of the breach. Art misappropriates the amount received for the property. Barb sells the property to Curt, who purchased for value and without notice of the breach. What are Barb's liabilities?[68]

d. Art, trustee, sells property in breach of trust to Barb. Barb has knowledge of the breach. Art misappropriates the amount received for

---

65.   Harris Trust & Sav. Bank v. Salomon Smith Barney Inc., 530 U.S. 238, 250 (2000) (citing authorities); *see also* RESTATEMENT (SECOND) OF TRUSTS § 291 (1959).
66.   RESTATEMENT (SECOND) OF TRUSTS § 291 cmt. d, illus. 1 (1959).
67.   RESTATEMENT (SECOND) OF TRUSTS § 291 cmt. e (1959).
68.   RESTATEMENT (SECOND) OF TRUSTS § 291 cmt. g, illus. 3 (1959).

the property. Barb sells the property to Curt, who purchased for value and without notice of the breach. What are Barb's liabilities?[69]

— — — — — — — — — — -

I. Punitive Damages

In *City of Hope v. Genentech*, discussed in Chapter Six, the court granted punitive damages as a remedy to the plaintiff.[70] This was a claim by a medical research center against a biotechnology company. The research center alleged breach of contract and breach of fiduciary duty, relating to a royalty agreement over patents for genetic processes that were invented at the research center.

The court wrote:

Punitive Damages.

Genentech attacks the $200 million award of punitive damages on two grounds. First, it claims that there was insufficient evidence to support a finding of fraud or malice. Second, it claims that the award was excessive because it did not act in a reprehensible manner. Both claims fail. . . .

. . . The courts examine three factors to determine whether an award is excessive. (1) The court looks at the particular nature of the defendant's acts in light of the whole record. "[D]ifferent acts may be of varying degrees of reprehensibility, and the more reprehensible the act, the greater the appropriate punishment, assuming all other factors are equal." (2) Next, the court must heed the amount of compensatory damages awarded. "[I]n general, even an act of considerable reprehensibility will not be seen to justify a proportionally high amount of punitive damages if the actual harm suffered thereby is small." (3) Finally, the court must take note of the defendant's wealth. "[T]he function of deterrence . . . will not be served if the wealth of the defendant allows him to absorb the award with little or no discomfort. By the same token, of course, the function of punitive damages is not served by an award which, in light of the defendant's wealth and the gravity of the particular act, exceeds the level necessary to properly punish and deter." . . .

Punitive damages may be awarded when there is clear and convincing evidence that a defendant is found guilty of fraud, oppression or malice. In this case, City of Hope sought to prove that Genentech's acted fraudulently and maliciously. Fraud "means an intentional misrepresentation, deceit, or concealment of a material fact known to the defendant with the intention on the part of the defendant of thereby depriving a person of property or legal rights or otherwise causing injury." Malice is "conduct which is intended by the defendant to cause injury to the plaintiff or despicable conduct which is carried on by the defendant with a willful and conscious disregard of the rights or safety of others." For conduct to be malicious, it must pass so far beyond the pale of the excepted norms of decency that it would be instantly condemned by any member of the citizenry as noxious to our sensibilities, our morals and our concept of right and wrong. . . .

In its opening brief, Genentech states: "Acting in accordance with a legally tenable (though erroneous) contract interpretation cannot be deemed 'despicable,' 'reprehensible,' 'vile,' or 'contemptible.' " We disagree. Whether a fiduciary acts in accordance with a legally

69. RESTATEMENT (SECOND) OF TRUSTS § 291 cmt. i, illus. 4 (1959).
70. City of Hope Nat'l Med. Ctr.v. Genentech, Inc., 20 Cal. Rptr. 3d 234 (Ct. App. 2004), *modified, reh'g denied*, No. B161549, 2004 Cal. App. LEXIS 1962 (Ct. App. Nov. 22, 2004), *review granted, depublished*, 24 Cal. Rptr. 3d 178, 105 P.3d 543 (Cal. 2005). *City of Hope* is an unpublished disposition issued before January 1, 2007, and as such may not be cited to Ninth Circuit courts except in certain limited circumstances. 9TH CIR. R. 36-3(C).

tenable contract interpretation does not end the inquiry. The dispositive question is whether the fiduciary was relying upon an interpretation it knew to be wrong in order to take advantage of the other party. Impliedly, the jury found that Genentech did exactly that. A review of the record reveals that this implied finding was supported by substantial evidence.

The evidence credited by the jury showed that the parties negotiated a deal whereby Genentech would pay when it used a Riggs-Itakura patent, and also when it licensed a Riggs-Itakura patent. . . . Further, there was evidence that Genentech engaged in a campaign to defraud and stonewall City of Hope. For example: By 1980, Genentech projected that it would earn $100 million through its license with Eli Lilly and believed that interferon, a drug that could be made with a Riggs-Itakura patent that Genentech had licensed to Hoffman La-Roche, could cure cancer. Rather than inform City of Hope of these facts, Genentech tried to buy down its royalty obligation in a move that would have cost City of Hope millions of dollars. . . . Finally, even after City of Hope made its interpretation known in the mid-1990's, Genentech did not disclose its licenses to Hoffman-La Roche or any other third parties.

Based on the evidence, the jury could and did reasonably conclude that Genentech understood the nature of the deal yet withheld royalties and actively concealed licenses in order to enrich itself. Such conduct, under the circumstances, amounts to fraud or malice and qualifies as being despicable, base and vile. . . .

Genentech focuses solely on reprehensibility . . . . By implication, it does not claim that the punitive damages award is disproportionate to the compensatory damages award. Nor does it claim that, in light of its net worth, the amount exceeds the level necessary to deter. It contends that a $200 million punitive damages award is excessive because its contract interpretation was legally tenable, it was not guilty of a widespread pattern or practice of wrongful conduct, and its conduct did not jeopardize anyone's life, safety, or health. Last, Genentech suggests that the economic nature of the harm, and also the sophistication of the two parties involved, calls upon us to reign in the award. . . .

The United States Supreme Court, in its recent decision instructed "courts to determine the reprehensibility of a defendant by considering whether: the harm caused was physical as opposed to economic; the tortious conduct evinced an indifference to or a reckless disregard of the health or safety of others; the target of the conduct had financial vulnerability; the conduct involved repeated actions or was an isolated incident; and the harm was the result of intentional malice, trickery, or deceit, or mere accident. The existence of any one of these factors weighing in favor of a plaintiff may not be sufficient to sustain a punitive damages award; and the absence of all of them renders any award suspect. It should be presumed a plaintiff has been made whole for his injuries by compensatory damages, so punitive damages should only be awarded if the defendant's culpability, after having paid compensatory damages, is so reprehensible as to warrant the imposition of further sanctions to achieve punishment or deterrence." . .

The jury found Genentech's contract interpretation to be a sham, so whether it was legally tenable is irrelevant. The withholding, as the jury found, amounted to fraud or malice. Not only that, but Genentech's scheme of concealing licenses and withholding royalties spanned decades. The conduct may not have been widespread as to the number of victims, but it was pervasive and continuous as to City of Hope. While Genentech did not directly jeopardize anyone's life, safety, or health, it damaged an entity that is in the business of providing medical care to the poor, often at City of Hope's own expense. Additionally, at the time Genentech offered to buy down the royalty rate, it knew that City of Hope was in need of money. Last, Genentech essentially cheated City of Hope out of a staggering amount of money.

These facts demonstrate that Genentech acted in a reprehensible manner. Because Genentech does not argue proportionality or net worth, we presume those issues support the judgment.

Genentech offers [a precedent] as the standard for what is reasonable in a commercial dispute. In [that case] the compensatory damages for fraud were $232,393, and the jury awarded $10 million in punitive damages. The . . . court reduced the amount to $2 million "to keep it in line with the actual compensatory losses suffered by buyers." [That case] offers Genentech no assistance. Here, the award was not proportionally high. Rather, it was only two-thirds of the compensatory damages award.

In any event, we take our cue from the Supreme Court.

In *TXO Production Corp. v. Alliance Resources Corp.*, the plaintiff suffered economic damages between $1 million and $4 million and was awarded $10 million in punitive damages. The Supreme Court upheld the punitive damages award, noting that the defendant had embarked on illicit, bad faith scheme to cheat the plaintiff out of lucrative oil and gas royalties. If the award and its proportion in *TXO* was constitutional, then the award against Genentech was constitutional as well.[71]

Punitive damages can be awarded in addition to other remedies. In *Action Marine, Inc. v. Continental Carbon Inc.*, Continental Carbon Inc.'s manufacturing plant emitted a pollutant into the air that damaged property.[72] Action Marine, the plaintiff, alleged that the emission damaged its inventory of boats and forced the company into bankruptcy. When the plaintiff could not meet its obligations with damaged boats, the creditors pursued a deficiency judgment against John Tharpe, Action Marine's sole shareholder and principal agent.

Action Marine sought "to recover for the lost value of its business" and punitive damages from Continental for "intentionally [choosing to] continue operating its Phenix City plant despite knowing that the plant's constant leaks were polluting their properties."[73] Tharpe also claimed emotional distress damages from the loss of his reputation as a reliable businessman, a claim that was dismissed by the district court on summary judgment.

The Eleventh Circuit upheld the district court's finding that Action Marine was entitled to compensatory business damages for the boat's lost value, the same position it would have been in but for Continental's actions. Denying that the $800,000 debt was a windfall to the plaintiff, the court wrote "Continental's actions led to Action Marine's demise and thus its inability to generate revenue and repay its debts."[74]

With respect to Action Marine's plea for punitive damages, the court reviewed the standard for awarding punitive damages "to further a State's legitimate interests in punishing unlawful conduct and deterring its repetition":

[The court presumes that] "a plaintiff has been made whole for his injuries by compensatory damages, so punitive damages should only be awarded if the defendant's

---

71. *Id.* at 354-58 (citations omitted).
72. Action Marine, Inc. v. Continental Carbon Inc., 481 F.3d 1302 (11th Cir. 2007).
73. *Id.* at 1307-08.
74. *Id.* at 1316.

culpability, after having paid compensatory damages, is so reprehensible as to warrant the imposition of further sanctions to achieve punishment or deterrence."

[Case precedent has also established guideposts to determine the constitutionality of the punitive damage award. These guideposts include:] (1) the degree of reprehensibility of the defendant's misconduct; (2) the disparity between the actual or potential harm suffered by the plaintiff and punitive damages award; and (3) the difference between the punitive damages awarded by the jury and the civil penalties authorized or imposed in comparable cases. . . .

Reprehensibility is the most relevant of the guiding posts because punitive "damages imposed on a defendant should reflect 'the enormity of his offense.'" The Eleventh Circuit upheld the district court's finding that Continental's actions were "so reprehensible as to warrant the imposition of further sanctions" beyond compensatory damages.

The court referenced evidence that "established a pattern of intentional misconduct . . . leading to repeated damage to Plaintiffs' properties." Furthermore, the court found that Continental tried to avoid accountability and described its approach to dealing with the public and the property owners as "less than honest."

Based upon documentation that carbon black may be a possible cause of cancer, the danger posed by the harmful emission also raises a public health concern as to legitimize punitive damages.

The court held that "the evidence supporting the district court's finding of reprehensibility alone justifies the punitive damages award."[75]

See also *OnePoint Solutions, LLC v. Borchert,* in which OnePoint alleged that the corporate founders authorized payments to themselves from the company after they were removed from the office.[76] OnePoint sought "treble damages under the Minnesota receipt of stolen property statute; punitive damages under the Minnesota civil theft statute; and attorney's fees and costs based on the 'third-party litigation' exception."

The court found that the founders violated their fiduciary duty by misappropriating corporate funds. With respect to remedies, the court wrote: "Minnesota law provides for a plaintiff alleging civil theft to recover the value of the property at the time it was stolen plus up to an equal amount of punitive damages."[77] Therefore, OnePoint could recover $66,000 for the value of the property stolen, plus $66,000 in punitive damages. OnePoint, however, was not entitled to recover the attorney's fees and costs.[78]

J. Dissolution of a Corporation

In *Kemp & Beatley, Inc. v. Gardstein (In re Kemp & Beatley, Inc.),* the court considered dissolution of a corporation as a remedy, when no other equitable remedies were available.[79] The Plaintiffs, Dissin and Gardstein, left their employment at Kemp & Beatley, the defendant

---

75. *Id.* at 1317-22 (citations omitted).
76. OnePoint Solutions, LLC v. Borchert, 486 F.3d 342 (8th Cir. 2007).
77. *Id.* at 350.
78. *Id.* at 352-53.

K. Criminalization — 275

corporation. The plaintiffs owned a combined 20.33% minority stake in the corporation. Because of the unfriendly circumstances surrounding their departure, Kemp & Beatley ceased to pay dividends, and eliminated their sharing in the corporation's earnings.

The plaintiffs alleged that the majority shareholders' change of the corporation's "long-standing policy to distribute corporate earnings on the basis of stock ownership" is "'fraudulent and oppressive' conduct by the company's board of directors such as to render petitioners' stock a 'virtually worthless asset.'"[80] The plaintiffs sought to dissolve Kemp & Beatley. In a hearing before this appeal, the Supreme Court stated that "[l]iquidation of the corporate assets was found the only means by which petitioners would receive a fair return" even if it is a "serious and severe remedy."[81]

The court agreed with the plaintiffs holding that

it was not unreasonable for the fact finder to have determined that this change in [the long-standing] policy [to pay dividends] amounted to nothing less than an attempt to exclude petitioners from gaining any return on their investment through the mere re-characterization of distributions of corporate income. Under the circumstances of this case, there was no error in determining that this conduct constituted oppressive action . . . .

[The majority shareholders have a] fiduciary obligation to treat all shareholders fairly and equally, to preserve corporate assets, and to fulfill their responsibilities of corporate management with "scrupulous good faith." . . . [Thus, when] it appears that the directors and majority shareholders "have so palpably breached the fiduciary duty they owe to the minority shareholders" [the court must exercise its equitable power to guarantee a fair return on the Plaintiff's investment].

[Therefore,] a forced buy-out of [the plaintiffs'] shares or liquidation of the corporation's assets was the only means by which petitioners could be guaranteed a fair return on their investments. [Given that the corporation has not offered to acquire the plaintiff's shares, dissolution is the alternative remedy in equity.][82]

K. Criminalization

In a number of situations, a breach of fiduciary duties can constitute a criminal offense, especially in the area of securities regulation. Insider trading can constitute a crime as well as a violation of a fiduciary duty.[83] We dealt with the issue posed by Samuel W. Buell, when the court recognizes relationships as fiduciary for the first time, and the question of fairness to the fiduciaries arises. As Samuel W. Buell noted, parties create new forms and incidences of fraud, and the law responds.[84]

We dealt with the issue posed by Buell, in situations in which courts recognize relationships as fiduciary for the first time, and the

---

79. Kemp & Beatley, Inc. v. Gardstein (*In re* Kemp & Beatley, Inc.), 473 N.E.2d 1173 (N.Y. 1984).
80. *Id.* at 1175-76.
81. *Id.* at 1176.
82. *Id.* at 1177-78, 1180-81.
83. Rule 10b-5, 17 C.F.R. § 240.10b-5 (2007). *See also* Investment Company Act of 1940, § 35, 15 U.S.C. § 80a-34 (2000).
84. Samuel W. Buell, *Novel Criminal Fraud*, 81 N.Y.U.L. REV. 1971, 2043 (2006).

question of fairness to the fiduciaries arises. That problem appears
often in situations involving fraud.[85] Here we just note that violations
of fiduciary duties are occasionally recognized as crimes. A general
prohibition on fraud should be insufficient to create a valid basis for
criminal prosecution. People should know the particulars of the
prohibited behavior. And yet, if the prohibitions are very specific, there
is a good chance for people to try and work around them. The balance
between general rules and specific rules is hard to achieve. The
following is an example of this dilemma.[86]

The Securities and Exchange Commission has issued a record number of rules directed
at the mutual funds advisory profession. From 1975 to 2000 the SEC enacted about 135
substantive rules. However, it has enacted 70 such rules over the five-year span from 2001
to 2006. These rules are progressively more specific, eliminating flexibility, putting the
profession in a straight-jacket, and imposing significant costs. The costs of these rules are
especially irritating to advisors who have done no wrong. Professional advisors blame the
SEC for being over-zealous, self-interested, and driven by ambitions and self-
aggrandizement. Yet, could it be possible that the professional managers and their advisors
are contributing to this rule avalanche?

The pressure for specificity

For the past 30 years mutual fund professionals and lawyers have demanded specific
rules from the SEC: "Tell us what to do or not to do. We will obey. But beyond the specific
rules, we are free to do or not to do as we please." Further, these specific rules are
interpreted literally. . . . When specific rules and literal interpretation do not limit all the
possible ways in which professional managers can unlawfully and unethically benefit from
their control of investors' assets, some professionals search for the ways which were not
specified. Competitors follow suit. The more innovative competitors uncover new ways to
benefit and hide the benefits. When this trend leads to blatant fraud and abuse of trust they
finally become public. Concerned that investors will "run" on mutual funds and the
securities markets, Congress and the regulators have reacted, but they have not changed
the approach of the current system. . . .

These specific rules obscure the heart of the prohibition: Professional advisers are
fiduciaries; they may not engage in conflicts of interest, regardless of how they do it;
regardless of the ways in which they hide the transactions. Innovative means of violating
the rule do not make the means legal. Rather than spelling out the prohibited objectives,
the SEC spells out the prohibited means, processes, documentation and alike by which the
wrongs can be perpetrated.

Justifications for specific rules and literal interpretation

Two main arguments justify the demand for specificity and literal interpretation. One
is efficiency and the second is the "rule of law." Another argument goes further to state that
there is no need for these rules; the markets will take care of the issues. These justifications
are weighty and honorable, but are faulty in the context of professional money
management. Specific rules are arguably efficient because the rules allow professional
managers to create and capture value. Specificity increases managers' freedom to gain
more from public clients and investors. That is fine, if professional managers are producers
and sellers of products. But they are fiduciaries, who must obey restrictions regarding other

85. *Id.*
86. Tamar Frankel, *Guest Column: Are Advisers Contributing to Fund Rule Avalanche?*, IGNITES, Apr. 2006, http://www.tamarfrankel.com/support-files/are-advisors-contributing.pdf (last visited Nov. 15, 2006) (edited).

people's money. Economists do not focus on enforcing this restriction, but law does. And the enforcement of specific rules is incredibly inefficient.

Standard-based rules involve some uncertainty, exposing professional managers to legal risks. Specific rules eliminate or reduce uncertainty and risks. Hence, managers can touch the prohibited line.

Gate keepers—lawyers, accountants and investment bankers—offer ways to reduce the risk of crossing the line by clamoring for more specificity, looking to form instead of substance, and ignoring the purpose of the rules. When the line is crossed, expect more specific rules to emerge to plug the "leaks." Thus, not only do specific rules lead to inefficient enforcement; they also lead to more (specific) rules.

The "rule of law," to which we all subscribe, does not justify specific rules, either. To be sure, people should know the rules. But, the rule for professional managers is clear: **The money they hold is not their money. It belongs to others.** Therefore, managers must receive permission to take any amount for themselves. The form of taking need not be specified, especially if it can be innovative and well hidden. It is still "taking what does not belong to you.". . .

Do these specific rules really make the "rule of law" more effective and fair to the managers? Specific rules come to bite the SEC as well. It is not surprising that the rules brought about attacks on the SEC's authority by honest managers. Some of these specific rules may have imposed on rogue managers the correct measure of control, but not on those who stayed and acted within the law.

Finally, there is the justification for limiting rules in scope and in number. Investors should trust the markets. Investors should take care of themselves. They can sell their shares if they are not satisfied, and they can elect other directors to represent their interests. However, some cannot take care of their own investments (for lack of knowledge or time). Markets are fickle. Investors may seem satisfied and then "run" and keep away for twenty years or only two.

Specific rules hurt professional managers and the regulators

When all is said and done professionals that ignore the problem the rules are designed to resolve will face criminal and civil charges and loss of customers.

"Gimmicks" and smart tricks covered by the specific rules do not resolve, but rather highlight, problems. When outrageous behavior re-appears, there is no escape from attacks on the wrongdoers. Above all, specific rules will bring more specific rules. Mutual fund professionals who seek specific rules and interpret them literally and circumvent them should expect more specific rules to address the circumvention. That is because the problems posed by those who hold other people's money remain unresolved.

— — — — — — — — — —

Discussion Topics

a. What are the effects of criminalization of civil laws on the view of criminal law?

b. Why do regulators criminalize the laws regulating fiduciaries, such as investment advisers? Do you agree with this trend?

— — — — — — — — — —

L. Breach of Fiduciary Duties Without Remedies

In *Wsol v. Fiduciary Management Associates, Inc.*, Judge Posner, writing for the Seventh Circuit, offered his views on the remedies of breach of fiduciary duties:[87]

The plaintiffs, trustees of a Teamsters pension fund [fund], brought this ERISA suit for breach of fiduciary duty by an investment advisor that the fund had retained, Fiduciary Management Associates [FMA], and an "introducing broker" that FMA had in turn retained, East West Institutional Services [East West]. [At the end of the plaintiffs' presentation the District Court dismissed the case on the ground that the plaintiff did not prove breach of fiduciary duty by FMA.] . . .

The appeals raise a number of questions, but one is dispositive and so we ignore the rest. The plaintiffs cannot prevail unless the breach of fiduciary duty either imposed a loss on the plan or generated a profit for FMA "through use of assets of the plan" by FMA. If the former, they are entitled to damages, and if the latter, to the recovery ("disgorgement," as the cases call it) of FMA's profit on a theory of unjust enrichment or, equivalently, constructive trust, a standard remedy against malfeasant fiduciaries. The plaintiffs have not established a basis for either remedy, however, and so they lose.

The keys to understanding the case are three terms, "introducing broker," "directed brokerage," and "best execution." An introducing broker (we'll get to the other terms later) is a broker who doesn't actually execute the customer's trades but instead acts as an intermediary between the customer and the executing broker, collecting a fee from the customer that covers the fee charged by that broker. East West was the introducing broker that FMA used on the trades it made for the plaintiffs' pension fund. FMA paid East West 6 cents per trade and East West turned around and paid the executing broker 2 cents. This spread is common, but the introducing broker does not pocket the entire difference; instead he passes part of it back to the customer (in this case FMA) in the form either of a rebate or of "soft money" consisting of securities analysts' reports and other investment information. The fund reimbursed FMA for the 6 cents that FMA paid East West.

It turns out that East West [the Introducing Broker] [bribed one of the Teamsters pension] fund's trustees (since indicted and convicted)[.] [These trustees then steered the Fund to FMA.] The plaintiffs argue in their main appeal that had FMA investigated East West, as it should in the exercise of due care have done, not only would it have discovered the unsavory connection between the trustee and East West; it would also have discovered that East West's principals were shady and the firm itself little more than a mailbox. Instead FMA treated the trustee [--] later unmasked as a crook [--] to expensive golf outings and hired East West as its introducing broker in order to curry favor with him.

The district judge found that FMA had exercised all due care. But if she was wrong, as the plaintiffs argue with particular vehemence . . . , [when presenting] newly discovered evidence of skullduggery, and not merely of negligence, by FMA, it makes no difference to the outcome of the case. For surprising as this may seem, the shady operation that was East West appears to have given the fund all the benefits it would have received had FMA either retained a reputable introducing broker or dealt directly with the executing brokers. In either case, FMA, which is to say the fund, would have paid 6 cents a share per trade; that is the standard fee and there is no proof that FMA could have obtained comparable trading services for less.

The fund could, it is true, have reduced the execution cost by "directed brokerage," that is, by directing FMA to execute trades through a particular broker. By thus bypassing the introducing broker, FMA and so the fund would have paid only 2 cents a share per trade. But with directed brokerage, the broker does not guarantee "best execution," which means getting the best terms for the customer that are available in the market at the time . . ., a duty the executing broker owes by virtue of his fiduciary relationship to his customer.

---

87.   Wsol v. Fiduciary Mgmt. Assocs., Inc., 266 F.3d 654 (7th Cir. 2001) (citations omitted).

For with directed brokerage the responsibility for making the best deal is with the director, that is, the fund manager. Anyway the fund's trustees had not authorized directed brokerage; so it's a moot point whether FMA would have conferred a net benefit on the fund if, at its customer's direction, it had bypassed East West and dealt directly with the executing brokers on a directed-brokerage basis, paying only 2 cents per trade rather than 6 cents but forgoing best execution.

Was "best execution" worth 4 cents per share? Because best execution has multiple dimensions that tend to be in conflict (such as speed of execution and transaction price), its net advantage seems unlikely to equal fully two-thirds of the total cost of executing the transaction, although remember that part of the 4 cents is rebated either in cash or in investment advice. But these considerations are not material in this case. What is material is that the district judge found as a fact that what the fund got for its 6 cents per share was as good as what it could have bought in a market free of kickbacks and undue influence and that her finding is not clearly erroneous on the record compiled at trial, even as supplemented by the additional evidence that the plaintiffs presented in their Rule 60(b) motion. Despite the disreputable character of East West and the scandalous provenance of its relationship with FMA, the fund received best execution at the same cost that it would have incurred had FMA hired a choir of heavenly angels as introducing brokers or had dealt directly with the executing brokers; and while 4 cents per share seems a stiff price to pay for best execution, it is the standard price and there is no proof that FMA could have gotten a lower price by using an introducing broker other than East West. Although it is conceivable that FMA received less valuable investment advice from East West than it would have from a reputable introducing broker and as a result made poorer investments for the fund, the district judge found the contrary and her finding is not clearly erroneous. So far as appears, FMA's investment performance was as good as it would have been had East West never entered the picture.

Nor is it contended that FMA's management fee was excessive; and the 6 cents a share per trade that it charged back to the fund was, as we have noted already, the standard charge. There is no evidence that FMA obtained a profit that it would not have obtained but for the alleged breach of its fiduciary obligation. If the newly discovered evidence that the plaintiffs unavailingly pressed on the district judge . . . is credited, not only would FMA not have gotten the fund's business had it not retained East West as introducing broker, but FMA knew about the crooked relationship between East West and one of the fund's trustees. But that is just to say that if the evidence is believed, FMA committed a very serious breach of its fiduciary duty. Even so, the fund was not harmed and FMA obtained no greater profit than it would have obtained had it not retained East West.

Besides FMA's management fee, the plaintiffs are seeking the profit that East West made from acting as introducing broker. But East West did not annex a profit opportunity that belonged to the fund. Had FMA used a reputable introducing broker, it might have received more valuable investment information and might as a result have given the plaintiffs better advice; but, as we have said, the plaintiffs failed to prove this.

The remedy of disgorgement is limited to cases in which the breach of the fiduciary obligation enables the fiduciary to make a profit "through [the fiduciary's] use of assets of the plan." The kind of misconduct contemplated is the fiduciary's appropriating plan assets or investing them in a risky fashion in order to maximize his fee. If no misuse of the funds occur, if no losses are incurred or profits obtained that differ from what they would have been had there been no breach of fiduciary duty, there is no remedy. Affirmed.[88]

---

88.   Tamar Frankel, *The Seventh Circuit Decision in Wsol v. Fiduciary Management Associates and the Amendment to Rule 12b-1*, INV. LAW., Aug. 2004, at 11.

- - - - - - - - - - - -

Discussion Topics

a. Who are the players in this case? What is the fund, and who acts for the fund? Who is the client of East West? Identify the status of each of the actors as the entrustor or fiduciary. How does the court describe the actors?

b. What was the claim of the trustee of the pension fund and against whom? The fund, namely the investors, paid commission of 6 cents a share while the execution of the fund's trades cost 2 cents a share. Who pocketed the difference? What would the fund's preference be: direct brokerage or indirect brokerage? Who would have decided the different ways of payment for execution? Did the fund lose any money?

c. Is it true that FMA gained no benefits, as the court notes? If the FMA did not benefit from the arrangement why did FMA hire an employee to get clients, and pay him? Why did the employee receive commissions rather than only a fixed salary?

d. The circuit court upheld the district court's denial of the pension trustee's claim on the ground that even if FMA were negligent in preventing its employee for arranging a referral scheme that led to bribing the pension fund the trustees of the fund would have no remedy. Did the circuit court have another rationale on which to base its decision?

e. Do you agree with the circuit court's holding that the broker's "shady operation" did not harm the fund: "[S]urprising as this may seem, the shady operation that was [Broker] appears to have given the fund [TFund] all the benefits it would have received had [Adviser] either retained a reputable soliciting broker or dealt directly with the executing brokers. In either case, [Adviser] which is to say the fund, would have paid 6 cents a share per trade; that is the standard fee and there is no proof that [Adviser] could have obtained comparable trading services for less." That is what everyone was paying, almost without exception, stated the court. Since TFund can expect to be charged the market price, said the court, TFund was not harmed. It received "best execution" and paid competitive commission rates.

f. Whose opinion do you prefer and why?

g. How does Judge Posner view the relationship between the pension funds and FMA and its employee, and the Introducing Broker?

- - - - - - - - - - - -

M. Chapter Review

After reviewing the many remedies discussed in this Chapter, which remedy is most extraordinary? If you represented a plaintiff client claiming breach of fiduciary duties, which facts would you seek in order to determine the proper remedies for the client?

Chapter Eight
Fiduciary Law around the Globe

Introduction. Fiduciary law is not unique to the United States or to common law countries. It seems that the same or very similar reasons for the appearance of this type of law emerged globally in societies and countries. Fiduciary law is also ancient. As we discussed in Chapter One, fiduciary law has been around for thousands of years. Mesopotamian law, Islamic law, Jewish law, Roman law, its successor—civil law, and common law have created similar types of legal relationships, and regulated them in similar fashions in response to similar issues.

However, societies differ in the roads they took and the emphasis they employed to reach these similar results. These roads and emphasis reflect the history of local law and culture of the community, balance of power among the parties, and social assumptions and sanctions on what these societies considered anti-social behavior. Past and current social and cultural pressures significantly influence the role of fiduciary law as they do laws generally. For example, in countries where shame in violating the duty of loyalty is dominant, the legal duty of loyalty is weaker than in cultures that exert less social pressure on disloyal actions. In some countries each supervisor in a large organization is responsible for whatever goes wrong in his or her unit. This principle applies to top supervisors' responsibility for what goes wrong in the entire enterprise. In such a country, responsibility cannot be shifted to underlings or to peers, and accountability is not mitigated at the top of the corporate pyramid. In such societies, the pressure on the top supervisor is socially greater and the law is likely to be weaker. Where the top supervisor's responsibility is more limited, the law is likely to "fill in" and be stricter.

Similarly, societies differ in their legal systems. For example, the common law and the civil law systems draw on different sources to classify fiduciary principles, even though many of the principles are similar. For example, the common law and its followers derive fiduciary law from property law and recognize "trust" that "splits" the property relationships into legal and beneficial property rights, duties and responsibilities. The civil law and its followers reject this split of the property relationships, and derive fiduciary rules from contract law. Fiduciary principles in the two systems rest in different legal categories. In the civil law systems, contract law embodies many rules similar to those of common law fiduciary duties while the common law contract rules intrude less on the parties' arrangements, and leave much room and effect for "hard bargains."

In addition, the common law and civil law systems tend to approach the law differently. Common law systems tend to approach the law from a bottom-up perspective. Many rules represent generalized holdings of cases dealing with specific situations. Legislation addresses specific problems, which the courts did not resolve or did not resolve to the satisfaction of the legislature. The civil law systems tend to view the law from a top-down perspective. Rules come first and are then "applied" to particular situations. Neither system has adopted purely one perspective. But their approaches lead to different starting points and to more flexible or more rigid rules.

Thus, even though the problems and the ultimate solutions are very similar in the common law and civil law fiduciary law systems, the routes that they have taken to reach these similar solutions may differ. And no system can fully adopt the other without some fundamental changes in either its property law or its contract law and perhaps in its general approach to law.

One commentator notes:

In contrast to the common law the civil law system relates the duty of loyalty to contract. Under the contract the agent promises to perform functions for another. And the duty of loyalty is grounded in this promise.

Such a duty of loyalty may arise from the performance of other services by anyone from a company director to a mere employee. [However it is not related to or derived from property law.] Continental jurisdictions do not consider conflicts of interest as such to be a problem. Decision making in a conflicted situation is not a breach of duty. Private law calls for at least prima facie evidence of damage or undue profits before condemning the conflicted actions.

Despite this historical difference, the gap between these two legal traditions is less significant than it appears, and there are certain convergences between Continental and Anglo-American legal systems. Indeed, it is indisputable that directors and officers owe a duty of loyalty to their companies, and that asset managers owe a similar debt to their clients.[1]

In addition, there is a strong movement to globally unify the laws, including fiduciary law.[2] In Europe, various organizations are working towards this end, including the Geneva conference (uniform law for bills and promissory notes), the Vienna conference (uniform law for international sales of goods), United Nations UNCITRAL and UNIDROIT and the European Community (legal rules for all member states). The European Parliament has declared that it is in favor of the eventual adoption of a common civil code for all of Europe. "Listing the reasons in favor of legal uniformity and unification is too simple. There

---

1.   Rashid Bahar & Luc Thévenoz, *Conflicts of Interest: Disclosure, Incentives, and the Market, in* CONFLICTS OF INTEREST: CORPORATE GOVERNANCE & FINANCIAL MARKETS 1, 3-4 (Luc Thévenoz & Rashid Bahar eds., 2007).

2.   Rodolfo Sacco, *Diversity and Uniformity in the Law*, 49 AM. J. COMP. L. 171, 171-72 (2001).

can be no doubt that conflicts of law are interfering with trade. Uniform law means cultural unity, and thus the elimination of misunderstandings and difficulties between different civilizations that must get on together. Listing the reasons at the root of the local character of legal solutions is also too simple. One could trace them to tradition, history, specificity of national cultures, lack of a supranational legislative authority, and lack of a common legal language. Because these circumstances are about the acceptance of diversity, they can make us skeptical or suspicious of any hypothesis in support of the global unification of the law."[3]

The world is shrinking as the Internet is expanding. Actors, including clients and their lawyers, are increasingly operating in the global arena. Even if the local lawyers abroad are involved in advising on local law, the American lawyer must understand not only the foreign local law but also how it affects the behavior of the local population.

This topic is vast and complex, even if we limit the discussion to fiduciary law, and this Chapter is not intended to cover it. We deal with the subject in a high general manner, and then focus on a few examples to demonstrate how fiduciary law rules evolved in different systems. Broad and incomplete as this survey is, it raises intellectually challenging and important implications. We learn from the topic something about our own system and approach. That is why we indulge in this bird's-eye view of global fiduciary law.

A. Continental Europe

1. How does European law deal with the concept of common law trust?

Rodolfo Sacco[4] hypothesized about European law's concept of common law trust. In English trust law ownership will be separated into legal title, which is vested in the trustee and allow the trustee to act as the owner towards third parties, and beneficial rights which belong to beneficiaries. The beneficial ownership entitles the owners to certain claims against the disloyal trustee. To be sure, the continental lawyer is surprised at this structure. Yet, in both systems the trustee in England and the contract-agent in the civil law system can bring an action against third parties as the owner. Even though the theories are different, the results are the same.

In England, whoever has a temporary right to physical control of a property is called the owner, the same as he who has a perpetual right. On the continent, indivisibility of ownership challenges temporary ownership. It is true that a temporary right may exist, but it will be called usufruct, usage, habitation, or temporary emphyteusis. Although the rules are uniform, taxonomy creates opposing classifications.[5]

---

3.   *Id.*
4.   Rodolfo Sacco, *Diversity and Uniformity in the Law*, 49 AM. J. COMP. L. 171 (2001).
5.   *Id.* at 181-82. See also Tamar Frankel, *Knowledge Transfer: Suggestions for Developing Countries on the Receiving End*, 13 B.U. INT'L L. J. 141 (1995).

2. How does the Swiss court deal with the same issue?

A Swiss court viewed a common law trust as follows:

As there exists in Swiss law no legal institution which corresponds in all its elements to the legal relationship created by the . . . [attempted trust], it is necessary to examine which legal institutions of Swiss law . . . [have] the closest resemblance. [T]he court determined that the trust had "certain elements of a contract of mandate, of a fiduciary transfer of property, of donation and of a contract for the benefit of a third party." In the words of another court in Hague: "[T]he mainstream in the civil law characterization of the trust . . . emphasizes its flexibility and sees it as a contract-like institution." . . . In Europe, contract does the work of trust.[6]

By examining the underlying principles, the courts have assimilated the two systems. So long as the principles are close and similar this assimilation system is likely to be successful.

-- -- -- -- -- -- -- -- -- -

Discussion Topics

a. The Hague Report views the civil law characterization of trust as a "contract-like institution" and concludes that the concept is therefore more flexible. Do you agree? Is the common law view of trust as an institution rigid? What mechanisms can render the concept more flexible even though it is not contract-based? Do courts in the United States evidence a disagreement that can render the trust institution and in fact the fiduciary law in general more or less flexible?

b. What did Sacco mean when he wrote that even though the solution in England and Germany is the same "it cannot be formulated without recourse to the idea of trust and to division of ownership, whereas in Germany the solution is presented as an obvious consequence of the fact that the agent has acted without contemplatio domini and that the management cannot be representative if the managerial act is separated from contemplatio domini"?

c. European jurists reject the trust structure, which separates legal from beneficial ownership. Apart from traditional and cultural view, do they have serious reasons for rejecting the Anglo-Saxon invention of the trust?

-- -- -- -- -- -- -- -- -- -

B. Japan

1. How does Japan absorb the common law concept of fiduciary duty?[7]

The traditional basic duty in Japan was the duty of care—Zenkan Chuui Gimu. "Japan established its Civil Code in 1898, which incorporated the Article of Zenkan Chuui Gimu (duty of care). Its

6.   John H. Langbein, *The Contractarian Basis of the Law on Trusts*, 105 YALE L. J. 625, 670-71 (1995) (citing Harrison v. Credit Suisse, Bundesgericht [Federal Court] Jan. 29, 1970, 96 Entscheidungen des Schweizerischen Bundesgerichtes 79 (Switz.)).

7.   Derived, with permission, from a comparative study by Ryuichi Nozaki & Yoshihisa Masaki, LL.M. students at Boston University School of Law, in satisfaction of the requirements of the seminar Fiduciary Law, Spring 2007. Edited and Abridged.

mandatory duties were influenced by the civil codes of Germany and France. Trust Law, enacted in 1922, was also influenced by the California Civil Code and the India Trust Law." The current fiduciary duties, which are similar to those of the common law (duty of care, the duty of loyalty, the duty not to delegate, and the segregation rule), are still based on Zenkan Chuui Gimu. "Recently, Japanese business law was drastically changed. In 2004, the National Diet of Japan (Japan's Congress) enacted a new Trust Business Law. In 2006, the Diet completely revised the Trust Law, for the first time in 84 years, as well as enacted a new Corporate Law, which reorganized the duties of directors and officers. In creating these new laws, Japanese legislators and academics considered the U.S. market and laws."

"The Japanese Commercial Code added the duty of loyalty of directors to Zenkan Chuui Gimu in the 1950 revision, under the influence of the United States occupation lawyers, based, with variations on the Illinois Business Corporation Act." Therefore, some Japanese scholars think that the duty of loyalty is different from the duty of care, "but the Japanese Supreme Court explains that the duty of loyalty of directors does not define a higher duty than the duty of care, it merely clarifies and amplifies the duty of care."[8]

Professor Kenjiro Egashira of the University of Tokyo explained [that the strict prohibition on violating the duty of loyalty in the common law as compared to the duty of care, and noted that] "this dichotomy is unnatural and unnecessary":

Culture affects the understanding of the director's role. In the United States, the director's role originated as the trustee for the company's shareholders. In Japan, the director's duties focus on the directors role as good supervisors or managers. Hence the main duty of the directors is to follow Zenkan Chuui Gimu—the duty of care. This is an objective, abstract care in performing one's or behaving in a social position. In this context, people's expectations of a director's position are relevant to determining the directors' duty of care. In Japanese tradition directors are selected from among the corporate officers or managers. Directors owe a duty to the shareholders to the company, to employees, customers, and the community. The director is a leader of the team of employees. While the stockholders' power under Japanese law is stronger than that of the shareholders' power under the United States law, the Japanese director's role as "trustee" is weaker than that of a U.S. director, but the scope of the Japanese director's supervision and management is broader.[9]

---

8. *Id.*
9. The Japanese business judgment rule is different than that in the U.S. In the U.S., courts will not decide whether a board's decisions are either substantively reasonable or sufficiently well informed. This protects directors from liability for breaching the duty of care. In Japan, the business judgment rule states the court will not decide whether directors violated their duty of care or of loyalty, unless the director's conduct was clearly irrational, if they were not sufficiently prudent to recognize facts that a reasonable director in the same industry knows or should have known.

The emphasis remains on the duty of care. Thus, the Supreme Court of Japan found the duty of loyalty to be a part of Zenkan Chuui Gimu (duty of care) and the test for violation of the duty of care is usually gross negligence. "The trend in Japanese Corporate Law has been to require clarification of the specific role and responsibilities of corporate directors and officers. And the basic liability rule has changed from absolute liability to negligence liability. These revisions then make it easier to limit the liability of directors. This trend of limiting the scope of liability is moving closer to U.S. law."

The regulation of top executives in Japan is relatively stricter than that under American law. Japanese directors often hold positions of executives as well. The liability of the company's head is often based on the person's oversight. Even if the company's head acted in good faith and couldn't have known of the problem, and even if his actions were not in conflict of interest, he will still be held accountable because he had a supervisory position.

Thus, in the *Daiwa Ginko Daihyo Sosho* case,[10] a manager of the New York branch of Daiwa Bank engaged in securities trading by secretly altering the books. He traded in this fraudulent fashion from 1984 to 1995. In 1995, he confessed to the president of the bank. Several board members investigated the matter and realized his confession was true. The board, however, kept the matter secret and submitted a false report to the Federal Reserve Bank of New York in an attempt to hide the problem from the inspectors. The bank was then indicted in the United States on 24 counts, including conspiracy, fraud, bank exam obstruction, record falsification, and failure to disclose federal crimes. In 1996, the bank agreed to pay a $340 million fine to avoid further legal battles. The stockholders of the bank brought a derivative suit against the current and former directors, contending that the damage should have been minimized by the internal control system, and that the directors breached their duty of care and of loyalty by failing to establish such an internal control system, and that the fine paid by the bank was caused by their breach of duty.

The Osaka District Court ordered each director to pay the bank the amount of damage which the director caused as restitution to the shareholders. The court found that the board had the duty to determine the risk control system of the bank and that each director had a duty to establish the internal control system in his particular department. The court also found that the content of the internal control system is a matter of business judgment, and that the president or vice president of a mega-bank can entrust each director to supervise and perform the work. Thus, ten directors were liable to the degree of their relation with the problem, but only three directors were liable for the failure to establish internal controls. The rest of the directors were held liable for

---

10.   Nishimura v. Abekawa (The Daiwa Bank Case), 1573 Shoji Homu 3 (Osaka Dist. Ct. 2000).

failing their supervisory responsibility even though they acted in good faith and had no knowledge of the problem.[11]

2. How has Japan dealt with trust law?[12]

Trust law has also seen changes in Japan. A new trust law was enacted in 2006, revising the 1922 version:

The drafters of the new revision recognized that there is a broad range of cases where typical conflicts of interest do not exist but trustees abuse their power and harm the beneficiaries and these should still be considered to be a breach of the duty of loyalty.

The former Trust Law prohibited trustees from taking trust property or obtaining rights to trust property in their individual capacity, but it lacked a provision about a duty of loyalty.[13] The new Trust Law declared the existence of a duty of loyalty. The new Trust Law also contained elaborate classifications of different types of conflict of interest.[14] The general provision concerning the duty of loyalty applies to all conduct in violation of the duty that the specific classifications don't cover.

Further, the new Trust Law seems to imply that the duty of loyalty extends to trustees' abuse of power even when no conflict of interest exists. This represents a broad comprehension of the duty of loyalty and is flexible enough to fit various trustee misconduct that could arise in the future.[15]

There is also a trend in Japan to broaden the power of the trustees, similarly to the trend in the United States. In the new Trust Law, the limitation on trustees' delegation of power to third party agents has been relaxed, for example, when the trust deed explicitly permits it, or when the delegation is proper in view of the purpose of the trust.[16] The new Trust Law allows the trust deed to clarify or loosen the duty of care.[17] The Law provides some exceptions to the prohibition on trustees' conflicts of interest, such as when the trust deed allows conflicts, or when there is a reasonable necessity and no harm is done to the beneficiaries.[18]

---

11. Derived, with permission, from a comparative study by Ryuichi Nozaki & Yoshihisa Masaki, LL.M. students at Boston University School of Law, in satisfaction of the requirements of the seminar Fiduciary Law, Spring 2007. Edited and abridged.
12. Derived, with permission, from a comparative study by Ryuichi Nozaki & Yoshihisa Masaki, LL.M. students at Boston University School of Law, in satisfaction of the requirements of the seminar Fiduciary Law, Spring 2007. Edited and abridged.
13. Former Japanese Trust Law § 22(1).
14. Trust Law §§ 31, 32.
15. In Hosei Shingikai Shintaku Ho Bukai (Legislative Council Trust Law Subcommittee in the Ministry of Justice) two hypothetical cases were discussed relating to the topic of expanding the scope of the duty of loyalty. The first was a case in which a trustee used information which he obtained through pursuing his duty as trustee. The second was a case in which a trustee constructed a building on a raw land. It was also pointed out that real cases which will rise in the future are far more various than as presently expected, and therefore it is important to set down a general provision of the duty of loyalty which is not limited to cases of conflict of interests and is open to various types of cases in the future. *Conference Minutes of Hosei Shingikai Shintaku Ho Bukai* (2004-2006).
16. Trust Law § 28.
17. Trust Law § 29(2).

Under the new Trust Law, beneficiaries are entitled to compensation for losses of trust property caused by a breach of the trustees' duty, and the amount of loss is presumed to be equal to the amount of profit which the trustees earned by their misconduct, in a breach of the duty of loyalty case.[19]

As in the United States trust law, Japanese trust law has developed a system to monitor trustees' administration to prevent trustee misconduct. The new Trust Law requires that trustees to furnish beneficiaries with information about the trust, regardless of whether the beneficiaries requested the information.[20] Japanese trust law is likely to evolve further with the evolution of trust relationships and the need for protecting beneficiaries. The new Law has provided the foundation for dealing with future developments and awaits its implementation.

C. China

1. How has China dealt with trust law?[21]

Since 2000, one of the main goals of the Chinese government has been investor protection. The Chinese central government has identified a correlation between investor protection and the development of equity capital markets. The government is therefore committed to protecting shareholders' interests. China continues to work to change its Company Law and Securities Law in order to create the legal framework necessary to develop a shareholder litigation system. In 2006, the New Company Law is the first legislation aimed at clearly establishing direct and derivative shareholder actions. However, the idea of shareholder litigation derives from Western legal concepts, particularly those of the United States. China faces the challenge of adopting ideas from foreign countries that have different cultures, economic philosophies, and judicial systems.

2. Many differences between China and the United States have prevented the quick and effective adoption of a shareholder litigation system

During the past decade, legislators in Taiwan have tried to formulate a more complete and demanding legal system.[22] In 2006, the

---

18.   Trust Law § 31(2).
19.   Trust Law § 40 (Unlike in the U.S., however, the presumption of the loss amount is rebuttable).
20.   Trust Law §§ 36, 37 (the Law and related regulations provide a detailed list of items that trustees must disclose).
21.   This discussion is derived from two papers by Tzung-Wei Chou and Pramod Thummala, students at Boston University School of Law, the former in satisfaction of the seminar on Fiduciary Law, Spring 2007 and the latter for an independent study with Professor Whitehead in 2007. The materials are used with the permission of the authors. They are edited and abridged.
22.   Legislators enacted the Fair Trade Law, the Financial Holding Company Act, the Securities and Exchange Act, and the Banking Act which all have very demanding requirements and harsh penalties. The Company Act, the Securities and Exchange Act and the Principles of Corporate Governance, in particular, discuss whether directors have a duty to ensure that the corporation complies with the related regulations.

Institute of International Finance (IIF) analyzed China's corporate governance regime and concluded that there was still room for improvement. The IIF found that while independent directors are given authority on paper, they still have only a limited power to influence the overall strategy of the company.[23] The new Company Law has further clarified and divided the duties of the supervisory board and the board of directors. In practice, however, the supervisory board in China is a rubber stamp for the board of directors. Members of the supervisory board and the board of directors are often friends, and that prevents effective monitoring.[24]

China's corporate governance regime has several problems as well. Managers are often so busy responding to central government inspections and requests that distract them from managing their company.[25] Shareholder meetings are ineffective at regulating the power of the supervisory board and the board of directors.[26] The central government can also control most shareholder meetings because the state is usually the dominant shareholder of a corporation.[27] In the U.S., the interests of the dominant shareholders are usually aligned with minority investors because generating profits is a common goal shared by all of the investors. When the government is the dominant shareholder, the interests of minority investors and the government might not be aligned. The government is interested not only in profits, but also in improving social welfare or maintaining government control of an industry. Senior management in these corporations often feel their job is to simply "keep[] the government happy at all costs." [28] The new Company Law still contains a provision requiring companies to open their doors to the Communist Party of China.[29]

3. China does not have a civil litigation system like the United States[30]

China has relied on traditional public enforcement and administrative and criminal punishment to prevent securities fraud.[31]

23.　*Id.*

24.　Cindy A. Schipani & Junhai Liu, *Corporate Governance in China: Then and Now*, 2002 COLUM. BUS. L. REV. 1, 50 (2002) ("The governing corporate bodies should assert claims whenever the corporate interest is damaged or threatened by directors' or executives' breach of duties. However, it is possible that the board of directors may refuse or fail to do so due to the amicable relationship between the wrongdoing directors and the remaining directors. The same phenomenon may occur with respect to the board of supervisors when some supervisors are close friends of the wrongdoing director.").

25.　*Id.* at 29.

26.　*Id.* at 36 ("[A]lthough legally the general meeting of shareholders is very powerful in China, in reality, the meeting is often simply a rubber stamp for the wishes of the majority of shareholders. There is little or no opportunity for minority shareholders to be heard. Oppression of minority shareholders is a serious issue.").

27.　*See id; id.* at 51 (noting concerns about abuse by state of controlling shareholder position).

28.　Johnny K.W. Cheung, *Shortcomings in China's Corporate Governance Regime*, CHINA L. & PRACTICE, Feb. 2007, LEXIS, News Library, Curnws File.

29.　New Company Law, art. 19 ("For the establishment of an organization of the Communist Party of China and the carrying out of party activities in a company in accordance with the charter of the Communist Party of China, a company shall provide the necessary conditions for the activities of the party organization.").

One of the first shareholder-initiated claims in China was a direct action alleging fraud, against the Guangxia Company in 2001.[32] After news spread about the claim, more than 1,000 cases were filed throughout China against the Guangxia Company.[33] In September 2001, before the trial, the Supreme People's Court (SPC) intervened stating that the court would not accept and hear any shareholder claims because the capital market was still developing and the current securities civil liability system was too weak. After significant opposition and uproar, the SPC reversed its position in January 2002. The SPC then stated that investors could bring direct actions for misrepresentation, but not for insider trading or market manipulation.[34] The SPC also disallowed class action lawsuits.[35] In February, 2002, the SPC further clarified the status of shareholder litigation by the Private Securities Litigation Rules (PSL Rules).[36] While the PSL Rules were more extensive and attempted to formalize direct shareholder suits, they still only allow misrepresentation cases.[37]

D. Taiwan[38]

1. How has Taiwan dealt with the fiduciary duty of directors?

Taiwan is a civil law country and legislators establish the legal system and write the laws before conflicts arise. In the courts, judges try to find applicable laws to apply, and when none are found, the judge will either extend a relevant law, or refrain from ruling in the case until new laws are enacted.

In Taiwan, in contrast to the United States, most public corporations are controlled by families or large shareholders. Usually outsiders own no more than 30% of the shares. Corporate directors, then, are representatives of the controlling shareholders, and follow

---

30.   ALBERT H.Y. CHEN, AN INTRODUCTION TO THE LEGAL SYSTEM OF THE PEOPLE'S REPUBLIC OF CHINA 217 (3d ed. 2004) ("[C]ivil litigation was never seen as a positive force promoting legal development . . . emphasis on social harmony and the fulfillment of moral obligations was accompanied by the discouragement of civil suits to pursue individuals' private monetary or proprietary interests.").
31.   Guiping Lu, *Private Enforcement of Securities Fraud Law in China: A Critique of the Supreme People's Court 2003 Provisions Concerning Private Securities Litigation,* 12 PAC. RIM. L. & POL'Y J. 781, 783 (2003).
32.   Katharina Pistor & Chenggang Xu, *Governing Stock Markets in Transition Economies: Lessons From China* 11 (Columbia Law School, The Center for Law and Economic Studies, Working Paper No. 262, November 2004), *available at* http://ssrn.com/abstract=628065.
33.   *Id.* at 11-12.
34.   *Id.* at 12.
35.   *Id.* (In China joint or group actions, called "gongtong," are different from class action lawsuits.)
36.   Hongchuan Liu et al., *Halfway to Effective Shareholder Protection,* CHINA L. & PRACTICE, Mar. 2003, LEXIS, News Library, Arcnws File.
37.   *Id.*
38.   This material is drawn, with consent, from a paper by Kye Chou in satisfaction of a seminar requirements on fiduciary law at Boston University Law School, Spring 2007. The paper is edited and abridged, and some of the footnotes were omitted.

their instructions. Directors are usually also the top management of the corporations.

As Christopher Gulinello wrote about the new Company Law in Taiwan, the 2001 revisions imposed an express duty of loyalty on directors, in addition to the express duty of care. Although "duty of loyalty" is not defined, Taiwanese legal scholars are influenced by U.S. law and thus U.S. law may influence its development.

The duty of loyalty addresses independence from both management and large shareholders, as Taiwanese companies tend to have large shareholders, and applies to supervisors in addition to directors; i.e., it applies to "responsible persons." [39]

2. What are some effects of Taiwan's new law?

As ownership in Taiwanese companies becomes more dispersed, management becomes more powerful; therefore, it is significant that the new law increases shareholder protection from management misconduct. The revision is also significant in that the duty of loyalty creates shareholder protection against self-dealing, as the express self-dealing prohibition applies only to directors. However, there is no provision for a shareholder derivative suit against managers, under the theory that a manager owes a duty of loyalty to the company rather than shareholders. Therefore, the board or supervisor must initiate an action. As ownership becomes less concentrated and management influence over the board increases, the lack of such a provision may impede shareholder protection. [40]

– – – – – – – – – – – –

Discussion Topics

a. If you had a choice to establish a trust in the United States, Japan or Taiwan, which country would you pick, and why?

b. What can we learn from Japan and Taiwan about fiduciary law?

c. What can we learn from these countries about preventing abuse of trust and breach of fiduciary duties?

– – – – – – – – – – – –

E. United Kingdom[41]

1. A pooled investment form was transported from the United Kingdom to the United States

Unit trusts are collective investment schemes where investors contribute to a pool of capital.[42] The profits of the pooled capital are

---

39. Christopher John Gulinello, *The Revision of Taiwan's Company Law: The Struggle Toward a Shareholder-Oriented Model in One Corner of East Asia,* 28 DEL. J. CORP. L. 75, 104-05 (2003).

40. *Id.* at 116-17.

41. This material is drawn, with consent, from a paper by Joclyn Chico in satisfaction of a seminar requirements on fiduciary law at Boston University Law School, Spring 2007. The paper is edited and abridged, and some of the footnotes were omitted.

42. KAM FAN SIN, THE LEGAL NATURE OF THE UNIT TRUST 1-6 (1997).

allocated to the units that investors hold, and each investor is entitled to part of the profit pro rata with each unit that he holds.

The Foreign and Colonial Trust of 1868 was the first British unit trust.[43] Its deed of trust was modeled after the deed of "deed of settlement" companies. It had fixed interest investment, gave fixed investment returns and investors were not expected to redeem all certificates for twenty-four years.[44] After some success, many of these unit trusts failed, and the unit trust lost ground to the company as the collective investment scheme of choice in England.[45] The predominant collective investment scheme in the United States from 1925 to 1929 had been the investment company.[46] But promoters often created these investment companies to dispose of unwanted stock and the shares in these investment companies plummeted in the October 1929 crash and during the Great Depression that followed.[47] Investors saw this as a result of abuses and malpractices by the management of investment companies.[48]

An American business man had created a unit investment trust in 1924 when he "'deposited' a share to his bank in exchange for ten bankers' receipts [representing] pro rata interests."[49] This was "[t]he form of the trust that influenced subsequent developments in England."[50] The *fixed* unit investment trust was governed by a contract between a management company and a trustee that left little discretion by specifying the securities against which certificates were issued and for that reason it became the choice of investment vehicle over the company.[51] But the advantages of empowering the manager with the ability to change the underlying securities in the portfolio of investments became clear by 1931 when the United States was clearly going through a severe economic depression.[52] That was how the *flexible* unit trust emerged in the United States.[53] This flexibility / discretion is what gives rise to fiduciary duties and the use of fiduciary law in the financial services context.

2. A pooled investment form was transported from the United States to the United Kingdom

In 1931, the U.K. imported the deed of an American mutual fund.[54] When First British Fixed Trust was formed in the U.K. in 1931, its trust deed was based on the deed of an American *fixed* trust—the All-America Investors Corporation Trust.[55] That was how the form of the

---

43.   *Id.* at 23.
44.   *Id.*
45.   *Id.* at 26-27.
46.   *Id.* at 28.
47.   *Id.*
48.   *Id.*
49.   *Id.*
50.   *Id.*
51.   *Id.* at 28-29.
52.   *Id.* at 29.
53.   *Id.* at 29-32.
54.   *Id.* at 29.

U.S. mutual fund migrated to the U.K. Both deeds of trust empowered the holder to surrender a unit in exchange for the underlying securities. But the First British Fixed Trust deed was different in one important aspect: the manager also agreed to "reacquire trust units at a *price* based on the value of the underlying investments."[56] The establishment of a trust by a contract between a professional manager and a trustee and the empowerment of the unit holder to exchange a unit for its underlying assets distinguished this arrangement from the investment trusts of the 19th century.[57]

3. The flexible unit trust emerged in 1934

The *flexible* unit trust that is closest to the modern British unit trust emerged in 1934: the Foreign Government Bond Trust.[58] It consisted of a pool of securities that was divided into "bond-units" representing changeable securities.[59] This flexibility based on the investor granting discretion to the fund manager gives rise to a fiduciary duty of loyalty that the fund manager owes the investor. The standard modern operation of today's British unit trusts appeared in December 1935 when the Limited Investment Fund offered subscriptions that did not require a cash deposit with the trustee.[60]

_ _ _ _ _ _ _ _ _ _ _

Discussion Topics

a. Why could the U.K. transport and import its forms of investment organization from the United States, while Japan, that had adopted the United States common law, has rejected it as a foreign implant for so many years?

b. As financial cultures become more global, could you predict whether the civil law or the common law forms would become more prevalent? Could you draw your answer from the prevailing use of the English language?

_ _ _ _ _ _ _ _ _ _ _

F. Culture and Impact of Social Controls on Law

If fiduciary laws in different countries are to be unified so that parties would be able to conduct their commercial activities and combine in institutional arrangements, we should understand the differences and find the common ground in their fiduciary laws. The language of the rules and their meanings are important, but just as important is the context in which these rules were adopted and practiced. And just as important is the heritage they carry and their place in the social culture. The following is an example of such an influence on the design and strength of fiduciary law.

---

55. *Id.* at 29.
56. *Id.* at 29-30 (emphasis added).
57. *Id.* at 30.
58. *Id.*
59. *Id.*
60. *Id.* at 31.

1. What is the role of shame, guilt and empathy?

In her book *Trust and Honesty*, Tamar Frankel discusses shame and the relation to trust of shame, guilt and empathy—emotions that humans have developed.[61] These emotions help human beings to reject the temptations to hurt others and to demonstrate their reliability to others:

> Shame and guilt can control the drive to cheat, even if it is "rational" to do so, and even if the cheaters have a good chance of "getting away with it." . . .
>
> Shame, guilt, and empathy are not identical with trustworthiness. People can be honest yet lack shame, guilt, and empathy. The law does not require people to experience these feelings. It is not a breach of a duty for corporate management to be insensitive to the pain of others. In fact, lack of empathy can be justified and approved when it might hinder helping others. Physicians and lawyers must control their empathy lest they become dysfunctional by suffering too much. This limitation is understood and accepted.
>
> And yet generally, when people lack these feelings, it is easier for them to harm others. That may include harm in legal and honest ways, as Scrooge did. It may include harm in illegal and dishonest ways as well. But these feelings are linked to honesty and trust because they help people to control their drive to hurt others. Therefore, people who show that they feel shame, guilt, and empathy demonstrate their reliability to others, and are more likely to be trusted. . . .
>
> Feelings of guilt, shame, and empathy are personal. They may be ingrained in some people more than in others. The depth of these feelings, and especially the desire to avoid inflicting pain on others, are influenced by the attitude of peers and the culture of the communities in which people live. In a culture that undervalues guilt, shame, and empathy, people can be under pressure to share passively in cruelty to others.[62]

2. What was the role of shame in Japan?

In an article about shame and culture, Toni M. Massaro discusses the shame culture of Japan:[63] Shame cultures use shame to control behavior. Ruth Benedict examined Japan's culture in 1946 and noted the strong concern about social judgment, especially in the closely knit society. Social standing is crucial, so much so, that if it is attacked, members of the family will not help.

"Public rebuke of an individual reared under these cultural conditions surely would strike deep and hard. Shame sanctions in Japan during this period therefore likely proved a significant deterrent to voluntary, socially disapproved behavior." Not much has changed in this respect in today's Japan. It is interesting to note how Japan refused to apologize to Korea for the treatment of Korean women during the Second World War. That apology has meant much both to the Koreans and to the Japanese.

3. What was the role of shame in colonial America?

Toni M. Massaro discusses shame in colonial America[64] as follows:

---

61. TAMAR FRANKEL, TRUST AND HONESTY: AMERICA'S BUSINESS CULTURE AT A CROSSROAD 109-110 (2006) (footnotes omitted).
62. *Id.*
63. Toni M. Massaro, *Shame, Culture, and American Criminal Law*, 89 MICH. L. REV. 1880, 1906-10 (1991).
64. *Id.* at 1912-15.

... A.M. Earle describes the colonists as "vastly touchy and resentful about being called opprobrious or bantering names; often running petulantly to the court about it and seeking redress by prosecution of the offender." This ultrasensitivity, she remarks, enhanced the effectiveness of . . . shaming sanctions. Moreover, the social intimacy of colonial communities meant that criminal offenders typically were known members of the group, not transient outsiders. Thus, the fear of disgrace before the community was considerable.

The sanction of "admonition" involved both state and church. In the process the heads of the community lectured to the violator who then confessed publicly. The sentence was suspended in whole or in part to show community forgiveness, which then brought the culprit back to the community. This process involved the state and the church. Sinners were forced to wear "signs or letters," or "stand in the pillory wearing a sign listing their crimes."[65] Perhaps the Puritan society was strict because of the belief in predestination: bad behavior meant an evil person, and evil was threatening. Hence the "formal public apologies and confessions" "to reinforce the strict moral order" and forcing criminals on death row to confess publicly (signalling consent to the punishment). This culture was inculcated in children, and resulted in "a harsh, disciplined life." This led to a very high sensitivity to "public exposure and shame" similar to that of the Japanese.[66]

— — — — — — — — — — —

Discussion Topics

a. What are the benefits and disadvantages of shaming as a mechanism to establish and control trustworthiness?

b. Under what conditions is such a mechanism effective?

c. What is the relationship between shaming and the law in the United States?

— — — — — — — — — — —

4. What is the role of "team" culture and "market" culture?

Here is a comment by Yoshihisa Masaki:[67]

Hello. I am Yoshi, a member of LL.M. in American Law. My country is Japan. The relation between the company and inventor is a big issue in my country. I suppose one of this site's purposes is to know what the other country's view. Therefore I would like to start introducing our country's R&D situation. . . . Japan encourages creators, inventors and researchers strongly. Accordingly, for example, our country's numbers of patent is top level of the world.[68] We are always competing with United States in this area. But the structure or circumstance of IP is different from U.S. Generally and roughly, the patent holders are individuals who research at the academic or public research institutes in the United States.

---

65. *Id.* at 1912-13.
66. *Id.* at 1912-15.
67. This is an abridged and edited comment that was sent by Yoshihisa Masaki [mailto:PXS04465@nifty.com] January 24, 2007 on the site of the InternetBar in which participants discussed culture of trust.
68. International IMD Competitiveness Scoreboard 2006/Overall ranking of all countries/regions, *available at* http://www.imd.ch/research/publications/wcy/competitiveness_scoreboard_ 2006.cfm?bhcp=1.

They establish business by the venture companies. On the other hand, in Japan, the patent holder is big company or employee of big company. A researcher uses the company's laboratory and other resources.[69]. . . Japanese business culture has been "team" culture. Individual character is not stressed. The team of employees has believed company returns to the profits to the workers, stockholders and society. Inventor is also a member of the team. But reflecting Americanization of economy, our mind has changed gradually.

Fifteen years ago, I could not imagine the Japanese baseball player use an agent lawyer and get the high salary for his pride and life (like Matsuzaka!). The Japanese baseball player's typical comment was "thanks to the team, I can keep playing my favorite sports. I am happy to play baseball with good teammates. I would like to contribute for the team." A[n] inventor [was] in the same situation. Major companies had a system of lifetime employment, under which employees were assured a job for life but were not rewarded based on performance. I suppose, in their recognition, there was a fiduciary relation between management (board) and working team or relation among teammates but rarely between the company and the individual researcher, because he is a part or body of the company.

Currently, an inventor has begun to contend own right to the invention. And the court took the course to support individual researchers. Recently, in the several "work made for hire" cases, the Japanese inventors awarded the compensation for their invention. Last year, the Tokyo High Court awarded an inventor 163 million yen (about 1.5 million dollars). His lawyer said he was paid only 118,000 yen (about 11 hundred dollars) for one of three patents he filed between 1973 and 1877 for technology used to read CDs and DVDs. It is seemingly that the concept of contract between the company and inventor arose. The warm family taste "team" relationship has declined through the long recession and world competition. We became to use legal language between the company and its worker, (like America). But in this context, I doubt that we have not established new fiduciary. The situation tells us declining reliance between the company and the researcher, but it does not construct new fiduciary relationship among them. . . .

In this situation, Professor Frankel's question: "when the parties start the collaborating" is really important and difficult. We would like to keep the strong point of team culture. When one team members invents or significantly develops part of the research should we separate and contract with him directly? If we do so at the beginning of the relation between the company and the researcher assessing the researchers' future value, the situation is similar to baseball team. But then the researcher can not keep a lifetime employment. In this case, each researcher tends to focus on own (small) subject of research and plan her goal in a short span.

The Japanese government revised the patent law in 2004. Under the revised law, the courts respect the company's contracts with the researchers and don't evaluate an invention value unless the company's rules are irrational. Under the revised rule, some Japanese companies are changing their rules and have increased the researchers' compensation but most of them have just revised "bonus" rule and provide lifetime employment. Some company established "the evaluation committee" in order to evaluate the employee's invention's value and his bonus. The management believes that the Japanese system should adopt the "contract" relation. The employee should contract when

---

69. *Id.* (noting that in the medical machine area, Japan's strong point is diagnostic machines and weak point is treatment machines. One reason for this is litigation risk; if the medical company made defective treatment machines, the damage might be a huge amount. If the company is a small venture, the company will just go to bankruptcy court. Thanks to the small scale, the influence is small. But for the big company, the damages might cause major consequences to the economy and society).

he starts work for company. Some inventors prefer fiduciary relationship rather than contract with the company, but want to contract when they produce valuable invention. . . . Both parties cannot feel "warm fiduciary relation," but they have business-like relation. . . .

In the United States, as the court noted, the government (patent system) "encourage(s) the sharing of new inventions so that they can be commercialized." Therefore both public policy and fiduciary law move in the same direction. On the other hand, Japan's inventors' sponsors are mainly big companies. Although Japanese government encourages inventors, we cannot use the American scale budget for the inventors. In order to keep "team" culture benefits, such as long term R&D and lifetime employment and to prevent high and unpredictable compensation, we should not follow the American fiduciary law between the company and inventor whether a researcher or employee.[70]

– – – – – – – – – – – –

Discussion Topics

a. Based on these readings, what role does culture and the society play in Japan's legal design?

b. Outline your preparation for negotiating with a Japanese counterpart. What questions would you ask an experienced lawyer who has been working in Japan for some time?

c. The separation of legal and equitable title is the central concept in Anglo-American jurisprudence in terms of the creation of trusts and the development of fiduciary law. Do those concepts really matter if other countries have functionally equivalent legal entities that accomplish the same thing?

d. Are these concepts so fundamental to our understanding of the base of fiduciary duties that they cannot be harmonized?

e. Analyze the difference between Japanese supervisors' duty of care and the United States directors' duty of care under Delaware law. How can you explain the difference? Is it justified? How can you unify the laws in the two countries? Do you need to unify the laws?

f. What do you think of the following dialogue between two students in the Fiduciary Law Seminar Class?[71]

Timothy: "Hey Ian, in class, you discussed how embarrassment in front of one's peers weighs more heavily on a would-be perpetrator than actual laws. You also said that the probability of getting caught is very minute (I believe he said in most cases it is less than 10% or so). I would imagine that the chances of getting caught breaching a fiduciary duty in many cases are very remote.

My question is whether breaches of fiduciary duties are as few and far between as you stated in class, or whether the fiduciary simply doesn't

---

70. This is an abridged and edited comment that was sent by Yoshihisa Masaki [mailto:PXS04465@nifty.com] January 24, 2007 on the site of the InternetBar in which participants discussed culture of trust.
71. This material is drawn, with consent, from a dialog between Ian Engstrand & Max Timothy Riffin in the seminar on fiduciary law at Boston University Law School, Spring 2007. The dialogue is edited and abridged.

get caught, so we never hear about the breach. Stated a different way: how can we be certain that most fiduciaries honor their duties when your research also stated that the odds of getting caught are so small? We would only hear of those who get caught. Just a question out of curiosity more than anything—which is why I held off using class time for it. I just wanted to get your thoughts on it since, in doing your research, you've read a lot more on the subject than I have.

Thanks! Sincerely, Max"

Ian: "So I think the short answer is that we can't be absolutely certain that most fiduciaries honor their duties most of the time. By its very nature, the fiduciary relationship is difficult, expensive and subversive to the utility of the relationship to monitor. Thus, I don't think there is going to be very good, if any, empirical data on the chances of fiduciaries getting caught. I certainly didn't come across any in my research. However, I think that in many cases there are societal and economic forces that promote honesty in the fiduciary relationship. For example, a lawyer has an economic incentive to fulfill his duties to his client (directly in a contingency fee arrangement and indirectly, through reputation and repeat business, in an hourly basis). The lawyer also is under societal pressure to fulfill his fiduciary duties because breach of those duties is generally considered morally repugnant. Additionally, and perhaps most importantly, the law firm itself promotes a culture of honesty-in-fiduciary-dealings that pressures the lawyer to be honest. I think this societal-structural pressure is important for most fiduciaries that are acting in their professional capacities.

. . . The culture in the brokerage firms prior to 2002 ran completely against the fulfillment of the analysts' trust relationship [with the public, which they advised]. Analysts' bonuses were contingent on hyping 'bad' stocks. Additionally, their coworkers pressured them to hype junk stocks to increase overall revenues for the firm (either through underwriting business or trading on brokerage's own account). Basically, the trust relationship broke down in that case because economic, social and structural incentives went directly against the keeping of the duties of honesty.

I think that the case of the research analysts is the exception rather than the norm. From what I have seen most professionals that act as fiduciaries are honest people that are kept honest in large part because of societal and structural pressures, not because of a fear of getting caught by the entrustor. If fiduciaries were to merely run a risk-reward calculation in their heads to determine whether to fulfill their duties for a given decision, they would betray their entrustors at every turn. The objective risk of getting caught is so low as compared to the monetary benefit of stealing, or skimming from your entrustor. If this were the case, then fiduciary relationships would be incredibly inefficient for entrustors. Since entrustors generally entrust because it is more efficient, it can be safely be said that there is something else besides a straight risk-reward calculation that keeps fiduciaries honest. I think that this something else is structural-societal pressure. Of course, as your question rightly points out, we cannot be absolutely certain of this contention because of a lack of empirical data. Hope this helps.

Best, Ian"

Chapter Nine
Role of Fiduciary Law in Facilitating Trust

A. The Nature and Role of Trust[1]

[Trusting can be defined as] "believing that others tell the truth and will keep their promises." [Because trust is a relationship, this] straightforward definition [becomes] as complicated as humans and their society.

With few exceptions trust is essential to economic prosperity. Thousands of people contribute to the sustenance and comfort of each of us, our dress and lodging, transportation and communications, education and entertainment. If we could not rely on the wholesomeness of the food we buy, the expertise of our physicians and lawyers, the honesty of our banks and mutual funds, or, as Sweeney Todd noted, the trustworthiness of the barber with his sharp shaving razor, our lives would be far more primitive.... Trust saves time and money. It allows people to believe other persons' statements without checking their truth, and to rely on other persons' promises, without demanding guarantees. It allows people to use the talents of strangers.

But there may be exceptions. Poor communities, such as the Eskimo community, may have deep trusting relationships.... In contrast, Russell Hardin notes small communities controlled by despotic masters that survive or even prosper on mistrust.... [S]preading mistrust can be useful, under certain circumstances, for example, to prevent prisoners from forging trust relationships and thus prevent riots and disruptions. Political competitors may spread mistrust of each other to their advantage....

Carol Rose has shown that, in theory, it may be irrational to trust or to be trustworthy. But the theory applies only in short-term reasoning, and when no emotions or other elements are in play.[2] In other words, the theory applies to hypothetical humans, not real ones, and to hypothetical societies, not real and prosperous ones. These exceptions to the rule that trust is crucial to our lives have not convinced the American society and its lawmakers. American law protects trust and punishes its abuse.

The following problem and the questions that follow highlight the ambiguity of trusting and trustworthiness.

Problem

NYC Cabbie Returns Bag of Diamond Rings. Osman Chowdhury, a native of Bangladesh, found 31 diamond rings in his taxicab "after dropping off [his] passenger, who [left him] a 30-cent tip on a $10.70 fare." "All my life, I tried to be honest," the New York cab driver said. "I'm proud of what I did so that people know New York taxi

---

1. TAMAR FRANKEL, TRUST AND HONESTY: AMERICA'S BUSINESS CULTURE AT A CROSSROAD 49-50 (2006) (Most footnotes and cites to authorities in the text have been omitted).
2. Carol M. Rose, *Trust in the Mirror of Betrayal*, 75 B.U. L. REV. 531, 534-35 (1995).

drivers are honest." Hours after dropping the woman off at her destination, the cab driver was alerted by three passengers that the woman's suitcase was in the trunk. After taking the suitcase to the Manhattan headquarters of the New York Taxi Workers Alliance, the cabdriver and the Alliance president opened the luggage and found the sparkling diamonds. They also found enough information to contact the woman. The woman offered Chowdhury a reward—a check for $100—which he at first refused, but then accepted due to his lost fares during the time he was attempting to find her. "I cannot take a penny for being honest," he said. "He reluctantly accepted the money to cover the fares he lost while trying to track her down." He said he never considered taking the diamonds. "I'm not going to take someone else's money or property to make me rich. I don't want it that way," said the cabdriver.

— — — — — — — — — — — -

Discussion Topics

a.   A person who takes a taxi expects a taxicab driver with the ability to take that person from point A to point B safely. This is the service that a person pays for when taking a taxi. What was the taxicab driver entrusted with? What falls within the realm of this entrustment?

b.   Which argument would you choose? A narrow view of entrustment would be that the passenger was merely entrusting the driver with providing her with a safe trip to the airport. Anything else is not included. The driver provided her with this service. For a narrow view of entrustment one could argue that, just as the taxicab driver can't be held liable if there is an accident and the passenger misses his or her flight, so the driver is not responsible for the luggage the passenger leaves behind. Why should the cabdriver be forced to look for the passenger when the driver's only obligation was to provide transportation to a desired destination? A broader view could be that the driver was entrusted not only with ensuring that she got a safe trip, but also that all of her possessions were also delivered safely.

c.   Was the driver honest or smart and risk-averse? Was he in danger of being caught if he kept the diamonds? Did it matter that he worked for a cab company? Did he owe anything to the passenger who tipped him 30 cents?

d.   Should we have faith in cabdrivers as an institution? Is it important for us to see that a cabdriver was honest? If the cabdriver had not returned the diamonds, would this shake our view of cabdrivers? If the cabdriver had not returned the diamonds, should the court have required him to do so? However, is there a greater duty here on a societal level? Essentially, does it matter if passengers trust cabdrivers? If not, what institutions should we and can we trust? When should the courts recognize a fiduciary relationship between cab driver and passenger and with respect to what?

e.   When is it important for our society to have trust? If we lose trust, will that make us less trustworthy, as well? Why or why not? Does trust breed trust? Fraud breed fraud? In light of the previous readings, should car mechanics be viewed as fiduciaries? Should services such as these, which literally and figuratively keep our towns and cities running, be viewed as containing fiduciary relationships?

f. Can you distinguish cleaning services from taxi services and mechanic services? What guidelines would you suggest to classify these services as fiduciary or non-fiduciary? What if the cabdriver tried to find the passenger unsuccessfully, and she did not make an effort to find the diamonds?

g. In determining whether property has been abandoned, certain factors must be considered: the property, time, place and circumstances, actions and conduct of the parties, opportunity or expectancy of recovery and all other facts and circumstances.[3]

h. Should the passenger bear any of the burden or is her offer of $100 at her discretion enough?[4] Is the cab driver entitled to more than his expenses? Is the issue a moral or legal issue?[5]

— — — — — — — — — — -

[Trust involves paradoxes][6]

During the Cold War negotiations with the Soviet Union, the late President Ronald Reagan often borrowed a Russian proverb: "Trust but verify." This statement drew chuckles. It seemed to be a contradiction in terms. After all, the very purpose and value of trust is to *avoid* checking the truth of what trusted persons say and the reliability of their promises. Yet, President Reagan (and Russian folklore) was right. There are reasons for encouraging people to trust each other. There are reasons for encouraging people to protect themselves from each other, and for criticizing those who unreasonably rely on others.

Thus, trust presents a paradox. To survive, individuals must both trust others and also protect themselves from others. The cause of this conflicted need to trust and yet verify seems to be rooted in the very nature and existence of humans. Without the support of others, humans cannot survive the dangers of the elements or provide for their needs. But if they rely on others, humans may not survive the danger of other humans' treachery. Wariness and alertness reduce our risks from others. Wariness has an added advantage. It

---

3. Verena Dobnik, *NYC Cabbie Returns Bag of Diamond Rings*, AP, Feb. 7, 2007, http://abcnews.go.com/US/wireStory?id=2857747 (summarized and edited).
4. Columbus-America Discovery Group, Inc. v. Unidentified, Wrecked & Abandoned Sailing Vessel, 742 F. Supp. 1327 (E.D. Va. 1990); Zych v. Unidentified, Wrecked & Abandoned Vessel, Believed to Be SB Lady Elgin, 755 F. Supp. 213 (N.D. Ill. 1990) (intent to abandon must be proven); Hoelzer v. City of Stamford, Conn., 933 F.2d 1131 (2d Cir. 1991) (to prove abandonment, there must be a showing of the owner's intent to abandon the property and some affirmative act or omission demonstrating that intention). Most state laws do not appear to be "finder's keepers," unless the property found has been abandoned (deliberately relinquished, not merely lost or misplaced). *See, e.g.*, Hener v. United States, 525 F. Supp. 350, 354 (S.D.N.Y. 1981) ("common law of finds" treats abandoned property as having no prior owner and person to reduce property to "possession" becomes owner) (citing RAY ANDREWS BROWN, THE LAW OF PERSONAL PROPERTY 15 (2d ed. 1955)).
5. *See* United States v. Taglione, 546 F.2d 194 (5th Cir. 1977) (the law entitles the finder of lost property only to his expenses, but he may ask for more so long as he does not extort more). Legally the cabdriver is not entitled to the diamonds through abandonment; the woman clearly did not abandon them but was negligent. Morally should the cabdriver have been entitled to the diamonds? *See* Bisignano v. Harrison Central School Dist., 113 F. Supp. 2d 591 (S.D.N.Y. 2000).
6. TAMAR FRANKEL, TRUST AND HONESTY: AMERICA'S BUSINESS CULTURE AT A CROSSROAD 50-51 (2006).

helps discover opportunities that would not be revealed if we fully relied on others. Thus, as we trust, we must also exercise a degree of caution. This leads to a second paradox.

To prosper, individuals and society must specialize. One look at the shopping mall in the United States shows the enormous specialization and its blessings. No one person or company can supply all the riches that are offered in that mall. To achieve this result, each person and enterprise must devote its energies and talents to a particular function. To enjoy the fruits of this specialization, individuals and societies must rely and depend on each other for products, services and knowledge.

But in order to specialize and create, individuals must become independent. Independence means precisely the opposite of relying on others. It means doing things for yourself, thinking for yourself, and deciding for yourself. And yet, only by relying on others for the things we need do we have the time to develop our own expertise (on which others rely). Therefore, the benefits of trusting others are accompanied by risks (and cost of self-protection). The benefits of relying on others are accompanied by the danger of undermining our independence from others. . . .

The Balance between "Trust" and "Verify" Depends in Part on the Particular Society. [The risk from other people's deception and the acceptable level of trust and mistrust depends on the society in which we live.]

Years ago, a person who visited a Mediterranean country told me the following story. A father puts his four-year-old son on a high stone wall and says: "Come, jump down. I will catch you." The child hesitates, and the father repeats the promise. After a few more assurances, the child jumps, and the father steps aside. The child falls on the hard ground and begins crying. The father kneels lovingly, picks the child up, and says: "This will teach you a lesson not to trust anyone, not even your father!" The implication for the child is broader. If the father is allowed to be untrustworthy, so can the child be untrustworthy. The lesson is: "Do not trust and do not be trustworthy." . . .[7]

. . . [I]n the United States, reputation for honesty is important to profitable trading on the eBay auction system. Traders are rated by the parties with whom they deal and the rating is published, thus determining the traders' reputation. Persons with lower reputation offer greater risks to the people with whom they deal. The eBay system operates as an auction. Therefore, those with reduced reputation will sell for less and buy for more. The offers of such persons will attract fewer offers or will cause the offerors to discount the prices for the risk in trading low-reputation persons. The system provides an incentive to be honest. [Barbara A. Misztal notes that] "[a] good reputation allows economic agents locked into the relation to cut the transaction costs and overcome limited information, and thus to facilitate efficient contractual relations."

The Balance between "Trust" and "Verify" Depends in Part on Costs and Benefits
When the cost of verifying the truth and honesty of the other party is negligible, and the potential losses from the transaction are relatively low, there is no need to trust. . . . The buyer of a newspaper need not trust the seller because the buyer can verify the nature and price of the paper and check whether the middle section of the Sunday paper is missing. Because the buyer does not have to trust the seller, the seller will not invest in guaranteeing his honesty. . . . The exchange is simultaneous: money for a newspaper. Therefore, neither party must [verify whether the other party is reliable and keeps his promises]. . . .

In contrast to newspaper buyers, investors who seek a mutual fund adviser to manage their life savings, must trust the adviser. That is because it is very costly for them to verify the truth of the adviser's stories and the reliability of the adviser's promises to act for the benefit of the investors and not to treat the entrusted money as his own. . . .

---

7.   *Id.* at 51-52.

The risk to investors is very high. Trusted persons do not break into investors' homes to take their money; they are offered money and assets voluntarily and even eagerly. Controlling enormous amounts of money could be tempting. There are so many easy-to-hide ways to help oneself to benefits from other people's money. Unless reminded time and again, and unless abuse-preventing mechanisms are in place, trusted persons might forget that entrusted money is not their money. Used to controlling other people's money, they may even begin to feel a sense of ownership and find reasons to justify it. Therefore, investors must rely on guarantors and verifiers in the markets, on the advisers' reputation, and on the law and the government to continuously maintain a high level of advisers' honesty.[8]

Discussion Topics

a. List the instances in which you trust others during one day. What induces you to trust them?

b. Can you justify your trust? What are the alternatives to not trusting? Is trusting rational? What makes the buyer of a washing machine pay hundreds of dollars without evidence that the machine is new? What prevents the seller of a washing machine from selling the customer a used one? What makes the seller accept a credit card from the buyer? Why do sellers of some items offer the buyers the option of returning the merchandise in 30 days?

c. A corrupt army official who ordered and received more wine bottles than his canteen consumed sold the rest through a dealer. The dealer took a percentage off the money he received and paid the rest to the official. Thus, the official came to trust the dealer. Years later the official was scheduled to retire and he told his friend the dealer that unfortunately their dealing will be terminated. The official sent the dealer the usual number of bottles but on the time for payment the dealer did not pay. The official came to the dealer and demanded payment, but the dealer refused. "How come?" said the official. "I trusted you all these years. Why do you betray me now? After all, you know that I cannot go to the authorities, and complain if you did not pay me, but you knew that I could not go to the authorities before, yet you never cheated me before." What, in your opinion, was the dealer's answer? Was there a trust relationship among the two? What were the underlying values of the dealer?

[How do Americans manage the paradoxes of trust?][9]

An effective way to increase trust is to establish trustworthy institutions and reliable systems. In spite of the risks, Americans are trusting people. Americans are proud of their independence and their ability to protect themselves from deception by others. Thus, we trust and rely on others; but we also seek independence and rely on ourselves.

If you were to ask most Americans, you would likely find that they rely on their financial system perhaps more than they rely on their brokers, advisers, and investment

---

8.   *Id.* at 52.
9.   *Id.* at 55-56.

bankers. You would also find that they trust the law perhaps more than they trust the lawyers, judges, and regulators. Americans have long felt confident in and admired the corporate system perhaps more than they trusted corporate management. Today, their trust in management is wavering, but it seems that their trust in corporations and financial institutions has remained intact . . . .

. . . Trust in institutions, systems, and ideas, is impersonal, unattached to any particular individual. After all, a system is a concept, or an expected pattern of behavior, within an organization or in society. A system can be inanimate, like the solar system, which is [trusted] to behave in a certain way. A system (even a chaotic system) may reflect a more predictable and less fickle pattern than the behavior of particular individuals. A system also signifies a consensus, or at least a significant following. Perhaps because Americans value individual freedom and independence, they trust their systems with something close to passion. This impersonal relationship allows them to "herd" by their own free will, without subjugation. This attitude may be one reason why Americans are so attracted to the invisible hand of the market system, its signals and its promises.

Besides, *it is efficient to trust institutions.* Throughout life, most people form personal, long-term relationships with not more than a couple of hundred people, [five hundred] at most. Because the number of institutions is smaller than the number of individuals, it is less costly to check out institutions before trusting. In addition, [trust] is easier to verify if it is limited to a particular context. Impersonal trust in business relationships is similarly "tailored" [and easier to verify]. For example, a bank verifies the borrowers' creditworthiness but little else. This limited context allows a bank to develop an efficient system to verify the creditworthiness of customers (or employ more persons to do just that).

While people can personally rely on a small number of businesses and few employees, trusting large institutions can expand reliance on thousands of employees, even if the employees are unknown and even if they change over time. While it is impossible to develop personal relationships with so many, it is possible to verify the honesty of the institutions that support their employees' honesty. Thus, trust in corporations with hundreds of thousands of employees, managers, and contracting parties, is efficient for the customers, for the institutions and for the economy as a whole. Americans are the masters of efficient organizations. No wonder they trust their own creations.

Americans' *trust in institutions is not complete, nor blind.* Perhaps the American experience involving serious frauds has introduced demand for guarantees, not only of individuals but also of institutions. America is covered with layers of private-sector guarantors of trust. Some guarantors are in turn insured by the government or by institutions that are supervised by the government.[10]

— — — — — — — — — — -

Discussion Topics

a. Can you list the ways in which the government guarantees truth and reliability of individuals, banks, corporations, and businesses?

b. How is trust established on the Internet?

— — — — — — — — — — -

---

10. *Id.* at 55-56.

B. The Barriers to Abuse of Trust and Dishonesty[11]

1. The barriers

There are many barriers to dishonesty, but among the main barriers are three. One is moral behavior, where trusted persons exercise self-control over temptations. The second is self-protection, when trusting people protect themselves with the help of market sanctions against abuse of trust. Market sanctions represent mostly self- protection of many people, each acting in his or her own interest. The third barrier to abuse of trust is the law. Morality reflects mainly the "trust" component in "trust but verify." One can trust people who exercise self-control in face of temptations. Self-protection and the markets reflect mainly the "but verify" component in "trust but verify." One must verify the other person's statements and promises. The law reflects and supports both the "trust" component and the self-protection "verify" component. Some rules are designed to put barriers to temptations. These rules are addressed to trusted persons. Some rules require . . . people to disclose true information. These rules are addressed to the recipients of the information, and they are expected to decide for themselves whether and how to engage in business with the disclosing parties. And some rules go further and withdraw legal protection from people who do not protect themselves from the fraud of others, even though they can do so.

Barriers to dishonesty are not free. They cost. Morality puts the burden on the trusted persons to withstand temptation. Law shifts the burden to the government and taxpayers to prevent trusted persons from succumbing to temptation. And the markets transfer the burden to the other parties to the relationships; they should protect themselves from trusted persons who cannot withstand temptation. However, by themselves, neither of these barriers to abuse of trust has been effective. Morality alone is not strong enough to enforce honesty. Markets alone do not achieve the goal either. And law on its own has not succeeded in imposing truth and trustworthiness. Each mechanism has supported the other and has drawn on the other for support. Together, they form a whole--a "diversified" package. The relative weight of the components in the package changes with the nature of the relationship among people and with the environment. As their balance changes, the costs that they impose change as well. But so do the deterrent and preventive effects of the barriers. The issue is not merely how much the barriers cost but also how much harm they prevent.[12]

2. Morality[13]

The idea of morality is complex and open to many interpretations and debates. For the purpose of this book, however, people are moral people if they control their temptations to do the wrong thing, and are inclined to do the right thing. The "wrong and right things" are narrowly defined to include a few principles. Moral persons do not abuse the trust that is vested in them and do not deceive. They refrain from misleading others intentionally or negligently, for their own benefit. Moral persons need not give, but they do not *take what they do not own* without the owners' permission. And, most important, they should behave in this manner *even if there are no police around,* that is, even when they are likely to "get away with it."

Moral people impose the rules of honesty on themselves. If people are *forced* to act according to the same rules, they are not moral. At least one reason for the distinction is that moral persons relieve society from the burden of enforcing its rules. For moral persons,

---

11.   *Id.* at 105-06.
12.   *Id.* at 106.
13.   *Id.* at 106-07.

a reward for doing the right thing is not only in the actual right behavior but ultimate power—the power of control: "No one tells me what to do." And even more importantly, the reward is the power of self-control: "I am the master of myself, and can control my weaknesses in the face of great temptations." From this point of view, rewards or punishments to do the right thing do not empower but signify the opposite. A person who is motivated by rewards or punishments submits to the control of others who can manipulate him by benefits and disadvantages. It is those others who decide how he would act, and have the tools to motivate him. This distinction is not lost on trusting persons. Therefore, they would trust those who impose limiting rules on themselves more than they would trust those who are forced to follow rules imposed by others.

On the other side of this coin are persons who may claim to be moral, but follow their own standards and own rules of morality. This attitude may lead trusting people to trust them less. The self-restraining morality according to one's moral standards is not self-restraining at all. If people reserve to themselves the right to define the temptations that they will withstand, there may be no real temptations. An aspect of moral behavior is self-negation in relation to others, and often for the benefit of others. And if people masqueraded as moral people according to their own rules, they could design rules for their own benefit and comfort, at the expense of those who trust them.

Educating Moral People, and the "Selfish Gene"

Learning moral behavior usually starts at an early age. Parents continuously tell children "not to." Children are admonished not to play with fire, not to hit the little brother, not to torture the cat. Most parents teach their children not to take what does not belong to them, to share their toys with other children, and to tell the truth. Just as important, children are taught to exercise self-restraint even if the parents are not around. Children are thus rewarded for policing themselves. Their self-interest is not dormant, however. What they learn is not necessarily self-sacrifice. What they learn is [self-limitation and avoiding anti-social behavior].

Because acting morally is necessarily a habit, [Emile Durkheim suggested that] morality should be instilled by education at an early age. [He viewed] "[c]ertain components of morality [to be] inherently matters of habit: to become attached to collective ideals, 'one must have developed the habits of acting and thinking in common; to assure regularity, it is only necessary that habits be strongly founded.'" We must create "a general disposition of the mind and the will": "a *habitus* of moral being."

For hundreds of years, philosophers, theologians, and scientists have debated the question of whether humans are born good and evil, selfish and unselfish, or whether they develop these tendencies depending on their environment. Researchers have found that people [have a tendency to selfishness, metaphorically called the "selfish gene"] that strives to ensure survival. Yet the "selfish gene" is compatible with moral sentiments. Rarely will the individual survive without a society; rarely will society survive if its members are intent only on taking, and each member must continuously protect himself from others....

One of Zimbardo's more famous studies is the Stanford Prison Experiment, where Zimbardo assigned 22 physically and mentally healthy young men to be either prisoners or guards in a simulated prison environment. The study was originally meant to continue for two weeks, but Zimbardo had to stop the experiment after only six days because of the developing behavior of the students. Five of the prisoners had to be taken out of the experiment because they began to suffer from extreme depression and anxiety. The prisoners as a whole lost their sense of identity, and began referring to themselves by their ID numbers. The prisoners that lasted the longest in the experiment were the ones that blindly followed the authority of the guards. Some of the guards became extremely cruel and abusive to the prisoners, and even acknowledged to the experimenters that they were taking pleasure from their role of authority and power over others. One guard tried to go beyond his assigned role by keeping a prisoner in solitary confinement past the time set out by the guards' rules, and tried to find ways to continue the prisoner's confinement without the other guards knowledge. Several guards worked overtime without pay. When the experiment was terminated, many of the guards actually became distressed at having to leave their roles behind. Not being tough and arrogant was a sign of weakness among the guards. While not all of the guards became abusive, the ones that did not still chose not to interfere or stop the cruelty. They continued to follow the orders of the more aggressive guards. One guard did report being upset over the suffering of the prisoners and expressed a wish to switch positions and become a prisoner instead, but he never did.[14] Thus, leadership and social pressure can determine social behavior.

_ _ _ _ _ _ _ _ _ _ _ -

Discussion Topics

a. Can you explain the behavior of the students in the case?

b. How can such a behavior be corrected?

c. Whom would you trust more: those who are under surveillance or those who are not?

d. Would you trust those who empathize with others more than those who do not? If empathy induces trust, how would you induce empathy?

e. The former president of American Airlines negotiated with the unions a reduction of 15% in salaries while increasing managements' pensions and making sure that even in the case of bankruptcy management's pensions would be paid. When this information became known the union rejected the agreement and the president had to retire. Is the resignation of the president of American Airlines justified? Assuming that he was a gifted and effective president, should he have been pressed to resign?

d. What arguments could you make against the resignation?

_ _ _ _ _ _ _ _ _ _ -

3. Law and culture[15]

Obedience to the law must be essentially voluntary. That depends on [culture]. Charles Camic describes Max Weber's views: "At the base of modern political-legal orders, ... 'the broad mass of the participants act in a way corresponding to legal norms,

---

14. *Id.* at 198; Philip G. Zimbardo, *A Situationist Perspective on the Psychology of Evil: Understanding How Good People Are Transformed into Perpetrators* 14 (2003), http://www.zimbardo.com/zimbardo.html (last visited Aug. 17, 2007); *see also* Craig Haney, Curtis Banks, & Philip Zimbardo, *A Study of Prisoners and Guards in a Simulated Prison* (1973), http://www.zimbardo.com/zimbardo.html (last visited Aug. 17, 2007).
15. TAMAR FRANKEL, TRUST AND HONESTY: AMERICA'S BUSINESS CULTURE AT A CROSSROAD 190 (2006).

not out of obedience regarded as a legal obligation but [in a great many cases] merely as a result of unreflective habit.'" If this cultural habit did not exist, and if a significant number of people did not obey the law, law enforcement in a democratic society would be impossible. The history of Prohibition in the 1930s teaches us this lesson.

Law is built on broad voluntary compliance. No matter how many laws are on the books, no matter how many police are on the beat, if the majority or leadership of the population does not obey the law, law is likely to remain a dead letter. Even in this litigious society, state and federal courts entertained only 15 million criminal cases in 2003. Assuming multiple convictions, that's less than 5% of the population involved in criminal litigation in a year. According to the Justice Department, only 2.7% of adults in 2001 had ever served time in prison. And these numbers strain the justice system. If the numbers were higher, law enforcement would be practically impossible. So, why do most people obey the law, knowing that their chances of being caught and punished are fairly slim? The rules within large corporations are enforced differently than the . . . law. But these rules, too, must be based on voluntary [compliance].

Voluntarily obedience to law [reflects] ethical and moral behavior.[16] [It cannot be coerced.] "We can't legislate ethics," said Commissioner Cynthia Glassman of the [Securities and Exchange Commission], in an interview with a *Christian Science Monitor* reporter in June 28, 2004. "But we can motivate people to do the right thing." However, she added: If fear of investigation (rather than ethical constraints) motivates the board of directors to enforce the law within their organizations, "that's OK with me." Yet, . . . fear of this sort may not be enough in the long run. . . . [T]here is little satisfaction in a fear-based behavior. [But if fear starts the process to produce satisfaction, then the fear of prosecution is OK, as the Commissioner stated.]

Edward Johnson, the head of Fidelity, the largest mutual fund complex in the United States, put it unconditionally: Nothing will be effective . . . but the "moral fiber" of the leaders. In [the same *Christian Science Monitor*] article I summarized this book's message: "Unless people are self-limiting, unless there is a culture of honesty, a law change won't work." And Charles Elson, a corporate governance expert at the University of Delaware, noted: "We have to look at our own culture." These statements raise awareness—the first step in a change of culture. But morality alone cannot change culture. It has no coercive power to begin the change. It can only strongly support it. The law can aim at the same objective as morality, and achieve it by *coercion*. Yet law alone cannot coerce a whole population. Law alone cannot change the habits of a society . . . . In a conflict between culture on one hand, and law on the other hand, culture [will] win.

. . . Millions of Americans work in corporations and large institutions. They are governed by internal corporate rules. These rules are backed by private sector sanctions and rewards, such as demotions and promotions. Law enforcement within organizations depends on their culture. Like culture in society, corporate culture, being the habit of members of the corporate community, evolves through repeated experience. This experience reflects the corporation's history, its population -- its old-timers and new recruits. But what most determines corporate culture are the attitude and the signals of top management; sometimes only one or two people at the head of the . . . pyramid. They set the tone and direction . . . . In corporations, the signals of top management are . . . watched and followed. When the chief financial officer throws a lavish party that costs $2 million and charges part of the expense to the corporation, the door opens to employees to help themselves to corporate assets[,] [perhaps on a smaller scale]. When top management travels frugally . . . , the word quickly spreads. Which employee would dare order the

---

16.   *Id.* at 191.

corporate jet for private travel? Top management can signal to obey the law or to ignore it. "Once you as CEO go over the line, then people think it's okay to go over the line." Lawrence Weinbach was quoted as saying.[17]

Why Do Most People Obey the Law?

[There is a rich literature on] the ways in which people can be induced to obey the law voluntarily, that is, to internalize the behavior and self-enforce it. But, as Alex Geisinger shows, there is no agreement on the [answer]. One reason for the disagreements could be that people obey the law for many different reasons.

Fear of punishment. [Professor] Gordon Tullock suggested that early detection and stricter laws and appropriate punishments induce people to obey the law. He believed that people obey the law for fear of punishment. . . . [If] punishment is unlikely, they will not obey. The past history of fraud and abuse may support this view. Fraud was not detected in time, and if it was detected it was not energetically prosecuted. The violation of the law was sometimes was eliminated by redefinition, or was made easier by explicit exemptions. Following Tullock's theories, swift detection, strict laws, and heavy punishments produce a culture of obedience to the law. The flavor of this culture is concern and fear.

Reciprocity by the members of the community. Professor Dan Kahan has a different view . . . . He suggests that people follow the law to gain favor and avoid disapproval of others. People assume that legal rules represent the views of the majority in the country. [And they] may feel a need to reciprocate and contribute to the general welfare, if others do the same. For example, if people believe that others pay their taxes, they too will pay their taxes. But if people believe that others do not pay their taxes, they will refrain from paying their taxes as well.

Following other people. An analysis of signaling leads to a similar conclusion. Most people follow the behavior and judgment of others, as well as [their] expressions and beliefs . . . .[P]eople wish to belong to a group, and are influenced by the attitudes and activities of their peers. They follow the leaders, doing good or evil, exercising mercy or cruelty. [Perception about how others behave is therefore a powerful signal that directs behavior.]

If everyone around obeys the law, a violator will be stigmatized and shunned. But if everyone around violates the law, a violator will not stand out and will not be shunned. His behavior conforms to the general behavior. Similarly, if most people in the community did not have a prison history, then the person who served a prison sentence is likely to be stigmatized. But if many community members spent time in prison, the sharpness of the stigma will be dulled. In that case the "square" or "preacher" will be stigmatized. In groups of white-collar criminals, the rights and wrongs differ from those of the law; but the same rules of stigmatizing apply. George C. Homans described high-crime areas where the criminals were "far from being neurotic and outcasts. They were healthy, hearty, happy, and much admired. . . . In these areas only a person who was not a criminal showed any sign of personality disorder." . . .[18]

Corporate leadership affects not only the culture of the corporations but also the general culture in the United States. On behalf of their corporations, management has contacts with the political leadership and the lawmakers. Through lobbyists, these leaders have access to the other powerful leaders here and abroad. Their attitudes toward the law affect the substance of the law as well as obedience to the law. Needless to say, corporate leaders also affect the marketplace, which can be a barrier to fraud. In many respects corporate America is not merely the leader but the keeper of American culture.

---

17. *Id.* at 192.
18. *Id.* at 192.

Members of American leadership have a culture of their own. They interact among themselves. They sit on each other's boards, share information networks, and gather in social affairs. They know each other or about each other personally, because their number is relatively small. Therefore, this group tends to be homogeneous, governed by a dominant culture.

Corporate employees spread their leadership's culture as well. They spend most of their waking hours within an organization, absorb its culture, and take home not only their pay and experience but also their assumptions about how people behave and should behave -- that is, the society's culture.

The leadership's attitude towards law is important to the culture of obedience to law. If the authorities, corporate leaders, and lawmakers denigrate the law and preach the market gospel, people will take these signals to heart and resist the law or tend to ignore [it] . . . . People need not be told what leadership's attitude is. They may even be told the contrary: to obey the law. But if the words come with conditions and strong criticism of the law, they will get the "correct and true" message, and follow it.

The same can be said of corporate leadership. [Dealing with corporate and organizational culture, Edgar H. Schein wrote:] "Culture and leadership are two sides of the same coin, in that leaders first create cultures when they create groups and organizations. Once cultures exist, they determine the criteria for leadership and thus determine who will or will not be a leader. But if cultures become dysfunctional, it is the unique function of leadership to perceive the functional and dysfunctional elements of the existing culture and to manage cultural evolution and change in such a way that the group can survive in a changing environment." And if leaders "do not become conscious of the cultures in which they are embedded, those cultures will manage them. Cultural understanding . . . is essential to leaders if they are to lead."[19]

If too many leaders belittle the law and criticize the very institution of the law, others will do the same. By so doing, they will cause enormous harm to the legal system, leading a movement that undermines the respect and obedience to law. Leaders may offer and request changes in the rules, but should do so with great caution and deference. They can provide justifications for relaxing the rules but take fraud prevention into account. If the influential members among American leaders talk disparagingly about the law and deny the legitimacy of its rules, those who listen to these leaders will follow in words and perhaps in deeds. They may accept the views of their own leaders rather than the views of the law enforcers. . . .

. . . [M]ost American business leaders are [true and honest, even as they criticize government regulation.] . . . [And yet, the recent scandals [starting with Enron corporation and continuing through the stock options manipulations] could have tarnished their reputation. But if they have a following, their actions will not tarnish their reputation. On the contrary, their actions will cause indignation, criticism, and resistance to the law. This is the power of a culture.]

. . . One reason people do *not* obey the law, says Professor Tom R. Tyler, is that they suspect the motivations of the authorities. A general perception that the enforcing authorities are the captives of corporate criminals prompts people to ignore and disobey the law. Therefore, the government's attitude toward law affects the culture of obedience to law. People tend to obey the rules if the government makes it clear that no complaint will be left untended, and no discovery of a wrong will be compromised, and that those who disclose fraud would be protected from powerful criminals.

---

19.   *Id.* at 193-94.

In sum, obedience to law must be largely voluntary. It is built on the perception that everyone else is complying with the law. This perception is affected by the behavior of leadership in the political and private sectors, the attitudes of peer groups, and the approach of the population at large. The pressures to conform to the culture of these groups bring about the voluntary obedience to the law.

It follows that people will **disobey** *the law for the same reasons that they obey it.* [Few will ignore the danger and disobey.] Obedience will erode as more and more people in the society, including leadership and peer groups, disobey the law, denigrate the law and belittle its enforcers. . . . That means that pockets of peer groups from students to athletes and from top management to healthcare providers . . . draw support for such a behavior. . . .

. . . "A society gets the culture it deserves." . . . But perhaps the American people are moving towards the culture that they do not deserve nor choose. They [follow passively.] They . . . do not get involved."[20]

C. Chapter Review

There are a number of ways to view trust. The following discussion topics consider a few. The first view is through the lens to cost and benefit. The second is through the lens of society's interests. The third takes the psychological approach.

— — — — — — — — — — -

Discussion Topic

Could you make a cost-benefit analysis to determine the costs of interaction between fiduciaries and entrustors? What will be the cost limit for the fiduciary to establish trustworthiness? What will be the limit for the entrustors to agree to trust? Taking cost into account, when will the two parties interact and when will they not?

— — — — — — — — — — -

Focusing on society's interests

a. Can trusting relationships be non-voluntary? To what extent should law interfere in the following transactions: buying a washing machine, buying a house, buying stock through a broker dealer, and entrusting one's savings to a money manager?

b. Why should society care about trust among these actors? What, in your opinion, is the cost of mistrust to society, if any? What will happen if the buyer of a washing machine does not trust the seller, or the saver does not trust the money manager? Does the law play a role in building trust relationships in these situations? Should it? Under what conditions should law interfere, if at all?

Taking the psychological approach

a. Does law increase trust and reduce mistrust?

b. If law interferes to support trust, is that support always positive? Can law undermine trust among people in society? Note the following ideas by Frank B. Cross:[21]

---

20. *Id.* at 194-95 (citing Tom R. Tyler, *Trust and Law Abidingness: A Proactive Model of Social Regulation,* 81 B.U. L. REV. 361, 366 (2001)).
21. Frank B. Cross, *Law and Trust,* 93 GEO. L.J. 1457 (2005), LEXIS. Lawrev Library, Geolj File (LEXIS summary).

Affective trust is akin to an emotion, while cognitive trust is more of a reasoned decision to trust another. . . . [and is therefore more pragmatic and deals with details, such as remedies]. [The writer deals with a number of questions.]

. . . First, what is the effect of the law upon relative levels of affective trust and cognitive trust? Second, which of these components, affective or cognitive, is the more critical to the overall production of the societal trust we desire? Third, should we prefer one of these types of trust, affective or cognitive, as the more desirable form of trust, as a societal matter? . . . . [The writer notices that the] monitoring associated with cognitive trust, which is integral to use of the law, may "poison" the preexisting affective trust. . . . [yet law] might help build affective trust over the long run, in addition to directly enhancing cognitive trust. . . . If this is true, legal structures that enhance cognitive trust will, over time, also enhance affective trust. . . . Affective trust or bonding social capital, without law, thus tends to racist, sexist, and generally xenophobic results.[22]

c. A student once told me that, in Cameroon, Africa, people do not usually bring their savings to a bank. They suspect that the government would borrow the money and not return it, rightly or wrongly. They do not trust the banks. But in most tribes and villages there is an older person, usually a woman, whom everyone knows and who knows everyone. A member of the community, who saved some money, would give the money to that older person and those who need money would get from that older person a loan and pay interest. The older person knows to whom to lend and to whom not to lend. In fact, Cameroon has many banks. What distinguishes these banks from the formal banks?

d. Historically, when gold was the currency, goldsmiths bought gold and also provided storage facilities. The gold depositors received the goldsmiths' receipts. In transactions, when gold had to pass hands, the parties usually transferred the goldsmiths' receipts rather than retrieve the gold from the goldsmiths only for the payee to return the gold for storage. And it was safer to carry the paper rather than the gold itself. The goldsmiths then realized that only a certain percentage of the depositors demanded the gold in specie in any given day. They then issued more receipts than they had gold in storage. That was the beginning of the banking system. What was the main characteristic of these banks? What was the main risk for the goldsmiths? How similar and different is the current banking system from the goldsmiths' system?

e. Can groups be trusted? Are groups separate from the individuals that compose them? Suppose you trust the teller of a bank, do you also trust the bank? Suppose you trust the bank. Do you also trust the teller? What is necessary for you to trust the teller? Would you trust the teller who recommended to you the bank's broker? Would you trust the teller if you knew that the teller was paid to recommend the broker?

f. Can a system be trusted? What does it mean to trust a *system,* for example, the financial system or the political system? Does it mean

22. *Id.*

also trusting brokers and politicians? If not, what remains from trusting the system?

g. Why do people obey the law? Why do people control temptation? Can you add reasons or observations to the written materials above?

h. How would you distinguish between con artists that mimic trustworthiness and true trustworthy people? What are the signs of a prosperous businessperson? How would you, as an investor, decide whether to trust the person with $10,000? Or with $100,000?

i. How would you verify trustworthy people who communicate with you through the Internet?

j. How different is a child's trust in parents from an adult's trust in a friend? Which of these types of trust should the law support more?

k. How do you explain the fact that, in Nazi Germany, the camp police exterminated Jews and others in gas chambers, and doctors experimented sadistically on human beings, yet these same persons were good devoted fathers and loving husbands?

l. There is a story about a mother who gave advice to her son before he went to war to fight the Turks. "Son," she said, "do not exert yourself. Shoot a Turk, then rest a little. Shoot another Turk, then rest some more." "But Mother," said the son: "What if while I am resting, the Turk shoots at me?" "Why, my son," said the mother: "What does the Turk have against you?" Is this story funny? If so, why?

m. The police in a "bad neighborhood" had great trouble receiving information about drug dealers. The residents in the neighborhood did not trust the police. How could the police establish a trust relationship? Tyler suggests that, when the police began to treat the residents with respect, they created a relationship of trust, received information and were in turn treated with respect rather than hostility. How can respect create such a change?

n. "Competition." Today there is a movement towards competitors that align and co-operate in some areas and compete in others. How can people compete and cooperate at the same time? Would courts tend to impose fiduciary duties on the parties that cooperate and compete? Does legal intervention comport with the parties' intent and with an effective co-operation among competitors? Do you think that the winner should get all, or that people who participated in the competition and tried hard but did not win should be rewarded as well? Is this solution fairer than the other—winner takes all? Is competing in sports different than competition in business? Are trust and mistrust synonymous with co-operation and competition? Can we have both? Should we?

o. Are trust and mistrust conflicting or complementary? Can the two complement each other? Are there relationships that require no verification? If not, the question is really how much do you need for trust and how much do you need for verification. That leads to quantification of trust. How should we quantify trust? Is it by the amount of money and costs involved? What about trust that does not concern business relationships? Is quantification in other relationships harder or easier? If the cost and risk are emotional, do these lend themselves to quantification? How?

p. Jennifer Halpern[23] hypothesized that "there are cognitive structures or *scripts* that incorporate roles and the ordering of events. . . . [such as scripts for interacting with friends and strangers, and transaction partners]. The script "includes universal understandings about maintaining the relationship into the future" and its voluntary nature as well as the "'liking' associated with the relationship" and achieving "equality, mutual self-disclosure, and future interaction."[24] Thus, when people bargain with friends, they are expected not to bargain very hard,[25] pay more when they buy from friends and charge less to friends. Among friends, the difference between offer and acceptance is smaller.[26] In sum, the desire to maintain friendship and trust is likely to bring commercial transactions to fruition more often. What is the relationship between friendship and trust?

q. Larry Ribstein wrote:[27] "Trust is a kind of social glue that allows people to interact at low transaction costs. Trusting people cooperate because it is in their nature or because they have been socialized to do it, not because some costly structure has been set up to ensure reliability. This implies that trust increases social wealth by permitting more investment in production. It is logical, therefore, to consider whether legal rules can contribute to trust." He argues that "trust does not provide a distinct justification for mandatory legal rules [to] supersede[] contract. Although regulation might lead parties to decide to rely on others, it does not produce the welfare-increasing 'trust' that makes costly constraints unnecessary. Moreover, this article shows that using mandatory rules to increase trust, in any form, may have precisely the opposite effect."

"This conclusion implies that a contractarian approach to law does not depend on a narrow 'economic' view of man." However, economic view is consistent with trust. "Indeed, expanding the model of human behavior makes mandatory rules even less defensible because contracts allow parties to avoid the trust-reducing effects of legal regulation." Does law support trust? Undermines trust? Is irrelevant to the establishment and maintenance of trust?

---

23.   Jennifer J. Halpern, *The Effect of Friendship on Personal Business Transactions,* 38 J. CONFLICT RESOL. 647, 648-49 (1994).
24.   *Id.* at 649.
25.   *Id.* at 650.
26.   *Id.* at 651.
27.   Larry E. Ribstein, *Law v. Trust,* 81 B.U. L. REV. 553, 553-55 (2001) (footnotes omitted).

Epilogue
Restoring Trust

Introduction. The issue of restoring trust is not directly related to fiduciary law. To be sure, trusting relationships are important to business, to economy and to society. But restoring trust is not necessarily a legal requirement. Yet, an important underlying objective of fiduciary law is to maintain trusting relationships, and loss of trust is often related to breach of fiduciary duties. Lawyers who advise businesses and especially fiduciaries may have to render advice to clients that have lost the trust of employees, clients, patients, investors and customers. The issue becomes an integral part of the lawyer's practice. Therefore we devote this Chapter to the issue of reducing the controlling the damage caused by violations of fiduciary law (among other actions).

Problems caused by violations of fiduciary law have persisted. Some violations date from 2000. Others have been perpetrated, discovered and litigated later. For example, the *Wall Street Journal* reported on August 1, 2006 that the Biovail chairman was accused of hiding family trust holdings (in the year 2003) in violation of Canada's securities laws.[1] Some executives "reaped millions" as they received stock options that were amended as to time or amounts, thus eliminating the risk that was designed to align their interests with those of investors.[2] The Securities and Exchange Commission reacted by enacting rules on executive pay and option grants.[3] Further, executive pay has been subject to criticisms for some time. On July 28, 2006, the *Wall Street Journal* read: "Are Deal Makers On Wall Street Leaking Secrets?" They collected high pay while the shares of their companies plummeted.[4] What if a corporation is required to restate its financial statements or a chief executive officer was found to have plagiarized pages from another book or adorned a resume with

---

1.   Elena Cherney, *Biovail Chairman Accused of Hiding Trust Holdings*, WALL ST. J., Aug. 1, 2006, at C3, LEXIS, News Library, Wsj File (he was living in Barbados, and did not own the controlling shares of the corporation. These shares were held by family trusts, but he was not a trustee of these trusts. Whether this situation constitutes a violation of the laws remains to be determined).
2.   Charles Forelle et al., *Executive Pay: The 9/11 Factor*, WALL ST. J., July 15, 2006, at A1, LEXIS, News Library, Wsj File.
3.   Kara Scannell & Joann S. Lublin, *SEC Issues Rules on Executive Pay, Options Grants*, WALL ST. J., July 27, 2006, at C1, LEXIS, News Library, Wsj File.
4.   Serena Ng et al., *Are Deal Makers on Wall Street Leaking Secrets?*, WALL ST. J., July 28, 2006, at C1, LEXIS, News Library, Wsj File.

unearned academic degrees? Some people might wonder whether other corporate actions are true and honest.

The following discussion focuses on issues and the suggestions that might help fiduciaries restore the trust they have lost. The first set of issues relates to what causes trust to fail in the first place. The second set relates to how trust could be restored. The two issues are connected. Unless one knows what caused or induced the loss of trust, it is hard to identify what problems should be addressed, and how they should be resolved.

A. Why and How Did Trust Fail?

1. Back to the definition of trust

The first step towards answering the question "why did trust fail" relates to the analysis of trust that we studied. Trust fails when *trusting parties believe that the entrusted persons or organizations do not tell the truth and do not fulfill their promises.* Communication is one component of trust. It relates to the belief that the trusted party is telling the truth. Evidence of failure to perform the promises is the second component. Loss of trust is loss of these beliefs.

Starting with the first component, we inquire into good and bad communications, establishing a dialog with other parties within and outside the corporation, connecting with the media, and communicating an apology that would restore trust. If the statements are important to the decisions of trusting persons, such as the financial statements of a corporation in which the trusting persons invest, then untrue statements may reduce trust significantly. Most importantly, untrue statements undermine trust not only with respect to the particular untrue statements, but raise suspicion as to every other statement and action: "What else did the management say that was untrue?"

"Some violators of trust protect themselves from the pain of guilt and shame by denial. White-collar offenders are "highly resistant to negative interpretations of their actions, [and] they rationalize their crimes even after conviction and display a remarkable inability to accept the moral implications of their convictions. . . . In rejecting negative labeling, they also reject or manage the accompanying emotions. Armed with this deep conviction, they avoid the internal conflicts and the feelings of guilt and shame, which usually accompany recognition that one's actions are wrong. Dr. Neal Shover and Glenn S. Coffey noted in their study of telemarketing con artists that they share a "strong culture of denial," according to the *Knoxville (Tennessee) News-Sentinel.* They typically dispute the very criminality of their behavior. They rejected the authorities' definition of wrong. The telemarketers refused to admit that they were criminals even after they were convicted. Most "rejected the words 'criminal' and 'crime' as being applicable to them and their activities." [5]

---

5.   TAMAR FRANKEL, TRUST AND HONESTY: AMERICA'S BUSINESS CULTURE AT A CROSSROAD 112 (2006) (footnote omitted); Don Jacobs, *Telemarketing Con Artists Do Not See Selves as Criminals; 47 Convicted of Fraud Subject of UT Study*, KNOXVILLE NEWS-SENTINEL, Dec. 10, 2001.

Culture might have the biggest impact of all. Leon Panetta wrote that our free market system is the strongest in the world and its fundamental strengths rest on imagination, creativity and leadership of America's business leaders. But just as our democracy depends on people's trust, so does our economy. That trust has been badly damaged in recent years. It cannot be legislated. Even if the nation passes stricter criminal laws and prosecutes more corporate criminals and sends them to jail and improves the regulation of corporations and the markets, the fundamental change depends on whether the current culture of business is willing to adopt a new set of values and business practices. That change cannot happen by changing laws. Change can happen by example of corporate leaders and investors who truly believe in accountability, transparency and integrity which are essential to doing business in a free enterprise system. "Only then will trust be restored to corporate America."[6]

2. How do entrustors react to abuse of trust?

Usually, entrustors react to false information by reducing their expectations and weakening their beliefs. They trust less; they suspect and question more. Depending on how deep their disbelief becomes they may assume that their expectations are faulty, or cease to expect trustworthiness altogether. That causes them to require more verification.

When a change in expectations and belief is widespread, and especially if it persists over time, culture is likely to change. If people find that others don't cooperate, the culture of cooperation may change to less or no cooperation. When a change in belief of statements is widespread, people increase their demand and need for verification.

A culture of mistrust differs from loss of trust by a particular person or institution or in a particular person or institution. When investors lose trust in a particular corporation, mistrust may spread both to other innocent corporations and to the stock market as a whole. Mistrusting investors might either sell their shares in the corporation, or sell their shares in all corporations and move to money market funds or bonds or CDs or land, or foreign currency, or gold or other alternative ways of investing their money.

Investors that are locked into pension funds and tax deferred plans may fret, and more likely try to escape as well. To be sure, Congress can and does sometimes help money managers draw more pension plan money notwithstanding the public's mistrust and desire to escape. These steps, however, may raise questions about the trustworthiness of congressional leaders. How much do they receive in campaign contributions from money managers? And how much do their advisers and supporting academics get paid? Suspicion is raised and mistrust is nurtured. The longer it lasts, the more entrenched it becomes. The more entrenched it becomes, the harder it is to restore trust and the

6.   Leon E. Panetta, *Restoring Trust in Corporate America,* MONTEREY COUNTY HERALD, July 14, 2002, LEXIS, News Library, Arcnws File.

longer it takes to reestablish it. This is the way of habits—by individuals and society.

Dishonesty is usually accompanied by justification. Let us be clear: people do not view themselves as dishonest. They find justifications for behaving in a dishonest way. For example, people who are deceived feel justified in deceiving. Or: "Others do not work as hard as I do." "I deserve this extra benefit." "Others would do the same if they were in my place." "Others are stupid, and deserve to be 'fleeced'" or "I am smarter and this is the world for smart people." These patterns of thought and behavior, however, include also: "Everyone is doing this." "If the leadership of corporate America is doing this, and if others benefit, why not I?"

— — — — — — — — — — -

Discussion Topics

a. Are investors and consumers really mistrustful? After all, they flock to the shops to buy products and to broker-dealers to buy stock. But suppose they do not trust corporations and the financial markets as they used to, what would be the difference? Who should care?

b. I heard a colleague claim that investors distrust regulators because the regulators sue corporations and cause the corporations to spend enormous money on defense and settlements. After all, these amounts are indirectly paid by the shareholders. What is your opinion?

— — — — — — — — — — -

B. What Should Be Done When Trust Is Lost?

a. Show self-limitation and reduction of self-benefits. Show that the truth is more important to you than the benefits you get from skirting around it[7]

Communicate the good and the bad. A first step to renew trust, assuming the speaker is honest, is to create an atmosphere of improved, open communication with all the stakeholders of the company. This advice is linked to the cause of mistrust when belief that the other is telling the truth is destroyed. To gain unqualified approval, the speaker must provide transparent, truthful information, and this information should project the company's values. Therefore, it is unacceptable to disseminate only good news and withhold the bad. It is unacceptable to tell the truth in details and describe the bad in "wishy-washy" generalizations that include every possible bad thing that might happen.

Managing reputation requires identifying potential business, as well as social and environmental problems. It requires addressing these problems before they become issues that are taken up by stakeholders, activists, and the media and before the regulators take action against the speaker.

---

7.   John DeFrancesco, *Restoring Trust in Your Company*, DYNAMIC BUS., Apr. 2004, *available at* http://www.smc.org/Article.cfm?id-296 (summarized).

Speaking the truth means being truthful *as the listeners define it*, and giving listeners the information, in which they are interested, even if it is not favorable to the speaker. This approach has two advantages. First, if the speaker limits the good information, and highlights the bad as well, and if the speaker does that voluntarily and not under a court's order, this self-policing and self-limitation creates trust. In addition, information of this sort can be protective. Such negative information clarifies the limits of the information, leaving less space for worse speculations by the listeners.

Communicate clearly, persistently, and consistently. It is important to tell the corporate story in a clear, precise, factual, and tight style. If a professional writer is hired, the writer must have the dull and correct information, with no embellishments. Otherwise the corporation risks compromising the integrity of the writer as well as its own.

Explain yourself. People usually give the benefit of the doubt when the suspected person or organization explains itself. Positive perceptions, attitudes, and beliefs return only when reality changes. A survey by Opinion Research indicated that half of the surveyed respondents would be less likely to buy the products from a company accused of misconduct. However, the survey also showed that Americans would give companies accused of wrongdoing the benefit of the doubt as long as the companies explain themselves fully to the public. People came down hard on companies that are tight-lipped.[8]

– – – – – – – – – – – –

Discussion Topic

a. "Restoring trust may take longer than it took the fiduciary to lose it."[9] Do you think that this statement is correct? If so, why?

– – – – – – – – – – – –

1. Truthful apology

An effective apology must be meaningful and convincing. The signals should demonstrate sincerity but most importantly risk taking rather than seeking safety. The language should be specific but not "lawyer's language."[10] The apology should be directed those who were harmed, and if possible in a personal meeting. The apologetic person should look the victims in the eye, describe the harm and avoid explanations, justifications, excuses, and blaming others. [11]

After the fact, when the negative information is discovered, it is not effective to explain why the information was not disclosed: "Everyone did it." "The lawyers and accountants said it was aggressive, but still OK." "Where was it written that we could not do this?" "A cost-benefit analysis justified it." Others "made us do it by inducement, pressures,

8.   *Id.*
9.   *Id.*
10.   *Id.*
11.   *Id.*

or threats." The "current woes were the responsibility of the prior management team"[12] may not be a good strategy. These statements do not repair the damage. The listeners hardly ever believe them.[13]

Most importantly, corrective actions should be spelled out. The apologies help "build credibility and reconciliation." But the main effect comes with "willingness to make things right." For example, paying back ill-gotten gains. And finally, "[w]hen all is said and done, don't expect everything to return to normal."[14]

2. Establish a dialog with corporate constituencies and especially the employees[15]

One means of restoring the employees' trust is to prepare for it.[16] Be forward and transparent which some senior managers find difficult to do. It is a mistaken to hide from employees the plan to outsource some of the company's operations. This behavior can undermine the trust of the remaining employees.[17] Trust is built on honest communications; preferably direct and personal.[18] One should tell them both the good and bad news. That creates a feeling of a partnership. Employees are no longer a mere audience.[19] As the relationship moves towards collaboration, communication themes stress new values such as dialogue, listening and asking [questions].[20]

Relationship with the media is also important. It connects the corporation with the public, and influences public opinion. Corporate managers should understand that the media's position is different from that of the corporation. The media posits itself as serving public interest, and its relationship with corporations has soured. To mend fences corporations should work with the media on a new basis by accommodating the media's preferences for the form and timing of the information.[21]

Thus, the Center for Media and Democracy published a list of corporations that hired Crisis PR Firms. These corporations include Halliburton, Adelphia, WorldCom, and Martha Stewart.[22] This form of

---

12. *APCO Helps WorldCom with "Transparency Initative,* [sic]*"* PR WEEK, July 15, 2002, available at http://www.prwatch.org/node/1302.
13. Mark S. Putnam, *Apology Accepted . . . Or Not: Handling the Fallout of an Ethical Crisis* (2003), http://www.globalethicsuniversity.com/articles/apologyaccepted.htm.
14. *Id.*
15. John DeFrancesco, *Restoring Trust in Your Company,* DYNAMIC BUS., Apr. 2004, *available at* http://www.smc.org/Article.cfm?id=296.
16. *Id.*
17. Boyd Neil, *Reaching Employees: It's the Message and the Medium,* AMPERSAND (Hill & Knowlton), Feb. 2005, *available at* http://www.hilland knowlton.com/ampersand/index.php/newsletter_articles/7.html.
18. *Id.*
19. John DeFrancesco, *Restoring Trust in Your Company,* DYNAMIC BUS., Apr. 2004, *available at* http://www.smc.org/Article.cfm?id=296.
20. *Id.*
21. *Id.*
22. Center for Media and Democracy, http://www.prwatch.org./taxonomy/term/104/9?from=90 (last visited Aug. 19, 2007) (citing *Washington Post*).

public communication on the Internet helps the company reach the public and influence public opinion in its favor.

_ _ _ _ _ _ _ _ _ _ -

Discussion Topics

a. Consider and comment on the following:

"Celebrity publicist Lizzie Grubman offered a tearful apology in front of reporters, but New York tabloids speculated that the sobs were orchestrated by her PR counsel, Dan Klores Communications, which specializes in 'crisis communications' for clients embroiled in scandals." Grubman might be charged for backing her car into a crowd in a fit of temper and injuring 16 people. Even in this case, some argue that PR firms can help revamping her image.[23] What do you think?

b. If you know that a corporation has hired consultants to contact the media, would that fact enhance or reduce your trust in the corporation?

_ _ _ _ _ _ _ _ _ -

3. Trust and cooperation on the Internet

What did companies do after they discovered e-mail-related frauds? How did they protect themselves? MasterCard International created a monitoring system to notify its members within four hours after a scam starts. It also utilized new technology to detect scams early. E-mail companies (AOL, etc.) agreed to have the same authentication standards. Large financial institutions developed a common database in order to share reports of attacks and responses. In addition, some banks changed how they used e-mail communication with customers. In general, firms that are competitors have been cooperating. Companies are now trying to work together. The danger and risk brought the competitors together.[24]

4. Establish trust by interpersonal relationship and norms[25]

Experience in a relationship can prove the extent, consistency and nature of the other person's trustworthiness. That is why trust among family members is deeper although it too can be destroyed. Even if the parties do not know each other there are trusted members of the group who can vouch for or warn against other members of the group. Trust within organizations is based on interpersonal relationship as well as the internal rules and practices that govern the relationship among the actors and the division of benefits and burdens among them. We call relationships among the actors "interpersonal relationships" and the rules and practices within the organization "cultural relationships." Thus, interpersonal relationship between two actors within an organization may be respectful and trusting or disrespectful and

---

23. *Id.*
24. Thomas Claburn & Steven Marlin, *Saving E-Mail—Phishing Attacks Are on the Increase, and They're Jeopardizing the Future of Business-to-Consumer Communications,* INFORMATIONWEEK., June 28, 2004, at 18, LEXIS, News Library, Curnws File.
25. FRÉDÉRIQUE SIX, THE TROUBLE WITH TRUST 45 (2005).

mistrusting, and the cultural relationship may be mutual respect, and mild mistrust, or complete obedience. Interpersonal relationships depend to a greater extent on the parties than do cultural relationships, but the two are interactive. Organizations' culture affects people's behavior, and people's behavior affects the organization's culture.[26]

A large organization usually consists of groups with different interpersonal and cultural relationships. Such diversity may depend in part on the functions and objectives of the particular groups, but most groups require some interaction and cooperation. Yet, researchers may require more interactions among themselves than salespersons that can work alone and interact with their customers more. [27]

Because establishing, maintaining and restoring trust in interpersonal and cultural relationships are based on the same principles some researchers do not separate the three. Rather they focus on ways in which trust is established (whether it exists, or existed before or has been destroyed and has to be restored). Under this approach, what is necessary to maintain and restore trust is a clear norm. According to Frédérique Six, a stable guiding normative frame is crucial to building interpersonal work relationships within an organization.[28] Six lists the following cultural arrangements that raise trust: norms and values, socialization, control, interdependencies, and human resource practices. For each she formulates a hypothesis worth repeating.[29]

The chances of establishing trust within the organization, Six maintains, can be increased with "explicit definition" of the norms and values that should operate within the organization and the "constant interpretation" of these norms and values.[30] In fact, Six suggests a system that is similar to lawmaking. Establish the law, define the directives and continue to interpret them. Thus, without clear norms, there is little chance of inculcating trust within an organization.[31]

Norms help establish trust within an organization. Frédérique Six focuses first on interpersonal relationships. It is easier to build trust, she writes, "[t]he more strongly the organization's values and norms stress 'other regard' [that is, considering others]."[32] In this respect she pays attention to the actors and their benefits: "[t]he more strongly the organization stimulates and supports the individual to develop his/her interpersonal skills,"[33] and "[t]he more the organization provides its

---

26. *Id.*
27. *Id.*
28. *Id.* at 28-29 ("The key argument put forward in this chapter is that for interpersonal trust to be built in work relations within organizations, both individuals in the relationship need to have their actions guided by a stable normative frame.").
29. *Id.* at 43-52.
30. *Id.* at 44.
31. *Id.*
32. *Id.* at 45: Hypothesis 4.1.
33. *Id.*: Hypothesis 4.2.

people with opportunities for continuous professional development, the more likely it is that trust can be built (between leader and subordinate)."[34] Similarly, with respect to newcomers, "[t]he more explicit and intensive the socialization process for newcomers, the easier it is to build interpersonal trust (between newcomers and tenured colleagues)."[35] She emphasizes the power of personal relationship. "The more people are able to meet informally, the easier it is to build interpersonal trust."[36] "Within relationships that have both personal and professional bases, trust can be built more easily and trouble can be resolved more easily."[37]

Interdependence is an aspect of trust building. "The higher the levels of functional interdependence, the easier it is to build interpersonal trust."[38] Interdependence can also be in terms of reputation, "[i]f third parties become active players, relating stories about the trustee to the trustor and vice versa, these indirect connections can affect both trust intensity and trust detection."[39] Similarly, "[t]he more homogeneous the important norms are throughout the organization, the easier it is to build impersonal trust."[40]

We can proceed by examining the norms governing the organization, and deal with the kind of controls that an organization should have. "The stronger the normative controls within the organization, the easier it is to build interpersonal trust."[41] A more effective control, she writes, is normative control that drives individuals "by internal commitment, strong identification with company goals and intrinsic satisfaction from work, then acting appropriately becomes the goal and a normative frame becomes salient."

In contrast, when control is used to enforce "obedience to the company rules, aimed at punishing disobedience, and is driven by the distrust that the controlling party has for the controlled party, then the controlling action will most likely be perceived as a negative relational signal and will probably lead to distrust (or at least low trust)."[42] Similarly, "[t]he stronger the bureaucratic controls within the organization, the more difficult it is to build interpersonal trust (and possibly also the higher the distrust)."[43]

---

34. *Id.* at 52: Hypothesis 4.11.
35. *Id.* at 45: Hypothesis 4.3.
36. *Id.* at 50: Hypothesis 4.8.
37. *Id.* at 51: Hypothesis 4.9.
38. *Id.* at 48: Hypothesis 4.5 (*But see id.* at 79, this hypothetical could not be empirically supported).
39. *Id.* at 49: Hypothesis 4.6.
40. *Id.* at 50: Hypothesis 4.7 (*But see id.* at 79, this hypothetical could not be properly tested).
41. *Id.* at 47: Hypothesis 4.4a.
42. *Id.* at 47.
43. *Id.*: Hypothesis 4.4b.

In addition, fair treatment in cultural relationship should be emphasized. "The more people consider performance-contingent rewards (such as bonuses and promotions) to be clearly and fairly formulated and executed, the easier it is to build interpersonal trust (between leader and subordinate)."[44]

In sum, the basis of the culture is clear and fair norms. Trust depends upon following organizational norms; fair treatment should be emphasized; and personal development and internal controls should be emphasized rather than punishment and external or bureaucratic controls.

C. Words Are Cheap. What Will You DO?

1. Voluntarily limit management's benefits and powers

One way to restore investors' trust relates to the executives' compensation including stock options.[45] A New York Stock Exchange proposal would require that all stock option plans be subject to shareholder votes. Further, stock options should be treated as expenses on corporate income statements. Moreover, corporate insiders would have to repay their gains from stock sales within less than a year before the corporation's bankruptcy. In addition, a majority of the board members of a public company should be independent directors. This form of trust creation is also based on reciprocity. It indicates that managers trust the investors and invites investors to trust management.

— — — — — — — — — — —

Discussion Topic

a. Please comment: There are arguments that reducing executive compensation will reduce the quality of the executives. That may not be true for all executives. There are few executives that declared a reduction of their own compensation.

— — — — — — — — — — —

2. Revamp corporate governance

To regain investors' trust corporations have revamped their governance structure. They found, however, that governance restructures without more do not assure or signify trustworthiness. Firms that were cited by the Securities and Exchange Commission as "fraudulently manipulating their financial statements" have adopted governance characteristics similar to other firms in terms of the numbers and percentages of outside directors, and exceeded other firms in "the number of audit committee meetings."[46]

---

44. *Id.* at 52: Hypothesis 4.10.
45. John A. Byrne, *Restoring Trust in Corporate America,* BUS. WK., June 24, 2002, at 30, LEXIS, News Library, Arcnws File.
46. David B. Farber, *Restoring Trust After Fraud: Does Corporate Governance Matter?* (current draft Oct. 4, 2004), http://papers.ssrn.com/sol3/papers.cfm?abstract_id=485403 (last visited Aug. 3, 2006).

The techniques of restoring trust by corporate restructure include: "Renewal" (refreshing the "self" and relationships); "Restart/repeat" (with different participants/ relationships); "Repair" ("mend fences"); "Relax/reduce" (increase tolerance regarding minor issues); "Retaliate" (against the offender); seek "Redemption" (by "[r]ely[ing] on a higher authority"), and "Reverse" (by "[d]eny[ing] trust . . . to affirm trust").[47]

The effect of these strategies depends on how they are used. If the strategies are applied by focusing on symptoms rather than the heart of the problem, the strategies can further destroy attempts to establish trust. Refreshing oneself depends on what needs refreshing. The same issue applies to restarting other relationships or repairing broken fences. If the main problem is not uncovered and clarified, these mechanisms could be ineffective. The results of relaxing controls or retaliating depend on why controls were tight in the first place, and why retaliation would be effective to ensure trustworthiness.[48]

Restructuring and revamping corporate governance is a form of restoring trust. After the WorldCom/MCI scandal, Richard Breeden prepared a report entitled "Restoring Trust" and recommended corporate governance reforms. Criticisms of these recommendations ranged from unduly restricting shareholder actions to too much shareholder influence, for example, over board nominations. The proposed restrictions on board composition (requiring all directors except the CEO to be independent; requiring qualification standards for members; requiring one director to be added (and one removed) each year) would reduce company's flexibility and ignore necessary qualities of board members.[49]

3. Build trust by reciprocity and signal to the other party a voluntary trust

Trust by reciprocity can be costly and risky. But it is an asset, "and companies very often underinvest in it,"[50] just as trust based on reputation is an asset. Parties will "rationally protect" reputation and it is based on information from many channels. It is unlikely that other parties will have an incentive to contribute to the reputation of a trusted party. However, technology facilitates multiple information channels and aggregates and publishes the results at low cost, for example, blogs, eBay, Amazon.com, and Google. The channels of communications can create different levels of trust. It is likely that consumers are influenced more by edmunds.com for car-buying

---

47. *Restoring Trust: Recovering and Rediscovering Trust: Overcoming a Legacy of Mistrust and Betrayal*, http://www.users.globalnet.co.uk/~rxv/trust/restore.htm (last visited Aug. 3, 2006).

48. *Id.*

49. Martin Lipton et al., *"Restoring Trust" or Losing Perspective?*, Memorandum of Wachtell, Lipton, Rosen & Katz (Aug. 27, 2003), http://www.realcorporate lawyer.com/pdfs/wlrk082803.pdf (the proposal, it was claimed, would risk election of "special interest directors" whose interests may not be the interests of the corporation or shareholders).

50. Philip Evans, *From Reciprocity to Reputation*, PERSPECTIVES (Boston Consulting Group), Apr. 2006, at 6-7, http://www.bcg.com/publications/files/425_Reciprocity_to_Reputation_Apr06.pdf (last visited Aug. 3, 2006).

information than by car manufacturer advertising. They are more likely to trust consumer posts (e.g., opinions) than telemarketing.[51]

4. Measure the "soft components" of trust within the corporation[52]

Experts have recommended measuring trust, and corporations such as General Electric and some analysts have been doing that.[53] The measurements include "customer satisfaction, innovation, human resources, . . . CEO's persona, the stability and talent level of senior executives, relations with the full range of stakeholders, consistency of policy, quality of strategic planning, persuasiveness of corporate vision, commitment of the board to shareholder interests, peer reputation, conduct and comportment of the CEO and top management."[54] These matters should be routinely considered because much of the corporate market value depends on them.[55] Trust is "earned, not managed." And the CEO may be the person to demonstrate the commitment to it.[56]

5. If trust was lost by a mistaken action then rectification of a mistake can be a powerful trust building block.[57]

It has been shown that "[c]onsumers are more willing to return to a company that has made a mistake but then rectified it, than to one that has not made a mistake in the first place."[58] Thus, when it was discovered that the United States Government used African-American men for a syphilis study without their knowledge and consent, President Clinton first apologized to the survivors and their family members, the city and county where it happened, the doctors "wrongly associated" with the study, and African-American citizens.[59] With the apology President Clinton promised concrete steps to make sure that this would never happen again.[60] He then set out specific steps to accomplish these goals (a memorial in the city, an increase in

---

51. *Id.* at 4-8.
52. Robert G. Eccles, *The Performance Measurement Manifesto*, HARV. BUS. REV., Jan.-Feb. 1991, at 131, 132 (contending that current metrics of a company's performance were assessing the consequences of yesterday's decisions rather than forecasting tomorrow's performance).
53. Council of Public Relations Firms, *A Time for Courage. A Time to Act. Let the Real Corporate Leaders Step Up,* http://www.prfirms.org/resources/research/courage.asp (last visited Sept. 22, 2007).
54. *Id.* ("A decade ago, *Fortune* did just that but the significance went unnoticed. The magazine's famed "most admired" rankings focused on intangibles—5 of 8 criteria—but the financials still received most of the attention.")
55. *Id.* ("Economic think tank Brookings says 70% of the value of a company roots in these soft values.").
56. *Id.*
57. *Restoring Trust: Recovering and Rediscovering Trust: Overcoming a Legacy of Mistrust and Betrayal,* http://www.users.globalnet.co.uk/~rxv/trust/restore.htm (last visited Aug. 3, 2006).
58. *Id.*
59. THE WHITE HOUSE, OFFICE OF THE PRESS SECRETARY, PRESIDENT CLINTON'S APOLOGY FOR THE TUSKEGEE SYPHILLIS STUDY (May 16, 1997), http://www.research.usf.edu/cs/library/docs/clintonapologyfortuskegee.pdf.
60. *Id.*

"community involvement" (especially minority community involvement) in research and health care, stronger researcher training in bioethics, a program to train bioethicists (especially African-Americans and other minorities), and the extension of the charter of the National Bioethics Advisory Commission.[61]

_ _ _ _ _ _ _ _ _ _ _ _

Discussion Topics

a. Which suggestions in sections B and C are more effective? On what would effectiveness of the suggestions depend?

b. What about the cost of these suggestions? How would you evaluate the benefits and the costs? After all, the objective of businesses is to make a profit.

_ _ _ _ _ _ _ _ _ _ _

D. What Are Desirable and Useful Attitudes?

1. Empathetic behavior helps restore trust

"Act in a way you would [expect] others to act toward you." This guide suggests that empathy towards others helps establish trust because others feel it and because they then relax their own self-protections. In sum, they rely. Author Six takes the same direction in another form when she suggests treating others for their own benefit.[62]

2. Useful tests

The utilitarian (benevolent) principle requires leaders to "Act in a way that results in the greatest good for the greatest number [of people]."[63] The action shows that the leaders exercised self-limitation and followed the obligation which they undertook to perform. Reliance is justified, especially if the leaders could breach their obligation but did not do so.[64]

Kant's categorical imperative directs leaders to follow "universal rules and be principled" rather than adopt exceptions, which may seem or be arbitrary.[65] Ethical behavior is a behavior which would be approved by "disinterested peers." This is another form of self-limitation, which invokes trust.[66]

The author suggests a four-way test: a decision is ethical if managers ask and answer yes to the following questions: "Is the decision truthful? Is it fair to all concerned? Will it build goodwill and better friendships? Will it be beneficial to all concerned?"[67]

61. *Id.*
62. *Id.*
63. *Social Responsibility and Organizational Ethics*, ENCYCLOPEDIA OF BUSINESS AND FINANCE (2001), *available at* http://www.enotes.com/business-finance-encyclopedia/social-responsibility-organizational-ethics (last visited Aug. 20, 2007).
64. *Id.*
65. *Id.*
66. *Id.*
67. *Id.*

The TV Test is asking: "Would I feel comfortable explaining to a national TV audience why I took this action?" Disclosure is one of the most powerful trust maintaining and restoring behaviors. It shows that leaders are not ashamed of their actions; that they are willing to withstand the judgment of the public on their taking the action. More so, they are willing to trust the public to judge their actions and themselves fairly. There is a reciprocal trust relationship that develops with truthful disclosure.[68] The legal test inquires whether the proposed action is legal.

3. Attitude toward people

Empathize. Empathy drives people to identify with others and that prevents them from harming others. If they do, they feel themselves feel the hurt. Hence empathizing people do not pose danger to others and that creates trust. [69]

There are a number of ways in which people steel themselves and reduce their feelings of empathy for their victims. "One way is by 'intellectualizing' and viewing humans as numbers. . . . Shareholders and bondholders can be aggregated into the right-hand side of the balance sheet. A common denominator, the dollar that represents them, makes them fungible. With this perspective, it is difficult to empathize with each of them or even . . . with them as a group. Generally, numbers don't raise feelings of identity. . . . Words like 'downsizing an enterprise' blur the reality of anxious and suffering people who lose their livelihoods. Thus, [an environment] can lower empathy even in people that naturally possess it."[70] This lowered environment can undermine trust.

4. Attitude toward the law

There is a need to change the "attitude" of CEOs, rather than their "aptitude." It is more important to conform to the spirit of the law than it is to the letter of the law.[71] The laws offer loopholes.

Proposals to reform the legal profession may guide reforms for corporate management and accounting.[72] But fierce competition already exists for the top positions even though the number of CEOs is small and is usually drawn from either a small group of outsiders or from insiders.[73]

The American Bar Association ethics commission proposed to add to its ethics rules "knowledge that the client was about to commit fraud" to the grounds permitting lawyers to reveal client confidences,

---

68.   *Id.*
69.   TAMAR FRANKEL, TRUST AND HONESTY: AMERICA'S BUSINESS CULTURE AT A CROSSROAD 111 (2006).
70.   *Id.*
71.   *Id.* at 148.
72.   Robert W. Gordon, *Portrait of a Profession in Paralysis*, 54 STAN. L. REV. 1427, 1438-40 (2002) (reviewing DEBORAH L. RHODE, IN THE INTERESTS OF JUSTICE: REFORMING THE LEGAL PROFESSION (2000)).
73.   Anup Agrawal et al., *Are Outsiders Handicapped in CEO Successions?*, 12 J. CORP. FIN. 619 (2006), *available at* http://bama.ua.edu/~aagrawal/succession.pdf.

but the proposed amendment was voted down at the annual meeting. The bar has called for "civility codes for litigators," "more pro bono service," and adoption of values other than profit-seeking. However, it is reluctant to suggest possibly more effective reforms, such as "relaxing unauthorized-practice prohibitions and licensing paralegal providers," "stringent regulation of overbilling," and "moderating its role-morality and ethical rules to take third-party, social interests, or even the effective functioning of the adversary system itself, into account."[74]

— — — — — — — — — — -

Discussion Topics

a. The problem of these guides is that truth, fairness, goodwill and friendships are not always clear. They often may be in the mind of the speaker or in the understanding of the group with which the speaker interacts almost exclusively. How do you resolve the issue?

b. Of the guidelines discussed above, which is the most effective and why?

— — — — — — — — — — -

E. Who Can Restore Trust?

The American public wants to trust, but not blindly. It demands evidence of trustworthiness.[75] The chief operating officer of a corporation is an important trust builder.

> "'CEOs are the ambassadors of the brand, the ones who set the tone and direction for trust in the brand by customers, investors, employees, marketplace partners and the communities in which the company does business. . . [T]he research makes one thing crystal clear: Americans expect CEOs to take the lead, make a meaningful commitment to trust-building, be accountable—and deliver on the promise of trust through corporate behavior.'"[76]

External auditors have power to restore trust. Tim J. Leech wrote that the Sarbanes-Oxley Act and related regulations gave external auditors, not internal auditors, "the primary role in restoring [public trust in corporate disclosures]." However, this is an opportunity for the internal auditing profession to increase its role and to "take the lead in restoring public faith."[77]

Internal auditors can provide additional feedback to the Public Company Accounting Oversight Board and SEC and suggest efficient ways to audit control of financial reporting, press the authorities "for

---

74.   Robert W. Gordon, *Portrait of a Profession in Paralysis*, 54 STAN. L. REV. 1427, 1438-40 (2002) (reviewing DEBORAH L. RHODE, IN THE INTERESTS OF JUSTICE: REFORMING THE LEGAL PROFESSION (2000)).
75.   *Trajectory of Trust in American Business Shows Signs of Improvement if Brands Act Decisively,* PR NEWSWIRE, Apr. 15, 2003, LEXIS, News Library, Arcnws File. ("Americans Are Willing to Trust Business Again if Companies Prove They Can Be a 'Trust-Builder' Not a 'Trust Buster'; "American companies that become positive, proactive trust-builders will be greeted enthusiastically by consumers . . . "; "Consumers . . . believe business can be trusted again - but only if business demonstrates trust in deeds, not words.").
76.   *Id.*
77.   Tim J. Leech, *Restoring Trust,* INTERNAL AUDITOR, Feb. 2006, at 38, 38, 40.

more specific guidance for management," and assist management in evaluating internal and external controls.[78]

Internal controls are crucial to the institutions. The controlling person may not be the one who has the discretion, however. A portfolio manager, should not enforce the limits on his own discretion, or evaluating and valuing the portfolio which is manages. His interest to show that the value of the portfolio rose may conflict with a true evaluation of the portfolio. Similarly, the broker that sold the illiquid securities to the manager should not value these securities (if there is no market price for them) because the broker's interest is to show the sale of "good stuff" to the manager so that the broker could sell more.

As a corollary, authority should be linked to accountability. Decision-makers must be accountable for their decision. They should not be permitted to shift to others either the authority to make (hard and risky) decisions or the responsibility for the decisions that they made. Achievement and cooperation in bringing about achievement should be rewarded to give incentives to the actors to provide rather than withhold information. If the winner takes all the glory the product may not be of the optimal quality. Finally, all tasks must have an early warning about risks, including the honesty risks.

F. How Can Employees' Trust Be Restored?

1. The current extent of employees' mistrust is a little surprising

Studies during the 1990s studies suggested that "employees have always considered their management's communication somewhat suspect," and "that 63% of employees believe management is often lying." "[E]mployees think management lies and is trying to cheat them." "[A]n employee's supervisor or manager [were considered] the most credible source of information on company issues. Employee meetings and co-workers rank third. The traditional tools used by communicators—print materials, web based information, and external media—come in a distant fourth, fifth and sixth." "[Employees doubt] the credibility of the words, and the believability of traditional channels . . . , especially in unionized work environments . . . ."[79] Assuming that building management credibility is a goal of an internal communications program corporate communicators must take a harder look at the substance and medium of their messages.

a. Suggested approaches to restoring employees' trust in management. What the employees should do?

The burden is on senior management to prove its trustworthiness. This can be done by increased transparency, sharing with employees the business strategy and true condition of the company. As one

---

78.   *Id.* at 40.
79.   Boyd Neil, *Reaching Employees: It's the Message and the Medium*, AMPERSAND (Hill & Knowlton), Feb. 2005, *available at* http://www.hilland knowlton.com/ampersand/index.php/newsletter_articles/7.html.

Canadian union leader put it, "Forget all the mission and vision bullshit; we want to know the facts. And we don't want to hear any more loyalty speeches either."[80]

What management should do. If possible, management should reduce outsourcing by educating employees.[81] The corporation might resort to other parties, including schools and universities,[82] alliance with other organizations and development of its own education and training.[83] The corporation can move toward "knowledge based work systems that allow front line workers to develop and utilize their skills at work."[84] Employees' personal and family needs should be taken into account. The corporation's culture should accept employees with reduced hours or part-time schedules and reject the view that they are less committed than others. Corporations should change the general position against family leave[85] and "help build the types of constructive and modern labor-management relationships and partnerships" that are sometimes necessary.[86]

Employees should receive information from employers through the Internet and new mediums.[87] The current trend of more women entering the human resources profession may be desirable, as women may be more supportive of employees' personal and family needs. [88]

2. The roles of punishment and attitude of management

Punishment stimulates aversion to wrongful behavior by inflicting unpleasant consequences.[89] However, people react differently to punishments. Therefore, "while rules should be consistent, they must reach the greatest number of employees."

Dan Hartshorn suggests a punishment program should be "clear, fair and enforceable" to be reviewed "with both employees and an attorney." The rules must be reasonable, state the dishonest behavior that will be punished (the severity of the punishment and the desired alternative behavior). Policies should not be too strict, or inflexible, or policies that cannot be reasonably monitored and enforced.

Wrongful action should be punished quickly, applied consistently, and be high enough to "hurt" to change in behavior, but not so high as to damage the employees' behavior in other areas. Shame, humiliation and embarrassment should be avoided. A dead letter rule is worse than no rule. Detection must include an effective monitoring. Remove

80.   *Id.*
81.   Thomas A. Kochan, *Restoring Trust in the Human Resource Management Profession,* MIT Workplace Center Working Paper No. WPC0013, at 5-7 (Sept. 2004), http://web.mit.edu/workplacecenter/docs/wpc0013.pdf (last visited Aug. 3, 2006).
82.   *Id.* at 6.
83.   *Id.* at 7.
84.   *Id.* at 8.
85.   *Id.* at 9-11.
86.   *Id.* at 12.
87.   *Id.* at 14.
88.   *Id.* at 15.
89.   Dan Hartshorn, *Punishing Unsafe Behavior,* OCCUPATIONAL HAZARDS, Oct. 1998, at 112, LEXIS, News Library, Arcnws File (quoting PSYCHOLOGY AND LIFE).

motivation to behave dishonestly. For example, every penny of the fruits of dishonesty must be fined (perhaps with an additional amount). Reinforce correct behavior.

Punishments can be designed by their degree of severity and progression: verbal warning, written warning, suspension, and termination. But this progression is not assured. Some companies, such as General Electric, note that certain transgressions lead automatically and directly to termination: "One strike and you are out." But otherwise, these graded punishments must be used with some discretion. Finally, punishment must be taken only with a review.[90]

— — — — — — — — — —

Discussion Topics

a. Which guidelines listed above are the most effective?

b. Would you change these guidelines depending on the business or size of the organization?

— — — — — — — — — —

H. What Can Each of Us Do? Conformity and Debate

Working in a group, each of us can confront conflicts. Should we follow, meld, and conform to the opinions and actions of the group to which we belong? Or should we speak out and express our opinions, even if the group and especially the leader-boss may have a different opinion? In fact, when the issue is whether to "stretch the envelope" or take an unwarranted risk of illegal action or lose a "fortune," and when the group tends to take the risk, the internal conflict of a person with different views can be very difficult. It has been shown that to disagree with the group opinion is psychologically (as well as sometimes politically) very painful for many people. Debate, arguments, and disapproval are difficult to tolerate. Yet, we are also often committed to ideas and ideals that we want to express as well as to lead the group rather than to be led by it. When and how should we act?

— — — — — — — — — —

Discussion Topics

a. What has the issue of debate and consensus, as interesting as it might be, to do with a class devoted to fiduciary law?

b. How would you deal with a situation in which you have doubts about the legality of certain activity, or the wisdom of a certain organizational legal structure, or the words of a press release or the treatment of an employee, and yet see no objection from the "group"?

c. How can you open the door to discussion about topics that may prove controversial, such as not taking and gaining from a situation that is not clearly illegal, without alienating and creating factions in the group?

---

90. *Id.*

d. How do you change a culture (whether towards women and minorities or towards violating the law just a little bit, or searching to compete in the gray areas of the law)? What are the reasons for demanding and expecting conformity and for resenting debate? Why does debate succeed in class and not in the workplace? What do you think would be more effective: talking about ethics or about trust? How do you create trust that would enable you to speak your mind? What is the trust component? How is it related to culture?

e. Do you agree with the following? The managing partner of Price Waterhouse Coopers in Denver noted that the Enron scandal shook the confidence in the accounting profession. He stated that, although "[y]ou can't prevent fraud," the accounting profession must take responsibility for it and "convince people that [accounting] is a good profession." He added: "I believe firmly that rebuilding the industry starts with the universities, getting people trained properly and having the right cultural attitude."[91]

---

91. Lynn Bronikowski, *Frank J. Puzio: Restoring Trust in Public Accounting,* ColoradoBiz, Mar. 2003, at 47 (available through ProQuest).

Table of Laws, Rules, Restatements and Secondary Sources

(References are to pages)

Secondary Sources

Foreign Laws

Table of Cases

(References are to page numbers)

G

H

I

J

K

L

M

N

O

P

R

S

Bibliography Table

(References are to page numbers)

___, Black's Law Dictionary (4th ed. 1968).. 9

___, The Code of Hammurabi 4 (Robert F. Harper trans., 1904) 10

___, The Code of Hammurabi (L.W. King trans., Richard Hooker ed., 1996)......... 8

___, Merriam-Webster's Collegiate Dictionary (10th ed. 1999)......................... 193

___, Social Responsibility and Organizational Ethics, Encyclopedia of
    Business and Finance (2001) 329

B

Bahar, Rashid, & Thévenoz, Luc, Conflicts of Interest: Disclosure,
    Incentives, and the Market, in Conflicts of Interest: Corporate
    Governance & Financial Markets (Luc Thévenoz & Rashid
    Bahar eds., 2007) 85, 282

Baker, J.H., An Introduction to English Legal History (3d ed. 1990)................... 20

Bogert, George G., The Law of Trusts and Trustees (rev. 2d ed. 2006) 128

Bogert, George T., Trusts (6th ed. 1987)... 20

Breasted, James Henry, A History of Egypt: From the Earliest Times
    to the Persian Conquest (2nd ed. 1919).. 10

Brown, Ray Andrews, The Law of Personal Property 15 (2d ed. 1955) 303

C

Caskey, John P., Fringe Banking: Check-Cashing Outlets, Pawnshops,
    and the Poor (1994) 91

Chen, Albert H.Y., An Introduction to the Legal System of the People's
    Republic of China 217 (3d ed. 2004) 290

Cook, Robin, Godplayer (1983)... 48

D

DeMott, Deborah, Fiduciary Obligation, Agency and Partnership:
    Duties in Ongoing Business Relationships 3 (1991)........................... 11

F

1 Farnsworth, E. Allan, Farnsworth on Contracts (3d ed. 2004) 268

2 Frankel, Tamar, & Schwing, Ann Taylor, The Regulation of Money
    Managers: Mutual Funds and Advisers (2d ed. 2001)...................... 85

2 Frankel, Tamar, Securitization (2d ed. 2006) 196

Frankel, Tamar, Trust and Honesty: America's Business Culture
at a Crossroad (2006) 116, 117, 245, 294, 301, 305, 307, 318, 330

Friedman, Lawrence M., A History of American Law (1973) 21, 22

G

Getzler, Joshua, Rumford Market and the Genesis of Fiduciary
Obligations in Mapping the Law: Essays in Honour of Peter
Birks (A. Burrows & A. Roger eds., 2006) 59, 62

Getzler, Joshua, The Road to Rumford Market: History and
Classification of Fiduciary Obligations 101

Gevurtz, Franklin A., Corporation Law (2000) 26

Gregory, William A., The Law of Agency and Partnership (3d ed. 2001) 26

Grisham, John, The Broker (2006) 52

H

The Hammurabi Code and the Sinaitic Legislation (Chilperic Edwards
trans., Kennikat Press ed. 1971) (1904) 10

Haney, Craig, Banks, Curtis, & Zimbardo, Philip, A Study of Prisoners
and Guards in a Simulated Prison (1973) 309

J

Johnson, Marcia K., & Hirst, William, MEM: Memory Subsystems as
Processes, in Theories of Memory 241 (Alan F. Collins et al. eds., 1993)..... 193

Johnston, David, The Roman Law of Trusts (1988) 15

L

Laws of Hammurabi, ¶ 125, in Martha T. Roth, Law Collections from
Mesopotamia and Asia Minor (1995) 9

Lewis, Michael M., Liar's Poker (1989) 123

Lipton, Martin, et al., "Restoring Trust" or Losing Perspective?,
Memorandum of Wachtell, Lipton, Rosen & Katz (Aug. 27, 2003) 327

Locke, John, Two Treatises of Government 306 (Cambridge
Univ. Press 2d ed. 1967) (1690) 42

8 Loss, Louis, & Seligman, Joel, Securities Regulation 3814
(3d ed. rev. 2004) 104

Luke 16:1-8 11

M

Maine, Henry James Sumner, Ancient Law (C. K. Allen ed. 1931) (1861) 49

Maitland, F.W., Equity: A Course of Lectures (1936) 20

McCormick on Evidence (Kenneth S. Brown et al. eds, 6th ed. 2006).................. 51

Mencken, H.L., A New Dictionary of Quotations 1220 (1960) 8

N

Noonan, Jr., John T., The Scholastic Analysis of Usury (1957)...................... 17, 18

P

Plucknett, Theodore F. T., A Concise History of the Common
Law (2d ed. 1936).. 17

Polinsky, A. Mitchell, An Introduction to Law and Economics (2d ed. 1989)..... 218

R

1 Rowley, Scott, The Modern Law of Partnership (1916) 17

S

Schafer, Stephen, Compensation and Restitution to Victims of
Crime 4 (1970) 10

Schmidt, David P., Quilting Professional Identities in Business, in Religion,
Morality and the Professions in America (1998) 47

1 Scott, Austin W., & Fratcher, William F., The Law of Trusts
(4th ed. 1987) 245

2A Scott, Austin W. , The Law of Trusts 509 (4th ed. 1987) 111

Scott, Austin W., Fratcher, William F., & Ascher, Mark L., Scott and
Ascher on Trusts (5th ed. 2006).. 26

Sin, Kam Fan, The Legal Nature of the Unit Trust (1997) 291

Six, Frédérique, The Trouble With Trust (2005).................................. 323, 324, 325

T

Tawney, R. H., Introduction to Thomas Wilson, A Discourse Upon Usury
(2d ed. 1963 (1925)... 18

Turow, Scott, The Billable Hour Must Die, in Raise the Bar: Real
World Solutions for a Troubled Profession (Lawrence J. Fox ed., 2007)...... 116

V

Van Ness, Daniel W., Restorative Justice, in Criminal Justice, Restitution,
and Reconciliation (Burt Galaway & Joe Hudson eds., 1990)........................ 10

W

Walzer, Michael, Spheres of Justice: A Defense of Pluralism and
Equality (1983) 19, 194

Wouk, Herman, Youngblood Hawke 89

Z

Zimbardo, Philip G., A Situationist Perspective on the Psychology of Evil:
Understanding How Good People Are Transformed into
Perpetrators 14 (2003)... 309

Table of Articles

(References are to page numbers)

Table of Law Reviews

(References are to page numbers)

G

H

K

L

O

Oppenheim, A.L., The Seafaring Merchants of Ur,
74 J. Am. Oriental Soc. 6 (1954) 10

Owen, David G., Problems in Assessing Punitive Damages Against
Manufacturers of Defective Products, 49 U. Chi. L. Rev. 1 (1982) 9

P

Peterson, Christopher L., Truth, Understanding, and High-Cost Consumer
Credit: The Historical Context of the Truth in Lending Act,
55 Fla. L. Rev. 807 (2003) 10

Puri, Poonam, Taking Stock of Taking Stock, 87 Cornell L. Rev. 99 (2001)....... 119

R

Resnicoff, Stephen H., Jewish Law and Socially Responsible Corporate
Conduct, 11 Fordham J. Corp. & Fin. L. 681 (2006) 14

Ribstein, Larry E., Law v. Trust, 81 B.U. L. Rev. 553 (2001)............................. 316

Romano, Roberta, Comment on Easterbrook and Fischel,
"Contract and Fiduciary Duty," 36 J.L. & Econ. 447 (1993) 211

Rose, Carol M., Trust in the Mirror of Betrayal, 75 B.U. L. Rev. 531 (1995)..... 301

Rubin, Edward L., Law and the Methology of Law,
1997 Wis. L. Rev. 521 (1997).. 194

S

Sacco, Rodolfo, Diversity and Uniformity in the Law,
49 Am. J. Comp. L. 171 (2001)... 282, 283

Salbu, Steven, Bribery in the Global Market: A Critical Analysis of the
Foreign Corrupt Practices Act, 54 Wash. & Lee L. Rev. 229 (1997)............. 153

Schipani, Cindy A., & Liu, Junhai, Corporate Governance in China:
Then and Now, 2002 Colum. Bus. L. Rev. 1 (2002) 289

Schlegel, John Henry, From High in the Paper Tower, an Essay on
von Humboldt's University, 52 Buffalo L. Rev. 865 (2004) 193

Schwarcz, Steven L., Financial Information Failure and Lawyer
Responsibility, 31 Iowa J. Corp. L. 1097 (2006).. 146

Scott, Austin W., The Fiduciary Principle, 37 Cal. L. Rev. 539 (1949)................. 11

Scott, Robert E., & Stephan, Paul B., Self-Enforcing International
Agreements and the Limits of Coercion, 2004 Wis. L. Rev. 551 (2004).......... 10

Shapiro, Susan P., Bushwhacking the Ethical High Road: Conflict of
Interest in the Practice of Law and Real Life,
28 Law & Soc. Inquiry 87 (2003) 115

Simmonds, Andrew R., Indirect Causation: A Reminder from the
Biblical Goring Ox Rule for Fraud on the Market Securities
Litigation, 88 Ky. L.J. 641 (2000) 9

Sitkoff, Robert H., An Agency Costs Theory of Trust Law,
89 Cornell L. Rev. 621 (2004)... 225

Sunstein, Cass R., On Analogical Reasoning,
106 Harv. L. Rev. 741 (1993) 194

Table of Media Documents

(References are to page numbers)

D

F

G

H

J

M

N

P

Table of Papers

(References are to page numbers)

Index

www.ingramcontent.com/pod-product-compliance
Lightning Source LLC
Chambersburg PA
CBHW080710220326
41598CB00033B/5365